Lost Kids

Edited by Mona Gleason, Tamara Myers,
Leslie Paris, and Veronica Strong-Boag

Lost Kids
Vulnerable Children and Youth
in Twentieth-Century Canada and
the United States

UBCPress · Vancouver · Toronto

17 16 15 14 13 12 11 10   5 4 3 2 1

Printed in Canada on ancient-forest-free paper (100% post-consumer recycled) that is processed chlorine- and acid-free.

Library and Archives Canada Cataloguing in Publication

Lost kids : vulnerable children and youth in twentieth-century Canada and the United States / edited by Mona Gleason ... [et al.].

Includes bibliographical references and index.
ISBN 978-0-7748-1686-1 (bound)
ISBN 978-0-7748-1687-8 (pbk.)
ISBN 978-0-7748-1688-5 (e-book)

1. Children with social disabilities – Canada – History – 20th century. 2. Children with social disabilities – United States – History – 20th century. 3. Youth with social disabilities – Canada – History – 20th century. 4. Youth with social disabilities – United States – History – 20th century. I. Gleason, Mona, 1964-

HQ792.C3L67 2010   362.70971'0904   C2009-903400-X

Canadä

UBC Press gratefully acknowledges the financial support for our publishing program of the Government of Canada through the Book Publishing Industry Development Program (BPIDP), and of the Canada Council for the Arts, and the British Columbia Arts Council.

This book has been published with the help of a grant from the Canadian Federation for the Humanities and Social Sciences, through the Aid to Scholarly Publications Programme, using funds provided by the Social Sciences and Humanities Research Council of Canada.

UBC Press
The University of British Columbia
2029 West Mall
Vancouver, BC V6T 1Z2
604-822-5959 / Fax: 604-822-6083
www.ubcpress.ca

For my parents, Margaret and William Gleason (1923-99) – MG

For my grandmother, Mable Nelson (1911-2009) – TM

For my parents, Roz and Joel Paris – LP

For my heroes, Stephen Lewis and Mary-Ellen Turpel-Lafond – VSB

Contents

Illustrations

Lost Kids

Introduction

Mona Gleason, Tamara Myers, Leslie Paris,
and Veronica Strong-Boag

Children and youth occupy important social and political roles, even as they sleep in their cribs or hang out on street corners. Conceptualized alternatively as harbingers or saboteurs of a bright, secure tomorrow, young people in various historical contexts have been central to adult-driven schemes to effect a positive future for children, families, communities, and nations.[1] In Western societies, children are believed to have become, as sociologist Viviana Zelizer argues, emotionally "priceless," gaining in social importance as their economic value waned in the industrial age.[2] Since the late nineteenth century, longer mandated periods of schooling and new age restrictions on workplace employment have shielded greater numbers of children from participation in wage labour; twentieth-century health advances such as the pasteurization of milk and the development of new vaccines have helped to protect them against potentially fatal illnesses; and protective legislation has formally recognized sexual relations between adults and minors as criminal.[3] In these ways and more, the past century was marked by a particular emphasis on improving children's lives and opportunities. Spurred on by the growing sentimentalization of childhood, twentieth-century children were to benefit from adult reform efforts intended to better protect them from risk and exploitation. But as we ask in this volume, which children benefited and which were left behind?

While those lucky youngsters raised to achieve their full potential provide a benchmark for societal evolution, their story has unfolded against a cast of girls and boys with more curtailed options who have experienced the sometimes contradictory outcomes of policies designed with "good intentions." Children today termed "at risk" – those who are considered to be more physically, economically, or socially vulnerable to becoming victims (or even perpetrators) of abuse – have long been the subjects of particular scrutiny among adults. These boys and girls turn up both in the popular Western imagination and in the real-life headlines that trumpet sad histories: the sexual and physical abuse of Aboriginal and Native American students at twentieth-century residential schools, the perils of long-term foster care, and the apparent ubiquity of drug use and violent acts within many adolescent cohorts. These stories remind us that childhood and adolescence constitute ambiguous social, cultural, and political territory in the world of adults: these young people appear at once to have been lost and found, understood and misinterpreted, valued and distrusted.

This volume concerns those vulnerable youngsters who have, for a variety of reasons, experienced fewer of the benefits the modern sentimentalization of childhood has had to offer, and the aspirations and judgments of the adults who have raised and supervised them. Boys and girls understood to be inadequate or at risk, whether disadvantaged by parental or community failings or by their own perceived characteristics, have been central to modern Western reform efforts – including philanthropy, policy making, therapeutic and educational support, and punitive options designed to contain the peril of disaffected or culturally distinct youth. Yet, as these essays suggest, although intermittent panics about the death of children in foster care or the discovery of high suicide rates among certain youthful populations have frequently elicited promises of reform, all too often these crises have faded away, leaving vulnerable children "forgotten" until the next crisis. For all the attention and outrage youth at risk in Canada and the United States have generated on rough streets, in overwhelmed institutions, and in troubled homes from the nineteenth century to the present, the most vulnerable youngsters continue to face higher risks and fewer opportunities than their better-off counterparts. Those children who deviate from the mainstream by reason of mental or physical disability, class, race, or simply age, or because their families cannot adequately care for them, have more often been "lost"; in this volume, we seek to "find" them and to showcase the importance of how the various debates about young people judged disadvantaged, vulnerable, or otherwise problematically "in need" have been framed. The chapters in this book remind scholars and practitioners working in various areas in childhood and youth studies that the varying experiences of disadvantaged youth are centrally implicated in state formation, class conflict, citizenship debates, and the cultural politics of identity. More broadly, we see how social inequalities are historically produced; young people, disadvantaged and otherwise, are central figures in the manufacture and maintenance of these hierarchies at the hands of parents, professionals, state representatives, and, sometimes, other children.

Lost Kids represents a collective effort by historians and social scientists to explore key difficulties faced by vulnerable children and their caretakers over the last hundred and more years in Canada and the United States. It marks an attempt to recast vulnerable children, their representation, their treatment, and their responses as social actors often *made additionally vulnerable* through the action and inaction of adults. Although children and youth experience a wide diversity of social locations based on their race, class, sex, and ability, they share a relationship to the power of adults that often places them at a distinct disadvantage. Yet, these children have often been resilient; many have carved out satisfying lives in spite of their difficult childhoods, enabled by or despite the efforts of adults.

As scholars, we endeavour to be attentive to how the conditions of children and youth deemed vulnerable have been alternately underrepresented and overdramatized in historical narratives of social, political, and cultural change in their contemporary iterations.[4] Marginalized children and youth around the world have appeared in adult narratives as waifs, as strays, and sometimes, as monsters. Some are construed as having lost their bearings, moral and otherwise, and being in need of correction or salvation. Some are deemed physically or intellectually deficient. Others, those who appear to represent less of a threat, are simply ignored. As Canadian editors, of one of the twenty-first-century nation-states whose history and current policies we probe in this book, we are motivated by efforts to connect past and present in ways that may illuminate the lives of such youngsters and the adults who plan for them.

Childhood in Canada and the United States

In the era considered in this book – the nineteenth century to the present – Canada and the United States share histories of investigating and attempting to improve and control children and youth. This has been an era of reform and child-saving, as well as of growing acknowledgment of children's rights. At the state level, early initiatives included Canada's Royal Commission on the Relations of Labor and Capital (1889), which devoted much attention to child labour, and the first American White House Conference on Dependent Children (1909), which supplied the momentum for the creation of the US Children's Bureau (1912). In both countries, the settlement house movement of the late nineteenth century onward had a significant focus on (mostly urban) youth; reformers also focused on institutional "care," including orphanages and industrial schools, the kindergarten movement, and new hygienic measures to preserve children's health. Overall, concern for children, especially those deemed at risk, was a central tenet of the developing social welfare apparatus in the two nations. Canadians and Americans were variously motivated by adult sentimentality, benevolence, and humanitarian concern. Reformers strove to integrate recent immigrants and racial minorities into the cultural mainstream, to prevent the economic drain of pauperism, and to produce industrious and self-reliant citizens. From juvenile courts that dealt both with dependent and delinquent children and kept minors out of the reach of criminal law, to international covenants recognizing the rights of children, the category of the child emerged as a fundamental political and social concern. In sum, social reform in the decades before World War One produced the institutions of modern child welfare.

These bold efforts had important results. Yet, a century later, many children in wealthy nations remain at risk or are understood as "trouble." Studies from provincial, state, and federal authorities, together with those from non-profit groups, have provided abundant empirical data on the difficulties facing vulnerable youngsters in both countries. For instance, the uncertain pace of improvement for indigenous girls and boys was recently signalled by Canada's 1996 *Report of the Royal Commission on Aboriginal Peoples.* In 2000, one in six of the "rich world's children" (residents of the thirty members of the Organisation for Economic Co-operation and Development) was estimated to live in poverty, placing them, as one UNICEF-commissioned study concluded, "at a marked and measurable disadvantage" in matters of physical and mental development, health, education, job prospects, income, and life expectancy.[5] UNICEF ranked Canada fourth (below South Korea, Japan, and Finland) in the percentage of children scoring below international benchmarks of reading, math, and science literacy, while the United States stood eighteenth.[6] The national pattern of births to teenage mothers, an especially vulnerable group, is similarly revealing: the United States had the highest rate in the developed world at 52.1 births per 1,000 fifteen to nineteen-year-olds; Canada came in twenty-first at 20.2.[7] Meanwhile, although evidence suggests that fewer children are victims of abuse than in the past, perhaps 3,500 youngsters under age fifteen in the industrialized world die from physical abuse and neglect every year.[8] Intra-country variations among classes and communities of residents are sometimes greater than international disparities, reflecting deep chasms of domestic inequality in the world's richest nations. Aboriginal youngsters and those from other minority racial groups, disabled boys and girls, and many from single-parent households have often faced particular difficulties.[9]

The rights of children to stable, safe, and rewarding lives have been widely acknowledged, most notably in the United Nations' 1989 Convention on the Rights of the Child (CROC) that, as of January 2009, had been signified and ratified by all members of the UN, except Somalia and the United States. Such recognition of the human rights of children is reassuring, inasmuch as it places their rights on many national agendas. Legal scholars, among others critically attuned to the need for vigilance in enacting such endorsements, have nevertheless pointed out that CROC's "implementation is left to the good will of nation states."[10] Thus, although the Canadian government ratified the CROC in 1991, it has yet to be fully implemented in the country's domestic laws.[11] The recently concluded administration of President George W. Bush rejected ratification, arguing that "the text goes too far when it asserts entitlements based on economic, social and cultural rights ... The human rights-based approach ... poses significant problems as used in this text."[12] Although governments would like to be seen to be promoting and protecting the national well-being of children, rights and emancipation remain contested, and the shifts in power relations that would be required for children's greater protection are clearly difficult to enact.

Scholarly Attention to Vulnerable Youngsters

The contributors to *Lost Kids* draw upon a number of theoretical perspectives, including feminism, critical race studies, and postcolonial studies, as they are employed in history, criminology, critical legal studies, and sociology. Foremost among these approaches is feminist scholarship, which has been influential in sensitizing us to the symbolic and material significance of children and youth, to questions of privilege and resistance, and to the value of recovering voices whose perspective has been so frequently ignored. Our work as historians and as scholars of contemporary child and youth studies is also marked by interdisciplinary and sometimes international linkages. These approaches make clear that particular ideas about, and treatment of, young people are historically constituted and indicative of unequal relations and often oppressive understandings of race, class, gender, sexuality, and ability.

Although the scholarly literature we draw on is vast, we direct readers' attention to three interrelated issues of particular concern to child and youth studies in Canada and the United States. First is the central place of the state – its evolving politics, procedures, and prejudices – in both the construction of and responses to vulnerable children. Second is the shifting context of families and households whose fundamental dynamics, occasionally quite in opposition to the priorities of the state, shape young lives. Finally, we consider the evolution of child welfare and criminal justice, two systems that are closely interconnected and have been likely to impinge on or even determine the future of disadvantaged girls and boys.

Early challenges to traditional interpretations of state intervention in vulnerable families, including, for example, Linda Gordon on American single women and welfare, Anthony Platt on juvenile justice in the United States, and Patricia Rooke, R.L. Schnell, and Neil Sutherland on the deinstitutionalization movement and child welfare in Canada, have provided astute critiques of social welfare politics.[13] Scholars in multiple national settings have described how ideologies became "modern" or "child-centred" as well as frequently "mother-centred" or mother-blaming in the last century and half, and how professionals became more and more powerful in setting the contours of public thinking about childhood. Increasingly, historians are highlighting a diversity of opinion about youngsters and their families. There is, for example, much evidence that Aboriginal communities have evolved different views of children than have settler societies and that the views of immigrant groups often differ from those of the mainstream. Thinking about young people in the two nations has ranged from the reactionary to the progressive, the punitive to the therapeutic, the clinical to the commercial, the idealistic to the pragmatic. Yet, it is difficult, as scholars have shown, for these groups to escape the disciplinary ideologies of childhood and youth propagated by schools, social welfare systems, and the popular media in both lands.[14]

Families and households, fundamental sites for the unfolding of lives, permit a close consideration of children's socialization as well as counter-discourses and resistance to mainstream norms. Early-twentieth-century reformers once largely idealized the domestic arrangements of middle-class white settlers, describing others as more likely to produce problem youngsters. That tradition has not entirely disappeared, but today's scholars are more likely to portray and appreciate the diversity of kin and residential arrangements and the ways that these work variously to support girls and boys, including non-standard arrangements where same-sex couples, grandparents, aunts, siblings, and other interested adults meaningfully care for girls and boys. There is also considerable recognition that particular families and households face tremendous threats, originating not only with poverty, addiction, and violence but also with the shortcomings of state regimes. In other words, critical studies of childhood and youth in Canada and the United States are increasingly aware of the ways in which class, race, gender, and ability matter a good deal when it comes to family opportunity.[15]

In both national contexts, scholarly examination of ideas about families and households has also regularly blended into discussions of the development of child welfare policy. This evolution has revealed long-standing assumptions that kin should properly care for their own (though the meaning of proper care has been contested), and that public aid should be directed, through both punishment and reward, to achieve this end. Canadian and American private and public assistance, ranging from the relatively generous to the deeply punitive, was never intended to undermine the pre-eminent obligation of family. Thus, relief, whether in the form of pensions, allowances, or workfare, has never provided financial options better than those available to families of the lowest paid wage earners. Linked to such assumptions and policies is a prevailing preference for men's commitment to breadwinning and women's to unwaged work for home and kin. Children everywhere have had the greatest claim on the hearts and the purses of the powerful and on tax dollars if their families were believed to match this portrait of responsible gendered parenting. That result has been especially clear in contemporary scholars' examination of the experience of those marginalized by class, gender, race, and disability in both nations.[16]

In the course of appraising ideas about children and youth, the role of families and households, and the emergence of child welfare, scholars have begun to recognize that vulnerable girls and boys have not necessarily been silent or powerless. Many seek to realize their own ambitions, to slip away from any too-ready supervision, and to resist the will of others. This has not always been to positive effect; but truancy, shoplifting, and joyriding, although different from the more socially approved options of academic or athletic prowess, also reflect young people's efforts to negotiate alternative realities for themselves. Such efforts at agency have had many outcomes, some more favourable to young people than others.[17]

Thinking about *Lost Kids*

In December 2006, funding from Canada's Killam Program enabled the editors to host an international workshop at the University of British Columbia. As members of the newly founded History of Children and Youth Group, now affiliated with the Canadian Historical Association, we wanted to engage with scholars who were doing stimulating new work in the North American context. Because we were further committed to fostering connections between historians and other social scientists addressing contemporary issues, we invited scholars in law, political science, and human kinetics. The ways in which our historically oriented workshop on vulnerable youngsters made connections to the present stand out as unusual. This volume affirms the significance of the connection between past and present for children as for adults.

Among the goals of *Lost Kids* is to highlight various ways in which scholars might approach vulnerable girls and boys. The keynote speaker at the workshop, historian Neil Sutherland, who contributes our postscript, pointed in particular to the possibilities of deriving children's stories from adult memories, while acknowledging the methodological concerns of doing so. And although young people's voices have been too often silent in the historical record, they surface here in numerous places. Mona Gleason uses interviews with adults as a way into a history of childhood illnesses. Tamara Myers, engages media interviews with youngsters targeted as potential trouble. Leslie Paris employs children's voices as they were recorded in contemporary newspaper and scholarly accounts. Wendy Frisby examines recent interviews with Aboriginal youth. In these sources, young voices are often mediated by adults but are revealing nonetheless.

Many contributors to this volume have mined institutional records. Veronica Strong-Boag uses ministerial and other public accounts to illuminate how disability has been understood and experienced. Hospital records provide Denyse Baillargeon with a perspective on patients at Montreal's Sainte-Justine Hospital. Juvenile justice records are central to William Bush's analysis of race and delinquency in Texas. An examination of expert thought on children and youth is central to Cynthia Comacchio's study of adolescence. The adoption files of child welfare agencies in Winnipeg and Montreal supply insights into cross-racial adoption for Karen Dubinsky.

Numerous contributors examine public policy more broadly. Molly Ladd-Taylor examines variations in the status of disadvantaged American children over the twentieth century. Law scholars Cindy Baldassi, Susan Boyd, and Fiona Kelly explore legal sources to suggest how adoption and the principle "in the best interest of the child" can be variously interpreted to raise questions about "normality." Stephen McBride and John Irwin employ contemporary Canadian public policy records. The array of sources used in *Lost Kids* illuminates the diversity of childhood and discourages the essentialism casually evoked in notions of the priceless child or the hopeless youth.

Several themes link the chapters in the book. One central concern is prejudice, and patterns of recurring discrimination that raise questions about whose interests were ultimately being served. Whether the spotlight is on white American elites' refusal to grant childhood to African American boys, as in Bush's study; Ladd Taylor and Strong-Boag's revelation of how ableism fuelled North American public policy in schools and child welfare; or Baldassi, Boyd, and Kelly's identification of the heterosexism of Canadian case law, the authors demonstrate the vexed nature of secular experts' claims to impartiality, and the ways in which child-management projects often served professionals' own claims to expertise.

The power of the child as a trope alternatively of innocence, vulnerability, and danger provides another recurring interest of contributors. Very often, youngsters emerge in public discourse as important indicators of the condition and future of the community or the nation more broadly. Dubinsky makes this connection in her comparison of the adoption of black and Aboriginal youngsters in Canada. Paris illuminates adult fears that rising American divorce rates signalled social disarray. Myers links debates about curfew laws to more general worries about nighttime social disorder and unease about youth's claim to public space. Comacchio emphasizes how adolescence invoked North America's anxieties about an immoral modernism freed of the constraints of propriety and custom. Gleason demonstrates how the small bodies were employed as symbols of both a strong citizenry and one in need of treatment and repair. Often, as these examples testify, cultural symbols of youngsters stand in the way of appreciating individual girls and boys.

The history of legal remedies for children in trouble or in need encompasses another shared theme for many of our contributors. How such children were to be assisted and straightened out has presented a recurring problem for the legal system, as Baldassi, Boyd, and Kelly demonstrate. Legislation to protect children from workplace exploitation, McBride and Irwin argue, continues to be compromised by the seemingly unassailable logic of consumer capitalism. Numerous authors remind us that public policy makers built edifices that allocated special and always inferior places and programs to those assumed to be hopeless or disabled. Ironically, such youngsters' lack of access to their fair share of funding often subsidized mainstream families' achievement of "normality."

The importance of what has been termed "the politics of identity" also regularly emerges in the following chapters.[18] Race looms particularly large in the discussions of Bush and Dubinsky, but it never stands alone. Black girls suffer different disabilities from their brothers. Class, race, and gender are invoked in the fears of adolescence uncovered by Comacchio and Myers. Frisby's teens would be hard put to know whether their recreational needs are ignored because of their age, their class origins, or, in some instances, their Aboriginality. The ideal and miscreant families described by Paris rise and fall in the public imagination and in state policy by virtue of their particular embodiment of racial and class ideals. Ultimately, these multi-faceted identities shape children's experiences. Some attributes, for good or ill, may be singled out for special attention.

To further complicate these stories, a number of the contributors point to global and transborder connections. Canadians and Americans have always been variously linked to near and far-flung communities and empires. Long after first contact, Aboriginal North Americans frequently ignored settler-imposed borders to travel for work and community. As Dubinsky points out, the adoption trade in indigenous youngsters was often equally transgressive. Few of the girls and boys recovered in these pages were unaffected by the global market in ideas about youngsters; some literally crossed frontiers in response to adult agendas. These themes of prejudice, cultural imagery, public policy, intersectionality, and border crossing invoke complicated histories that stand close to the heart of modern life. Youngsters do not constitute an isolated cohort. As members of intergenerational communities, they embody the preconceptions and the priorities of their larger societies.

In the mould of pioneering feminist historians such as Mary Quayle Innis in Canada and Mary Ritter Beard in the United States, we believe that past and present operate in tandem, and that illuminating the connections between them helps us understand both better.[19] To take only one example, Aboriginal residential schools (and, as the Law Commission of Canada has argued, children's institutions in general) have scarred far more than the generations they actually abused.[20] Survivors have sometimes passed on their trauma in the course of their own parenting, schooling, and employment. Equally dangerous have been some of the conclusions drawn by political elites who see such children's subsequent difficulties as proof of their inferiority and not as most properly an indictment of mainstream indifference, neglect, and abuse. The pattern of vulnerable children and youth we see around us in the world today is ultimately the legacy of past choices. The Child Welfare League of Canada has recently produced resource papers that review key contemporary child protection issues. Many echo the issues treated in this collection: children in institutional care, Aboriginal youth, youth homelessness, children and juvenile delinquency, and working conditions for youngsters.[21] We hope that readers of *Lost Kids* will not only better understand the past but also be able to make the critical linkages that will help us to understand the conditions of childhood in the present.

Acknowledgment

We would like to thank the Killam Program of the Canada Council for funding the workshop for which most of these chapters were produced and for its contribution to the publication of this volume. We are also grateful for the support of SSHRC and our university departments at the University of British Columbia: Women's and Gender Studies, Educational Studies, and History. We also thank the graduate students who have assisted this project at various stages, notably Laurie Parsons, Beth Stewart, and Dilek Kayaalp. Finally, the enthusiasm and patience of our UBC Press editors, first Jean Wilson and now Darcy Cullen, transformed this hard work into a pleasurable experience.

Notes

1 Canadian scholarship includes Patricia Rooke and R.L. Schnell, *Discarding the Asylum: From Child Rescue to the Welfare State in English-Canada, 1800-1950* (Lanham, MD: University Press of America, 1983); Neil Sutherland, *Children in English-Canadian Society: Framing the Twentieth Century Consensus* (Toronto: University of Toronto Press, 1976); Cynthia Comacchio, *Nations Are Built of Babies: Saving Ontario Mothers and Children, 1900-1940* (Montreal and Kingston: McGill-Queen's University Press, 1990). In the American literature see, for example, Kriste Lindemeyer, *A Right to Childhood: The U.S. Children's Bureau and Child Welfare, 1912-46* (Urbana, IL: University of Illinois Press, 1997); and Judith Sealander, *The Failed Century of the Child: Governing America's Young in the Twentieth Century* (New York: Cambridge University Press, 2003).

2 Viviana Zelizer, *Pricing the Priceless Child: The Changing Social Value of Children* (New York: Basic Books, 1985).

3 See Matthew Waites, *The Age of Consent: Young People, Sexuality and Citizenship* (Houndmills, UK: Palgrave Macmillan, 2005).

4 There is a significant historical and contemporary literature on "children at risk." In particular, juvenile delinquency, children and drug use, sexuality, and children at the centre of moral panic have received extensive exploration in numerous national contexts. Less scholarly attention has been paid to children labelled "disabled," particularly in historical and non-therapeutic literature, though that is slowly changing. See, for example, Richard J. Altenbaugh, "Where Are the Disabled in the History of Education? The Impact of Polio on Sites of Learning," *History of Education* 35, 6 (2006): 705-30.

5 UNICEF Innocenti Research Centre, "A League Table of Child Poverty in Rich Nations," *Innocenti Report Card* 1 (June 2000): 3. See also UNICEF Innocenti Research Centre, "Child Poverty in Rich Countries, 2005," *Innocenti Report Card,* 6 (2006); and John Micklewright, "Child Poverty in English-Speaking Countries," Innocenti Working Paper No. 94 (UNICEF Innocenti Research Centre, Florence, 2003).

6 UNICEF Innocenti Research Centre, "A League Table of Educational Disadvantage in Rich Nations," *Innocenti Report Card* 4 (November 2002): 4.

7 UNICEF Innocenti Research Centre, "A League Table of Teenage Births in Rich Nations," *Innocenti Report Card* 3 (July 2001): 4; see "Juvenile Justice," *Innocenti Digest* 3 (1998).

8 UNICEF Innocenti Research Centre, "A League Table of Child Maltreatment Deaths in Rich Nations," *Innocenti Report Card* 5 (September 2003): 2. The figures are averaged over five years.

9 See Maggie Black, "Children and Families of Ethnic Minorities, Immigrants and Indigenous Peoples: Global Seminar Report," Innocenti Global Seminar, 1995 ser., 7 (UNICEF ICDC,

Florence, 1997). See also the National Clearinghouse on Family Violence, *The Abuse of Children with Disabilities* (Ottawa: Family Violence Prevention Unit, Health Canada, August 2000).

10 Melinda Jones, "Changing Families, Challenging Futures" (paper presented at the 6th Australian Institute of Family Studies Conference, Melbourne, 15-27 November 1998), http://www.aifs.gov.au/institute/afrc6papers/jones.html.

11 See Canadian Children's Rights Council, "About the U.N. Convention on the Rights of the Child (UNCRC)," http://www.canadiancrc.com/UN_CRC_webpage/UN_CRC.htm; Australian Human Rights and Equal Opportunity Commission, "Children's Rights," http://www.humanrights.gov.au/human_rights/children/index.html.

12 World Net Daily, "Bush Team Signals New U.N. Direction," http://wnd.com/news/article.asp?ARTICLE_ID=21590.

13 See, for example, Linda Gordon, *Pitied but Not Entitled: Single Mothers and the History of Welfare, 1890 to 1935* (New York: Free Press, 1994); Anthony Platt, *The Child Savers: The Invention of Delinquency* (Chicago: University of Chicago Press, 1977); Patricia Rooke and R.L. Schnell, *Discarding the Asylum: From Child Rescue to the Welfare State in English-Canada, 1800-1950* (Lanham, MD: University Press of America, 1983); and Neil Sutherland, *Children in English-Canadian Society.*

14 For an introduction to these concerns see Neil Sutherland, *Children in English-Canadian Society* (Waterloo, ON: Wilfrid Laurier University Press, 2000) and *Growing Up: Childhood in English Canada from the Great War to the Age of Television* (Toronto: University of Toronto Press, 1997) and Kriste Lindenmeyer, *A Right to Childhood: The U.S. Children's Bureau and Child Welfare, 1912-1946* (Urbana, IL: University of Illinois Press, 1997).

15 See Margrit Eichler, *Families in Canada Today: Recent Changes and Their Policy Consequences* (Toronto: Gage, 1988); and Sherri Broder, *Tramps, Unfit Mothers, and Neglected Children: Negotiating the Family in Nineteenth Century Philadelphia* (Philadelphia: University of Philadelphia Press, 2002).

16 Christopher Walmsley and Diane Purvey, eds., *Child and Family Welfare in British Columbia: A History* (Calgary: Detselig Enterprises, 2005); Patricia T. Rooke and R.L. Schnell, *Discarding the Asylum;* Patricia Monture, "A Vicious Circle: Child Welfare and the First Nations," *Canadian Journal of Women and the Law* 3, 1 (1989): 1-17; Janet Golden, Richard A. Meckel, and Heather M. Prescott, *Children and Youth in Sickness and in Health: A Historical Handbook;* Lori Askeland, ed., *Children and Youth in Adoption, Orphanages, and Foster Care: A Historical Handbook and Guide* (Westport, CT: Greenwood, 2006); LeRoy Asby, *Endangered Children: Dependency, Neglect and Abuse in American History* (New York: Twayne, 1997); Marilyn I. Holt, *Indian Orphanages* (Lawrence, KS: University Press of Kansas, 2001); and Linda Gordon, *Pitied but Not Entitled.*

17 Tamara Myers, *Caught: Montreal's Modern Girls and the Law, 1869-1945* (Toronto: University of Toronto Press, 2006); for first-person accounts see Evelyn Lau, *Runaway: Diary of a Street Kid* (Toronto: HarperPerennial, 1996). More representative of the vulnerable were the lives of the murdered young prostitute and addict recalled in Maggie de Vries, *Missing Sarah: A Vancouver Woman Remembers Her Vanished Sister* (Toronto: Penguin, 2004) or the sad-eyed foster child whose suicide was immortalized in *Richard Cardinal: Cry from the Diary of a Métis Child* by Aboriginal filmmaker Alanis Obomsawin (Montreal: National Film Board of Canada, 1986).

18 See Leslie McCall, "The Complexity of Intersectionality," *Signs: Journal of Women in Culture and Society* 30, 3 (2005): 1771-1800; and Patricia Hill Collins, "It's All in the Family: Intersections of Gender, Race, and Nation," in Uma Narayan and Sandra Harding, eds., *Decentering the Center: Philosophy for a Multicultural, Post-Colonial, and Feminist World* (Bloomington, IN: Indiana University Press, 2000), 156-76.

19 See Mary Ritter Beard, *A Woman Making History: Mary Ritter Beard through Her Letters*, edited with an introduction by Nancy F. Cott (New Haven, CT: Yale University Press, 1991); Beverly Boutilier and Alison Prentice, eds., *Creating Historical Memory: English-Canadian Woman and the Work of History* (Vancouver: UBC Press, 1997); and Anne Innis Dagg, "Mary Quayle Innis," in Mary Ann Dimand, Robert W. Dimand, and Evelyn L. Forget, eds., *Women of Value: Feminist Essays on the History of Women in Economics* (Aldershot, UK: Edward Elgar, 1995).

20 See Law Commission of Canada, *Restoring Dignity: Responding to Child Abuse in Canadian Institutions* (Ottawa: Law Commission of Canada, 2000).
21 Child Welfare League of Canada, *The Welfare of Canadian Children: It's Our Business* (Ottawa: Child Welfare League of Canada, 2007).

Part 1
Wanted Kids? Institutions, Fostering, and Adoption

"Every Child a Wanted Child" has long been the slogan of Planned Parenthood. Its message has angered opponents of women's access to birth control and abortion, who dream of good homes for every child. However, as the chapters in this section remind readers, children have never been regarded as equally desirable. Even when public enthusiasm for adoption has been at its height, numerous youngsters have gone unparented. As Karen Dubinsky and Veronica Strong-Boag demonstrate, differences of race, gender, class, religion, ethnicity, and disability have all affected the prospects of girls and boys in need of assistance.

A long history of childhood neglect and abuse within families and in varied societies provides ample evidence of human shortcomings across generations. Today, lower child mortality rates and shifting sensibilities tend to make the unequal experiences of children across lines of difference even more visible. At the same time, history shows that adult champions of children and youth, inspired variously by religious and personal values, have advocated on their behalf in varied contexts. The emergence of a sentimental version of childhood in the eighteenth- and nineteenth-century Western world drew on compassionate impulses; indentures, orphanages, reformatories, and hospitals have everywhere acted to discipline and control, but they have also embodied reformers' hopes for children.

Karen Dubinsky explores the changing parameters of transracial and transnational Canadian adoption in the postwar years. Contrasting the adoption of Aboriginal and black children by white parents, Dubinsky examines significant differences in parental intent and community support in these two cases, and the effects of these specific adoption climates. Veronica Strong-Boag, meanwhile, examines the changing ideals of "worthiness" through which Canadian children have been fostered, institutionalized, or adopted. As she argues, the history of children with disabilities suggests the challenges of parenting, as well as the vulnerability of some of the most needy.

1

A Haven from Racism? Canadians Imagine Interracial Adoption

Karen Dubinsky

Children suffer the paradoxical burden of both over- and under-representation. The under-representation of children is what brings this book together as contributors explore how children have been excluded, marginalized, and ignored in everything from playgrounds to political economy, past and present. Yet, over-representation is, in a sense, the flip side of powerlessness. Because what is socially peripheral is often symbolically central, children strike it rich in symbolic power. The insight that women have acted historically as "bearers but rarely makers of social meaning" applies even more so to children.[1] Through the nineteenth and twentieth centuries, "childhood" was invented and then universalized, so much so that, today, nations are increasingly judged on the basis of their ability to provide for their citizens a universal (and highly circumscribed) "childhood." I argue that the relatively recent (and by no means uncontested) creation of a single, global meaning of "child" explains much about the contemporary controversies accompanying transracial and transnational adoption. In this sense, the adopted child joins other globally controversial children, including the labouring child and the child soldier, who are understood to be subject to adult imperatives.[2]

My current project is a history of interracial and international adoption in various locations in the Americas. My main theme is the extraordinary symbolic power of children, and my goal is to try to move our understandings of interracial and international adoption past the binaries of "kidnap" versus "rescue." Adoption controversies are never just about children. The history of interracial adoption provides enormous scope for those interested in both the social and the symbolic history of children and childhood. In the latter part of the twentieth century, as mainstream adoption policy and practice moved from matching and secrecy toward a degree of openness, the placement of black and Aboriginal children in white homes, and the subsequent creation of visible, multiracial adoptive families, sparked significant and ongoing debate. Adopted children merit more than a mention on the list of so-called emblematic cases of childhood, because their circumstances have triggered such intense, and often contradictory, responses. Here I want to consider two such differing histories from Canada: the adoption stories of black children in the 1960s and Aboriginal children in the 1970s and 1980s.

It is widely held in Canada that the adoption of Aboriginal children by white parents has been an almost unmitigated disaster. Individual horror stories of Aboriginal kids "gone wrong" – abused, addicted, and acting out – circulate widely. One of these horror stories involves the troubled son of Canada's former prime minister – adopted from an Inuvik orphanage in 1970 when Jean Chrétien was minister for Indian Affairs. The sad life and legal troubles of Michel Chrétien have become the elephant in the room in the production of commonsense knowledge of Native adoption in Canada. The adoption of Aboriginal children in Canada in this era is popularly known as the "Sixties Scoop": the timing is a bit off, but the politics are clear.[3] "Cultural genocide" is another common term, given mainstream legitimacy by a Manitoba government inquiry into Native adoptions in 1983.[4] The adoption of Aboriginal children by whites is now invoked, constantly and almost automatically, by Aboriginal and non-Aboriginal writers and scholars alike as an instrument of colonization. To activist and writer Winona LaDuke, for example, adoption joins eugenics and blood quantum as "the new mechanisms to cause the elimination of nations of indigenous peoples."[5] Social workers and other adoption professionals acknowledge the profound lack of empirical research on the lives of cross-culturally adopted Aboriginal children. Yet, anecdotal evidence and practical experience lead many high-profile Aboriginal adoption professionals to oppose cross-race placements. For Kenn Richard, social work professor and director of Toronto's Native Child and Family Services Centre, "far too many Aboriginal to non-Aboriginal adoptions break down ... and cultural dynamics must play a significant role in this process."[6] Here the United States looms as the more progressive country; a rare thing indeed in Canadian political discourse, especially on social welfare or race relations. Opponents of Aboriginal adoption in Canada cite the US Indian Child Welfare Act of 1978 (a product of a decade-long struggle by US Aboriginal groups appalled by the high rates of children "in care"), which limited cross-racial adoption of Aboriginal children, approvingly and enviously.[7]

Less well known today but just as emblematic in its day is the history of the adoption of Canadian black children by white parents.[8] This tale plays very differently. The decision by a Montreal agency to cross adoption's colour bar in the 1950s and place black children with white parents led to the creation of an integrationist discourse of adoption, which positioned interracially adopted black children as innocent bearers of racial reconciliation. The high media profile of this version of adoption was initiated by an enthusiastic group of white adoptive parents, the Open Door Society, formed in Montreal in 1959. In this story, Canadians saw interracial adoption as a hopeful sign of cross-racial tolerance and a measure of our progressive values.[9] Here Canadians occupied the more familiar (and definitely more comfortable) role of moral superior to our southern neighbours. American liberals, including an approving Martin Luther King Jr., looked longingly at Canada's adoption pioneers. As one American journalist noted, "Only in Montreal are mixed race adoptions an honor, not a stigma."[10] Although a few Canadian blacks saw this as a story of the political weakness of their community, including persistent discrimination by the child welfare system, this version of interracial adoption was rarely mobilized as a symbol of racism or colonialism. This story disappeared from public view as adoption's era of integrationist fervour subsided in the 1970s. But this narrative still makes the occasional appearance, including a recent feature in the *Globe and Mail*, in which Canada was positioned as a land of "racial tranquility," more suitable for US adopted black babies than the "muggy heat and segregation of the Deep South."[11]

Adoption historian Ellen Herman writes that adoption is "good to think with."[12] In this chapter, I want to use the subject of adoption to think about the different trajectories of Aboriginality and blackness in Canada – a huge project, to be sure. Fifty years of transracial-adoption debate in this country shed light on what US adoption scholar Sara Dorow calls "flexible racialization." In her work on Chinese adoptions in the United States, Dorow illustrates how, to many adoptive parents and adoption professionals alike, the "rescuability" of Chinese children stands in stark contrast to the abjectness and general hopelessness of domestic black children. As she puts it, to many, both Chinese and black children need to be rescued, "but it was easier to imagine the former being absorbed into White kinship."[13] What makes one group a "model minority" – and hence a good "bet" for adoption, and another a risk? Reflecting on his troubled adopted son, former Prime Minister Chrétien told his biographer, "Nobody told us there was a big problem to take Indians, that their record was not good."[14] Another white adoptive parent of a Native son gone terribly wrong, and author of a recent book about "adoption breakdown," sadly recalled the words of her father when she announced her adoption: "You can't make a White man out of an Indian."[15] In stark contrast to the discourse of black adopted child as harbinger of racial peace, the Aboriginal adopted child seemed, to some, almost freakish. "By treating him White, [they] rubbed away his native soul," one reporter has explained the unfortunate Chrétien family.[16] In what follows, I want to try to take these stories past such essentialist territory, and explore how transracial adoption can mean both cross-racial solidarity and colonial conquest.

We cannot contrast the various commonsense understandings or public narrative of Native and black adoption with an objective truth from the adoption case files.[17] It would be simplistic indeed to suggest that the adoption of black children by whites was inherently progressive while the adoption of First Nations children by whites was wholly reactionary. Relations between birth parents, adoptive parents, and social workers narrated through the framework of "the case file" – the official dossier of adoption – confirm and depart from these public narratives. It would be naive to believe everything one reads in an adoption file. In the era of closed adoption, social workers were like directors in a strange drama in which the actors were unseen by each other. The historical traces left in the case file are mostly told to and through the social worker. When the perspective offered by adoption's private, official record seems out of sync with adoption's public profile, the issue is not which story is wrong. Rather, I want to explore why such different ranges of understandings and beliefs about interracial adoption emerged at all. The intense emotional attachments between adults and children in our world are too complicated to fit into simple binaries; certainly, almost none of the hundreds of adoption case files I have examined could be described in the stark terms of "kidnap" or "rescue" alone. What accounts for such different public understandings of interracial adoption? Despite the universality of the concept, the symbolic child in the case file had many faces. The black child in Montreal meant something very different from the Aboriginal child in northern Manitoba.

The most obvious difference between the adoption of Aboriginal and black children in Canada is numbers. About 350 children labelled "non-white" (mostly black) were placed for adoption in Montreal between 1955 and 1969. These are figures from one agency in one city, although as Montreal's Children's Service Centre was widely recognized as an interracial adoption pioneer, these figures probably represent the apex of black placements in Canada. Even the province of Nova Scotia, home to a sizable black community, placed adoption ads in Montreal newspapers.[18] The statistical picture for Aboriginal adoption is complicated, but by whatever measure, Native children have been vastly over-represented in the child welfare system since the 1950s. Native children have been placed in state care at a rate as high as four and a half times that of other Canadian children; in the four western provinces they represent at least 40 percent of the children "in care." Thus, here we are speaking of thousands, not hundreds, of adoption placements. Manitoba recorded the highest number of adoptions in the country. An internal file review conducted by the Manitoba Department of Family Services in 2004 calculated that between 1960 and 1980 almost five thousand children were placed outside Manitoba, two-thirds within Canada, the rest to the United States.[19] Encounters between Native children and child welfare systems mushroomed during the 1960s, when Aboriginal social welfare was transferred from the federal government to provincial governments.[20]

Thus, it is in no way surprising to discover a wealth of stories of apprehension in the Aboriginal case files. Children took many routes into the world of child welfare, for Aboriginal families imploded in ways that ranged from the dramatic to the mundane. Fathers shot mothers and/or themselves. Fathers abandoned families. Fathers lost their jobs. Mothers went to jail. Parents responded to the pressures of poverty and violence by neglecting or bullying their children; they beat them, they abandoned them, they did not feed or clothe them. In one instance, parents locked their children in a car overnight because they could not stand their crying. Children responded to such dysfunctional and abusive behaviour in kind.

In approximately half of my sample of two hundred files, direct intervention and apprehension by social workers is discernable. What makes these stories different from other encounters between the poor, their children, and the state?[21] Numbers provide part of the answer: over-representation is simply the racialization of poverty. But so too are the historical interactions of colonialism, which have consistently produced infantilized relations between Aboriginals and the Canadian state. These infantilized relations, enacted in encounters between social workers and Aboriginal families (as they were in other realms with police, doctors, and teachers, to name a few) worked to undermine one of the mainstays of North American culture: that the family takes care of its own. "Children have historically been the battleground on which the struggle between Indigenous People and newcomers has been waged," declared the Union of British Columbia Indian Chiefs in 2002. The child welfare system simply replaced residential schools as a mechanism for removing and assimilating Native children.[22] In what other circumstances can we imagine children living with their grandparents described as "deserted"? What is necessarily "irresponsible" about leaving one's children with one's own parents? Why was it not even possible to redeem good-parent status when children were in the care of grandparents while parents were away working?[23] That in such situations some grandparents turned to the state for assistance was not necessarily a referendum on permanent custody. In a perceptive study on shared parenthood among the Brazilian poor, Claudia Fonseca asks whether the basic premises of legal adoption are intelligible to those who are most involved: "the poverty-stricken families from which adoptable children are drawn." Are "abandonment," "foster care," and "adoption" – presented as obvious in the offices and courtrooms of the child welfare system – understood in the same terms by all?[24] Did the widowed birth father who requested temporary care for his son while he spent a summer looking for work expect to lose permanent custody? Even the potentially more ambiguous tales from the social work archive, such as the parents whom, according to caseworkers, "would simply drop the children off with anyone who would look after them," appear startling when the trajectory leads from this to legal apprehension, sibling separation, and adoption to families in Minnesota and Pennsylvania.[25]

Child welfare systems normalize and promote a universal definition of parenthood and family life in which the experiences and cultures of the Anglo middle class are privileged. This applies to Aboriginal people in Canada, and to poor people all over the world.[26] Nothing explained this better to me than a jolting personal/archival moment as I was doing this research. During my research time in Winnipeg, at the offices of the Department of Family Services, I began my day, as was customary, by opening an adoption case file from a large pile. This birth mother, described, incidentally, as "an unkempt woman who presents herself as being quite dull and confused, and looks like she has just come off a binge" seemed to "require time out from parenting, so would leave the children with whomever would look after them."[27] That very morning I had left my then three-year-old son, who accompanied me on the research trip, at a new daycare. Sure, he was in the company of the child of a friend, in a perfectly reputable, state-licensed daycare, to which I paid a lot of money. But these truths did not change the fact that I, too, needed "time out from parenting" and had just left my child with someone who would "look after him." (I had not, I realized, even caught the name of his caregiver that morning.)

The contradictions in (and profound racialization of) the production of normative parenthood leap from almost every page of the social work archive. Consider this description of a birth family in the malevolent terms it was intended to invoke: "A large collection of extended family living in one house."[28] What did it mean to describe Aboriginal parents who consistently "drifted," "wandered," or "rambled from one place to another," and how might this contrast to other parents – like me, perhaps - who "travel"? In cases of severe family implosion, such as the deaths of birth parents, why were extended family deemed inappropriate, their motives for wanting custody, questionable?[29] Indeed, why were extended family not contacted at all, in some cases learning about parentless children only after adoptions had been finalized? When social workers described someone who had a "higher degree of responsibility to their children than most Métis," or warned potential adoptive parents that Métis children have a "lower mental potential" because it was usually "a low class White man who would rely on Indian women for his sexual gratification," or attributed the repeated and increasingly hostile attempts of a birth father to regain custody of his children to "more [of] an ego blow than anything else," the compelling force of the kidnap narrative comes into view.[30] "Cradle snatchers. That's the whole long and short of it, nothing more than common kidnappers!" declares a character in Drew Hayden Taylor's play *Someday,* describing her experience as a birth mother whose child was apprehended in the 1960s. Children were taken simply "cuz we were Indians. Things were different way back then."[31]

At the same time, Native women were, in some areas in North America, subject to forced sterilization at rates twice as high as poor white women, and so it is not surprising that the politics of reproductive rights looked different in these communities.[32] The full story of the First Nations response to adoption and child welfare issues has yet to be fully told. Certainly, within the child welfare system some social workers, at least, were aware of Native opposition since the early 1970s, and some took pains to at least appear sensitive to Aboriginal concerns.[33] First Nations women voiced their public opposition to transracial adoption placements in various national and provincial women's organizations in 1974. That same year, the North American Council on Adoptable Children, a lobby group, approved a Native-initiated resolution that asked agencies to work "WITH" [sic] Native communities to strengthen families, find Native adoptive homes, or, in the last resort, "find good people" to care for Native children.[34] First Nations communities, especially women, also worked locally to provide shelters and other forms of housing for Native women with children, in order to keep their children out of the child welfare system.[35] Aboriginal publications constantly stressed the need for Aboriginal adoptive and foster homes, and many published lengthy stories, complete with photographs, of children in need of adoptive homes.[36]

No wonder, then, adoption as a form of colonial kidnap came to characterize the discourse of Native activism in the 1970s. Aboriginal politics, particularly the Red Power variant, drew inspiration from global movements for decolonization in the era, and children have always been stark and powerful symbols of anti-colonial solidarity.[37] A cartoon printed in the Aboriginal publication *Akwesasne Notes* tells the story of the "rescue" of Vietnamese children by US forces from the perspective of those on the losing end, by depicting an American couple shopping for orphans as though for souvenirs. The accompanying story was headlined "Another Native People Lose Their Children."[38] This transnational solidarity perhaps explains why when child welfare issues hit the political radar, the so-called export of Aboriginal children to adoptive homes in the United States seemed to sharpen the pain of child apprehension, particularly as interracial placements in the United States were coming to an end, and it was thus more difficult for white parents south of the border to adopt domestically. Almost all political interventions by Aboriginal activists on child welfare issues highlighted the exportation issue. In March 1976, for example, fifty Aboriginal and Métis people occupied the office of the deputy minister of social services in Saskatoon. Their general concern, about what they termed the "rapid increase in the intrusion of social workers into Native family life," was triggered by one especially high-profile case of Native children recently sent from Aboriginal foster parents in Saskatchewan to adoptive parents in Michigan.[39] The forced removal of Aboriginal children for adoption to the United States fit easily into a general discussion of imperialism and colonialism when Montreal's Black Power student-leader Rosie Douglas toured Indian reserves across Canada in the summer of 1975.[40] One Aboriginal publication, *New Breed,* even featured an Aboriginal cartoon superhero, who rescued Native children from US adoptive parents.[41]

Virtually the same conditions applied in the United States: high rates of Aboriginal children in state care; the popularization of transracial placements through an active promotion program by the Child Welfare League of America; horror stories of unjust apprehensions, which occasionally made the papers; and Aboriginal organizations increasingly committed to resisting what they saw as the incursions of the child welfare system. This resistance caught the attention of James Abourezk, senator from "Indian Country," South Dakota. Abourezk, the first Arab American elected to the US Senate, had an affinity for unpopular causes – he left politics after one term to found the American-Arab Anti-Discrimination Committee. But he did some remarkable things in office, including helping to organize Senate hearings on Aboriginal child welfare in 1974, in which dozens of Aboriginal people told their stories of forced removal of their children. In 1978, the United States' Indian Child Welfare Act (ICWA), which made the adoption of Aboriginal children by those without tribal affiliations extremely difficult, became law.[42]

This legislation, clearly a political victory for Indian tribes in the United States, had immediate reverberations. Researcher Patrick Johnson stressed the enormous symbolic importance of ICWA, the very existence of which, he argued, "increased the demands made on the Canadian government to find solutions." Canadian commentators and activists cited the US precedent sympathetically. At the same time as Canada appeared as a bastion of multicultural harmony for encouraging cross-racial adoptions of black children, the United States appeared as the more progressive place for prohibiting the same thing for Aboriginal children.[43]

The highlight of the kidnap narrative was the multi-year Kimelman Inquiry (the Review Committee on Indian and Métis Adoptions and Placements) in Manitoba, which began in 1982. Justice Edwin C. Kimelman and his committee spent many months touring the province, and issued an exhaustive and hard-hitting final report – referred to by historian Veronica Strong-Boag as a "wake-up call" – in 1985.[44] The committee provided a forum for a steady stream of Aboriginal people from across the province to speak publicly, and often bitterly and sadly, of their experiences with the child welfare system. Isaac Beaulieu of Brandon spoke for many when he declared, "In the eyes of our people, the agencies that care for children are looked upon as policemen, not a helping agency."[45] Here, too, the pain of losing children to American adoptive homes dominated. Peter Kelly, veteran Red Power activist from northern Ontario, was blunt: "What is objectionable is to take some dried up old prune in a suburb of Philadelphia who couldn't bear a child and take an Indian child from Canada and place them with that prune in Philadelphia. That kind of trafficking is what is objectionable."[46] While Kelly harnessed sexism to buttress his point, a particular form of anti-imperialism fuelled the issue. "Big shiny American cars would come onto the reserve, followed by the social worker's car," an Aboriginal social worker in Manitoba recalled; "when they left, there'd be a little Indian child sitting in the back of the American car bawling their eyes out."[47] It is possible to argue – as the *Winnipeg Free Press* did – that it was this trope of adoption that created the Kimelman Inquiry itself. In March 1982, the newspaper published a series of sensational stories about "child export" to the United States. It found a voluble foil in the form of Richard Zellinger, a former Ontario childcare worker turned director of a private Louisiana adoption agency. Zellinger claimed to have a long waiting list of Americans who wanted "those beautiful Canadian children," most of whom, he went on, "take to their new homes like a duck to water." The press dutifully reported that such talk "riled" and "stirred up" local Native leaders and quoted a chief who "condemned Zellinger and said he should be 'hanged.'"[48] A week later, out-of-province placements were banned, and Kimelman's committee was convened.[49]

Yet, we need to make room in this discussion for the less straightforward tales for which "kidnap" – always an abstraction – is also a distortion. Of the almost one hundred life stories of adopted Aboriginal adults gathered by researchers in recent years, a small minority – 8 percent – believe their adoptions were illegal or improper. The vast majority were either relinquished or apprehended as a result of neglect, abuse, or some form of family dysfunction.[50] These stories, of course, represent a tiny fraction of the total, and, in making the argument for a more complicated understanding than the discourse of "scoop" provides, I in no way diminish or disbelieve the pain of those who had horrific experiences. But "scoop" is heavy-handed and leaves out a lot.

Birth parents tend to disappear when adoption is narrated in the abstract terms of either cultural genocide or humanitarian rescue, and none more so than the Aboriginal birth mothers who requested adoption for their children. A relatively unambiguous request for adoption is discernable from about a quarter of my sample. Birth mothers of Aboriginal children had some of the same reasons for requesting adoption as did other women of the era. Their boyfriends – Native and non-Native – abandoned them. They had affairs with married men. They were raped. They had several children and could not cope with more. "She is not content being a single parent on welfare," a social worker reported of one woman who had two children and a dysfunctional husband. "She would like to improve her conditions by furthering her education. Her family is not in favour of the relinquishment." Adoption promised secrecy, even from immediate family who, as one single woman explained, "would put considerable pressure on her to keep the child."[51] Some of the birth mothers were white woman with Native boy-friends and furious, racist parents. Here, too, the secrecy promised by adoption in this era was paramount.

Historian Veronica Strong-Boag warns us not to glamorize what she terms the "classical family of Native nostalgia," which can, of course, both inspire and homogenize.[52] To some Manitoba young women, the bonds of Aboriginal community felt closed and restrictive. One woman entered a maternity home in order to hide her pregnancy and refused to register her child as Indian so as to leave no trace for her reserve. Some were students who did not want to interrupt their studies. "This is the most heart-breaking decision I have had to make," explained one such young woman, surprised by a pregnancy as she was about to enter nursing school.[53] "As she is Indian I feel she is showing a great deal of initiative in choosing adoption and should be encouraged to continue her education," wrote a social worker of another woman in 1966, a rare indication that adoption as a strategy of upward mobility – common for single white girls of the era – was occasionally seized by others.[54] Others relinquished their children after trying, and failing, to raise them on their own. One such mother said she wanted adoption but also feared that her child, being Native, would never find a secure adoptive family (a fear echoed by many Montreal mothers of black children.) In all these examples, the circumstances that produced such narrow choices should not be conflated with the absence of adult subjectivity itself.

Historical memory is always complicated, and women reflected on their experiences as birth mothers differently with the passage of time.[55] The archive of Native adoption often brings the story forward as parties attempted to find each other later in life. In a trove of remarkable stories, these offer a kaleidoscope of emotions – among them chiefly grief and forgiveness – and testify to the immense continuing damage this era of adoption inflicted. But here, too, the lines between kidnap and rescue are sometimes difficult to see precisely. Fifteen years after her children were apprehended by the state, one mother wrote what she titled "A Mother's Anguish" and asked the Children's Aid Society (CAS) to send it to her sons. In it she recounted her story of severe abuse by her husband, divorce, poverty, and serious alcoholism. "I had no right to drag my beautiful babies to my level, so I got up the last bit of decency in me and took them to the CAS and left them there to be put up for adoption," she explained. "All the people I knew told me what a horrible person I was, even drunken women threw it in my face: 'at least they kept their kids.' But for what? Those kids with the drunken mothers turned out to be hoodlums and prostitutes, which I had not wanted for my boys ... I know in my heart that I made the right decision at the time."[56] That even a handful of Aboriginal women narrated their stories of relinquishment like this, as decency, obliges historians not to let such voices disappear.

The kidnap narrative of Aboriginal adoption relies on a unitary view of Native birth mothers. The notion that the adoption of black children was unambiguously heroic also functions on half-truths. One of the long-standing, and highly romantic, beliefs about interracial adoption in this era is that most of the "black" adopted children circulating through the agency in Montreal were mixed race, the offspring of liaisons between white women and black men. This narrative of doomed interracial romance certainly fuelled media interest in and public representations of needy black children, especially as interracial dating was emerging as an issue of civil rights. Yet, even as adopting a black child was becoming an act of goodwill, giving birth to one signified immorality.[57] White women with black boyfriends and those same scandalized parents produced about a third of Montreal's adopted black children. Of course, when the public face of interracial adoption was the mixed-race child, white adoptive parents found another claim upon which to base their parenthood. In all of this, however, almost no one saw the extraordinary struggles of black birth mothers (of whom there were twice as many); many of them assisted immigrant domestics, newly arrived from the West Indies. The very existence of a global black underclass in Canada complicated our beloved national narrative of anti-conquest; no wonder their tale has been eclipsed by feel-good stories about the rescue of their children.

Despite what a Montreal social worker described as a "strong cultural need" among West Indian women to keep their children – ironically in this instance because the unmarried mother in question arrived at the agency having survived a botched abortion – half of my sample of black women in Montreal did not keep their children, and opted instead for adoption. This is despite that black birth mothers were generally encouraged by social workers to plan to keep their child, advice rarely dispensed to white women. Usually, this took the form of repeatedly warning them that their child – particularly if "full Negro" – would fare poorly in the adoption system and might stay in the foster system indefinitely. Even during the high point of integrationist fervour in Montreal, when interracial adoption activism seemed everywhere, pregnant black women considering adoption were told they should wait until after birth to decide, when "the full force of her emotional feelings will have a different meaning to her."[58] Hundreds of case files later, I simply cannot imagine a young unwed white woman of the era hearing this. Black women, such as the twenty-two-year-old Barbadian who arrived in Canada pregnant and who wanted neither single parenthood nor even marriage because, as she said, "people in the West Indies get married too early," often had to fight their way into the adoption system.[59] Too much social welfare for some, too little for others; this is one of the great paradoxes of the child welfare system historically.

These varied experiences of birth mothers point toward fundamental distinctions in the discourses of adoption in different communities. These differences include vastly contrasting circumstances of adoption, differently motivated adoptive parents, and different agency practices. All of these suggest a different cultural and political understanding of the meaning of race as applied to different racialized groups.

Most Aboriginal children experienced the ragged edges of adoption practice: multiple placements, at an older age. Two or three placements in foster care was average, and as many as six was in no way unusual. The high number of apprehensions, of course, also determined a very different pattern of adoption: adopted Native children were older, and often more than one child was involved and many siblings were separated. Montreal's black children were spared most of these problems.

There were also fundamental differences in the demographic profile, motivation, and politics of adoptive parents, all of which produced different cultural milieus for adopted children. To simplify, the typical destination for a black adopted children was a middle-class family, headed by a teacher or an engineer, in Montreal's West Island suburbs. Native kids were adopted by families headed by electricians in small-town Ontario or small businessmen in rural Minnesota. Also to simplify: secular humanism became the idiom of Montreal's adoptive parents. They described themselves as "freethinkers," "internationalists," or "rebels at heart." One mother was described by her social worker as "inclined to get on a soapbox."[60] Social workers looked for signs – generally expressed in what we might now call the language of therapy or personal growth – that parents understood interracial adoptions were different from same-race adoptions. "I went into their attitudes towards Negroes quite fully with them and found they did not have the strength," wrote one social worker of a couple she rejected. Wrote another, approvingly: "They have the necessary streak of independence and unorthodoxy, they are not concerned about what other people think."[61]

In the case of Aboriginal-adopting parents, it was more common to hear religious, rather than secular, motivations. Adopting an Indian child, explained a Presbyterian couple from West Virginia, was possible only because they had attained sufficient "faith." A Baptist couple in North Carolina had recently undergone a religious conversion, which, as they described it, saved their marriage and started them thinking about adoption. "Their recent success in business and recent discovery of Christ made them feel strongly that they need to share what they have with an Indian child," their social worker explained, approvingly.[62]

Perhaps the greatest difference in these stories is how race was conceptualized. Here we see both similarities and differences, and I do not want to overstate either. Culturally shared ideas about what I call the "racelessness of babies" was alluring and no doubt comforting for many adoptive parents as they contemplated their voyage across the chasm of race in North America. "Both parents agreed they were not adopting a child of native background but a human being," wrote one social worker.[63] "You've got to accept them as babies and forget about the rest," declared a Montreal mother of two black children.[64] To aid in this forgetting, some adoptive parents tried to reimagine their black child's bodies as white, likening their skin, for example, to a tan. The belief that children had mutable racial beliefs and boundaries – that "children have no prejudice" – is obvious in these debates about interracial adoption but also evident in this era in discussions of desegregation in the American South, for example, where it was believed that "children were particularly vulnerable to the effects of integration."[65] It's not surprising, therefore, that people who believed themselves to be behaving honourably, as I think white adoptive parents did, found some solace, at least temporarily, in race transcendence. It's more interesting that some, especially parents of black children, did not and instead attempted to raise racially conscious children. And this stemmed from politics; the different ways in which adoption and race were imagined by various protagonists.

Montreal's Open Door Society quickly outgrew its origins as a white parent support group and became an active civil rights organization, dedicated to a unifying politic of adoption. This group maintained for almost twenty years an extensive international communications network, lobbied governments, and organized international conferences. Most significantly, it worked with Montreal's black community to promote civil rights and teach black history and culture. It helped to organize a school for black children of white parents, taught by blacks; members held workshops in black beauty salons to learn how to care for their children's hair, they maintained a library of multiracial children's literature, they organized community Christmas parties and picnics at Montreal's Negro Community Centre. Members also maintained an unusually close association with the Children's Service Centre, the Montreal adoption agency. They became, effectively, part of the screening process, as parents considering cross-racial adoption were directed by the agency to attend Open Door Society functions and read its literature. Probing the race consciousness and politics of prospective parents became part of the casework at this agency, and it constantly encouraged parents to "stretch" – a favourite social work word.

So in these various ways, something like a community of interracial adoption was created in and around Montreal. This community believed that the families they had created through adoption embodied the possibility of racial equality. The social meaning of "blackness" and "race" were fluid and certainly non-unanimously understood, but notions such as "race pride"; respect for black knowledge, history, and culture; and the importance of relations with other black people were paramount. The force, and uniqueness, of this community of interracial adoption was evident particularly in contrast to other communities with other politics. For years, Open Door Society parents in Montreal received requests from anxious American white adoptive parents who wondered which US hotels and restaurants might welcome mixed-race families, and even which US cities had integrated neighbour-hoods. In the early 1970s, during a period of highly contested adoption politics, a black social work consultant from Missouri approached the group, offering his services to educate white adoptive parents. He was politely re-buffed, the group noting that it had already had such an education program in place for several years and had no trouble finding speakers from Montreal's black community. It encouraged him "to continue to offer services to parent groups in the US."[66] On one rare occasion, a kidnap narrative was voiced by a Canadian black organization, in an article critical of transracial adoption first published in the *Village Voice,* then reprinted in *Contrast* in 1972. The Open Door Society's letter to the editor extolling the virtues of how trans-racial adoption was practised in Canada was printed with a polite note: "Your points are sincerely well taken."[67] Again, the United States functioned as Canada's racial foil, to reflect back multicultural tolerance.

For all the reasons I have explored, there was little sense of a community of interracial adoption created around Manitoba's Aboriginal children. They were widely disbursed geographically, often in rural areas and small towns. While individual families may have aligned themselves with adoption ad-vocacy groups, there was no Open Door Society equivalent operating in Manitoba.[68] Adoptive parents never spoke with one voice (in Montreal or in Manitoba), but the defensiveness of some white parents of Aboriginal children is striking. A Brandon-based group of adoptive parents testifying at the Kimelman Inquiry in 1985, for example, rebuffed the arguments of Aboriginal spokespeople as "making the issue into a racial confrontation."[69] The institutional practices of agencies working with prospective adoptive parents of Aboriginal children were extremely different. Social workers rarely engaged prospective parents in extended discussions on racial identity or racism. Indeed, in many case files, race was barely mentioned, and when it was, it was simply another way of saying "appearance." Parents might ex-plain, for example, that they were willing to adopt an Aboriginal child be-cause others in the family had dark hair or a swarthy complexion, and thus the child would not feel different. If the idiom of Montreal was that the parents should "stretch," in Manitoba the favoured phrase was that the children should "fit in." An adoptive father declared his intention to send his son to Boy Scouts and Sunday school in order to "learn to mix with White children at a young age, so he could function effectively in White society."[70] In this climate, it is not surprising that discussions of race pride and con-sciousness could take superficial forms. Were the parents who dressed their child in an Indian chief costume for a party and explained this to their social worker as an example of pride in heritage typical? It's difficult to know, for the discussion of this topic, among my sample of social workers and adoptive parents at least, was barely audible. In a perceptive reflection on the "Sixties Scoop," adoption scholar Raven Sinclair has argued that it's not just that the occasional weekend foray to a powwow was an insufficient basis for cultural learning. The issue is that such idealized versions of Aboriginal culture do not square with the rest of life. "What the adoptee may not know," writes Sinclair, "is that they are not seeing Aboriginal culture; they are seeing the vestiges of colonization and a neo-colonial society's construction of Aboriginal culture."[71] But who was going to explain that?

As comforting as the "haven from racism" model might be to Canadian sensibilities, these different moments of adoption politics in this country suggest that how one imagines children, race, and racial hierarchies is more significant than where. The differences in perceptions of black and Aboriginal transracial adoptions cannot be accounted for solely by a "progressive" record on the one hand, and a "failure" on the other. How can black children in white families be bearers of reconciliation, but Aboriginal children in white families be monuments to colonialism? Perhaps the problem lies in the inherent instabilities of using symbolic children to gauge, illuminate, and solve adult social problems?

Acknowledgment
Thanks to Susan Belyea, Karen Dyck, Roberta Hamilton, Scott Rutherford, and Barrington Walker for their help with this work. Thanks also to the editors of this volume for their help and their patience.

Notes

1 Judith Walkowitz, *City of Dreadful Delight* (Chicago: University of Chicago Press, 1993), 21. On the symbolic links between women, gender, and nation, see also Anne McLintock, *Imperial Leather: Race, Gender and Sexuality in the Colonial Context* (New York: Routledge, 1995).

2 Elizabeth Chin, "Children Out of Bounds in Globalising Times," *Postcolonial Studies* 6, 3 (2003): 312. See also Jo Boyden, "Childhood and the Policy Makers: A Comparative Perspective on the Globalization of Childhood," in Allison James and Alan Prout, eds., *Constructing and Reconstructing Childhood: Contemporary Issues in the Sociological Study of Childhood* (New York: Falmer Press, 1990), 184-215.

3 Patrick Johnston, *Native Children and the Child Welfare System* (Toronto: Canadian Council on Social Development, 1983), 23, takes the phrase the "Sixties Scoop" from a self-reflective BC social worker, herself a participant in the removal of Native children from their communities, on what she later referred to as "the slightest pretext." Other important commentaries on the politics of Aboriginal adoption in Canada are Margaret Ward, *The Adoption of Native Canadian Children* (Cobalt: Highway Book Shop, 1984); Brad McKenzie and Pete Hudson, "Native Children, Child Welfare, and the Colonization of Native People," in Kenneth L. Levitt and Brian Warf, eds., *The Challenge of Child Welfare* (Vancouver: UBC Press, 1985), 125-41; Suzanne Fournier and Ernie Crey, *Stolen from Our Embrace: The Abduction of First Nations Children and the Restoration of Aboriginal Communities* (Vancouver: Douglas and McIntyre, 1997); Patricia A. Monture, "A Vicious Circle: Child Welfare and the First Nations," *Canadian Journal of Women and the Law* 3, 1 (1989): 1-17; Geoffrey York, *The Dispossessed: Life and Death in Native Canada* (Boston: Little, Brown, 1990); Christopher Bagley, "Adoption of Native Children in Canada: A Policy Analysis and a Research Report," in Howard Alstein and Rita Simon, eds., *Intercountry Adoption: A Multinational Perspective* (New York: Praeger, 1991), 55-79; Marie Adams, *Our Son a Stranger: Adoption Breakdown and Its*

Effects on Parents (Montreal and Kingston: McGill-Queen's University Press, 2002); Shandra Spears, "Strong Spirit, Fractured Identity: An Ojibway Adoptee's Journey to Wholeness," in Bonita Lawrence and Kim Anderson, eds., *Strong Women Stories* (Toronto: Sumach Press, 2003), 81-94.

4 E.C. Kimelman, *No Quiet Place: Review Committee on Indian and Métis Adoptions and Placements* (Winnipeg: Manitoba Department of Community Services, 1985).

5 Winona LaDuke, Forward to Bartholomew Dean and Jerome M. Levi, eds., *At the Risk of Being Heard: Identity, Indigenous Rights and Postcolonial States* (Ann Arbor: University of Michigan Press, 2003), x.

6 Kenn Richard, "On the Matter of Cross-Cultural Aboriginal Adoptions," in Ivan Brown, Ferzana Chaze, Don Fuchs, Jean Lafrance, Sharon Mckay, and Shelley Thomas-Prokop, eds., *Putting a Human Face on Child Welfare: Voices from the Prairies* (Regina: Prairie Child Welfare Consortium, 2007), 189.

7 See, for example, Renate Andres, "The Apprehension of Native Children," *Ontario Indian* 4, 4 (1981): 32-46; McKenzie and Hudson, "Native Children, Child Welfare," 137. On the campaign for the Indian Child Welfare Act in the United States, see Laura Briggs, "Communities Resisting Interracial Adoption: The Indian Child Welfare Act and the NABSW Statement of 1972" (paper presented at the Adoption and Culture Conference, Tampa, Florida, October 2005).

8 Karen Dubinsky, "We Adopted a Negro: Interracial Adoption and the Hybrid Baby in 1960s Canada," in M. Fahrni and R. Rutherdale, eds., *Creating Postwar Canada: Community, Diversity and Dissent, 1945-75* (Vancouver: UBC Press, 2008), 268-88.

9 At the same moment in Sweden, some of the first formal mechanisms of international adoption were created, which also confirmed to their proponents Sweden's egalitarian ideology. See Barbara Yngvesson, "'Un Niño de Cualquier Color': Race and Nation in Inter-Country Adoption," in Jane Jenson and Boaventura de Sousa Santos, eds., *Globalizing Institutions: Case Studies in Regulation and Innovation* (Aldershot, UK: Ashgate, 2000), 182.

10 Claude Rose, "Should White Parents Adopt Colored Babies?" *Coronet*, December 1964: 42.

11 Jane Armstrong, "A Canadian Haven for Black U.S. Babies," *Globe and Mail*, 1 October 2005. See also the response by Karen Balcom and Karen Dubinsky, "Babies across Borders," *Globe and Mail*, 13 October 2005.

12 Ellen Herman, "Modern Culture and the Many Meanings of Adoption," keynote address, Conference on Adoption and Culture, University of Tampa, 17-20 November 2005.

13 Sara K. Dorow, *Transnational Adoption: A Cultural Economy of Race, Gender and Kinship* (New York: NYU Press, 2006), 55-56.

14 Brad Evenson, "The Sixties Scoop," *Calgary Herald*, 19 April 1998.

15 "I deliberately chose to downplay his warning, not because I believed he was necessarily wrong, but because I had faith in the current belief that the environment was more important in the upbringing of all children. His comments still haunt me." Adams, *Our Son a Stranger*, 104.

16 Brad Evenson, "The Sixties Scoop," *Calgary Herald*, 19 April 1998.

17 This work is based on a 20 percent sample of case files from the Montreal Children's Service Centre between 1956 and 1969 (approximately eight hundred cases) and a 13 percent sample of the extant files of the (former) Manitoba Children's Aid Society, from 1961 to 1980.

18 Charles Saunders, *Share the Care: The Story of the Nova Scotia Home for Coloured Children* (Halifax: Nimbus, 1994), 138.

19 The figures are as follows: total number of children placed outside Manitoba, 4,824; total within Canada, 3,649; total placed in the United States, 1,149; total outside North America, 16. Of these placements, 274 were Caucasian, 170 were of unknown racial origin, the rest were Aboriginal or Métis. Manitoba Department of Family Services, "Out of Province Adoptions," internal report, 2004.

20 Suzanne Fournier and Ernie Crey report the following national statistical trend: in 1959, Native children represented 1 percent of children "in care"; by 1969, this figure had climbed to between 30 and 40 percent. Fournier and Crey, *Stolen from Our Embrace*, 83. See also Canada, *Report of the Royal Commission on Aboriginal Peoples*, vol. 3, *Gathering Strength* (Ottawa: Ministry of Supply and Services, 1996), 24-26; and Marlee Kline, "Child Welfare Law: Best Interests of the Child; Ideology and First Nations," *Osgoode Hall Law Journal* 30 (1992): 375-426.

21 Another statistical survey of Aboriginal adoption in Manitoba found a higher rate. Using a list from the Department of Indian Affairs in Ottawa, Josette Lukowycz sampled ninety-five adoptions of Aboriginal children between the 1950s and 1984 and found that 80 percent were non-voluntary relinquishments. Josette Lukowycz, "An Exploratory Study of the Adoption of Indian Children in Manitoba" (MA thesis, University of Manitoba, 1985), 48.

22 Ardith Walkem, "Calling Forth Our Future: Options for the Exercise of Indigenous Peoples' Authority in Child Welfare" (Vancouver: Union of British Columbia Indian Chiefs, 2002), 9. See also the various articles in D. Memee Lavell-Harvard and Jeannette Corbiere Lavell, eds., *"Until Our Hearts Are on the Ground": Aboriginal Mothering, Oppression, Resistance and Rebirth* (Toronto: Demeter Press, 2006).

23 All citations from Manitoba Children's Aid Society Case Files (hereafter cited as CAS file).

24 Claudia Fonseca, "Patterns of Shared Parenthood among the Brazilian Poor," in Toby Alice Volkman, ed., *Cultures of Transnational Adoption* (Durham, NC: Duke University Press, 2005), 157. This point has also been made by commentators on Aboriginal adoption; see Pauline Turner Strong, "To Forget Their Tongue, Their Name, and Their Whole Relation: Captivity, Extra-Tribal Adoption, and the Indian Child Welfare Act," in Sarah Franklin and Susan McKinnon, eds., *Relative Values: Reconfiguring Kinship Studies* (New York: Oxford University Press, 2001), 468-94.

25 CAS file.

26 Boyden, "Childhood and the Policy Makers," 184-215; Erica Burman, "Local, Global or Globalized? Child Development and International Child Rights Legislation," *Childhood* 3, 45 (1996): 45-66.

27 CAS file.

28 Ibid.

29 In a particularly tragic example, children were given instead to an adoptive family that used torture, sexual and physical, as discipline. CAS file.

30 CAS file.

31 Drew Hayden Taylor, *Someday* (Saskatoon: Fifth House, 1993), 14.

32 Andrea Smith, *Conquest: Sexual Violence and American Indian Genocide* (Cambridge, MA: South End Press, 2005).

33 In 1973, the director of the Adoption Resource Exchange of North America (ARENA, an extension of the Indian Adoption Project, which promoted cross-border and cross-racial placements) underlined that "since the Indian people have the same resistance to their children being placed transracially as the Blacks, we continue to use the resources of ARENA to make known the need for Indian families." Karen Balcom, *The Traffic in Babies: Cross-Border Adoption, Baby-Selling and Child Welfare in the United States and Canada, 1930-1972* (Toronto: University of Toronto Press, forthcoming), 451.

34 "Good Intentions Not Enough!" *Akwesasne Notes,* Early Summer 1974, 41. Resolutions calling for Aboriginal control over the child welfare system were passed by the National Association of Native Women and the Indian Homemakers Association of BC in 1974. "Native Women Exhorted to Become More Active," *Thunder Bay Chronicle Journal* 26 (August 1974); Walkem, "Calling Forth Our Future," 15.

35 Nancy Janovicek, "Assisting Our Own: Urban Migration, Self-Governance, and Native Women's Organizing in Thunder Bay, Ontario, 1972-1989," *American Indian Quarterly* 27, 3-4 (2003): 548-64.

36 See, for example, the "Today's Child" column in the *Toronto Native Times,* which ran in the mid-1970s.

37 Scott Rutherford, "Canada's Other Red Scare: The Anicinabe Park Occupation, Indigenous Radicalism and the Circulation of Global Culture and Politics, 1965-1975" (PhD dissertation, Queen's University, n.d.).

38 "Another Native People Lose Their Children," *Akwesasne Notes,* Early Summer 1975, 26.

39 "Department of Social Services Steals Children," *New Breed,* September 1975.

40 Library and Archives Canada, RG 146, RCMP files, Native People's Friendship Delegation, vol. 1, 14.

41 *New Breed,* November-December 1975.

42 The most complete account of the Indian Child Welfare Act campaign is found in Steven Unger, "The Indian Child Welfare Act of 1978: A Case Study" (PhD dissertation, University

of Southern California, 2004). See also Laura Briggs, "Communities Resisting Interracial Adoption: The Indian Child Welfare Act and the NABSW Statement of 1972" (paper presented at the Adoption and Culture Conference, Tampa, Florida, October 2005.)

43 Patrick Johnston, *Native Children and the Child Welfare System* (Toronto: Canadian Council on Social Development, 1983), 90; Renate Andres, "The Apprehension of Native Children," *Ontario Indian* 4, 4 (1981): 32-46; and McKenzie and Hudson, "Native Children, Child Welfare," 137.

44 Veronica Strong-Boag, *Finding Families, Finding Ourselves: English Canada Confronts Adoption from the Nineteenth Century to the 1990s* (Toronto: Oxford University Press, 2006), 169.

45 Review Committee on Indian and Métis Adoptions and Placements, *Transcripts and Briefs* (Winnipeg: Manitoba Community Services, 1985), 15.

46 Review Committee, *Transcripts and Briefs,* 464.

47 Fournier and Crey, *Stolen from Our Embrace,* 89. The "foreign car" is shorthand for a globalized fear. See, for example, Luis White, "Cars Out of Place: Vampires, Technology and Labor in East and Central Africa," *Representations* 43 (Summer 1993): 27-50; Abigail Adams, "Gringas, Ghouls and Guatemala: The 1994 Attacks on North American Women Accused of Body Organ Trafficking," *Journal of Latin American Anthropology* 4, 1 (1999): 112-33.

48 Maureen Brosnahan, "Child Export for Adoption Riles Natives," *Winnipeg Free Press,* 4 March 1982.

49 Mary Ann Fitzgerald, "Judge to Review Native Adoptions," *Winnipeg Free Press,* 13 March 1982. One of the dramatically failed Louisiana placements, the story of the Gott children, is explored in Colleen Rajotte's documentary series "Confronting the Past." See http://www.rajottedocs.com.

50 Raven Sinclair, "All My Relations: Native Transracial Adoption; A Critical Case Study of Cultural Identity" (PhD dissertation, University of Calgary, 2007), 258.

51 CAS file.

52 Strong-Boag, *Finding Families, Finding Ourselves,* 138.

53 CAS file.

54 See, for example, Strong-Boag, *Finding Families, Finding Ourselves;* Ricki Solinger, *Beggars and Choosers: How the Politics of Choice Shapes Adoption, Abortion and Welfare in the United States* (New York: Hill and Wang, 2001); Barbara Melosh, *Strangers and Kin: The American Way of Adoption* (Cambridge, MA: Harvard University Press, 2003); and Julie Berebitsky, *Like Our Very Own: Adoption and the Changing Culture of Motherhood, 1851-1950* (Lawrence, KS: University Press of Kansas, 2000).

55 See Ann Fessler's sensitive collection of interviews with birth mothers, *The Girls Who Went Away: The Hidden History of Women Who Surrendered Children for Adoption in the Decades before Roe v. Wade* (New York: Penguin, 2006).

56 CAS file.

57 Renee C. Romano, *Race Mixing: Black-White Marriage in Post War America* (Cambridge, MA: Harvard University Press, 2003), 75.

58 Montreal Children's Service Centre Case File (hereafter cited as CSC file).

59 Ibid.

60 Ibid.

61 Ibid.

62 CAS file.

63 CSC file.

64 Chris Davies, "Society Discusses Aims and Problems," *Lakeshore News,* 2 June 1960.

65 Romano, *Race Mixing,* 161.

66 Open Door Society correspondence files, 1972.

67 "Article Considered Disservice," *Contrast,* 2 February 1973.

68 Project Opikihiwawin, a group of adoptive parents of Aboriginal children, started in Winnipeg in 1979.

69 Review Committee, Michael Malazdrewicz, Westman Adoptive Parent Group, *Transcripts and Briefs,* 12.

70 CAS file.

71 Raven Sinclair, "Identity Lost and Found: Lessons from the Sixties Scoop," *First Peoples Child and Family Review* 3, 1 (2007): 73.

2

"Forgotten People of All the Forgotten": Children with Disabilities in English Canada from the Nineteenth Century to the New Millennium

Veronica Strong-Boag

Birth announcements invite public celebration. Some new arrivals, such as the thalidomide-affected infant born to a Kitchener, Ontario, couple in the spring of 1962 and the conjoined twins and fragile sextuplets born in Vancouver, British Columbia, in December 2006 and January 2007, respectively, also invoke consternation and, sometimes, state intervention.[1] These newsworthy examples, like the girls and boys with autism spectrum disorder featured in the *Vancouver Sun* in the spring of 2007, are only the most visible of a broad sweep of youngsters with disabilities of every sort.[2] Impairments may occur at any point in childhood and youth, and Canadian numbers, although generally uncertain, have been significant.[3] Many children and youth have been handicapped in some aspect of their physical and mental functioning and disabled in their performance of normality. Pervasive prejudice in most times and places has further deepened vulnerability.

Whenever they happen and whatever form they take, disabilities present girls and boys, mothers and fathers, and communities with challenges, sometimes short-term and sometimes ongoing, that are not always easily reconciled with prevailing preferences or the demands of day-to-day life. Generating feelings variously of love, sympathy, discomfort, frustration, and despair, such girls and boys have disappeared from much of history. To everyone but those who love them, they, as one Canadian observer lamented in 1949, readily recede from public consideration to become the "forgotten people of all the forgotten."[4]

This chapter sets out to jog our collective memory of one part of the story of English Canada's youngsters with disabilities. It begins with a review of their commonplace evaluation by society and experts, next suggests the strength and vulnerability of birth families, and focuses finally on the evolving options for children with disabilities in twentieth-century English Canada. If precedent is any indication, the prognosis for twenty-first-century Vancouver's fragile twins and surviving sextuplets, like that of the victim of thalidomide in 1962, leaves much to be desired.

Defining Normality for Children and Youth

Disadvantage and disability are always socially constructed. Youngsters who are racialized, classed, and gendered as inferior by the dominant society are handicapped before they explore life's paths. They are hard put to attain the dominant definition of normality, their families struggle against greater odds, and private and public initiatives of every sort regularly embody prejudice. I have elsewhere described how race, class, gender, and disability created vulnerabilities in adoption in Canada, and the many intersections of disadvantage provide the critical backdrop for the discussion here as well.[5] By the end of the twentieth century, Canadian welfare authorities acknowledged the social construction of disability by grouping youngsters racialized as Native or African as "special needs" alongside those with presumed physical and mental handicaps.

In the modern world, scientific and social scientific definitions of normality became increasingly powerful for parents, communities, and governments.[6] Where imperfection might be previously assumed to be divine design, supposed defects were less taken for granted in a more secular climate. Canadians have had great hopes for advances in medical science, not to mention diets, clothing, and exercise regimes, and these contributed to shifts in what was viewed as acceptable and possible for all ages. For some youngsters, developments such as vaccinations against polio and measles and surgery for cleft palates and club foot could well better lives.[7] Old injuries lost some of their power, especially in the context of public medicare, beginning in Saskatchewan in 1946, and governments' increasing willingness to fund preventative programs and remedial treatments. Gains could be very real.

Nor were modern Canadians unanimous about the appropriate standards for judging human beings. Communities of every sort maintained some part of traditional responses that might contradict or confirm new assessments.[8] Discrimination was never readily given up. Human rights movements, especially after the Second World War, nevertheless directed attention to inequities of ability, as well as of class, race, and gender, and they helped to inspire new advocates for a fair deal. Some children identified with disabilities benefited from a new spirit of acceptance and inclusion.[9]

For those who could not or would not be "improved" along up-to-date lines, however, new standards sharpened the boundary between supposedly normal and abnormal populations and readily consigned the latter to evaluation as inferior. In schools, hospitals, and clinics, girls and boys, and their parents, quickly learned just how they were to be valued and regulated. New systems of categorization and discipline informed twentieth-century eugenics and the related ideologies of racism, sexism, and ableism. Flagrant abuses, such as those epitomized by Nazi concentration camps, curbed open enthusiasm in many quarters but negative eugenics, with its invocation of sterilization, and positive eugenics, with its pronatalist agenda, have threaded through Canadian life.[10]

Ontario's first inspector of the feeble-minded (1915) and first chief of the Child Welfare Division of the federal Department of Health (1920), Dr. Helen MacMurchy embodied the close connections between the promise of more scientific human measurement and suspicion of some forms of diversity.[11] Her 1920 book, *The Almosts: A Study of the Feeble Minded,* made it quite clear that progress demanded the containment of supposedly blighted human stock. Mental disability was identified as a threat to the body politic, and youngsters with disabilities became both the products and the producers of familial and national tragedy.[12] Few public commentators were as explicit as MacMurchy, but her overall assessment fitted comfortably with much policy over the course of the twentieth century.

Disabilities and health impairments were used to justify exclusion of immigrants from 1886 to 2001: the 1952 Immigration Act specified "idiots, imbeciles or morons," the "insane," "psychopathic personalities," persons with "epilepsy," and those who were "dumb, blind, or otherwise physically defective." In the twenty-first century, Canada prohibited the entry of those who would put "excessive demand on health or social services." In a similar vein, not until 1986 did the Supreme Court require that a daughter with a mental handicap give her consent to the sterilization requested by her mother.[13] Accommodation, or "reasonable accommodation" as it is more often termed, in order to ensure access to public spaces such as polling stations, schools, transportation, and streets, awaited the last decades of the twentieth century and remained far from complete.[14]

Native, minority ethnic communities, and the poor in general were especially vulnerable to being singled out as failing the test of the survival of the fittest, often equated with dominant groups or the so-called normal. The Better Baby and beauty contests that flourished for much of the twentieth century spelled out the details of exclusion. So did seemingly innocuous developments such as the increasing emphasis on high school and university completion, markers of the new normalcy that were regularly celebrated in local newspapers.[15] Even as late as 2008, a major report on Aboriginal youngsters concluded that "early childhood screening and assessment tools and school-readiness inventories currently used in Canada have been developed, normed and validated in research involving predominantly English-speaking children of European and Asian heritage living in middle-class urban settings."[16] Whatever their competencies, youngsters from disadvantaged communities have frequently been subject to scrutiny that often took their inferiority for granted. They readily emerged, as one brutal commentator put it, "spoilt goods" in the view of many mainstream observers.[17]

The recurring failure of care confirms pervasive beliefs that some lives are simply worth less than others. Recent polls make the same point. The failure to live up to standards of what counted as normal could be very dangerous. Many modern Canadians sympathized with so-called mercy killings of those who suffered painful conditions.[18] Estimates that Canadians with disabilities were five times more at risk of abuse from family members and others told the same story.[19] In a few extreme cases, despair, lack of financial and emotional support, and generally limited options have driven desperate parents to murder their offspring and sometimes themselves.[20] Public response to such tragedies has often confirmed that youngsters with disabilities are frequently viewed as having a lesser right to life. To be considered abnormal is to be especially vulnerable to such judgment.

Domestic Strength and Fragility

The fate of all youngsters is inextricably tied to families, and this is especially true for those with disabilities. Families everywhere constitute the first line of support. Even if they sometimes yearned for respite from responsibility, they have often taken for granted the need to shelter and protect dependents, and the great majority has not readily surrendered offspring who did not match the standards of the day. Disproportionately expected to deal with family health and children, mothers also took the lead in dealing with impairments. Until vaccinations helped reduce the toll, recurring diseases such as scarlet fever, which blinded and/or deafened many thousands of youngsters, kept women busy.[21] For many years, they could nevertheless be suspect, since maternal influences on developing fetuses were sometimes blamed for physical and mental injuries.[22] The rise of Freudian-influenced psychology and psychiatry offered another form of mother-blaming.[23] Guilt readily added to the mix of feelings found in families.[24] Many women also interpreted their tasks to include public and private advocacy for their charges, and they have been prominent in equality-seeking movements.[25] Mothers were not alone in these roles but fathers were more likely to meet expectations by bringing in money to support domestic needs.[26] Many Canadians were more likely to count on female relatives, notably grandparents and aunts or sisters, to shoulder physical and emotional duties.[27]

Over the course of the twentieth century, kin became steadily more visible in demanding services from schools and health care authorities. Many Anglo-Celtic women were early supporters of specialized schools as a means of improving opportunities.[28] Some also placed their hopes on inclusion in mainstream institutions, such as special-education classes in public schools. There are many early examples of maternal activists, such as Adelaide Hunter Hoodless (1858-1910) of clean milk fame, confronting disease but post-Second World War Canada produced them in abundance.[29] In the 1950s and 1960s, the most famous maternal crusade was the Marching Mothers, who campaigned in Canada and the United States for a cure for polio. Ellen Fairclough (1905-2004), Canada's first woman cabinet minister, was one such advocate. She demanded treatment and research when her only son contracted polio in 1947.[30] Polio's mothers had many counterparts. In 1952, the Council for Retarded Children of Southern Alberta was very much the initiative of local mothers. One typical activist, Christine Meikle-Campbell (1908-97), a former nurse and a mother of eight, including one boy with Down syndrome, dedicated her life to improving options.[31] In 1976, provincial groups led in large part by parents formed the Coalition of Provincial Organizations of the Handicapped (later the Council of Canadians with Disabilities), while others formed the Autism Society of Canada. Maternal activists used the United Nations' International Year of Disabled Persons to advance their cause in 1981 and helped secure protection from discrimination as invoked in section 15 of the Charter of Rights and Freedoms in the same year.[32] At the beginning of the twenty-first century, mothers of youngsters diagnosed with autism were similarly outspoken about rights to government support.[33] The emergence of the community living movement, with its emphasis on inclusion, owed much to such activists.[34] Although studies are still rare, immigrant women have also championed offspring with disabilities.[35]

Kin were not always, however, part of the solution. Family relations readily succumb to dreams of the "classical family of western nostalgia" or that of "native nostalgia,"[36] but they may be fraught with tension and violence. Parents, siblings, and other relatives may share assumptions of normalcy with the wider society and regard disability as a source of shame and anger. The reality of anticipated reciprocity and unequal power similarly provides a useful antidote to any celebration of pre-industrial "practices of community responsibility for poverty and disability" and to singling out modern stigmatizing regimes as especially brutal.[37] Kin and communities are not necessarily "preferable, less controlling, less intrusive and less oppressive." State agencies often came into being to protect the vulnerable.[38] Recurring private violence against children has created moral space for intervention. That states may fail in their trust only underscores the pervasiveness of abuse. As Australia's Robert van Krieken has put it, youngsters pay "a high price for our continued indulgence in fantasy and nostalgia about the self-sufficient extended family groups."[39] The demands associated with disabilities can shatter households. In 1928, British Columbia's Royal Commission on Mental Hygiene found that retention in "the average home is too great a burden and often results in break-down of other members of the family."[40] A 1989 task force offered an equally bleak assessment:

> The drug thalidomide caused indescribable mental anguish for the parents of children who were disfigured or otherwise damaged by its ravaging effects

... in some cases, the psychological consequences experienced by the mothers and fathers had the unfortunate result of creating additional hardships for the thalidomide victims.

Many parents did cope and should be commended accordingly. Notwithstanding, statistical evidence in our surveys indicates that the rate of divorce and separation among thalidomide parents was significantly higher than the norm. There were, as well, a sizeable number of desertions, particularly where there were a large number of other children or where the financial circumstances of the family presented very real hardships.[41]

At the beginning of the twenty-first century, families with members who were disabled could still be capsized only too easily by poverty and other stresses.[42]

Improvements in support were glacial. The introduction of school health-screening programs beginning in the late nineteenth century clearly benefited some families but failed others.[43] Pupils and their parents encountered professional standards that singled them out as mentally, physically, or socially inadequate but found little aid meeting needs.[44] As one assessment of Ontario in the 1980s concluded, "Non-compliance with necessary diagnostic, therapeutic, and preventive follow-up for children with positive screening tests" was a major problem.[45] Although that study did not elaborate, the high cost and limited availability of treatment regularly undermined care.

First Nations youngsters, whose parents have been more likely than others in Canada to be poor, have suffered more disabling illnesses and conditions and fewer efforts at remediation. The young boy who died in a Winnipeg hospital in 2003, far from his Norway House Cree Nation reserve, because federal and provincial authorities could not agree on who was financially liable for his medical costs, symbolized the continued shortfall. Despite governments' supposed adoption of Jordan's Principle, which was to prioritize care over liability, 2008 saw thirty-seven children with disabilities from the same community still unable to access services at home.[46] Yet, even as race remained a substantial factor in determining vulnerability, Canadian youngsters from diverse backgrounds also faced long waits if they needed rehabilitation services. Only the richest of parents could afford to circumvent the prejudices that helped keep assistance in short supply everywhere.[47]

Over time, as distinctions between abled and disabled youngsters sharpened and as the growth in urban living made domestic inclusion sometimes more difficult, nonfamilial options became increasingly significant. One sign of this shift appeared in the national census. Between 1871 and 1911, enumerators asked households if they included the blind, deaf, or "simpleminded." By 1921, these questions had disappeared.[48] Their omission hinted at growing stigmatization, institutional alternatives, and perhaps new agreement that such family members were more appropriately cared for by others.

More than anything, the change captured the reality that families regularly required external supports if disabled members were to share in the benefits of modern life.

Shifting Options

Widespread public exposure of the unmet needs of special needs youngsters occurred only at the end of the twentieth century, but the "third wave" of advocacy, the demand for "inclusion with full civil and legal rights," had emerged by the Second World War.[49] Special needs youngsters were sometimes swept up in the sentiments that supported the UN's Universal Declaration of Human Rights in 1948 and the first National Conference on the Rehabilitation of the Physically Disabled in 1951. Telethons and other media blitzes featured attractive girls and boys who were intended to empty the pockets of the charitably minded. The singular absence of adults in such sentimentalized portraits suggested that disability was especially worth addressing in the young. What happened when children grew up went largely unmentioned.[50] Despite their obvious shortcomings, such campaigns helped put disabilities on the public agenda. Families sometimes benefited.

While the term "respite care" is modern, it captures the long-standing desires of many Canadian households.[51] Shorter or longer periods with lessened immediate caregiving demands could do much for family stability. It is from this perspective that it is useful to consider traditional options such as care by neighbours or by women who were readily and negatively judged by authorities as "baby farmers" but who might well be local people helping out in short or prolonged emergencies. Governments have attempted to regulate such arrangements, but steady demand made informal operations a fact of life throughout the twentieth century.[52] Most such women coped with a handful of children at a time, but numbers could sometimes be considerable. In the 1950s, Ontario's notorious Mrs. Bertha Whyte, or "Mom" Whyte, housed over a hundred girls and boys at a time, many of them with special needs. Despite her lack of records, her unauthorized transfers of children elsewhere, and at least one or two deaths, this Protestant evangelical and her husband prided themselves on accepting youngsters with handicaps from overwhelmed parents.[53] When the general public and Ontario authorities became increasingly alarmed, Mrs. Whyte simply set up a children's home in British Columbia and an orphanage in Nigeria.[54] Even regulated arrangements were not, however, foolproof. In the summer of 2008, for example, Canadians were enraged by the death of a vulnerable Native seven-year-old in Toronto. She was the victim of a neighbour and supposed friend (and her boyfriend) selected by the birth mother to assume legal guardianship while she fought addiction.[55]

Although they were less likely to attract public notice, middle-class and elite households have also sought substitutes for their own direct care. A notable example is Canada's first prime minister, Sir John A. Macdonald, who had a much-loved daughter, Mary, born in 1869, who was severely disabled with hydrocephalus. Her care quickly put him in debt and depression.[56] In 1923, Canadian's director of child welfare described recurring desperate requests for relief from a wide range of Canadians.[57] Responsibilities could break middle-class families just as they might the households of the poor.

When they survived but could not be accommodated at home, youngsters could well end up in a wide variety of orphanages, hospitals, asylums, reformatories, and residential schools. The results of such inclusion could be brutal and short. No wonder specialized institutions were regarded as an advance. Respectable solutions included schools and hospitals dedicated to the disabled. Children with hearing and sight difficulties were the first to be separately accommodated.[58] Residential schools providing for the hard-of-hearing appeared, for example, in Quebec City in 1831; in Belleville, Ontario, in 1869; and in Winnipeg, Manitoba, in 1888. Montreal made initial provision for blind youngsters in 1861, Halifax in 1871, and Toronto in 1872.[59] Children identified as "idiots" and "morons" were more likely to remain alongside adults, though some settings such as Ontario's Orillia Hospital started separating patients by age by the late nineteenth century.[60] For many years, in face of relentless evidence that undifferentiated institutional care shortchanged youngsters with special needs, progressive views favoured specialized sites. In the particular context of a provincial Poor Law that made few distinctions among Nova Scotia's disadvantaged residents as late as the 1950s, reform-minded citizens, for example, echoed old hopes in anticipating "sympathetic training" and a "better day" in segregated institutions.[61] Once set up, however, such facilities could hardly meet nationwide demand. Girls and boys with disabilities continued to turn up in county homes, residential schools, reformatories, and in state care more generally. In such settings, treatment was essentially nonexistent.

Special sites were, however, by no means certain. Authorities, fearing ongoing responsibility, regularly resisted the additional expense youngsters with disabilities represented. The persisting lack of welcome, and often brutal treatment, of young immigrants identified as abnormal was part of the same story.[62] When they dealt with citizens, governments and philanthropies always preferred families to retain their suspect members. As the director of the Children's Aid Society in Pictou, Nova Scotia, typically explained in 1946, "We are in the anomalous position of being able to make no immediate provision for the inferior or abnormal unwanted child of an unmarried mother. We can only persuade or coerce the inferior or abnormal mother to take her child."[63] Richer jurisdictions, such as Alberta, were similarly reluctant. As social work leader Charlotte Whitton discovered, "In cases of children suffering physical defects, mothers or relatives are generally persuaded to assume responsibility for their care. Otherwise they are placed in institutions or hospitals for crippled children where they may spend most of their life or remain until coming of age."[64] That frosty reception persisted at every level. In 1988, for example, one Ontario birth mother found herself in a familiar predicament. She had optimistically hoped for an open adoption, but the diagnosis of Down syndrome deterred the parents she had selected, and she was confronted with an infant that no one immediately wanted.[65]

In the second half of the twentieth century, new therapeutic models sometimes sparked hopeful institutional initiatives.[66] Adolescents who were particularly likely to resist insertion into foster families helped retain such options. A post-Second World War generation of therapeutic group homes resembled smaller traditional orphanages and cottage systems, but there were larger initiatives as well. The result was a combination of initiatives. In 1957, Ontario introduced the nation's first mental hospital specifically for children, later the Thistletown Regional Centre. In the next decade, Toronto's Warrendale Residential Treatment Centre for Emotionally Disturbed Children offered further therapies.[67] The Ottawa Welfare Council, Community Chest, and Children's Aid were among those with high hopes for "children's villages" in assisting the "emotionally disturbed ... whom no one wanted." Up-to-date treatment promised to make troubled children newly "constructive, respectful, trustful, and ... worthy and loved." Graduates were supposed, like their normal counterparts, to move on to foster parents.[68] The appearance of L'Arche homes for people with developmental disabilities, initially established in the 1960s by Jean Vanier, the son of a Canadian governor-general, was part of extensive efforts to bridge standard institutions and normal households.[69] Despite great hopes for such strategies, demand once again proved overwhelming and remedies insufficient.[70]

Institutions of every kind weighed on miserly public treasuries and regularly became associated with abuse.[71] In 1996, the Royal Commission on Aboriginal Peoples reported on the typical damage inflicted by residential schools. In 2000, the Law Commission of Canada added reformatories, orphanages, and schools for youngsters with disabilities to the list of injurious sites. A similarly brutal picture emerged in an assessment by the provincial ombudsman of the 120-year history of British Columbia's Woodlands School for those with mental disabilities.[72] Such disclosures and disillusionment fuelled demands for deinstitutionalization and community integration that began after the Second World War but flourished especially in the 1980s and 1990s.

The deinstitutionalization movement relied on alternate community living supports for youngsters and adults.[73] In the first instance, hopes rested on good funding for family-based care. The election of neo-conservative regimes federally and provincially in the 1980s and 1990s meant that deinstitutionalization frequently descended into an exercise in cost-saving as part of attacks on social security entitlement.[74] Youngsters and adults with disabilities quickly confronted limited institutional supports and few other options. The near absence of inclusive daycare was a typical constraint, placing families under enormous strain, especially when two wage earners became increasingly essential in households.[75] In 2005, Ontario's ombudsperson summed up a dismal picture familiar across the country. His report, *Between a Rock and a Hard Place,* described how parents had to surrender custody and guardianship – effectively identifying themselves as neglectful – in order to get help.[76]

Institutions were not the only options with chequered histories. After the Second World War, social workers increasingly explored the alternatives of fostering and adoption and grew initially more optimistic about "stretching" potential adopters. In 1949, a Canadian social work thesis articulated the emerging faith that "there is no clear-cut line between the non-adoptable and the adoptable child."[77] Even normal families had "skeletons" and it was "only humane to give the child the benefit of the doubt."[78] In 1952, a Nova Scotian summed up hopes for greater inclusiveness: "The child's handicaps should be minimized and not emphasised."[79] Social workers experimented with matching demand and supply. When 1950s polio epidemics resulted in children with disabilities that birth parents could not cope with, Manitoba child welfare authorities sought adults who "have suffered from the same handicap, and their sympathy and understanding are a great help."[80] By the late decades of the twentieth century, provinces also slowly introduced additional financial and institutional supports to foster and adoptive families with special needs youngsters.

In the 1960s and 1970s, authorities campaigned hard to insert previously unplaceable girls and boys in good homes. The *Toronto Telegram* typically used its Today's Child column to spotlight disadvantaged provincial wards, while British Columbia heard Dr. Sydney Segal, Vancouver's influential pediatrician, explain that adopters were now "more willing to take their chances as do natural parents and will still love and look after a child that turns out to have a health problem."[81] Those who sought defect-free white newborns were told there might "*never* be a child" and urged to be flexible. Children's rather than adults' needs supplied matching's new baseline. "Special parents" were sought for children with special needs. Even if "the child with an emotional or behaviour problem is not an easy child to love," "consistent understanding and security" could triumph.[82] Such sentiments explain the *Vancouver Sun*'s advertisements, in the mid-1980s, for adoption of youngsters with cerebral palsy, congenital heart conditions, epilepsy, behavioural problems, or histories of abuse.[83]

Authorities also regarded adults whose age, income, race, or single status disadvantaged them as candidates for adoptive offspring as potential solutions. In dealing with an "East Indian couple" in the 1970s, Ottawa's Children's Aid social worker cited policy forbidding placement of "a white child with brown parents" and offered "an abnormal, retarded or native Indian child."[84] Other nonpreferred applicants for parenthood, such as unmarried women, were also likely to be offered hard-to-move girls and boys, but these less than blue-ribbon adopters also resisted restricted choices. Their reluctance made hard practical and personal sense in the context of the persisting absence of medical, academic, housing, and other supports. The scenario worsened as the numbers of youngsters with special needs in state care steadily mounted during the twentieth century.[85] Boys and girls assigned to the bottom of the "hierarchy of preference" proved difficult to place even with adoption subsidies and higher foster care rates.[86] As federal and provincial regimes slashed social security, child welfare workers moved desperately both to bolster fragile birth families and to find resilient foster parents.[87]

Conclusion

In the first decade of the twenty-first century, essential supports remain few and far between. Deinstitutionalization has brought only limited help. The slow and patchwork evolution of federal and provincial allowances and tax benefits for rearing youngsters with disabilities rarely matched needs.[88] Respite care was hard to find and to access everywhere. In 2002, a major assessment grimly concluded that "despite a large body of literature that shows the importance of respite to promoting well-being ... issues have changed little in the last few decades. Access is particularly difficult for families in rural areas and for children who have particular support needs like complex health issues, or behavioural disabilities."[89] Early twenty-first-century Canada for the most part continued to require parents to lobby hard for treatments and care.

The pervasive failure to support family-based care and the particular needs of some youngsters kept institutions a fact of modern life. Indeed, politicians, sometimes the very ones who had initiated welfare cuts, murmured about expanding institutionalization.[90] Like their predecessors, modern parents remained divided. Although institutions produced obvious tragedies, deinstitutionalization offered its own betrayals. Growing rates of homelessness and inadequate supports for community living were far from the dream of integration.[91] Opposition to closures was one result.[92] Scholars also began to reconsider congregate arrangements, arguing that institutions sometimes supplied nurture for youngsters and respite for parents.[93] Some investigators discovered comradeship among those who have lived collectively.[94] Such observations suggest that institutions might, under certain conditions, support relations and development better than single households. Adult failure and abuse occur after all in both domestic and institutional settings.

Canada's recurring failure to meet the diverse needs of young disabled citizens cannot be linked solely to the particular choice of families or institutions. It lies, rather, in the persisting temptation to judge humans as more or less worthy by reference to an idealized standard and in the continuing vulnerability of families. Institutions, foster care, and adoption cannot compensate for original sins. Unfortunately, the will to change has always seemed uncertain. In 2006, young Canadians, such as the Vancouver newborn sextuplets and conjoined twins, faced hardships far beyond their original disabilities. In the twenty-first century, as in the past, Canadians are likely to "see only the disabilities" and ignore the "strengths" of such youngsters.[95]

Notes

1 On the transfer of the child suffering the effects of thalidomide to the Waterloo County Children's Society two months after birth, see "Armless Baby Made Children's Aid Ward," *Toronto Star*, 20 July 1962. On the other cases, see the extensive coverage in these months in the *Vancouver Sun*.
2 See Peter McMartin's six-part series, "Faces of Autism," *Vancouver Sun*, 21-27 April 2007.
3 Problems of disclosure and definition make it impossible to know how many Canadians experience disability at any time. For example, the International Human Rights Monitor has recently noted that one authority suggests that "1.6 percent of all children 0-4 years and 4.3 of children 5-14 years" have a disability, while the National Longitudinal Survey of Children and Youth in Canada and the Canadian Council on Social Development report much higher numbers at 13 percent of all Canadian youngsters aged eleven or younger. Center for International Rehabilitation, IDEAnet, "International Disability Rights Monitor (IDRM) Publications – IDRM – Canada 2004," http://www.ideanet.org/content.cfm?id=535C.
4 Letter to the Editor, "Asks Square Deal for Disabled Persons," *Western Producer*, 30 April 1949.
5 See my *Finding Families, Finding Ourselves: English Canada Confronts Adoption from the Nineteenth Century to the 1990s* (Toronto: Oxford University Press, 2006) and "'Children of Adversity': Disabilities and Child Welfare in Canada from the Nineteenth Century to the Twenty-First," *Journal of Family History* 32, 4 (2007): 413-32.
6 See Mona Gleason, *Normalizing the Ideal: Psychology, Schooling, and the Family in Postwar Canada* (Toronto: University of Toronto Press, 1999); Julia Grant, *Raising Baby by the Book: The Education of American Mothers* (New Haven, CT: Yale University Press, 1998); and Douglas C. Baynton, "Disability in History," Forum on Disability in History, *Perspectives* 44, 8 (2006): http://www.historians.org/perspectives/issues/2006/0611/0611for1.cfm.
7 On some benefits see Arthur Allen, *Vaccine: The Controversial Story of Medicine's Greatest Lifesaver* (New York: W.W. Norton, 2007); R.A. Meckel, "Levels and Trends of Death and Disease in Childhood, 1620 to the Present," in J. Golden, R.A. Meckel, and H.M. Prescott, eds., *Children and Youth in Sickness and Health: A Handbook and Guide* (Westport, CT: Greenwood Press, 2004), 3-24; and A. Chase, *Magic Shots: A Human and Scientific Account of the Long and Continuing Struggle to Eradicate Infectious Diseases by Vaccination* (New York: William Morrow, 1982).
8 On the role of some traditional views see Rick Biesinger and Hiroko Arikawa, "Religious Attitudes and Happiness among Parents of Children with Developmental Disabilities," *Journal of Religion, Disability and Health* 11, 4 (2007): 23-34. For useful discussions of different cultural views of disability see also M. Miles, "Disability in an Eastern Religious Context: Historical Perspectives," *Journal of Religion, Disability and Health* 6, 2-3 (2002): 53-76; M. Miles, "Disability on a Different Model: Glimpses of an Asian Heritage," *Journal of Religion, Disability and Health* 6, 2-3 (2002): 89-108; M. Miles, "Disability in South Asia-Millennium to Millennium," *Journal of Religion, Disability and Health* 6, 2-3 (2002): 109-16; M. Miles, "Some Influences of Religions on Attitudes towards Disabilities and Peoples with Disabilities," *Journal of Religion, Disability and Health* 6, 2-3 (2002): 117-30; J.L. Connors and A.M. Donnellan, "Citizenship and Culture: The Role of Disabled People in Navajo Society," *Disability, Handicap and Society* 8 (1993): 256-80; and J. Scheer and N. Groce, "Impairment as

a Human Constant: Cross-Cultural and Historical Perspectives on Variation," *Journal of Social Issues* 44 (1988): 23-37.

9 See Strong-Boag, *Finding Families, Finding Ourselves,* esp. chaps. 5-7.

10 See Angus McLaren, *Our Own Master Race: Eugenics in Canada 1885-1945* (Toronto: McClelland and Stewart, 1990). See also Martin Pernick, *The Black Stork: Eugenics and the Death of "Defective" Babies in American Medicine and Motion Pictures since 1915* (New York: Oxford University Press, 1996). For one example of the close association between ideas of disability and racialization, see the documentary film "The Sterilization of Leilani Muri," dir. Glynis Whiting (Ottawa: NFB, 1996).

11 See Dianne Dodd, "Advice to Parents: The Blue Books, Helen MacMurchy, MD, and the Federal Department of Health, 1920-1934," *Canadian Bulletin of Medical History* 8 (1991): 203-30.

12 Helen MacMurchy, *The Almosts: A Study of the Feeble Minded* (Boston: Houghton Mifflin, 1920). See also Douglas Morecroft Criffin, Samuel Ralph Laycock, and William Line, *Mental Hygiene: A Manual for Teachers* (Toronto: W.J. Gage, 1940), for a much moderated view of the need to protect communities; and Harley D. Dickinson, "Scientific Parenthood: The Mental Hygiene Movement and the Reform of Canadian Families, 1925-1950," *Journal of Comparative Family Studies* 24, 3 (1993): 387-402.

13 See Canadian Association for Community Living, "Immigration and Disability: Submission to the Standing Committee on Citizenship and Immigration," April 2005, http://www.cacl.ca/backup/english/GovLegalAffairs/docs/CACLCIMMBrief2005.pdf. Such regulations were in force even as Canada imported medical professionals from around the world, in the process undermining local health services.

14 For an up-to-date assessment, including the situation of children, see the work of the Learning Disabilities Association of Canada, http://www.ldac-taac.ca/LDandtheLaw/toc_Law-e.asp. See also Robert F. Drake, "Welfare States and Disabled People," in Gary L. Albrecht, K.D. Seelman, and M. Bury, eds., *Handbook of Disability Studies* (Thousand Oaks, CA: Sage, 2001).

15 See Gerald Thomson, "'A Baby Show Means Work in the Hardest Sense': The Better Baby Contests of Vancouver and New Westminster Local Councils of Women, 1913-1929," *BC Studies* 128 (2000/2001): 5-35; and Jane Nicholas, "The New Muse: Canadian Beauty Contestants in the 1920s" (paper presented to the annual meeting of the Canadian Historical Association, Vancouver, 2008). See also A.M. Stern, "Making Better Babies: Public Health and Race Betterment in Indiana, 1920-1935," *American Journal of Public Health* 92 (2002): 742-52; Sarah Banet-Weiser, *The Most Beautiful Girl in the World: Beauty Pageants and National Identity* (Berkeley and Los Angeles: University of California Press, 1999); and Caroline Daley, *Beauty Queens and Physique Kings: A History of New Zealand Beauty Contests* (Auckland: University of Auckland Press, 2009).

16 Jessica Ball, "Promoting Equity and Dignity for Aboriginal Children in Canada," *Choices* 14, 7 (2008): 8, http://www.ecdip.org/docs/pdf/Ball%20Choices.pdf.

17 L.E. Lowman, "Mail-Order Babies," *Chatelaine,* April 1932, 34.

18 See the December 2000 Canadian poll reported in Willamette University College of Law, "Recent Developments in Physician-Assisted Suicide," March 2001, http://www.willamette.edu/wucl/pdf/pas/2001-03.

19 The National Clearinghouse on Family Violence, *The Abuse of Children with Disabilities* (Ottawa: Family Violence Prevention Unit, Health Canada, 2000), 1.

20 Although the Latimer case in which a Prairie father killed his twelve-year-old daughter, Tracy, in 1994, is the most notorious example, it is not unique. In September 2004, a Montreal nurse's aid assisted her adult playwright son, Charles Fariala, in suicide. See Amy Hasbrouck, "Society Should No Longer Tolerate Assisted Suicide," *Montreal Gazette,* 6 February 2006. In 1996, another mother from the same city drowned her six-year-old, who suffered from autism. See Council of Canadians with Disabilities, "The Toll Mounts: Another Child Killed," http://www.ccdonline.ca/en/humanrights/deathmaking/latimer/2001/03. See also R. Enns, *A Voice Unheard: The Latimer Case and People with Disabilities* (Halifax: Fernwood, 1999).

21 Margaret A. Winzer, *The History of Special Education* (Washington, DC: Gallaudet University Press, 1993), 152.

22 See ibid., 162-63.

23 On this see Denise P. Sommerfeld, "The Origins of Mother Blaming: Historical Perspectives of Childhood and Motherhood," *Infant Mental Health Journal* 10, 1 (2006): 14-24.

24 See the moving recognition of this in War Amputations of Canada, "Thalidomide Task Force Report" (Ottawa: 1989), 1:108-11.

25 Melanie Panitch, "Mothers of Intention: Women, Disability and Activism," in Deborah Stienstra and Aileen Wight-Felske, eds., *Making Equality: History of Advocacy and Persons with Disabilities in Canada* (Concord, ON: Captus Press, 2003); and Philip M. Ferguson, *Abandoned to Their Fate: Social Policy and Practice toward Severely Retarded People in America, 1820-1920* (Philadelphia: Temple University Press 1994), 11 and passim.

26 On the similar role of fathers see Veronica Strong-Boag, "Judging Men: Assessments of Fathers in Canadian Adoption Circles," *Adoption and Culture* 1, 1 (2007): 69-100.

27 See Marilyn Callaghan, Leslie Brown, Patricia Mackenzie, and Barbara Whittington, "Catch as Catch Can: Grandmothers, Raising Their Grandchildren and Kinship Care Policies," *Canadian Review of Social Policy* 54 (Fall 2004): 58-78; E. Dowdell Burgess, "Caregiver Burden: Grandmothers Raising Their High Risk Grandchildren," *Journal of Psychosocial Nursing* 33, 3 (1995): 27-30; and Veronica Strong-Boag, "Sisters Are Doing It for Themselves, or Not: Aunts and Caregiving in Canada," *Journal of Comparative Family Studies*, forthcoming. See also the taken-for-grantedness of maternal care of young children with chronic conditions in Dorn L. Hatton, Connie Canam, Sally Thorne, and Anna-Marie Hughes, "Parents' Perceptions of Caring for an Infant or Toddler with Diabetes," *Journal of Advanced Nursing* 22, 3 (1995): 569-77; and Claudia Malacrida, *Cold Comfort: Mothers, Professionals and Attention Deficit Disorder* (Toronto: University of Toronto Press, 2003), which examines mothers in the United Kingdom and Canada who moved from paid work to home.

28 Unfortunately, as a leading scholar in the field notes, the early history of special education in Canada, and the contribution of women in particular, have yet to be written. Winzer, *The History of Special Education*, xii. See also her "Education, Urbanization and the Deaf Community: A Case Study of Toronto, 1870-1900," in J.V. van Cleve, ed., *Deaf History Unveiled: Interpretations from the New Scholarship* (Washington, DC: Gallaudet University Press, 1993).

29 See Bruce Uditsky, "From Integration to Inclusion: The Canadian Experience," in Roger Slee, ed., *Is There a Desk with My Name on It? The Politics of Integration* (London: Routledge, 1993), 79-92. This supplies a useful chronology of change but ignores the gender of the leading activists. See, too, Terrence Crowley, "Hunter, Adelaide Sophia (Hoodless)," in Ramsay Cook and Jean Hamelin, eds., *Dictionary of Canadian Biography* (Toronto: University of Toronto Press, 1994), 16:488-93.

30 See the website of March of Dimes Canada, "About March of Dimes Canada," http://www.marchofdimes.ca/dimes/national_programs/about_us/about_march_of_dimes_canada/. See also Ellen L. Fairclough and Margaret Conrad, *Saturday's Child: Memoirs of Canada's First Female Cabinet Minister* (Toronto: University of Toronto Press, 1995); and Daniel J. Wilson, *Living with Polio: The Epidemic and Its Survivors* (Chicago: University of Chicago Press, 2005).

31 See Glenbow Archives, Christine Meikle-Harris Fonds.

32 On the struggle for inclusion see Yvonne Peters, "Canadians with Disabilities Take Their Rightful Place in Canada's Constitution," in Stienstra and Wight-Felske, *Making Equality*, 119-36; and Norman Boucher, Patrick Fougeyrollas, and Charles Gaucher, "Development and Transformation of Advocacy in the Disability Movement of Quebec," in Stienstra and Wight-Felske, *Making Equality*, 137-62.

33 For example, Dr. S.K. Freeman, a sociologist and parent of a daughter with autism, is the executive director and founder of Families for Early Autism Treatment of British Columbia (established 1996). See http://www.featbc.org. See also Peter Carver, "Disability and the Allocation of Health Care Resources: The Case of Connor Auton," *Health Ethics Today* 12, 1 (2001), http://www.phen.ab.ca/materials/het/het12-01b.asp.

34 See, for example, Ontario Association for Community Living (1953), Canadian Association for Community Living (1956), Fort St. John Association for Community Living (1960). See also "Disability Rights in Canada: A Virtual Museum," http://disabilityrights.freeculture.ca.

35 For an unusual study see Yuan Lai and F. Ishu Ishiyama, "Involvement of Immigrant Chinese Canadian Mothers of Children with Disabilities," *Exceptional Children* 71, 1 (2004), 97-108.
36 Veronica Strong-Boag, *Finding Families, Families Ourselves* (Toronto: Oxford University Press, 2006), chap. 1.
37 Sharon L. Snyder and David T. Mitchell, *Cultural Locations of Disability* (Chicago: University of Chicago Press 2006), 37-38.
38 Robert van Krieken, *Children and the State: Social Control and the Formation of Australian Child Welfare* (Sydney, Australia: Allen and Unwin, 1991), 143.
39 Ibid., 181.
40 Cited in Nic Clarke, "'Sacred Daemons': Exploring British Columbian Society's Perceptions of 'Mentally Deficient' Children, 1870-1930," *BC Studies* 144 (Winter 2004/2005): 75. On the difficulties of families see also Thierry Nootens, "'For Years We Have Never Had a Happy Home': Madness and Families in Century Montreal," in James E. Moran and David Wright, eds., *Mental Health and Canadian Society: Historical Perspectives* (Montreal and Kingston: McGill-Queen's University Press, 2006), 49-68.
41 War Amputations, "Thalidomide Task Force Report," 108.
42 Louise Hanvey, "Children with Disabilities and Their Families in Canada: A Discussion Paper" (Ottawa: National Children's Alliance for the First Roundtable on Children with Disabilities, 2002), 9.
43 See Neil Sutherland, who identifies school health programs as one of the twentieth century's success stories in *Children in English-Canadian Society: Framing the Twentieth-Century Consensus* (Toronto: University of Toronto Press, 1976; Waterloo, ON: Wilfrid Laurier University Press, 2000), esp. chap. 3. This and all subsequent citations are to the 2000 edition.
44 On the problems encountered by children and their parents by school inspections, see Mona Gleason, "Race, Class, and Health: School Medical Inspection and 'Healthy' Children in British Columbia," in Cheryl Krasnick Warsh and Veronica Strong-Boag, eds., *Children's Health Issues in Historical Perspective* (Waterloo, ON: Wilfrid Laurier University Press, 2005), 287-304.
45 David Cadman, Larry W. Chambers, Stephen D. Walter, Ruth Ferguson, Nancy Johnston, and Jane McNamee, "Evaluation of Public Health Preschool Child Developmental Screening: The Process and Outcomes of a Community Program," *American Journal of Public Health* 77, 1 (1987), 50.
46 This case caused considerable outcry and produced Jordan's Principle, which states that the welfare of the child is paramount and responsibility for expenses are secondary. See First Nations Child and Family Caring Society of Canada, "Joint Declaration of Support for Jordan's Principle to Resolving Jurisdictional Disputes Affecting Services to First Nations Children," http://www.fncfcs.com/more/jordansPrinciple.php. See also Noni MacDonald and Amir Attaran, "Jordan's Principle, Governments' Paralysis," *Canadian Medical Association Journal* 177, 4 (2007): 1; and Dan Lett, "Whatever Happened to Jordan's Principle," *Canadian Medical Association Journal* 178, 12 (2008): 1534-35. On the special health problems of Native children, see "Hope or Heartbreak: Aboriginal Youth and Canada's Future," *Horizons* 10, 1 (2008): 68-72, http://www.policyresearch.gc.ca/doclib/HOR_v10n1_200803_e.pdf.
47 On, for example, the long wait times reported for a diverse population for services even on the Island of Montreal, see D.E. Feldman, F. Champagne, N.K. Bitensky, and G. Meshefedjian, "Rehabilitation Services for Physically Disabled Children in Montreal," *Abstract for Academy for Health Services Research and Health Policy Meeting* 18 (2001): 70, http://gateway.nlm.nih.gov/MeetingAbstracts/ma?f=102273285.html. See also Ball, "Promoting Equity," 14.
48 For examples of disabled kin staying in families see Hilda M. Campbell, Joanne Robinson, and Angela Stratiy, *Deaf Women of Canada: A Proud History and Exciting Future* (Edmonton: Duval House, 2002), and Clifton F. Carbin, *Deaf Heritage in Canada: A Distinctive Diverse and Enduring Culture* (Toronto: McGraw-Hill Ryerson, 1996).
49 Neufeldt, "Growth and Evolution of Disability Advocacy in Canada," 22.
50 For an excellent assessment see Doris Z. Fleischer and Frieda Zames, *The Disability Rights Movement: From Charity to Confrontation* (Philadelphia: Temple University Press, 2001), 10-11.

51 See the Alberta study of S.M. Neufeld, B. Query, and J.E. Drummond, "Respite Care Users Who Have Children with Chronic Conditions: Are They Getting a Break?" *Journal of Pediatric Nursing* 16, 4 (2001): 234-44.

52 Many orphanages and infants' homes in Canada, as elsewhere, were established to counteract so-called baby farmers. See Sonia Michel, *Children's Interests/Mothers' Rights: The Shaping of America's Child Care Policy* (New Haven, CT: Yale University Press, 1999). On female baby farmers accused of murder see Annette Ballinger, "The 'Worse' of Two Evils? Double Murder Trials and Gender in England and Wales, 1900-53," in Alana Barton, Karen Corteen, David Scott, and Dave Whyte, eds., *Expanding the Criminological Imagination: Critical Readings in Criminology* (Uffculme, UK: Willan, 2007); and Bronwyn Dalley, *Family Matters: Child Welfare in Twentieth-Century New Zealand* (Auckland: University of Auckland Press, 1998), 52.

53 See "Plan Tighter Act on Placing Child," *Toronto Star,* 7 January 1959, and "Good Intention Enough, Kim Placed without Real Probe," *Toronto Star,* 7 January 1959.

54 Sidney Katz, "What Can We Learn from Mom Whyte?" *Canadian Welfare* 33, 7 (1958): 331, and "Missing Persons: Whatever Became of Mom Whyte?" *Star Weekly,* 24 April 1971, 10.

55 This is the case of Katelynn Sampson. See coverage in the *Globe and Mail* and *Toronto Star* during the first two weeks of August 2008 and the editorial "How We Failed Katelynn," *thestar.com,* 14 August 2008, http://www.thestar.com/article/477995.

56 For this story see Patricia Phenix, *Private Demons: The Tragic Personal Life of John A. Macdonald* (Toronto: McClelland and Stewart, 2006).

57 Helen MacMurchy, *Handbook of Child Welfare Work in Canada* (Ottawa: King's Printer, 1923), 87-88.

58 On this in the United Kingdom see Anne Borsay, *Disability and Social Policy in Britain Since 1750: A History of Exclusion* (Basingstoke, UK: Palgrave, 2005).

59 Aldred H. Neufeldt, "Growth and Evolution of Disability Advocacy in Canada," in Stienstra and Wight-Felske, *Making Equality,* 17; and James Roots, "Deaf Education and Advocacy: A Short History of the Canadian Association of the Deaf," in Stienstra and Wight-Felske, *Making Equality,* 76-77.

60 See Jessa Chupik and David Wright, "Treating the 'Idiot' Child in Early Twentieth-Century Ontario," *Disability and Society* 21, 1 (2006): 77-90.

61 Nova Scotia, Director of Child Welfare, *Annual Report* (30 November 1951), 10. On the continuation of the Poor Law, see Janet Guildford, "The End of the Poor Law: Public Welfare Reform in Nova Scotia before the Canada Assistance Plan," in Judith Findgard and Janet Guildford, eds., *Mothers of the Municipality: Women, Work, and Social Policy in Post-1945 Halifax* (Toronto: University of Toronto Press, 2005), 49-75, and Jeanne Fay, "The 'Right Kind' of Single Mothers: Nova Scotia's Regulation of Women on Social Assistance, 1956-1977," in Findgard and Guildford, eds., *Mothers of the Municipality,* 141-68.

62 For many such stories see Joy Parr, *Labouring Children: British Immigrant Apprentices to Canada 1869-1924* (Toronto: University of Toronto Press, 1994).

63 A.C. Mackenzie, Nova Scotia Director of Child Welfare, *Annual Report* (fiscal year ending 30 November 1946), 92.

64 IODE, Alberta provincial chapter, *Welfare in Alberta: The Report of a Study* (1947), 61.

65 See Anonymous, "Open Adoption," *Ontario Association of Children's Aid Societies' Journal* 32, 3 (1988): 2-4.

66 On the shift in psychiatry from psychoanalytical explanations, often mother-blaming, to organic explanations and treatments, see Andrea Tone, "Listening to the Past: History, Psychiatry, and Anxiety," *Canadian Journal of Psychiatry* 50 (2005): 373-80. See also Neil Sutherland, "North America Perspectives on the Historiography of Child Health in the Twentieth Century" (paper presented at the McGill-McCord colloquium Comparative and Interdisciplinary Approaches to Child Health in the Twentieth Century, Montreal, 28-29 October 2004). My thanks to Neil Sutherland for providing me with an electronic version of this very useful paper. See also Wendy Kline, *Building a Better Race: Gender, Sexuality and Eugenics from the Turn of the Century to the Baby Boom* (Berkeley: University of California Press, 2001).

67 See Sheila H. Kieran, "Where Disturbed Children Learn to Live Again," *Maclean's,* 19 February 1966, 17-19, 24, 26-27.

68 Preceding three quotations from Alan Phillips, "The Home That Rebuilds Children's Lives," *Maclean's*, 28 March 1958, 13.
69 On L'Arche see John Lord and Peggy Hutchison, *Pathways to Inclusion: Building a New Story for People and Communities* (Concord, ON: Captus Press, 2007), esp. 62, and E. McDonald and Christopher B. Keys, "L'Arche, the Successes of Community, the Challenges of Empowerment in a Faith-Centered Setting," *Journal of Religion, Disability and Health* 9, 4 (2005): 5-27.
70 For developments in one province see Ontario, Ministry of Community and Social Services, Policy Development, *Three Decades of Change: The Evolution of Residential Care and Community Alternatives in Children's Services*, November 1983.
71 See, for example, the Winnipeg Welfare Council's concern over the costs of institutionalizing "paraplegics and crippled children," *Manitoba Medical Review* 33, 7 (1953): 387. On the dangers see also A. Paul and P. Cawson, "Safeguarding Disabled Children in Residential Settings: What We Know and What We Don't Know," *Child Abuse Review* 11, 5 (2002): 262-81.
72 Canada, *Report of the Royal Commission on Aboriginal Peoples*, Part 2 (Ottawa: Ministry of Supply and Services, 1996); Law Commission of Canada, *Restoring Dignity: Responding to Child Abuse in Canadian Institutions* (Ottawa: Law Commission of Canada, 2000); and Dulcie McCallum, *The Need to Know: Woodlands School Report; An Administrative Review* (Victoria: Ministry of Children and Family Development, 2001).
73 A typical policy document in this vein is *Community Living for the Retarded in Ontario: A New Policy Focus* (Toronto: Provincial Secretary for Social Development, March 2006).
74 On the costs of neo-conservatism see J.F. Conway, *The Canadian Family in Crisis* (Toronto: James Lorimer, 2003), and Sylvia Bashevkin, *Welfare Hot Buttons: Women, Work, and Social Policy Reform* (Toronto: University of Toronto Press, 2002).
75 On this situation see G. Allan Roeher Institute, *Right Off the Bat: A Study of Inclusive Child Care in Canada* (North York, ON: Roeher Institute, 1993).
76 André Marin, *Between a Rock and a Hard Place: Final Report* (Toronto: Ombudsman of Ontario, 2005), http://www.ombudsman.on.ca/media/3277/between_a_rock_and_a_hard_place_20050520.pdf.
77 Rosemary L. Lansdowne, "The Concept of Non-Adoptability: A Study of the Effect of the Concept of Non-Adoptability on Case-Work Services to the Unmarried Mother, and the Examination of the Validity of this Concept" (MA thesis, University of British Columbia, 1949), 19.
78 Ibid., 65.
79 Nova Scotia, Director of Child Welfare, *Annual Report* (1952), 8.
80 Rita Loadman, "What's New in Adoption," *Canadian Welfare*, 15 March 1956: 336.
81 "Appendix D: Dr. Segal's Summary; Sunday Morning, December 10, 1967," *Adoption Conference: Dec. 8th, 9th and 10th, 1967, Victoria, BC*, typescript pamphlet, Koerner Library, University of British Columbia, 4.
82 British Columbia, BC Department of Rehabilitation and Social Improvement, *Annual Report for the Year Ended March 31, 1971*, 31.
83 See the *Vancouver Sun*'s descriptions of Carol (28 January 1986), Down syndrome; Penny (1 April 1986), Down syndrome; Alyssa (15 April 1986), cerebral palsy; Jeff (22 April 1986), mentally handicapped; Darren (6 May 1986), developmentally delayed, congenital heart condition, skin rash; Robbie (8 July 1986), "multi-handicapped"; Daniel (15 July 1986), developmentally delayed; Scotty (28 October 1986), cerebral palsy, delayed mental development; Christian (18 November 1986), cerebral palsy; Mark (2 December 1986), epileptic seizures; Jean (31 March 1987), not walking and a squint; Robby (21 April 1987), mentally handicapped.
84 "Ottawa CAS Criticized for Race Adoption Policy," *Globe and Mail*, 7 March 1978.
85 The growing numbers in care has many causes, including higher survival rates for disabled children and the conflict between heightened need for parental care and the associated expenses that required two breadwinners in families. Mandatory reporting of abuse and neglect also brought more youngsters into care. On the latter see Heather Whiteford, "Special Needs Adoption: Perspectives on Policy and Practice" (MA thesis, University of British Columbia, 1988), 15-16.

50   *Veronica Strong-Boag*

86   Ibid., 22.
87   See Margaret Hillyard-Little, "The Limits of Canadian Democracy: The Citizenship Rights of Poor Women," *Canadian Review of Social Policy* 43 (Spring 1999): 59-76; Sylvia Bashevkin, *Women on the Defensive: Living through Conservative Times* (Chicago: University of Chicago Press, 1998).
88   For an introduction to the issues see Steven Hick, *Social Work in Canada: An Introduction* (Toronto: Thompson Educational Press, 2004), and his *Social Welfare in Canada: Understanding Income Security* (Toronto: Thompson Educational Press, 2004). On the reality for a Toronto family with a son with autism, see Thelma Wheatley, *My Sad Is All Gone: A Family's Triumph Over Violent Autism* (Lancaster, OH: Lucky Press, 2004).
89   Hanvey, "Children with Disabilities and Their Families in Canada," 22-23. See also H. MacDonald and P. Callery, "Parenting Children Requiring Complex Care: A Journey through Time," *Child: Care, Health and Development* 34, 2 (20 November 2007): 207-13; G. Damiani, P. Rosenbaum, M. Swinton, and D. Russell, "Frequency and Determinants of Formal Respite Service Use among Caregivers of Children with Cerebral Palsy in Ontario," *Child: Care, Health and Development* 30, 1 (2003): 77-86; A. Cocks, "Respite Care for Disabled Children: Micro and Macro Reflections," *Disability and Society* 14, 3 (2000): 507-19; and A. Geoffrey Abelson, "Respite Care Needs of Parents of Children with Developmental Disabilities," *Focus on Autism and Other Developmental Disabilities* 14, 2 (1999): 96-100.
90   See Premier Gordon Campbell of British Columbia to the Union of BC Municipalities in Victoria on 27 October 2006, "Campbell pledges more help for welfare recipients, mentally ill," 27 October 2006, CBCNews.ca. For one criticism see Gary Mason, "For the Most Helpless of the Homeless," *Globe and Mail*, 31 October 2006.
91   On the danger of homelessness for children whose families can no longer cope and can find no substitute caregiving arrangements, see Jayne Barker, "Out-of-Home Care for Children and Youth with Serious Emotional Disturbances" (MA thesis, Royal Roads University, 2000), esp. 5.
92   See Kathy Jones, "Listening to Hidden Voices: Power, Domination, Resistance and Pleasure within Huronia Regional Centre," *Disability and Society* 7, 4 (1992): 339-48. See also Harvey G. Simmons, *From Asylum to Welfare: The Evolution of Mental Retardation Policy in Ontario from 1831-1980* (Downsview, ON: National Institute on Mental Retardation, 1982).
93   Kenneth Cmiel, *A Home of Another Kind: One Chicago Orphanage and the Tangle of Child Welfare* (Chicago and London: University of Chicago Press, 1995). See also Nurith Zmora, *Orphanages Reconsidered: Child Care Institutions in Progressive Era Baltimore* (Philadelphia: Temple University Press, 1994). In Canada, the reconsideration of orphanages began with Bettina Bradbury, "Pigs, Cows, and Boarders: Non-Wage Forms of Survival among Montreal Families, 1861-1891," *Labour/Le Travail* 14 (1984): 9-46. It is echoed in popular accounts such as Judy Gordon, *Four Hundred Brothers and Sisters* (Montreal: Lugus, 2003).
94   See Jones, "Listening to Hidden Voices."
95   Commission on Emotional and Learning Disorders in Children, *One Million Children: The CELDIC Report; A National Study of Canadian Children with Emotional and Learning Disorders* (Toronto: L. Crainford, 1970), 2. See also the moving philosophical reflection in Stanley Hauerwas, "Community and Diversity: The Tyranny of Normality," in Stanley Hauerwas and John Swinton, eds., *Critical Reflections on Stanley Hauerwas' Theology of Disability* (Philadelphia: Haworth Press, 2005), 37-44.

Part 2
The Trouble with Adolescents – Law, Experts, and Institutions Target Youth

Perhaps no youthful cohort generates more ambivalence than teenagers. Seemingly a danger to themselves and to others, adolescents are feared, fretted over, and the cause of much anguish and hope. It was just a century ago that adolescence was recognized as a separate life-stage category, generating social science research, public policy, and law specific to the teenager. The liminal nature of adolescence – caught between childhood and adulthood, dependence and independence – inspired adults to establish youth-specific institutions to help direct adolescents' transition to maturity. We see this in particular in the first half of the twentieth century with the expansion of high schools, the implementation of child welfare and juvenile justice regimes, and the innovation of medical and psychological specialties devoted to the adolescent. Although well-meaning adults have created these institutions to protect the vulnerable as well as the at-risk, too often protection has translated into policing and surveillance, as the chapters in this section reveal. The "trouble" with adolescents, it seems, was adolescence itself.

The three chapters in this section examine the category of adolescence and how certain groups of adolescents were cast as problematic at different historical moments. Cynthia Comacchio shows that for the generation that came of age after the First World War, adolescence was defined as a modern social ill. Youth specialists classified adolescents as lost or, to use the modern term, broadly "maladjusted" and in need of management or surveillance. If these professionals generally perceived youth to be trouble, they were particularly concerned by working-class and immigrant youth, whom they took to be inherently troubled and thus overly subject to the relatively new juvenile justice system.

William Bush demonstrates the importance of considering race when examining the episodic moral panics over teenagers in his chapter on the post-Second World War juvenile justice system in the American South. Bush sees the African American teenager denied the promise of juvenile justice and therefore, an adolescence. Juvenile justice, born alongside the discovery of the adolescent, was intended to promote a gentler form of legal process for youngsters who required treatment and guidance. Yet, this justice was denied to boys incarcerated at the Gatesville, Texas, reformatory, where no one tended to their education, care, or upbringing.

The "good intentions gone bad" storyline is also evident in Tamara Myers's piece on the history of curfew laws in Canada. In 1908, Canadian legislators created the Juvenile Delinquents Act, which established juvenile courts and the government's commitment to an *in loco parentis* role. A fine example of the state's embracing this role is in the use of juvenile nocturnal curfews. Curfews, which have been used in Canada since the late nineteenth century, demonstrate effectively the profound ambivalence over young people: the law criminalized the presence of youth on the streets after a set time each evening – for their own, and society's, protection.

The trouble with adolescents has not yet been resolved. Today, threatening and vulnerable youth continue to capture headlines in our newspapers. Canadian Justice Minister Rob Nicholson promises "to get tough on youth crime," while youth curfews in the United States are embraced as a prophylactic against growing violence.[1] As the authors of the chapters in this section argue, the "problem with youth" has beset modern society for a century and has given rise to a variety of well-meaning but short-sighted experiments in youth "management."

Note

1   Jim Brown, "Justice Minister Promises New Moves to Get Tough on Youth Crime," *Canadian Press Online*, http://www.westislandchronicle.com/article-cp99296040-Tory-government-promises-new-moves-to-get-tough-on-youth-crime.html. Many US cities have implemented youth curfews to curb violence, including Rochester, New York, and Hartford, Connecticut.

3
Lost in Modernity: "Maladjustment" and the "Modern Youth Problem," English Canada, 1920-50
Cynthia Comacchio

In the Western world, the years immediately succeeding the First World War heralded the dawn of a "new generation." Carried along in an international tide of violence, working-class unrest, the undermining and collapse of political and social institutions, the proliferation of radical ideas, and the apparent loosening of moral standards, the generation born into the prewar world came of age in one that had changed irrevocably from that time not so long past.[1] Perhaps even more than the material challenges facing Canadians at this time, their socio-cultural implications aroused foreboding about the collapse of cherished institutions and the historic relations of authority that sustained them, including intergenerational ones. Contemporary discourses about a multitude of "modern problems" consistently reveal a subtext of anxiety about the future. Racialized and class-based apprehensions about disorder, degeneration, and crisis, much of the rhetoric echoing concerns in Great Britain and the United States, imbued public discourses about the condition of youth. Such public anxieties about youth are no more exclusive to modernity than they are unique to Canadian society. Yet, within the setting of a new worldwide awareness of youth as a modernizing force, as well as the young Dominion's own experience of liminality in striving to become modern, adolescence was configured as "the problem of modern youth."

For those disturbed by the evident unmooring of tradition more than they were beguiled by modernity's promises, the young were further characterized as a "lost generation." Although the term signifies a postwar cultural movement of writers and artists, those concerned about the so-called problem of modern youth applied the notion of a generation adrift much more broadly.[2] To many Canadians, it appeared that the times had spawned certain destabilizing trends of fearsome potential. As generational explanations gained momentum, adolescence came to be regarded as a social problem primarily because its constituents were coming of age in the modern age. Their specific life stage coincided with a historic moment that marked them as generationally distinct, but also distinctly disadvantaged, fundamentally maladjusted, lost. They were young in dangerous times, and consequently a danger for being young.

Thus a "youth problem," more specifically, "the problem of modern youth," distinguished the postwar generation from all its predecessors. Despite the absence of any proven direct causal relationship, youth experts increasingly associated adolescent maladjustment with the pressures of modernity, adding their "science" to popular ideas about the so-called lost generation.[3] As befitting such an amorphous classification, maladjustment could manifest in any number of ways, from broad-spectrum delinquency and promiscuity, often the same "problem" where girls were concerned, through anorexia, depression, and, at its extreme, suicide. It was not only age-determined but also a gendered condition with its own generation-specific racial and class dimensions. In the shaky aftermath of the First World War, these worries were not so much about the medical and psychological problems relevant to the adolescent years as about middle-class ideals regarding how adolescence should be managed as a healthy transition to adulthood. Young Canadians were seen to be incapable of navigating a wholesome, socially approved accommodation to the complexities of the modern age. Within the context of emergent theories that conceptualized adolescence as a troubled, and troublesome, life stage, the young could not be left to work out a healthy self-individuation on their own, nor to do so within their uninformed families, and especially not within their suspect peer group.[4]

Medicine and the social sciences, especially the modern fields of psychology and sociology, extended their reach beyond clinic and classroom just in time to supply an appropriate typology for the problems that appeared to be destabilizing youth, family, and nation in the early twentieth century. Eugenic theory, a distortion of genetics that sought to control the reproduction of the supposedly unfit – so classified in blatantly class and racialized terms – captured the popular imagination, lending dubious support to child-saving campaigns. Inspired by American developments in the field of mental hygiene, which focused largely on public education in the interests of preventing mental illness, the Canadian National Committee for Mental Hygiene was inaugurated in 1918. Not surprisingly, considering the eugenicist, educational, and preventive elements of the mental hygiene campaign, children and youth became a central focus.[5] Finally, in Canada as elsewhere, the language of citizenship permeated child welfare discourses in the First World War's aftermath. Children and youth became "national assets" whose well-being was the concern of the expansionary state as much as that of the private family. The futurist orientation of the modern, as expressed in pervasive concerns about public health, national welfare, and "racial hygiene," demanded that youth be rescued from "the unholy trinity of Mammon, Bacchus and Priapus."[6]

For all that worries about the young can be tracked throughout history, the early twentieth century consequently saw adolescence gain legitimacy as a subject of scientific research. Derived from a varied disciplinary base, with much cross-fertilization and not a little imagination, theories about adolescence did not simply expand existing knowledge; they operated in a fundamentally political manner as they interacted with public concerns about the national importance of childhood and youth, the cultural implications of modernity, the maintenance of civil order, and the training of a citizenry to meet certain prescribed "modern" ends. In these modern times, individual age and the age group became useful instruments for sorting and classifying human beings; identifying status, civic rights, and duties; and defining the appropriate means and methods of regulation. The study of adolescence would give rise to numerous attempts to manage the actual members of that life stage. Such campaigns were not in and of themselves a modern phenomenon either, as the complex schooling, apprenticeship, inheritance, and marriage laws of earlier times demonstrate. What is different – modern – about early-twentieth-century approaches is the extent and uniformity of theorizing about, and surveillance of, young people, as reflected in public discourses, professional studies, government surveys, and all manner of reform campaigns common to Western industrial nations at the time, including Canada. Nor were such broadening, at times escalating, anxieties about young people contained at the discursive level. In Canada, as elsewhere, they took form in an intricate network of state policies and legislation designed to address such related "problems" as those of youth recreation, labour, schooling, vocational training, "social hygiene," and juvenile corrections – to name the most prominent – that made up the multifarious modern youth problem.[7] Since adolescence was the prime training ground for citizenship, and since the decline of family, church, community, and other traditional agencies of socialization was seen to be the foremost of worrisome modern trends, expert direction and state involvement were entirely justified.

Growing public acceptance of ideas about childhood as an especially vulnerable stage that demanded parent education and expert supervision also helped to extend the experts' vigilance beyond childhood's end. By the 1920s, adolescence was newly regarded as a unique opportunity for special – and specialized – attention to the needs of the young. The ideal was a partnership of informed parents and professionals, but the balance of power, as in the wider "scientific parenthood" campaign, was steeply inclined toward the experts. In laying claim to adolescence, modern experts expanded their authority over parents and children of all ages.[8]

What was easily the modern era's most important study on adolescence actually predated the First World War, gaining influence in professional circles and among the educated public, with scarce contestation, throughout the first half of the twentieth century. In his multivolume 1904 work *Adolescence: Its Relation to Physiology, Anthropology, Sociology, Sex, Crime, Religion, and Education,* American psychologist G. Stanley Hall delineated the modern experience of becoming adult. A pioneer in the psychology of child development, Hall worked within a recapitulation paradigm borrowed from evolutionary theory and cultural anthropology. Recapitulationism correlated individual human development with the larger process of human evolution. Childhood and adolescence reflected the prehistoric state of humanity, the primitive and savage. Each succeeding stage of "normal" development, successfully negotiated, would bring the young closer to the evolutionary apex represented in adulthood, hence the modern age. Finding resonance within a context of conflicting and even contradictory ideas about modernity, Hall's theories affirmed that adolescence constituted the critical gap between primitive childhood and the "more perfect form" of civilized adulthood.[9]

In focusing on the moral, sexual, and psychological upheaval that he related exclusively to the onset of biological puberty, Hall produced an enduring portrayal of "normal" adolescence as an episode of "physical and mental anarchy" during which the young demonstrated a "peculiar proneness to be either very good or very bad."[10] This emphasis on youth morality, as measured by judgment and behaviour more so than the quality of mental and physical health, underlay the period's understandings of "maladjustment" among the young, bolstering the experts' insistence that all responsible adults must work toward "the stabilization of youth during this important period."[11] Moreover, in the view of Hall and his followers, the moral foundations of adolescent maladjustment were directly related to the biological changes of puberty. In this manner, the physiological process of puberty became conflated with the socio-cultural experience of adolescence. Paradoxically, for all the experts' insistence on the modern scientific bases of their views, they continued to be informed by Victorian Christian moralism, especially in the critical matters of gender and sexuality. They might well recognize that the times demanded adaptation, but experts such as Hall were nevertheless intent on using science to support their own conservative positions.

Although the storm-and-stress model did not go entirely unchallenged even in Hall's time, its imprint on the body of twentieth-century theories of adolescence has been remarkably tenacious. The biological approach to the concept of the psyche held by his famous contemporary, Sigmund Freud, clearly fits with Hall's own biological determinism. Both the psychoanalytic and recapitulation approaches depict adolescence as phylogenetic, involving a staged process of psychosexual development that is genetic and therefore not greatly affected by environment; in short, "anatomy is destiny," as Freud would phrase it. Although there is no obvious link between Hall's ideas and the psychoanalytical method of Sigmund Freud, Hall did much to introduce North Americans to the Freudian thought that would so influence modern psychology.[12] Most important, like Hall, Freud stressed the critical relationship between the physiological manifestations of puberty and the growth of the psyche, reinforcing the "storm and stress" perspective on sexual maturation.[13]

In the end, more synthetic than innovative, moralistic than scientific, homiletic than analytical, Hall's theory of adolescence was not modern in the sense of diverging greatly from its antecedents. What made his ideas uniquely tenable was their introduction at a notable historical conjuncture. Socio-economic transformation had prepared a receptive audience for so-called scientific theories that explained current ills and suggested ways to mitigate or at least to regulate them.[14] Along with those of other American experts and reformers who specialized in youth issues, such as Jane Addams, his writings were cited in Canadian publications and professional journals, as well as in newspapers and mass-circulation magazines, both Canadian-produced and those of American origin that had a wide Canadian readership. Presented without fail as though their findings were directly applicable to Canadian conditions, they reached a growing audience of both experts and predominantly middle-class readers by the time of the First World War. Canadian medicine, psychology, and sociology were increasingly affected by these new ideas about the nature of adolescence and its social import.[15]

As did most of the period's physicians and psychologists, Canada's pre-eminent pediatrician, Dr. Alan Brown, drew a direct line of causation between the "rapid physical and mental growth" of the teen years and their characteristic "emotional confusion." Also commonplace were Brown's views about the inadequate socialization that thrust adolescents, without adequate preparation, into the "hostile world" of adult customs. Anxiety and alienation were the inevitable, indeed the natural, outcome: it was "not to be wondered that so many ... break down physically or mentally, but the wonder is that so many survive the ordeal with the little health supervision and health knowledge they receive." If biology were destiny, the worried public needed to understand that destiny could be positively affected by intervention, regulation, and management of the problem, in this instance, the adolescent.[16] The challenge lay in the fact that the young also appeared best qualified to adopt and popularize the modern age's darker elements.

By the 1920s, sociology was opening up a promising area of specialization in family studies, especially at the renowned University of Chicago, from which emanated the modernization hypothesis that would dominate North

American family sociology for at least the next half century. Sociologists in Canada, many of them Chicago-trained and working out of McGill University, took active part in examining the array of social problems identified under the modernization heading. These studies were intended to gauge the effects of modernization on both internal family dynamics and the relations of family and society; a necessary corollary, consequently, was its generational impact. A number of surveys highlighted the complications of coming of age in a time of rapid change, emphasizing the generational conflict inherent in the relations of modern youth with their less-than-modern parents. Although these emphasized environment – the changes in the family's outer world in relation to changes within – they nonetheless assumed adolescent angst to be a normal feature of the life stage, in these instances exacerbated by the tensions between old- and new-world cultures.[17]

Commentators of all stripes therefore gave signal importance to the "hectic modern times" that rendered adolescence "characteristic of and created by our form of civilization."[18] Yet, even as the historic moment was ascribed explanatory force, the young person's inability to cope with problems peculiar to both the age group and "the times" was still explained biologically. In his 1932 popular advice manual for parents, *Normal Youth and Its Everyday Problems,* whose very title captures the idea that the adolescent experience is normally troubled, American psychologist D.A. Thom found no "specific psychological principles applicable to the adolescent period." Echoing Hall, he did find "certain physiological factors and psychological situations that are not met elsewhere, or are met here for the first time, or are met more frequently here than at any other time," so that adolescence was inevitably a stage "when all of life seems to be dominated by the intensity of the individual's own feelings."[19] The boundaries between mental and physical health and what was considered healthy social functioning were nowhere as ambiguous as in discussions about this life stage.

Despite the standardizing intentions of those who classified by age, the factors of class, race, and gender remained key signifiers of what made the young a problem or at least what made some young Canadians more a problem than others. What were considered the normal psychological patterns of adolescence were themselves abnormal in reference to the only standard that mattered, that of the mature adult, with the white adult male standing tall at the evolutionary pinnacle. In 1920, Dr. C.K. Clarke, psychologist, founder of the Canadian Mental Hygiene Association, and dean of the University of Toronto medical faculty, reminded his audience of eight hundred teachers that "upon them fell the duty of saving the race" from the repercussions of the "deplorable depravity" of Canadian youth. Clarke had discovered girls as young as thirteen suffering from venereal diseases, some becoming unmarried mothers, others "commencing lives of shame," with not much to tell the difference between these paths. He had also seen boys who had acquired habits associated with "only the most hardened moral perverts." In his view, the source was "organic": the "moral depravity" of many of these young people was largely attributable to feeble-mindedness. He might well have made class and race the primary causes, as he contended that feeble-mindedness disproportionately affected the families of workers and immigrants.[20] Clarke's views on youthful "perversion" and criminality found solid support in those of Hall, who maintained that these were biologically based, that adolescence "is pre-eminently the criminal age when most first commitments occur" and that juvenile delinquency was "everywhere increasing."[21]

Clarke's characterization of troubled and consequently dangerous youth shared, and undoubtedly reinforced, the racialized profile that underpinned many of the period's discourses of anxiety. Not only were the foreign-born felt to be more inclined to deviance at all ages, "aliens" provided the settings most conducive to it. The *Toronto World* reported in 1918 that aliens owned most of the city's licensed poolrooms: a reporter who visited fourteen poolrooms in the Queen and Bathurst district "found himself as in a strange country ... a stranger among the elect ... No one spoke either French or English." Worst of all, "the preponderance of youth was noticeable."[22] Moreover, the "foreign" neighbourhoods, with their crowded and substandard housing, harboured any number of "crime-producing tendencies." Young people inevitably strove to "escape as often as possible from their cramped quarters ... They drift to sidewalks, to gatherings under street lights, or to shops and dance-halls, anywhere where they may find space and light, and if the weather is cold, warmth." If they justifiably ventured out to seek light, warmth, and companionship, they invariably found "opportunity for mischief that sometimes degenerates into serious misdemeanour."[23]

Nor was this evidence of maladjustment among "foreign" youth merely an urban phenomenon. Sociologist Charles Young claimed to have personally observed much fighting in the Ukrainian settlements of the west, most of it resulting from "the capers of the young males," usually touched off by drinking. The situation was decidedly worse for Ukrainians in urban areas, where he thought he saw definite signs of the breakdown of parental authority and "misbehaviour among large numbers of the younger generation." In particular, the young men, "surer of foot, more accustomed to the ways of the new world and slightly contemptuous of the old" had "gone their own way," in many instances making "a sorry mess of things." Their gangs and wild parties were largely responsible for incidents of disorder in the Ukrainian communities. Settlement teachers reported that "the imperfectly assimilated adolescent," who knew little English and lacked "character training" opportunities, all the while "shut off" from the traditional prohibitions of the older generation, was becoming "a serious menace." According to Young, national duty demanded that "inclusive programmes" be implemented to prevent the social disorganization that immigrant communities were evidently suffering because of the generational clash and the youthful [male] propensity for inflammatory action.[24]

If adolescence were a dangerous passage for all, young women, as Clarke's views suggest, were thought to be predisposed by nature to an inestimable variety of potential physical and mental health complications. Hall saw women as perpetually adolescent, their psychological formation never completed, never approaching the evolutionary summit claimed by adult men. As he contended, "woman's body and soul are phylectically older and more primitive, while man is more modern, variable and less conservative." He insisted that feminists persistently ignored "the central importance of reproduction in women's lives," much to their physical and emotional detriment in adolescence, and what could only be their further deterioration in adulthood.[25]

Although Hall actually acknowledged that gender roles are in part socially constructed, he warned that, because they are fundamentally biologically determined, their modification could not be countenanced in the long term: "Nature decrees with advancing civilization that the sexes shall not approximate but differentiate." The specialization and rationalization central to modern progress would necessarily apply to gender roles. Caught up in such modern trends as urban living and employment, best left to men, young women were pushing beyond their natural limitations and resisting their naturally evolving womanly specialization, which actually resembled their traditional roles as wives and mothers. They were "fired" with ambitions that they could not safely and effectively attain, and therefore condemned to the unhealthy condition of what Hall termed "a suppressed semi-erotic state with never-culminating feeling." Unable to "fix their attentions properly" on womanly things, they were "lapsing into mannish ways, methods and ideals."[26] Paradoxically, even as they became mannish, modern young women seemed to be transforming themselves into "mere figurines" and "grow[ing] dollish" by resorting to commercial amusements and shopping to pass their time, rather than taking up their ordained vocation in homemaking.[27]

The girl runaway was a hot subject in the press during the 1920s, fuelling public worries about the seemingly new propensity for dangerous adventuring among young women. In 1925, the *Globe*'s regular Homemaker's Page featured a detailed interview with Mary E. Hamilton, identified as New York's best-known policewoman, who estimated that some five thousand girls disappeared in the United States every year.[28] Hamilton's view of the girl runaway situation was true to Hall's theories: she believed that the young were "apt to go to extremes, emotionally and mentally," simply because of the fragile condition that was adolescence. Hurt feelings, a desire to be alone, rebellion against authority, boredom, love of adventure, and a "desire to see the world" were the principal motives.[29]

Running away was the ultimate show of adolescent rebellion, an extreme form of individuation, and therefore maladjustment. In one reported instance, two fifteen-year-old Toronto girls left home to "be in the movies." One of the girls claimed to have two sisters who were actresses and "to this influence the police ascribe[d] the determination of the two girls to leave home." They were ultimately tracked down by police, after several days' search, at the Metropole Hotel in Detroit.[30] The flight across the border is common enough in these escape stories to qualify as a trope. Another two girls, aged fourteen and fifteen, escaped from the Ursuline Academy in Chatham, Ontario, only to be picked up by police after a few nights in Windsor and returned to their school. The runaways confessed to have been "looking for adventure, which they expected to find in Detroit." Penniless and hungry when found, the girls said that they would go back gladly.[31] Some parents felt the need to turn in their seemingly intractable offspring when they were unable to deal with them, at times sparking serial escape attempts by those confined against their will. Such was the case of sixteen-year-old Kathleen, committed to the Orillia, Ontario, industrial refuge by her father, who reportedly felt assured that a year's confinement would "cure his daughter of all her waywardness." After her first successful escape, she spent the months from May to September in "the north," where she was taken in by a sympathetic family. Something appears to have gone awry in that arrangement, because she was soon sent to live with an aunt; the aunt quickly asked to have her recommitted because she had run away to Buffalo and "was not doing at all well." The hapless Kathleen once again fled the refuge within days of her involuntary return but was located two days later, suffering from exposure.[32]

The "revolution in morals" of the new day was so closely associated with the so-called flaming youth of modernity that the flapper came to be its emblem, a sort of folk devil for the times.[33] American psychologist W.I. Thomas was one of many experts who stirred controversy on the subject of the sexual proclivities of modern young women in his "shocking" 1923 study, *The Unadjusted Girl, with Cases and Standpoint for Behavior Analysis*. Thomas proclaimed the adolescent girl's "lack of adjustment" to be outright demoralization due to a sexual delinquency attributed unequivocally to "today's unrest."[34] Nonetheless, echoing Hall and ignoring Freud, he insisted that "the sex passion" played an insignificant role in female sexual delinquency. He claimed to have three thousand documented cases revealing that girls had "usually become wild before the development of sexual desire," and that "their casual sexual relations do not usually awaken sex feeling." It appeared instead that these demoralized young women, evidently unadjusted to society's expectations of womanhood, deployed sexuality as "their capital," as "a condition of the realization of other wishes."[35] Put simply, the sexuality of adolescent girls was pathological. Although the modern girl, the flapper, was possibly the most frighteningly maladjusted of adolescents, all those who failed to learn sexual self-control were well "on the road to becoming sexual perverts."[36] As warned by Dr. Thom, heterosexuality had to be accomplished during those critical years or it would "never be accomplished in a normal way," but only by means of "some technical interference ... only after much conflict, failure and illness."[37] Given the magnitude and intensity of public anxiety about adolescent sexuality, the sexual regulation of the young was easily the issue that drew the most attention from youth-watchers during the first half of the twentieth century, and one that would remain a constant and remarkably consistent theme despite changing generational and historical contexts.[38]

At a time when Hollywood and advertising agencies were ever more intently selling the freshly coined "sex appeal," or "IT," as a package wrapped in youth and beauty, experts were quick to pick up on the health repercussions of the exacting new physical standards that sexiness entailed, especially for young women. Visiting Montreal families during the Depression, a McGill University social worker was struck by the extent to which adolescent girls were affected by the idea that they were not attractive by current standards, and how this notion undermined their social confidence. One of her case studies, Anne, from a middle-class anglophone family, had become so self-conscious about her height that she had withdrawn almost entirely from the company of her peers, believing that she was "not one of them."[39] A familiar theme in autobiographies, memoirs, and diaries is the sense of young women's confusion about their bodies that often accompanied the arrival of puberty, of which menstruation was the crowning manifestation. Growing up in Winnipeg in the 1920s, Lillian Allen was raised from early childhood by her widowed father and unmarried aunt, neither of whom prepared her for sexual maturation. The last of her friends to develop physically, Allen was "terribly scared" when she began to menstruate at age thirteen. Her very religious father, finding her in bed with "periodic pains," would ask her, "What have you done that God is punishing you?" thus inspiring in her a "fear complex" about her own feminine body.[40]

The notion of body image is a late-twentieth-century phenomenon, but the ideas at its base go back to the century's early years, gaining particular force after the First World War. Awareness of both a certain physical ideal and the degree to which the individual falls short of its achievement is central to the process of self-formation that takes place during adolescence. Joan Brumberg's studies effectively demonstrate that "every girl suffers some kind of adolescent angst about her body; it is the historical moment that defines how she reacts to her changing flesh."[41] Young women do not stand alone before their mirrors; reflected back to them are the ideals that are conceptualized, disseminated, and construed as the norm. The ongoing medicalization of women's bodies provided women with a scientific vocabulary to describe their bodily concerns and functions. But modern medicine, technology, and popular culture, as well as informing, also allowed for an increasingly pervasive understanding of what constituted the ideal body and, consequently, that which deviated from it. Ultimately, idealized body types are made to correspond to ideal moral types, the acknowledged "good citizen"; hence, the healthy, beautiful citizen is the good citizen, an application especially pertinent to young women in their specialized social role as future mothers.[42]

Although the science of nutrition did not become established until the 1930s, doctors early on recognized the importance of nutrition to guard against chlorosis (anemia) in adolescent girls in order to ensure that it would not do "permanent damage to the future wife and future mother."[43] With its new emphasis on the straight, angular, androgynous flapper physique for women, the 1920s brought the concepts of slenderizing and slimming into the popular consciousness more than ever before.[44] During the 1930s, in light of public health concerns about Depression-induced deprivation, health professionals were worried about the findings of dietary surveys that consistently showed adolescent girls to have the poorest diet of any family member in every economic class. They attributed this not to ignorance about nutrition nor to lack of adequate food, especially for those families on relief, but to "the urge for slenderness and the compulsion to do as the group does."[45]

It appeared that new pressures exerted by the increasingly commercialized popular culture of the day, especially the movies, the dance hall, and mass-circulation magazines, and fortified by the newly important, high school-based peer culture, were pushing a dangerous obsession with thinness among the nation's prospective mothers at the crucial point of their physiological development.[46] Whether the problem was poor eating habits or actual eating disorders – clearly a broad spectrum of "maladjustments" – most important is the fact that they were all considered to be an outcome of age compounded by the matter of gender. Adolescent girls were prone to such maladjustments because they were uniquely vulnerable to social pressures as well as to psychological disorders: the two were often intertwined. Anorexia nervosa, a "feminine" problem, was also an adolescent one. It was believed to materialize "following some emotional disturbance."[47] The sufferer typically showed symptoms of "an active morbid or fanatic aversion to eating high caloric foods; perverse habits of eating, often pretending to eat and throw food away" and, ominously, amenorrhea (absence of menstruation) was a "constant finding."[48] Removal from the home, where, it was surmised, there were almost invariably troubled relations with parents, especially mothers, to a hospital under close regulation and constant surveillance by a team of nurses, physicians, and psychologists, had already come to be the favoured remedy by the Second World War.[49]

If girls were seen to be inclined to promiscuity and self-starvation to assuage their adolescent angst, or at least to draw attention to it, among boys, besides the gang membership, hooliganism, and petty criminality classified as delinquency, suicide was the extreme manifestation of maladjustment. Because boys were perceived to be naturally more impulsive than girls, more aggressive and violent, and given to immediate action, experts reasoned that self-annihilation was a problem – a tragic solution – that afflicted adolescent boys more than girls. The suicides of numerous teenage male immigrants from Great Britain during the 1920s sparked a public outcry sufficient to bring about an investigation into their treatment and prompted calls, ultimately successful, for severe restriction of the immigration schemes.[50] An inquest into the 1923 suicide by hanging of sixteen-year-old Charles Bulpitt, a British farmhand sent to Goderich, Ontario, saw a courtroom filled to capacity, as well as detailed press coverage.[51] Ontarians were again shocked when, within days of young Bulpitt's death, John Payne, another juvenile immigrant working on a farm in Emily Township in eastern Ontario, killed himself by ingesting the common household poison Paris Green, which induced a slow and agonizing death. It was felt that the Bulpitt case had inspired Payne to consider suicide.[52] A decade later, much attention was paid to the notion that the Depression had spawned a generation more truly lost than any before, as opportunities to come into their own eluded the young. It was argued that unemployment caused more damage among young people than among adults: "It confuses them in a period of adaptation and development, undermines their confidence in life and can even destroy their latent possibilities."[53] Despite the lack of any concerted state effort to ameliorate the lot of this generation of modern youth, their elders' worries about desperation leading to subversion, rising youth crime, and the "tragic waste" entailed in youth suicide were not realized, insofar as the available statistics can reveal.[54]

Before the first week of 1945 had closed, the *Toronto Star* was reporting on the suicide of a promising young man, a resident of the city's Forest Hill Village. President of the student council of Northern Vocational School, where he was in his graduating year, he was described by family, friends, and teachers as "among the most popular students at school." The seventeen-year-old was found shortly after midnight in a parked car not far from his home, shot in the temple, a .22 calibre revolver on the seat beside him. Police investigation revealed that he was "believed to have been depressed since receiving his report card" the previous week. Stunned by the outcome, the school's principal and the Toronto Board of Education's superintendent both observed that he had always done well academically and could readily have improved his score on the final examinations to achieve matriculation that year, that he had been active in extracurricular activities and as student council president, and that "he did not appear depressed or despondent to his teachers or classmates."[55]

In a plaintive editorial under the declarative heading "Nobody Really Knew Him," a *Toronto Star* editor interpreted the schoolboy suicide as "a tragic reminder of the inadequate mental hygiene services" and health supervision in the nation's high schools, "something for which welfare and parents organizations [had] agitated for some time without success." In the editor's view, "had there been such a service, this boy's suicide might have been prevented and his life made happier. No one among those with whom he mingled really knew this lad. What loneliness and torture he must have experienced as he approached the fatal moment! ... His case should serve as a severe warning to health and school authorities; to parents and all who care about the happy development of children. The science of psychology is far enough developed today to provide the means of preventing some of these tragedies." The conclusion drawn, the warning issued, were those that had underlain discussions about lost youth for a quarter century by this time: "It is costly to neglect the youth of the nation."[56] For, as one early-twentieth-century expert had observed, "Suicide accompanies civilization and education as an unerring index of maladjustment in society and defects in education."[57]

Conclusion

At the beginning of the twentieth century, G. Stanley Hall contended that to study the changing meaning of adolescence was to gain understanding of the nature of modernity: "Other oracles may grow dim," he argued, "but this one will never fail."[58] Age became an instrument for assessment and classification, standardization and regulation, as the social sciences, medicine, and psychology expanded their influence over the population. Modernity's dangers were perceived to be peculiarly dangerous to the young, thus endangering the future that they embodied. Much like the larger youth problem in its vagaries, the problems of the young as individuals were encoded in the decidedly nonspecific term "maladjustment."

The maladjustment classification favoured by doctors, psychologists, social workers, and educators had the dual benefit of being sanctioned by modern science and yet so embedded with facile popular assumptions that it could be easily and broadly applied. As it came to be the catch-all diagnosis for myriad adolescent mental and physical health concerns, it reinforced the Hall model of adolescence as a normally volatile life stage, feeding social constructions about typical teenage behaviour, individual and generational. It made patients of virtually all adolescents, openly maladjusted or just assumed to be, treated or left untreated, on their own and as a cohort, thereby medicalizing the adolescent experience. And the effects have been enduring,

as witnessed in the manner in which the universal designation of "maladjustment" continues to support the paradox at the heart of modern adolescence.
Normalizing maladjustment has inflated concerns about the problems of
youth, and of youth as a social problem; at the same time, it has allowed
for ready dismissal as mere teenage angst what might well have been – and
continue to be – very real problems tending toward self-destructive practices
and even suicide. Despite the many challenges to these ideas during the past
century and into our own, this modern definition of adolescence has proved
to be remarkably tenacious, complicating understandings of adolescence
and the policies and programs intended to help those who lose their way
on the path to adulthood.

Notes

1 Robert Wohl, "Heart of Darkness: Modernism and Its Historians," *Journal of Modern History*
74, 3 (2002): 576, 614-15. On modernity as process and condition see also Marshall Berman,
All That Is Solid Melts into Air: The Experience of Modernity (New York: Simon and Schuster,
1982); William R. Everdell, *The First Moderns: Profiles in the Origins of 20th Century Thought*
(Chicago: University of Chicago Press, 1997); Keith Walden, *Becoming Modern: The Industrial
Exhibition and the Shaping of a Late Victorian Culture* (Toronto: University of Toronto Press,
1997); and David Harvey, *The Condition of Postmodernity: An Enquiry into the Origins of Cultural
Change* (London: Blackwell, 1990), as well as the expansive synthesis by Peter Watson, *A
Terrible Beauty: The People and Ideas That Shaped the Modern Mind* (London: Phoenix Press,
2000), esp. chap. 16, 273-99. Allan Levine discusses "the modern" in Canada within a North
American context in A. Levine, *The Devil in Babylon: The Fear of Progress and the Birth of
Modern Life* (Toronto: McClelland and Stewart, 2005).
2 The "lost generation" classification is associated with Ernest Hemingway's 1926 novel *The
Sun Also Rises*, though Hemingway attributed the phrase to Gertrude Stein. For contempor-
ary views, see the essays in V.F. Calverton and Samuel D. Schmalhausen, eds., *The New
Generation: The Intimate Problems of Modern Parents and Children* (New York: The Macaulay
Company, 1930), especially the introduction by Bertrand Russell, 17-24; also Karl Mannheim,
"The Problem of Generations" (1927), in Karl Mannheim, *Essays on the Sociology of Knowledge*
(1952; repr., London: Routledge and Keegan Paul, 1972), 320. For an overview of the "soci-
ology of generations," see June Edmunds and Bryan S. Turner, "Introduction," 2-3, and
Bryan S. Turner, "Strategic Generations: Historical Change, Literary Expression, and Generational Politics," in June Edmunds and Bryan S. Turner, eds., *Generational Consciousness,
Narrative, and Politics* (Lanham, MD: Rowman and Littlefield, 2002), 15.
3 Contemporary commentaries include T.R. Robinson, "Youth and the Virtues," *Social Welfare*,
October 1928: 9; H. Dobson, "Youth: Scapegrace or Scapegoat," *Social Welfare*, July 1929:
228; Editorial, "Hygiene of Recreation," *Canadian Practitioner* 49, 6 (1924): 309. These
anxieties are further discussed in Cynthia Comacchio, *The Dominion of Youth: Adolescence
and the Making of Modern Canada, 1920-50* (Waterloo, ON: Wilfrid Laurier University Press,
2006), esp. chap. 1, 17-44. On childhood and youth in Canada in the early twentieth
century, see Neil Sutherland's inaugural, and unsurpassed, *Children in English-Canadian
Society: Framing the Twentieth-Century Consensus* (Toronto: University of Toronto Press, 1976;
Waterloo, ON: Wilfrid Laurier University Press, 2000) (all subsequent citations are to the
1976 edition); Veronica Strong-Boag, *The New Day Recalled: Lives of Girls and Women in
English Canada, 1919-1939* (Toronto: Penguin, 1988); Karen Dubinsky, *Improper Advances:
Rape and Heterosexual Conflict in Ontario, 1880-1929* (Chicago: University of Chicago Press,
1993); Jeffery Taylor, *Fashioning Farmers: Ideology, Agricultural Knowledge and the Manitoba
Farm Movement, 1890-1925* (Regina: Canadian Plains Research Center, 1994); and Carolyn
Strange, *Toronto's Girl Problem: The Perils and Pleasures of the City, 1880-1930* (Toronto:
University of Toronto Press, 1995). On post-Second World War developments, see M.L.

Adams, *The Trouble with Normal: Postwar Youth and the Making of Heterosexuality* (Toronto: University of Toronto Press, 1997), and Mona Gleason, *Normalizing the Ideal: Psychology, Schooling, and the Family in Postwar Canada* (Toronto: University of Toronto Press, 1999). Among the seminal works on the historical experience of adolescence are J. Kett, *Rites of Passage: Adolescence in America* (New York: Basic Books, 1977); J. Springhall, *Coming of Age: Adolescence in Britain, 1860-1960* (London: Oxford University Press, 1986); J. Modell, *Into One's Own: From Youth to Adulthood in the United States* (Berkeley: University of California Press, 1988); R. Wegs, *Growing Up Working Class: Youth in Vienna, 1870-1920* (Philadelphia: University of Pennsylvania Press, 1989); D. Linton, *"Who Has the Youth Has the Future": The Campaign to Save Young Workers in Imperial Germany* (Cambridge, MA: Harvard University Press, 1990); H. Hendrick, *Images of Youth: Age, Class, and the Male Youth Problem, 1880-1920* (London: Oxford University Press, 1990); J. Neubauer, *The Fin-de-Siecle Culture of Adolescence* (New Haven, CT: Yale University Press, 1992); M. Childs, *Labour's Apprentices: Working-Class Lads in Late Victorian and Edwardian England* (Montreal and Kingston: McGill-Queen's University Press, 1993); and David Fowler, *The First Teenagers: The Lifestyle of Young Wage-Earners in Interwar Britain* (London: Woburn Press, 1995).

4 Erik H. Erikson, *Identity, Youth and Crisis* (New York: W.W. Norton, 1968), 102; also Erik H. Erikson, *Identity and the Life Cycle* (New York: W.W. Norton, 1959), 17-18, 94-96. On Erikson's influence as the foremost theorist of human development of the latter part of the twentieth century, see J.E. Cote and A.L. Allahar, *Generation on Hold: Coming of Age in the Late 20th Century* (Toronto: Stoddart, 1994), 70-75.

5 Pre-eminent Toronto psychiatrists Dr. Charles K. Clarke and Dr. Clarence Hincks figured strongly in the association's inception and program during the interwar years. Clarke served as its first medical director. J.D.M. Griffin, "The Contribution of Child Psychiatry to Mental Hygiene," *Canadian Public Health Journal* 29 (1938): 550. See also David Wright and James E. Moran, eds., *Mental Health and Canadian Society: Historical Perspectives* (Montreal and Kingston: McGill-Queen's University Press, 2006), 5; Charles Roland, *Clarence Hincks: Mental Health Crusader* (Toronto: Hannah Institute/Dundurn Press, 1990). On the mental hygiene movement in the United States and Canada, and especially its links to child study, see Theresa Richardson, *The Century of the Child: The Mental Hygiene Movement and Social Policy in the United States and Canada* (Albany, NY: State University of New York Press, 1989); see also Gleason, *Normalizing the Ideal*.

6 Editorial, "Hygiene of Recreation," 309.

7 Victoria Getis, "Experts and Juvenile Delinquency, 1900-35," in Joe Austin and Michael Nevin Willard, eds., *Generations of Youth: Youth Culture and History in 20th Century America* (New York: NYU Press, 1998), 30-31. For a discussion of similar themes and issues, see William Bush, Chapter 4 of this volume, and Tamara Myers, Chapter 5 of this volume. Myers provides full treatment of girl delinquency in *Caught: Montreal's Modern Girls and the Law, 1869-1945* (Toronto: University of Toronto Press, 2006).

8 On the subject of changing views of childhood, and the development of child welfare movements, see N. Sutherland, *Children in English-Canadian Society*; T.R. Richardson, *The Century of the Child*; C.R. Comacchio, *Nations Are Built of Babies: Saving Ontario's Mothers and Children, 1900-1940* (Montreal and Kingston: McGill-Queen's University Press, 1993), esp. chap. 2, 16-42; and K. Arnup, *Education for Motherhood: Advice for Mothers in Twentieth-Century Canada* (Toronto: University of Toronto Press, 1994).

9 Hall adhered to the Lamarckian premise that evolution consists of the incremental acquirement of memories and characteristics over time, a popular scientific theory prior to any understanding of genetics. See G. Stanley Hall, *Adolescence: Its Psychology and Its Relation to Physiology, Anthropology, Sociology, Sex, Crime, Religion and Education* (New York: D. Appleton, 1904), 1:vii, 614. The massive two-volume work, with over 1,300 pages, sold a remarkable twenty-five thousand copies. See Jeffrey Jensen Arnett and Hamilton Cravens, "Introduction: G. Stanley Hall's *Adolescence*: A Centennial Reappraisal," *History of Psychology* 9, 3 (2006): 165-71. Hall (1844-1924), who pursued graduate studies under William James at Harvard University, was awarded the first doctorate in psychology in North America, in 1878. He became the first chair of psychology at The Johns Hopkins University in 1884; in 1888, he became president of the newly established Clark University in Worcester,

Massachusetts. He is considered one of the founding fathers of experimental psychology, and child psychology in particular, as well as the leading American figure in the child study movement. He tells his own story in Hall, *Life and Confessions of a Psychologist* (New York: D. Appleton, 1923). See N. Lesko, "Denaturalizing Adolescence: The Politics of Contemporary Representations," *Youth and Society* 28, 2 (1996): 144-47; and Rolf E. Muus, *Theories of Adolescence*, 5th ed. (New York: Random House, 1988), 17-21. On Hall and recapitulation theory, see Kett, *Rites of Passage*, 218-19, and Adams, *The Trouble with Normal*, 43-47. The definitive biography remains D. Ross, *G. Stanley Hall: The Psychologist as Prophet* (Chicago: University of Chicago Press, 1983), 332-33. See also Jeffrey Jensen Arnett, "G. Stanley Hall's *Adolescence: Brilliance and Nonsense*," 186-97, and Hamilton Cravens, "The Historical Context of G. Stanley Hall's *Adolescence*," 172-85, in the special centennial reappraisal volume of *History of Psychology* 9, 3 (2006).

10 G. Stanley Hall, *Youth: Its Education, Regimen and Hygiene* (New York: D. Appleton, 1907), 135; and H.P. Chudacoff, *How Old Are You? Age Consciousness in American Culture* (Princeton, NJ: Princeton University Press, 1989), esp. chap. 4, 65-91. Hall's 1907 volume is the popularized, condensed version of the 1904 study.

11 Dr. D.A. Thom, *Normal Youth and Its Everyday Problems* (New York: D. Appleton, 1932), ix; see also Dr. A. Goldbloom, "Problems of the Adolescent Child," *Canadian Medical Association Journal* 43, 4 (1940): 336-39, and Hall, *Adolescence*, 1:xvi-xvii.

12 Muus, *Theories of Adolescence*, 270. If, as Rolf Muus contends, "the hypothesis of a universal period of storm and stress is no longer tenable," it is clear that it remains an important characteristic of the life stage for at least some of our present-day experts, as well as for much of the public. See, for example, A.C. Petersen and B. Taylor, "The Biological Approach to Adolescence: Biological Change and Psychological Adaptation," in J. Adelson, ed., *Handbook of Adolescent Psychology* (New York: Wiley, 1980). See also Arnett, "G. Stanley Hall's *Adolescence*," 186-87.

13 As president of Clark University, Hall invited Freud to give a lecture series in 1909 and wrote the preface to the American edition of Freud's *A General Introduction to Psychoanalysis* (New York: Liveright, 1920). See Muus, *Theories of Adolescence*, 45, and Cravens, "The Historical Context of G. Stanley Hall's *Adolescence*," 173.

14 It is clear that Hall was inspired not only by Darwinian and Lamarckian evolutionary theories but also by the ideas of French Enlightenment philosopher Jean-Jacques Rousseau and the German Romantic school of *Sturm und Drang*. See Kett, *Rites of Passage*, 221; Sutherland, *Children in English-Canadian Society*, 6-13; and Harvey Graff, *Conflicting Paths: Growing Up in America* (Cambridge, MA: Harvard University Press, 1995), 302.

15 Hall's views on child development were making their mark in Canadian educational and medical circles even before the publication of *Adolescence*. See, for example, Hall, "The New Psychology," *Canadian Educational Monthly and School Magazine* 16 (April 1894): 151; see also editorial comments in *Canadian Educational Monthly* 20 (April 1898): 128; *Canadian Educational Monthly* 20 (April 1898): 20; *Canadian Educational Monthly*, August-September 1898: 262; *Montreal Medical Journal* 26, 1 (1897): 75; *Educational Journal of Western Canada* 3, 10 (1902): 306; and *Canadian Practitioner* 30, 7 (1905): 374. On Addams's influence see Cathy L. James, "Practical Diversions and Educational Amusements: Evangelia Home and the Advent of Canada's Settlement Movement, 1902-09," *Historical Studies in Education* 10, 1-2 (1998): 49-51.

16 Preceding four quotations from Dr. A. Brown, "Toronto as a Paediatric Centre," *Canadian Medical Monthly* 5, 6 (1920): 205. Heather Munro Prescott, *A Doctor of Their Own: The History of Adolescent Medicine* (Cambridge, MA: Harvard University Press, 1998), 14, 24-25, notes that this cross-training in medicine and psychology was actively promoted by the Commonwealth Fund during the 1930s. For Hall's views on medicine and psychology, see *Adolescence*, 1:xvi-xvii, 438-39. See also Gleason, *Normalizing the Ideal*, and Adams, *The Trouble with Normal*, on mutually supportive applications of psychology and medicine to children and youth.

17 The interactionist approach was imported to Canada by the University of Chicago-trained Carl Addington Dawson, who was instrumental in establishing sociology at McGill University. With Warner Gettys, Dawson produced an influential textbook, *An Introduction to*

Sociology (New York: Ronald, 1929), in which they catalogued modernization's undermining impact on families. Ostensibly targeting the relations of industry and community during the economic crisis of the 1930s, McGill's Social Science Research Project discussed family as an integral player in these interactions. Examples of this approach in relation to youth of the time can be found in Charles H. Young, *The Ukrainian Canadians: A Study in Assimilation* (Toronto: Thomas Nelson and Sons, 1931); Carl Dawson, *Group Settlement: Ethnic Communities in Western Canada* (Toronto: Macmillan, 1936); and Horace Miner, *St. Denis, a French-Canadian Parish* (Chicago: University of Chicago Press, 1939). Dawson mentored both Young and Miner. See Marlene Shore, *The Science of Social Redemption: McGill, the Chicago School, and the Origins of Social Research in Canada* (Toronto: University of Toronto Press, 1987), xvi, 118, 227-30.

18 Dr. W.T.B. Mitchell, "The Clinical Significance of Some Trends in Adolescence," *Canadian Medical Association Journal*, 22, 30 (1930): 183. Similar views are found in Thom, *Normal Youth and Its Everyday Problems*, ix–xi.

19 Thom, *Normal Youth and Its Everyday Problems*, 18, 19; Hall, *Adolescence*, 1:237-38.

20 Clarke cited in Editorial, "A Deplorable Depravity of Young Girls and Boys," *Globe and Mail*, 3 April 1920; also P.J. Bend, "Juvenile Delinquency: Its Causes," *Social Welfare*, March 1919: 126; "Records Indicate Crime Increasing among Youths," *Globe and Mail*, 6 January 1920; and Judge E. MacLachlan, "The Delinquent Girl," *Social Welfare*, December 1921: 56.

21 Hall, *Adolescence*, 1:325, also 335 and 396-400.

22 Editorial, "Many Aliens Hold Licenses in City," *Toronto World*, 1 January 1918.

23 Editorial, "A Deplorable Depravity," 3; see also A Juvenile Court Probation Officer, "As the Twig Is Bent: What Are We Doing to Keep Children from the Reformatory?" *Chatelaine*, March 1928, 3-6, and D.N. McLachlan, "The Spiritual and Ethical Development of the Child," *Social Welfare*, December 1929: 68. Historical treatments include R. Coulter, "Not to Punish but to Reform: Juvenile Delinquency and the Children's Protection Act," in R.B. Blake and J. Keshen, eds., *Social Welfare Policy in Canada* (Toronto: Copp Clark, 1995), 137-52, and Bryan Hogeveen, "'The Evils with Which We Are Called to Grapple': Élite Reformers, Eugenicists, Environmental Psychologists, and the Construction of Toronto's Working-Class Boy Problem, 1860-1930," *Labour/Le Travail* 55 (Spring 2005): 37-68.

24 All quotations in this paragraph from Young, *Ukrainian Canadians*, 282-83. See also W. Burton Hurd, "The Decline in the Canadian Birth Rate," *Canadian Journal of Economics and Political Science* 3, 1 (1937): 40-57.

25 Hall, *Adolescence*, 2:566, 624, also 572, 646; on menstruation, which he called "periodicity," see Hall, *Adolescence*, 1:xiv, 472, 494.

26 Hall, *Adolescence*, 1:325, 335, 396-400.

27 Hall, *Adolescence*, 2:617.

28 The Homemaker's Page, "Among Ourselves: Runaways," *Globe and Mail*, 25 September 1924.

29 Ibid., 16.

30 "15-Year-Old Toronto Girls Run Away to Join Movies," *Globe and Mail*, 4 March 1920.

31 "Seeking for Adventure; Glad to Go Back Home," *Globe and Mail*, 19 January 1920. See also Editorial, "Runaways," *Toronto World*, 2 March 1918.

32 "Girl Returns after Escape from Refuge," *Globe and Mail*, 4 March 1920. The difficulties of "delinquent girls" have been thoroughly examined by Joan Sangster, *Regulating Girls and Women: Sexuality, Family, and the Law in Ontario, 1920-1960* (Don Mills, ON: Oxford University Press, 2001); see also Myers, *Caught*.

33 The terms "folk devil" and "moral panic" are attributed to Stanley Cohen, *Folk Devils and Moral Panics* (1972; repr., Oxford: Basil Blackwell, 1990). For contemporary views about these fears, see Lorine Pruette, "The Flapper," in Calverton and Schmalhausen, *The New Generation*, 572-90. Pruette was a Columbia-trained psychologist and author of a biography of G. Stanley Hall, whose views on women she disputed. See also E. McLaughlin, J. Muncie, and G. Hughes, "Introduction," in John Muncie, Gordon Hughes, and Eugene McLaughlin, eds., *Youth Justice: Critical Readings* (London: Sage, 2002), 19-21; John Clarke, "The Three Rs: Repression, Rescue and Rehabilitation: Ideologies of Control for Working-Class Youth," in Muncie, Hughes, and McLaughlin, *Youth Justice*, 121-37.

34 W.I. Thomas, *The Unadjusted Girl, with Cases and Standpoint for Behavior Analysis* (Boston: Little, Brown, 1923), xi.

35 Thomas, *The Unadjusted Girl,* xvi-xvii, 109. Similar views are discussed in G. Pringle, "Is the Flapper a Menace?" *Maclean's,* 15 June 1922, 19; Thom, *Normal Youth and Its Everyday Problems,* 69-70; W.F. Roberts, Minister of Public Health, New Brunswick, "The Reconstruction of the Adolescent Period of Our Canadian Girl," *Social Welfare,* January 1920: 100; and Phyllis Blanchard and Carolyn Manassas, *New Girls for Old* (New York: The Macaulay Company, 1930), cited in Pruette, "The Flapper," 583.

36 F.E. Williams, *Adolescence, Studies in Mental Hygiene* (New York: Appleton-Century, 1932), 54; and Thom, *Normal Youth and Its Everyday Problems,* 69-70.

37 Thom, *Normal Youth and Its Everyday Problems,* 60.

38 See, for example, T.G. Hunter and Dr. C.H. Gundry, "School Health Practices: Ritualistic or Purposeful?" *Canadian Journal of Public Health* 46, 1 (1955): 9-14.

39 Inez LePage, "Group Organization and the Development of the Adolescent Girl" (MA thesis, McGill University, 1932), 27.

40 University of Manitoba Archives, Lillian Beatrice Allen papers, MSS 45, Box 14, file 1, typescript, undated, "Growing Up," 21, 23. Allen was born in Winnipeg on 9 November 1904. She was the only daughter of Frank Allen, the first physics professor at the University of Manitoba. She earned a master's degree in home economics at the University of Syracuse in 1947 and lectured at Manitoba's Faculty of Agriculture and Home Economics.

41 J. Brumberg, *The Body Project: An Intimate History of American Girls* (New York: Random House, 1997), xvii; J. Brumberg, "Chlorotic Girls, 1870-1920: A Historical Perspective on Female Adolescence," *Child Development* 53 (1982): 1468-1477; for Canada, see Wendy Mitchinson, *The Nature of Their Bodies: Women and Their Doctors in Victorian Canada* (Toronto: University of Toronto Press, 1991).

42 Brumberg, *The Body Project,* 96.

43 Editorial, "The Care of Growing Girls," *Canada Lancet,* September 1907: 93.

44 Brumberg, *The Body Project,* 99-100.

45 Dr. J.F. Webb, "Horizons in Child Health Supervision," *Canadian Public Health Journal* 50, 12 (1959): 491-95.

46 E.W. McHenry, "Nutrition and Child Health," *Canadian Public Health Journal* 33, 4 (1942): 152-57; Canadian Council on Nutrition, "A Dietary Standard for Canada," *Canadian Nutrition Notes* (1949): 6-10.

47 R.F. Farquharson and H.H. Hyland, "*Anorexia Nervosa:* The Course of 15 Patients Treated from 20 to 30 Years Previously," *Canadian Medical Association Journal* 94, 2 (1966): 411. This study returns to seven teenage patients treated for anorexia between 1932 and 1937, and eight patients treated between 1936 and 1943.

48 Ibid., 413.

49 Ibid., 414.

50 "British Youngsters Arrive on Prairies," *Globe and Mail,* 19 March 1924; "Lonely 'Home' Boy, Licked by Farmer, Hanged Himself," *Globe and Mail,* 23 January 1924; "London Wants Probe into Tragic Deaths of Immigrant Boys," *Globe and Mail,* 31 January 1924; "Two Months in Prison for Bulpitt's Employer," *Globe and Mail,* 1 February 1924; "Farmer Sent to Jail for Assaulting Boy Who Hanged Himself," *Globe and Mail,* 2 February 1924. See also Library and Archives Canada, MG 28, I 10, Canadian Welfare Council, vol. 6, file 33, 1928, Charlotte Whitton, Letter to Miss Gladys Pott, Society for Overseas Settlement of British Juveniles, 16 August 1928, 2. Whitton was the council's executive secretary; in this letter criticizing the juvenile immigration scheme, she refers to the "suicides of recent years."

51 "Urge a Readjustment: Children's Aid Staff," *Toronto Star,* 28 February 1924; also "Seek to Guard Young Who Come to Ontario," *Toronto Star,* 8 May 1924.

52 "Funeral of Home Boy Moves Many to Tears," *Globe and Mail,* 28 January 1924; "Farmer Exonerated at Omemee Inquiry into Boy's Suicide," *Globe and Mail,* 3 February 1924.

53 B. Davies, *Youth Speaks Its Mind* (Toronto: Ryerson Press, 1948), 62-63; 65; Canadian Youth Commission, *Youth and Jobs in Canada* (Toronto: Ryerson Press, 1945), 54.

54 Editorial, "The Revolt of Youth," *National Home Monthly,* June 1934, 3; D.L. Ritchie, "The Plight of Youth," *Social Welfare,* June 1934: 50; G. Arnold, "Flaming Youth," *Maclean's,* 1

July 1934, 13; H. Weir, "Unemployed Youth," in L. Richter, ed., *Canada's Unemployment Problem* (Toronto: Macmillan, 1939), 146. See also J.P. Huzel, "The Incidence of Crime in Vancouver during the Great Depression," *BC Studies* 69-70 (1986): 211-48, and B. McCarthy and J. Hagen, "Gender, Delinquency and the Great Depression," *Canadian Review of Sociology and Anthropology* 24, 2 (1987): 153-77.

55 "High School Student Found Dead in Car," *Toronto Daily Star,* 9 January 1945.

56 Editorial, "Nobody Really Knew Him," *Toronto Daily Star,* 10 January 1945. See also "Studies Not Cause for Boy's Suicide," *Toronto Daily Star,* 12 January 1945. The *Globe* was not as interested in the story, running only one short report, "Boy Self-Slain in Parked Car," 9 January 1945.

57 James Gibson Hume, "The Significance of Suicide," *Philosophical Review* 19 (1910): 179-80; cited in "Classics in the History of Psychology," developed by Christopher D. Green, York University, Toronto, Ontario, http://psychclassics.yorku.ca/. Hume (1860-1949) was professor of philosophy at the University of Toronto, 1891-1926. The historic silence that surrounds suicide means that there is still relatively little historical work on the subject. See Georges Minois, *History of Suicide: Voluntary Death in Western Culture* (Baltimore: Johns Hopkins University Press, 1999); for contemporary views, see Keith Hawton, Emma Evans, and Karen Rodham, *By Their Own Young Hand: Deliberate Self-Harm and Suicidal Ideas in Adolescents* (London: Jessica Kingsley, 2006).

58 G. Stanley Hall, "Child Study and Its Relation to Education," *The Forum* 29 (August 1900): 689.

4

James Dean and Jim Crow: Boys in the Texas Juvenile Justice System in the 1950s

William Bush

One of the first scenes in the iconic American film *Rebel without a Cause* (1955) takes place in a Los Angeles juvenile hall. Jim Stark, the affluent and alienated teenage rebel played by James Dean, has just been arrested on a charge of underage drinking, much to the chagrin of his parents, who come across as caricatures of the dysfunctional middle-class family popularized by 1950s psychiatrists. Jim's father, a befuddled executive, wonders aloud how a boy showered with "anything he wants" could become a delinquent; his mother, portrayed as a domineering shrew, worries about what the neighbours will think. Finally, Officer Roy intervenes, rescuing Jim from his parents' bickering. In his office, the juvenile officer provides Jim with the kind of patient but tough mentoring that the boy's own father seems incapable of dispensing.[1] Encapsulated in this scene was the film's larger message that juvenile delinquency was no longer merely a problem of the urban, immigrant working classes that had preoccupied reformers and experts during the previous half century. After the Second World War, delinquency wore a different face. Located in the emerging suburbs, the old social malady now stemmed from different causes and called for new remedies. In articles featuring clean-cut, white, middle-class teenagers, popular magazines such as *Look* and *Newsweek* espoused the need to combat emotional "maladjustment."[2] Media outlets borrowed much of their language from social scientists with an increasingly psychiatric orientation who studied middle-class teenagers.[3] Experts also began analyzing urban, working-class teenagers through a similar lens, in a raft of studies portraying youth gangs as delinquent subcultures that functioned in pathological opposition to the normative values of mainstream society.[4]

So pervasive was this imagery that even juvenile justice agencies and institutions adopted it. The notion that delinquency grew out of emotional rather than material poverty reflected the expansion of mental health services aimed at middle-class needs.[5] However, it also dovetailed particularly well with an optimistic new movement in juvenile justice administration that aimed to coordinate prevention, adjudication, and rehabilitation programs within a single state agency. One of the first of these youth authority programs, the Texas Youth Council (TYC), is the subject of this chapter. Inaugurated in 1949, TYC's key mission was to reduce the number of delinquent boys incarcerated in large and overcrowded institutions. In the process, TYC helped popularize narratives and images of juvenile delinquency that echoed those put forth in popular culture. As has often been the case in the history of juvenile justice, however, reality diverged sharply from rhetoric. During the 1950s, budget cuts, entrenched ideologies of punishment, and shifting inmate demographics limited TYC's activities to juvenile corrections. Few delinquent boys under state custody had much in common with Jim Stark, while their adult caregivers generally bore even less resemblance to the sensitive and professional Officer Roy. In the same decade that Americans embraced the teenager as a cultural ideal, the number of juvenile offenders incarcerated in prison-like conditions skyrocketed, driven largely by disproportionate increases in African American and Mexican American inmates. I argue here that black and Latino youth, subject to the racialized politics of juvenile justice in the American South, were excluded from the protected, and ultimately privileged, categories of child and youth. Although James Dean may have represented the juvenile delinquent, Jim Crow – the legal system of segregation that took on the nineteenth-century minstrel character's name as a shorthand reference – shaped the reality of juvenile justice, even in the civil rights era.

At the centre of the postwar expansion of juvenile corrections in Texas was the Gatesville School for Boys, which housed all delinquent boys committed to state custody. By the end of the 1950s, Gatesville had become the largest juvenile training school in the United States, with triple the number of new inmates it had admitted a decade earlier. Male commitments grew at such a fast rate, from about six hundred to over two thousand, that overcrowding was a regular concern discussed at the monthly meetings of the TYC board. The training school was one of the largest employers in the rural town of Gatesville, in central Texas, with a longer history than any of its counterparts in the American South. Gatesville opened as a juvenile reformatory in January 1889, followed by others in Virginia (1889), Kentucky (1891), and Alabama (1900).[6] Until 1913, Gatesville functioned under a strict regimen of hard labour, much of it designed to support the institution and earn it a profit. Juvenile inmates spent their days toiling in cotton fields, some owned by the state and others owned by private farmers, under the watch of armed guards. Progressive reformers, led by the Texas Federation of Women's Clubs, excoriated Gatesville as "a convict farm for boys under sixteen years of age" and demanded changes.[7] In 1913, the state legislature renamed Gatesville as a "training school" and mandated a program of academic and vocational education. For about two years, the institution was led by an educated superintendent who installed qualified teachers, an accredited curriculum, extracurricular activities such as sports and music, a merit system of rewards and punishments, and military discipline. However, these reforms soon became mired in electoral politics. The election of James "Pa" Ferguson as Texas governor in 1914 resulted in the ouster of progressive reformers from the board of trustees that supervised Gatesville. In June 1915, the reconstituted board fired the "reform" superintendent in favour of a farmer and businessman who had no background in education or corrections.[8] During the interwar era, therefore, the institution maintained its educational programs but largely reverted back to emphasizing labour under the guise of vocational training. Most boy inmates divided their days evenly between classwork and field work, a practice that earned sizable sums for the institution; in one four-year period, 1920 to 1924, the boys' agricultural labour earned about $63,000 for Gatesville.[9] Until a sustained public outcry in fall 1927, boys were hired out as convict labourers, even though the legislature had banned the practice in adult prisons more than a decade earlier. The end of juvenile convict leasing still left hundreds of acres of state-owned land for boys to work throughout the Depression years.[10]

Among the labourers were a disproportionate number of African American juvenile inmates over the age of sixteen, who were excluded completely from the education program because of a combination of racial discrimination and overcrowding. Organized like Southern public schools according to Jim Crow segregation, Gatesville had allotted black inmates only one schoolteacher, a former night watchman with no educational training. This arrangement quickly proved inadequate as the institution was overwhelmed with far more black inmates than it could accommodate. When Gatesville opened in 1889, 46 of the first 68 inmates had been African American. By 1917, about 250 black inmates crowded into a congregate dormitory intended to house 125 inmates.[11] Throughout the period, Gatesville officials complained bitterly that black inmates "were never supposed to have been placed" in an institution that had "no provision" for their education.[12] Calls for the establishment of a completely separate training school for black delinquent boys went largely unheeded; in 1917, the legislature passed a statute establishing such a school but neglected to appropriate any funds for it. Thus, black inmates were relegated to farm labour, which school officials claimed was vocational training, even though most of the boys came from cities and were unlikely prospects for future farmers.[13] Nevertheless, the prevailing attitude was expressed in a 1927 letter from the Gatesville superintendent claiming that "some of the best Negro farmers in the country" had gotten their start in the Gatesville cotton fields. "If these boys are not taken care of in this way," the letter went on, "they must be kept at the institution and taught to play games, but I must confess that a buck negro looks better to me with a goose-necked hoe in his hand than he does with a baseball bat or a golf club."[14] A specially prepared 1932 yearbook shows an all-white inmate staff working in the blacksmith and printing shops, and an all-black workforce posing glumly in front of the "Cotton Fields of Dixie."[15] Segregation shaped even the geographic layout of the ever growing Gatesville compound. A state highway bisected the institution and functioned much the way railroad tracks did in dividing black and white areas in towns throughout the South. As the institution added new buildings, this division became more pronounced, with black inmates' dormitories located on the west side, and white inmates, the administrative offices, and utility buildings on the east.[16]

These patterns of overrepresentation and discrimination were not unusual for the period. According to a 1923 federal census of children in US institutions, half of all black delinquents were placed in prison-like settings (prisons, jails, workhouses, or reformatories), compared with only about a fifth of their white counterparts.[17] The roots of such disparities ran back to slavery and shaped the thinking of child savers who created juvenile justice and corrections. Put simply, white reformers did not include black children in the emerging idea of modern childhood, and unequal treatment largely persisted despite the strenuous efforts of African American reformers. Rather than malleable blank slates capable of being rehabilitated, black children and adolescents were viewed by many whites as hard clay fit only for manual labour and social control.[18] Thus, juvenile courts and institutions discriminated against African Americans by allocating fewer resources to their treatment, which had the effect of narrowing the range of options to punitive ones such as incarceration. For example, the only book-length study to date of Southern juvenile justice illustrates how the Memphis juvenile court increasingly resolved African American delinquency cases by commitment to the city's training school, which quickly became "a predominantly black institution" and "a holding station and short-term jail."[19] Similarly, in Texas, African Americans consistently experienced the harshest treatment within an already harsh institution, a situation that remained essentially unchanged throughout the interwar period.

After the Second World War, racial disparities in both the incarceration and treatment of male juvenile delinquents began a precipitous rise. The context for this shift was a major overhaul of juvenile justice at a state-wide level, prompted in part by concerns about conditions at Gatesville. Despite earlier reforms, Gatesville had amassed a notorious reputation as "the favourite prep school for Huntsville," the state prison. A 1948 study found that almost half of Gatesville's inmates were repeat offenders, while nearly two-thirds of the state's prisoners described themselves with wry humour as "graduates" of Gatesville. The study was performed by the Texas Training

School Code Commission, created in 1947 by the legislature to investigate and recommend improvements in the state's programs for juvenile rehabilitation. The commissioners described Gatesville as a house of horrors, with unsanitary cafeterias and hospitals, a dangerously neglected physical plant, and abusive punishments that included severe whipping, excessive solitary confinement, and, in extreme cases, the so-called water cure, in which guards fired a high-pressure hose at the inmate's groin. So widespread was word-of-mouth knowledge about Gatesville that several juvenile court judges confessed to dismissing all but the worst delinquency cases.[20]

By this time, many officials were equally concerned about predictions of a future surge in the adolescent population because of the baby boom, which was expected to hit with particular force in Texas. In the decade of the 1940s alone, the state gained 1.2 million in total population, with those who lived in urban areas rising from 45 to 60 percent. Immigration, as well as natural increase, fuelled population growth as job-hungry Americans from rural areas of Texas and Louisiana flocked to cities that became centres of military-related industries. So sudden was this influx of migrants that it quickly overwhelmed housing and service capacities and in some instances caused social upheaval. A case in point was Houston, a military, petroleum, petro-chemical, and defence industry centre that became the fifth largest American city by 1960.[21] In 1942, the Texas office of the US Census Bureau estimated that about 10,000 people were immigrating to Houston each month, a staggering amount for a city that had numbered less than 400,000 in 1940.[22] Local newspapers lamented the number of unsupervised youth roaming the streets, while the city's police department logged record numbers of juvenile arrests. According to the Crime Prevention Division of the Houston Police Department, a unit organized in 1941 specifically to handle youthful offenders, juvenile arrests increased by nearly half, from 4,258 in 1942 to 6,618 in 1945.[23]

The perception of more juvenile delinquents coupled with fewer constructive institutional responses was not unique to Texas. Reformers in California had embraced the Youth Authority Model Act, prospective legislation written and circulated by the American Law Institute, a legal reform group based in Philadelphia.[24] The act envisioned all of a given state's institutions for juvenile delinquents operating under the supervision of a single agency, which would devise diagnostic, classification, and treatment programs based on child psychology rather than penology. Each child adjudged delinquent in juvenile court was to be sent to a single diagnostic centre, where a team of psychologists, psychiatrists, and social workers would decide on disposition and treatment. The youth authority agency's other task was to aid local governments in organizing non-institutional programs of prevention and diversion, such as youth recreation and probation. This emphasis reflected the influence of consultants from the US Children's Bureau and the Osborne

Foundation, whose director, Austin MacCormick, was the leading expert in the field of correctional education.[25] Thus, the Texas report called for Gatesville to jettison its previous commitment to "the whole correctional system and philosophy" of mass custody and control, in favour of "diagnosis, treatment, and rehabilitation."[26] The tone of the report echoed that of national reformers, who were optimistic that new knowledge about the life stages of childhood and adolescence could revitalize the enterprise of juvenile justice.

In spring 1949, that sentiment emerged clearly in a public campaign on behalf of proposed legislation establishing the Texas State Youth Development Council, the forerunner of the Texas Youth Council (TYC).[27] Its supporters toured the state, addressing civic groups and holding press conferences touting TYC's virtues. The most forceful advocate was Walter Kinsolving Kerr, who had served as vice-chairman of the Code Commission. The son of a lumber and cotton businessman from East Texas, Kerr had developed a knack for performing in front of audiences in previous stints as a stage performer, a radio personality, and pastor of the Central Methodist Church in downtown Austin, the state capital, which was attended by many of the state's political power brokers.[28] Kerr had recently completed a master's thesis at the University of Texas based on his development of one of the state's first juvenile detention centres in south Austin.[29] In short, Kerr's political connections, expertise, and charisma made him an ideal choice to spearhead TYC. In early 1949, while the TYC bill made its way through the legislature, Kerr effectively promoted its potential contributions to public safety, social progress, and child welfare, all with a low price tag.[30]

Kerr and his compatriots used sweeping language in describing the need to modernize an antiquated system, often comparing Gatesville unfavourably with its counterpart institutions in California. Reformers' appeals also employed specific narratives and images of the delinquents themselves meant to sway public audiences. Almost always, these representations distinguished young, neglected children, who could benefit from TYC's programs, from hardened offenders, who were beyond help. The ideal recipient of TYC's attention appeared on the cover of the Code Commission's official report, which was circulated at press conferences across the state (see Figure 4.1). Neatly combed, white, freckle-faced, and clearly pre-adolescent, "Bill" wears a western-style belt buckle over a tucked T-shirt emblazoned with a cowboy. His determined stare toward the horizon, taken from a lower, heroic camera angle, seems meant to arouse a collective purpose and may have evoked nostalgia for a rural childhood uncomplicated by the state's urbanization and industrialization. A similar image graced the cover of the June 1944 issue of *Our Community,* the monthly newsletter of the Houston YMCA. The cover of this special issue devoted to the problem of juvenile delinquency featured a rendering of a freckle-faced white boy gazing wide-eyed and

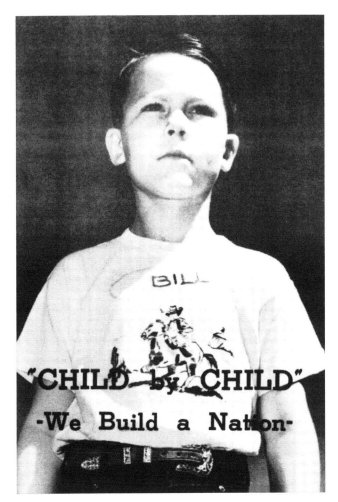

Figure 4.1   Cover, *Child by Child We Build a Nation: A Youth Development Plan for the State of Texas* (Austin: Texas Training School Code Commission, 1949)
Source: Archives and Information Services Division, Texas State Library and Archives Commission

admiringly at a father figure whose hand rests on the boy's shoulder. Entitled "Man of Tomorrow," the image was disconnected from the actual character of Houston's wartime delinquency problem. The previous summer, the city's police had initiated a crackdown on Mexican American youth gangs, spurred in part by reports of the Zoot Suit Riots in southern California. Racial tensions also ran high between the city's all-white police force and African American youth at the time; police regularly raided black juke joints in search of underage drinkers and curfew violators, and had been accused of coercing false confessions from African American juveniles. The gulf in Houston between law enforcement and child welfare responses to juvenile delinquency, each targeting distinct populations, was repeated a few years later in the state-wide campaign for TYC.[31]

Appearing alongside phrases such as "Man of Tomorrow" or "Child by Child We Build a Nation," these images suggested which boys were worthy of the state's (and by extension the citizenry's) investment of time and resources. Who was to be included in the "nation" or the "community" that captioned these photographs? Moreover, the image of the wholesome yet at-risk youth, the misguided boy next door in need of professional mentoring, not only erased any socio-economic context but also diverted attention from the actual population of juvenile delinquents. This delinquent was a far cry from Stanley the jack-roller, profiled famously in Chicago sociologist Clifford Shaw's 1930 study, a product of urban poverty and the clash of immigrant and native cultures.[32] Instead, this new boy was, like James Dean's Jim Stark, suffering from psychologized problems of self-esteem or inadequate parenting, removed from any meaningful socio-economic context. The "problem" of inadequate parenting, especially individual parent-child relationships, perhaps accounts for a number of images featuring boys alongside surrogate father figures.

Although most scholarly studies of gender and delinquency focus on girls, gender anxieties also shaped official approaches to male delinquency.[33] The norms of hegemonic masculinity in postwar American society were severely restricted, partly because of the emerging Cold War, which made it more crucial than ever that boys grow into men capable of supporting families and leading the nation.[34] Thus, the images of at-risk boys were fraught with tension as well as optimism. Many of them feature an adult male with his hand rested reassuringly (to whom?) on the boy's shoulder (see Figure 4.2). Rather than profile adjudged delinquents already in the juvenile justice system, who might have elicited less public sympathy, the new reformers invented wholesome composite characters for public consumption, mixing their hopes for the future with examples of the least serious cases on record.

Lost in all of TYC's optimistic promotions was the incarcerated juvenile population for which it became responsible in September 1949. Official statistics on this population clashed almost completely with the public image TYC constructed. The most obvious differences fell in the area of race, with white juvenile inmates making up a minority of the Gatesville population (see Table 4.1).[35] Meanwhile, the percentage of African American inmates was, at 27 percent, more than twice that of the state's general population of fifteen- to nineteen-year-old African Americans (13 percent). Overall, the general inmate population tended to be older than the younger boys presented to the public: 3,964 of the 5,436 boys admitted to Gatesville between

Where Credit Is Due

Figure 4.2   "Where Credit Is Due," *Tyler Morning Telegraph* (5 May 1951)
Sam Nash cartoon, reprinted with permission of the *Tyler Courier-Times-Telegraph*,
Tyler, TX

1935 and 1950 were at least fourteen years old. In contrast to the frontier
imagery of TYC literature, nearly a third of inmates came from urban areas
with a population of at least 100,000, more than double the second-largest
category. Economic hardship also marked their backgrounds, according to
a partial survey of the families of boys committed to Gatesville between
1936 and 1945 (see Table 4.2). The majority of African Americans and Mexican Americans came from households headed by unskilled labourers, while
whites were distributed more evenly between skilled, unskilled, and on relief
– a category that almost certainly meant temporary employment via a New
Deal agency such as the Works Progress Administration. The higher representation for poor whites in the on-relief category also may have reflected
the racial discrimination practised by New Deal administrators in Texas, part
of a larger regional pattern.[36] Few boys came to Gatesville from the professional middle class, but of those, most were white.

Excluded from TYC's loftier rhetoric of protection and rehabilitation,
African American inmates figured tacitly in proposed reforms for Gatesville.
An interesting example was TYC's expressed desire to introduce "facilities

Table 4.1

Boys admitted to Gatesville, in five-year increments by race and ethnicity, 1935-50

Year of commitment	Total cases*	White/ Anglo		Mexican American		African American	
		#	%	#	%	#	%
1935	550	281	51.1	92	16.7	177	32.2
1940	463	185	40.0	104	22.5	174	37.6
1945	571	269	47.0	144	25.2	158	27.7
1950	621	300	48.3	149	24.0	172	27.7

* For fewer than 1% of inmates, race and ethnicity were listed as "undetermined."
   Discrepancies in totals or percentage figures are due to this.

Table 4.2

Economic status of parents of boys admitted to Gatesville, 1936-45

	Total cases	White/ Anglo	Mexican American	African American
Unemployed	282	123	91	68
On relief	521	311	59	151
Unskilled	1,138	329	223	586
Skilled	530	377	91	62
Professional	69	47	8	14
Farmer	346	184	29	133
Prison	36	18	3	15
Total	2,922	1,389	504	1,029

for classification or segregation" along lines adopted by prisons in the 1930s.[37] On its face, this meant separating inmates according to offence category, age, and behaviour; in practice, however, "segregation" meant precisely what it did outside the institution's walls. School administrators, all of whom were white, claimed that African American inmates would disrupt any attempt to relax the strict military routine that previously had characterized daily life in Gatesville. TYC's introduction of a diagnostic program that included intelligence and psychometric testing lent "scientific" weight to such arguments.[38] The centrepiece was an intelligence test, the contents of which were described vaguely in official documents but that were probably little changed from the Binet tests on which they were based.[39] Given the biases built into the most widely used intelligence tests of the period, the large proportion of Gatesville inmates working far below grade level, and the reduced opportunities for schooling for African American inmates, one can speculate that this test was highly likely to produce results that left the racist treatment of blacks unchallenged. The test examiners added another distorting element to the mix, however, by administering the test selectively, seemingly to achieve desired results. They gave the test to all the African American inmates but, allegedly due to time constraints, only to sample groups of white and Mexican American inmates. Four-fifths of black inmates tested at or below an intelligence quotient of seventy, putting them in the category of "feeble-minded." The mean score, respectively, of Mexican Americans at eighty-five ("borderline") and whites at ninety-one ("low normal") made them better candidates for rehabilitation.

On this basis, TYC called for the removal of all African American inmates from Gatesville, in a virtual replay of the interwar era. The request was repeated to no avail for the next several years. Throughout the 1950s, annual reports published similar test scores and complained that "feeble-minded Negroes" undermined institutional goals. In the same breath, TYC reports made excuses for white delinquents who scored poorly on the intelligence tests. Low intellect among white boys was attributable to "poor environment, lack of opportunity, lack of parental love and guidance, and not necessarily to low mental capacity." Even those few whites who tested below the cut-off score of seventy could not "be taken at face value" and probably performed badly because of "emotional disturbance."[40] Officials thus explained away the substandard scores of white inmates while exaggerating the significance of poor non-white performance – surely not an unprecedented phenomenon in the sorry annals of juvenile justice history, but a particularly anachronistic example for the early 1950s, a time when most clinicians had long since dispensed with categories such as feeble-mindedness.

While TYC scientists attempted to demonstrate innate deficiencies in intelligence, popular news reports bolstered the notion that non-white delinquents harboured a unique proclivity for violence. Reports of Mexican American youth gangs had appeared regularly in big-city newspapers since the Second World War, while reports of African American juvenile offences conspicuously highlighted the race of the offender. These sorts of stories took on a special significance, however, when an especially egregious crime was committed by a former Gatesville inmate. Whether they were parolees or escapees, ex-inmates became lightning rods for concerns about public safety, particularly after TYC took control of Gatesville. Local residents in central Texas, especially in the town of Gatesville, began to question whether a program of juvenile rehabilitation was compatible with public safety.[41] This discussion suggested that juvenile delinquents, especially if they were black, would be viewed not as confused teenagers but as dangerous criminals.

The fears of the most fervent law and order advocates were realized with the escape from Gatesville of Walter Johnson, a fifteen-year-old African American inmate from Austin, on a Monday morning, 15 August 1950.[42]

Johnson was a first-time offender who had been committed only three weeks earlier for a series of grocery store burglaries. That afternoon, Johnson allegedly broke into the home of a Gatesville farmer and seized a Winchester rifle. The farm owner, a fifty-five-year-old white man named Walter Mack, surprised and confronted the boy. Although no official incident report survives, news accounts portrayed Johnson as a rampaging predator who shot Mack twice in the back after he pleaded for his life and attempted to flee. These same accounts had Johnson – consistently described as "the Negro" – helping the seriously wounded Mack onto his bed and promising to seek help. Within hours, Johnson was picked up by military police at nearby Fort Hood, an army base from which Gatesville recruited much of its correctional staff. His escape foiled, the presumably terrified Johnson confessed to everything, enabling authorities to locate the shooting victim in time to get him to a hospital.

Although Mack survived the incident, his shooting provoked public outrage. Local residents blamed soft-hearted TYC reformers for meddling with long-standing Gatesville policies, particularly corporal punishment, which had been the traditional penalty for running away. TYC had banned whipping only months earlier and had fired the Gatesville superintendent for his defiance of the new rule. At the time, the TYC board had stated its belief that escapes were motivated by several causes, chiefly rebellion against authority, and had suggested that the school's obsession with escapes only encouraged them. In fact, the escape rate had dropped slightly in the first year after the abolition of corporal punishment, from an average of eight to six per month.[43] This trend was lost on local critics, who demanded either the reinstatement of whipping or the removal of the school altogether. At a town meeting held shortly after the Johnson incident, an angry crowd of farmers and small-business owners shouted down TYC officials and vowed to shoot all runaways on sight. The prospect of a black escapee shooting a local white farmer had inverted the historical power relationships that had characterized the institution's prior existence, when black juveniles worked as convict labourers on white farms. An "ugly mood" swept across central Texas, ensuring that any further reforms of Gatesville would be closely watched and criticized by enraged critics.[44]

On the heels of this affair, TYC's leadership began to articulate a proposal to replace Gatesville with four smaller institutions. In TYC's view, this change would allow the state to put its diagnostic classification system to concrete use and, it was hoped, quell growing public anger. The proposal was first spelled out in TYC's first annual report, published mere weeks after the Johnson affair. This document offered the first full description of the intelligence test results, implying that runaways like Johnson not only influenced other inmates but also posed too great a danger to public safety to be included in a program of juvenile rehabilitation. All African American inmates, under this plan, were to be housed in a segregated Jim Crow facility, while the remaining inmates would be placed in three separate facilities for maximum, medium, and minimum custody. The four institutions were to be located near urban centres rather than in the rural backwater of Gatesville, which would encourage cooperation between state schools and local juvenile courts (and make supervised probation and parole more meaningful enterprises).[45] Hailed as "real" reform, the breakup promised to separate first-time offenders from "the toughies," the negative influences that prevented younger delinquents from responding to education, recreation, and individual treatment.[46] The wholesale association of African Americans with these undesirable offender types suggests that they represented the worst of the worst, offenders for whom age- and offence-based classifications were unnecessary. Like their progressive predecessors, TYC's architects simply did not view African American delinquents as candidates for rehabilitation.

TYC director Kerr requested a $2.5 million appropriation from the state legislature for the construction and staffing of the new juvenile facilities. Because the legislature was notoriously stingy in funding social programs, Kerr launched another public relations campaign similar to the one that had helped win passage of the bill creating TYC. The centrepiece of this campaign was a mobile diagnostic clinic that conducted child guidance demonstrations in eight locations over a period of six months, from February to July 1951. Its purpose was to demonstrate community-based and institutional services that TYC could provide if given the necessary funds, including those needed to replace Gatesville. By all accounts, the clinic won praise everywhere it went, treating 152 children in all and concluding that the vast majority of them suffered from emotional problems caused by "weak or inadequate parents."[47] These findings were far less severe than those arrived at in diagnoses of Gatesville inmates, but comparisons are difficult because the only report on the mobile clinic lacks any demographic information on the children treated, compiling only a few anecdotal descriptions clearly meant to elicit sympathy for less serious delinquents locked up with older offenders.[48]

In May 1951, the expanded TYC budget bill went down to defeat in the legislature, which appropriated a fraction of the requested amount.[49] The vote was the first of several legislative setbacks. Especially hard hit were non-institutional prevention and diversion programs, as the legislature itemized appropriations for the training schools. In May 1953, Gatesville received "one of the best appropriations in its history," while the non-institutional positions of director of community service, recreation consultant, clinical psychologist, as well as those of four field representatives were eliminated.[50] By 1955, budget cuts forced TYC to abandon its advising and grant programs for local juvenile courts, civic groups, and youth recreation clubs. Finally,

TYC's once diverse scope of activity narrowed to a single task: the management of the state's three juvenile training schools, the largest of which was Gatesville.[51]

This shift coincided with the rise to power of James Turman, who took over the agency in 1957 after stints as TYC's director of clinical psychology, consultant on juvenile delinquency, and director of institutions. Turman had designed and supervised Gatesville's diagnostic services, including its psychometric intelligence testing. He had led the charge to convince the legislature to transfer African American inmates from Gatesville to an institution for the mentally handicapped. A former army captain, engineer at the DuPont corporation, and psychology graduate of Abilene Christian College, Turman earned his master's degree in educational psychology at the University of Texas. Turman's thesis, completed in January 1951 amid his Gatesville activity, extolled the potential benefits of school desegregation and admiringly quoted anti-racist intellectuals such as Gunnar Myrdal and Gordon Allport.[52]

Already uncertain, Turman's avowed commitment to racial integration was tested further by an explosion in the juvenile inmate population in the 1950s. TYC's earlier promises to improve conditions at Gatesville, combined with rising juvenile crime rates across the state, freed juvenile court judges from their previous reluctance to commit delinquents to state custody. The estimated delinquency rate in Texas jumped from fifteen per thousand in 1953 to nineteen in 1955 and to twenty-three in 1964.[53] Over a thirteen-year period, the increase in new Gatesville inmates overwhelmed the institution's capacity to house them (see Table 4.3). The "crisis" of overcrowding was a

Table 4.3

Boys admitted to Gatesville, in irregular increments by race and ethnicity, 1952-65

Year of commitment	Total cases*	White/ Anglo		Mexican American		African American	
		#	%	#	%	#	%
1952	669	328	49.0	174	26.0	167	25.0
1955	881	395	44.8	239	27.2	247	28.0
1958	1,598	655	40.9	563	35.3	380	23.8
1961	2,016	721	35.7	726	36.0	569	28.2
1962	1,867	618	33.1	607	32.5	642	34.4
1963	2,184	735	33.6	664	30.4	785	36.0
1964	2,091	660	31.5	635	30.4	796	38.1
1965	2,274	736	32.3	640	28.1	895	39.4

* For fewer than 1% of inmates, race and ethnicity were listed as "undetermined." Discrepancies in totals or percentage figures are due to this.

regular subject of discussion in TYC board meetings throughout the 1950s; as early as 1952, the Gatesville superintendent admitted to an unofficial policy of releasing two inmates daily, regardless of their individual progress, to compensate for the average daily admission of two new inmates.[54] This revolving-door tactic failed to stem the tide; although the average stay for inmates dropped from fourteen to nine months during this period, the facility's average daily population typically exceeded capacity by at least two hundred. Much of this growth was driven by the rising number of African American inmates, which actually surpassed that of whites in raw and percentage terms by the early 1960s. It seems likely that these figures reflected a disproportionate sentencing of African-Americans to institutions within the juvenile court system. In 1958, the last year for which juvenile court data by race were tallied, until the 1970s (a curious decision in itself), the number of white cases dwarfed those of African Americans (see Table 4.4). Comparing data sets from Gatesville and the juvenile court for 1958 suggests that most official resolutions of African American delinquency cases resulted in institutionalization.[55] By the end of the decade, an agency forced to abandon lofty goals for delinquency prevention and juvenile rehabilitation found itself saddled with an inmate population that it had categorically excluded from consideration. The stage was thus set for a more repressive response to juvenile delinquency.

During the mid-1950s, with delinquency on the rise, Turman lobbied the legislature to upgrade TYC's status from a division of the state Department of Welfare. He pointed to statistics for the previous five years showing a 13 percent increase in the adolescent age population and a 51 percent rise in delinquency cases.[56] He also contended that a separate, independent youth agency would be freer to work more directly with the state Department of Corrections. These arguments proved successful and, in September 1957, TYC was reconstituted as the Texas Youth Council, with a three-member directorate appointed by the governor and Turman permanently ensconced as the executive director.

Table 4.4

Resolution of boy delinquency cases in Texas juvenile courts, 1958

	Total cases**	White/Anglo*		African American	
		#	%	#	%
Official	3,278	2,799	85.4	479	14.6
Unofficial	14,009	11,829	84.4	2,180	15.6
Total cases	17,287	14,628	84.6	2,659	15.4

*   "White" in this report includes all Mexican American cases.
** Based on 124 of 264 (47%) of counties reporting.

Meanwhile, a new rash of isolated incidents created the perception that violent juvenile crime was also on the rise, which provoked calls for tougher punishments, including the juvenile death penalty.[57] As early as 1956, the TYC board presented to the legislature its unanimous opinion that "certain juveniles have taken advantage of the law, escaped punishment, and flaunted the juvenile law in the faces of law enforcement officers after the commission of such crimes and have sometimes continued such behavior with the knowledge that they could not be prosecuted as adults."[58] Lending impetus to TYC's policy position was a drive-by shooting, on Christmas Day 1957, of a teenage boy in his own driveway in an upscale Houston neighbourhood by four Gatesville parolees joyriding in a stolen car. That the victim was previously unknown to his assailants only added to the hysteria. Local citizens organized a neighbourhood council, warning that "any family's child, even yours" could be a victim of "teen-ager terrorism."[59] In January 1958, the Houston parents' group issued a blueprint that recommended trying violent juvenile offenders as adults, and building more training schools. In the midst of this recharged cycle of outrage, TYC director Turman urged the construction of a maximum-security facility for those delinquents whom he described in a major speech to a law enforcement convention as inhabiting a "twilight zone between adolescence and complete adulthood."[60] Endorsing the Houston plan, in a sweeping reversal of his juvenile justice predecessors, Turman also advocated easier certification of adolescents to adult court. "In some instances," he suggested, violent juvenile offenders were "overprotected ... at the expense of society."[61] Even the rhetorical commitment to juvenile rehabilitation seemed to have come to an end, a view shared in full by the legislature, which eagerly appropriated funds for a youth prison that far exceeded what it had been willing to approve for smaller, community-based programs a few years earlier.

In the early 1960s, while TYC embraced "get tough" policies, national policy makers began to rediscover delinquency in the cities. Under the Kennedy and Johnson administrations, the federal government awarded a series of large grants supporting community action projects to combat delinquency in several American cities.[62] One of the first such projects, Houston Action for Youth, enlisted TYC's assistance in an expensive media campaign to raise public awareness about delinquency.[63] The centrepiece, a made-for-television film entitled *The Lonely Ones,* won an award at the 1963 San Francisco Film Festival and was the subject of a panel presentation at that year's annual meeting of the American Psychological Association. The film aired simultaneously on all three major television networks, as well as on the public television channel, in prime time on a Saturday night in December 1962. Thus, a fairly captive audience viewed profiles of three archetypical delinquents, drawn from the case files of the Houston Juvenile Probation Department. Two of the three vignettes featured white characters, including

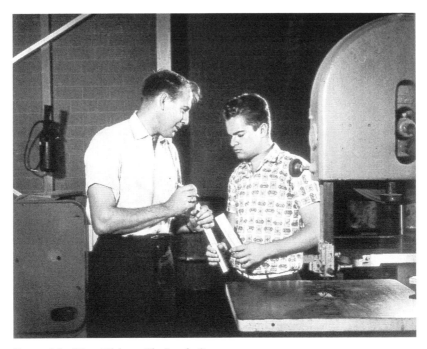

Figure 4.3   Film still from *The Lonely Ones*.
Source: Sutherland (Robert Lee) Papers, Barker Center for American History, University of Texas at Austin

"Jimmy," whose clean-cut and stylish appearance resembled James Dean's Jim Stark in *Rebel without a Cause* but concealed a messier and more impoverished existence. Jimmy lived in a housing project with his mother, a divorcee with five children fathered by four different men. In the film, Jimmy's mother regularly parades strange men in front her children, driving her son to binge drinking and petty crime. Unlike *Rebel's* Stark, however, Jimmy's alienation lands him in juvenile court and an institution that turns out to be none other than Gatesville. Shot on location, the film portrays the notoriously overcrowded and regimented facility as a clean and orderly setting, where Jimmy found in his shop teacher a fatherly mentor along the lines of *Rebel's* Officer Roy (see Figure 4.3). After lavishing on Jimmy an unlikely level of individual attention, Gatesville paroles him to a "loving" foster family on a country ranch. But Jimmy is too far gone; within days, he falls in with "the wrong kind of friends" and goes on a drunken joyride in a stolen car. A police chase ends in a crash killing all of the teenage passengers except Jimmy. As the police haul him off to jail, a narrator laments Jimmy's inability to overcome a "lifetime of deprivation," embodied not by his economic

Figure 4.4 Exterior shot of Mountain View during construction, 1962
Source: Photographs, Records, Texas Youth Commission, Archives and Information Services
Division, Texas State Library and Archives Commission

poverty but by his rebellion against "the lonely position." In the end, alienation and "maladjustment" were Jimmy's greatest problems.[64]

That same year, TYC's lobbying efforts resulted in the opening, a mere
stone's throw from Gatesville, of the Mountain View School for "violent and
serious" juvenile offenders.[65] Surrounded by high barbed-wire fences (see
Figure 4.4) and patrolled by armed guards on horseback, Mountain View
harkened back to the reformatory era. It lacked an academic educational
program but featured a massive isolation ward. In less than a decade, Mountain View would achieve a level of notoriety that dwarfed the fearsome
reputation achieved by Gatesville over a much longer period. Graphic tales
of abuse and brutality leaked to a newly skeptical press; by 1980, the institution would be ordered closed in the wake of a massive federal civil rights
lawsuit. This news appeared to the public as a series of revelations that should
not have surprised anyone. Its power to shock drew on a kind of wilful
blindness, the enduring gulf between rhetoric and reality, a widely shared
way of seeing the typical juvenile delinquent in ways that masked entrenched
and emerging injustices.

Clearly, by the early 1960s, "Jimmy" was an anachronism belying the state's general abandonment of juvenile rehabilitation and seeming return to the pre-TYC era of punishment. This state of affairs proved to be short-lived, however. Within a few years, real-life juvenile inmates, black, brown, and white, forced their way in front of the cameras to describe their often horrific experiences to reporters, judges, legislators, attorneys, and anyone else who would listen. Acting collectively in a host of ways, they propelled sweeping action. In 1968-69, both houses of the Texas legislature conducted well-publicized and embarrassing investigations of TYC. National newspapers and television outlets gave critical portrayals, most notably in the 1971 NBC news documentary *This Child Is Rated X*, in which former Gatesville inmates described being starved, beaten, and locked in filthy isolation wards. That same year marked the start of a landmark class-action lawsuit, *Morales v. Turman*, which resulted in the closing of both Gatesville and Mountain View, the deinstitutionalization of hundreds of incarcerated juveniles, the resignation of TYC director James Turman, and a major overhaul of TYC.[66]

The rights revolution in juvenile justice was in part a response to the contradictions of the 1950s, a crucial period for understanding the historical development of juvenile justice, corrections, and the exclusive category of "child" worthy of protection. Racial disparities in the treatment of at-risk youth grew beneath national discourses of delinquency that separated whites from non-whites, and less privileged from more affluent youth. Juvenile justice reformers, sometimes without forethought, helped promulgate different ways of seeing delinquent youth from disparate social and economic backgrounds. As we struggle to understand and reverse the trend toward locking up "other people's children" in prison-like institutions even for nonviolent offences, we must tackle the continuing gap between the promise of childhood's universality and the all too frequent reality of childhood denied.

Notes

1 Nicholas Ray, dir., *Rebel without a Cause* (Hollywood, CA: Warner Bros., 1955), filmstrip; for a recent analysis, see Leerom Medovoi, *Rebels: Youth and the Cold War Origins of Identity* (Durham, NC: Duke University Press, 2005), 177-91.
2 For example, see "How American Teen-Agers Live," *Look*, 23 July 1957; or, "Our Good Teen-Agers," *Newsweek*, 23 November 1959.
3 The most obvious example was *Rebel* itself, which was very loosely based on Robert M. Lindner, *Rebel without a Cause: The Hypnoanalysis of a Criminal Psychopath* (New York: Grune and Stratton, 1944). For a survey of mid-century scientific literature, see Edmund W. Vaz, ed., *Middle-Class Juvenile Delinquency* (New York: Harper and Row, 1967).
4 Albert K. Cohen, *Delinquent Boys: The Culture of the Gang* (Glencoe, IL: Free Press, 1955), and Richard A. Cloward and Lloyd E. Ohlin, *Delinquency and Opportunity: A Theory of Delinquent Gangs* (Chicago: University of Chicago, 1960).
5 Kathleen W. Jones, *Taming the Troublesome Child: American Families, Child Guidance, and the Limits of Psychiatric Authority* (Cambridge, MA: Harvard University Press, 1999).

6 See Donald R. Walker, *Penology for Profit: A History of the Texas Prison System, 1867-1912* (College Station, TX: Texas A&M University Press, 1988), 72; Vernetta D. Young, "Race and Gender in the Establishment of Juvenile Institutions: The Case of the South," *Prison Journal* 73, 2 (1994): 244-65; and, John Garrick Hardy, "A Comparative Study of Institutions for Negro Juvenile Delinquents in the Southern States" (PhD dissertation, University of Wisconsin, 1946).

7 Mrs. E.W. Bounds, "The Transformation of the State Juvenile Training School," address to the Texas Conference of Charities and Corrections, Fort Worth, TX, 30 November 1913, reprinted in *Biennial Report of the State Juvenile Training School, 1913-1914* (Austin: Von Boeckmann-Jones Printers, 1914), 44-48.

8 The firing is described in *Biennial Report of the State Juvenile Training School, 1915-1916* (Austin: Von Boeckmann-Jones Printers, 1916), 3-4. On Ferguson, see Randolph B. Campbell, *Gone to Texas: A History of the Lone Star State* (New York: Oxford University Press, 2003), 347-51.

9 *Report of the State Juvenile Training School to the State Board of Control, 1920-1924* (Austin: Texas State Board of Control, 1924).

10 The public attack on juvenile convict leasing began with a single editorial, "Juvenile Peons of Texas," *Galveston Tribune*, 12 September 1927; within weeks, the state was forced to outlaw the practice by executive order.

11 *Biennial Report of the State Juvenile Training School, 1917-1918* (Austin: Von Boeckmann-Jones Printers, 1918).

12 *Report of the State Juvenile Training School to the State Board of Control, 1924-1926* (Austin: Texas State Board of Control, 1926), 121.

13 Ted Winfield Brumbalow, "An Analysis of the Educational Program of the State Juvenile Training School" (MA thesis, University of Texas, 1937), 57-64.

14 Charles E. King to R.B. Walthall, 16 August 1927, Chairman R.B. Walthall files, Board members files, Records, Texas State Board of Control, Archives and Information Services Division, Texas State Library and Archives Commission.

15 *State Juvenile Training School Pictorial Review* (Gatesville, TX: State Juvenile Training School, 1933), 12-20.

16 *Texas' Children: A Report Prepared by the Bureau of Research in the Social Sciences* (Austin, TX: University of Texas, 1938), 340-43.

17 The data are reproduced in *The Delinquent Child* (New York: The Century Company, 1932), 322-24, which originally appeared as White House Conference on Child Health and Protection, *The Delinquent Child: Report of the Committee on Socially Handicapped Delinquency,* Section 4 (Washington, DC: US Children's Bureau, 1930).

18 See Geoffrey K. Ward, "Color Lines of Social Control: Juvenile Justice Administration in a Racialized Social System, 1825-2000" (PhD dissertation, University of Michigan, 2001), esp. 40-117. See also Jennifer Trost, *Gateway to Justice: The Juvenile Court and Progressive Child Welfare in a Southern City* (Athens, GA: University of Georgia Press, 2004); David M. Oshinsky, *"Worse Than Slavery": Parchman Farm and the Ordeal of Jim Crow Justice* (New York: Free Press, 1997), esp. 46-48; and, Young, "Race and Gender," 244-65.

19 Trost, *Gateway to Justice*, 152, 155.

20 Texas Training School Code Commission, *Child by Child We Build a Nation: A Youth Development Plan for the State of Texas* (Austin: Texas Training School Code Commission, 1949), 9-25.

21 Campbell, *Gone to Texas*, 396; Bruce Schulman, *From Cotton Belt to Sunbelt: Federal Policy, Economic Development, and the Transformation of the South, 1938-1980* (New York: Oxford University Press, 1991), 135-59.

22 Official quoted in "Workers Pour by Thousands into City," *Houston Post*, 4 September 1942.

23 "Houston Children and the Police," *Social Statistics* (Houston Council of Social Agencies) 2, 2 (April 1946): 5.

24 For an excellent recent study of the youth authority movement and its first trial run, see Laura Mihailoff, "Protecting Our Children: A History of the California Youth Authority and Juvenile Justice, 1938-1968" (PhD dissertation, University of California at Berkeley, 2005).

25 In addition to Mihailoff, "Protecting Our Children," the youth authority movement is described in Bertram M. Beck, *Five States: A Study of the Youth Authority Program as Promulgated by the American Law Institute* (Philadelphia: American Law Institute, 1951). See also Robert H. Bremner, ed., *Children and Youth in America: A Documentary History*, vol. 3, *1933-1973* (Cambridge, MA: Harvard University Press, 1974), 1060-68. For more on MacCormick, see Steven Schlossman and Amy R. deCamp, "Correctional Education," in Marvin C. Alkin, ed., *Encyclopedia of Educational Research*, 6th ed. (New York: Macmillan, 1992), 244-47.

26 Texas Training School Code Commission, *Child by Child We Build a Nation*, 34.

27 For clarity's sake, the abbreviation "TYC" refers to both the Texas State Youth Development Council (1949-57) and the Texas Youth Council (1957-83).

28 "Jester Will Recommend Adoption of Extensive Youth Program," *Houston Chronicle*, 6 February 1949; "A Crusader for Freedom," *Dallas Herald*, 21 October 1962; all at "Walter K. Kerr" Vertical File, Barker Center for American History, University of Texas at Austin.

29 Walter Kinsolving Kerr, "Juvenile Detention in Austin and Travis County" (MA thesis, University of Texas, 1949).

30 "16-Member State Youth Council Urged," *Houston Post*, 6 February 1949; "Jester Will Offer Delinquency Plan," *Big Spring Herald*, 6 February 1949; "Integration of State and Local Child Agencies Urged by Group," *Fort Worth Star-Telegram*, 8 February 1949; "New Plan for Youths," *Abilene Reporter News*, 15 February 1949; "Youth Development Measure Filed with Aim of Correcting Delinquency," *Austin American-Statesman*, 18 February 1949; "New Juvenile Bill," *San Angelo Standard Times*, 19 March 1949; all in the State Youth Development Council early history scrapbooks, Records, Texas Youth Commission, Archives and Information Services Division, Texas State Library and Archives Commission (hereafter cited as TYC Scrapbooks).

31 Arnoldo de Leon, *Ethnicity in the Sunbelt: A History of Mexican Americans in Houston* (Houston: University of Houston, 1989); Howard Beeth and Cary D. Wintz, eds., *Black Dixie: Afro-Texan History and Culture in Houston* (College Station, TX: Texas A&M University Press, 1992); and Robert D. Bullard, *Invisible Houston: The Black Experience in Boom and Bust* (College Station, TX: Texas A&M University Press, 1987).

32 Clifford R. Shaw, *The Jack-Roller: A Delinquent Boy's Own Story* (Chicago: University of Chicago Press, 1930).

33 Rachel Devlin, "Female Juvenile Delinquency and the Problem of Sexual Authority in America, 1945-1965," in Sherrie A. Inness, ed., *Delinquents and Debutantes: Twentieth-Century American Girls' Cultures* (New York: NYU Press, 1998), 83-106; also Mary E. Odem, *Delinquent Daughters: Protecting and Policing Adolescent Female Sexuality in the United States, 1885-1920* (Chapel Hill, NC: University of North Carolina Press, 1995).

34 For an overview see Michael S. Kimmel, *Manhood in America: A Cultural History*, 2nd ed. (New York: Oxford University Press, 2006), 147-72.

35 The following discussion, including Tables 4.1 and 4.2, draws on four main sources: US Bureau of the Census, *Texas: General Social and Economic Characteristics, 1950* (Washington, DC: Government Printing Office, 1951), 64-66; *Texas Juvenile Court Research Reports* (Austin: December 1948); Dana Buckley MacInerney, "A Statistical Survey of Commitments to the Gatesville State Training School for Boys and the Gainesville State Training School for Girls, 1936-1945" (MA thesis, University of Texas, 1951), 11-64; and Texas State Youth Development Council, *First Annual Report of the State Youth Development Council to the Governor of Texas* (Austin: Texas State Youth Development Council, 1950).

36 An exception to this rule was the National Youth Administration (NYA), whose national director, Aubrey Williams, was a white anti-racist from Alabama, and whose Texas director, Lyndon Johnson, worked quietly with African American educators and community leaders to divert federal educational aid to black institutions. Christie L. Bourgeois, "Stepping Over Lines: Lyndon Johnson, Black Texans, and the National Youth Administration, 1935-1937," *Southwestern Historical Quarterly* 91, 2 (1987): 149-72. For more on the NYA, see Richard A. Reiman, *The New Deal and American Youth: Ideas and Ideals in a Depression Decade* (Athens, GA: University of Georgia Press, 1992).

37 Texas State Youth Development Council, *First Annual Report of the State Youth Development Council*, 27-28.

38 Ibid., 51-58.

39 On the Binet tests see Elizabeth Lunbeck, *The Psychiatric Persuasion: Knowledge, Gender, and Power in Modern America* (Princeton, NJ: Princeton University Press, 1994), 54-61; and Paula S. Fass, "The IQ: A Cultural and Historical Framework," in *Children of a New World: Society, Culture, and Globalization* (New York: NYU Press, 2007), 49-73. On their use with racial and ethnic minorities see Anne Meis Knupfer, *Reform and Resistance: Gender, Delinquency, and America's First Juvenile Court* (New York: Routledge, 2001), 35-46.

40 Texas State Youth Development Council, *First Annual Report of the State Youth Development Council*, 65-66.

41 "Coryell Jury Blasts Escapes at Gatesville Boy's School," *Waco News-Tribune*, 9 June 1950; "Police Clear Six Thefts by Arrest of Juvenile from Reform School," *Austin Statesman*, 16 June 1950; "Texas Youth Delinquency Unsolved Yet," *Austin Statesman*, 16 August 1950; all in TYC Scrapbooks.

42 "Austin Youth Held in Affray," *Austin Statesman*, 16 August 1950; "Walter Mack Better after Gunshot Wound by Walter Johnson," *Coryell County News*, 18 August 1950; in TYC Scrapbooks.

43 Texas State Youth Development Council, *First Annual Report of the State Youth Development Council*, 43-46.

44 Quotation from "Mass Meeting Favors Removal of School from Gatesville," *Fort Worth Star-Telegram*, 17 August 1950; see also "Gatesville Wants Problem Solved," *Dallas Morning News*, 24 August 1950; "Runaway Boys Should Be Whipped," *McKinney Examiner*, 25 August 1950; all in TYC Scrapbooks.

45 Texas State Youth Development Council, *First Annual Report of the State Youth Development Council*, 31-32.

46 Quotation from "Small Unit Breakup for Gatesville Set," *Houston Post*, 22 September 1950; see also "Youth Council Says Split School for Boys to Divide Sheep, Goats," *Austin American*, 22 September 1950; "Real Reform: That Is Texas' Need," *Lubbock Morning Avalanche*, 27 September 1950; all in TYC Scrapbooks.

47 Quotation from "Two Juvenile Girls to Take 'Spot' Psychological Exams," *Tyler Courier-Times*, 6 March 1951; see also "Juvenile Diagnostic Clinic to Bring Mobile Unit to Edinburg," *McAllen Valley Evening Monitor*, 5 April 1951; "Youth Council Clinic to Be Here Next Week," *Nacogdoches Daily Sentinel*, 21 July 1951; all in TYC Scrapbooks.

48 Texas State Youth Development Council, *Third Annual Report of the State Youth Development Council to the Governor of Texas* (Austin: Texas State Youth Development Council, 1952), 52-62.

49 "$669,000 Will Improve School," *Waco Times-Herald*, 20 May 1951; "Bellamy New Head of Gatesville," *Austin Statesman*, 20 July 1951; in TYC Scrapbooks.

50 State Youth Development Council minutes, 21 May 1953, Minutes, State Youth Development Council and Texas Youth Council, 1949-65, Box 1999/115-1; Meeting minutes and agenda, Records, Texas Youth Commission, Archives and Information Services Division, Texas State Library and Archives Commission (hereafter cited as TYC Minutes).

51 Texas State Youth Development Council, *Sixth Annual Report of the State Youth Development Council to the Governor of Texas* (Austin: Texas State Youth Development Council, 1955), 1-2.

52 James Aubrey Turman, "A Comparison of Negro and White Teacher Attitudes toward Non-Segregation" (MA thesis, University of Texas at Austin, 1951).

53 Texas State Youth Development Council, *Texas' Teenagers in Trouble: 1955 Statewide Delinquency Survey* (Austin: Texas State Youth Development Council, April 1956); Texas Youth Council, *Texas Juvenile Court Statistics for 1958* (Austin: Texas Youth Council, May 1959); and Texas Youth Council, *Texas Juvenile Court Statistics for 1964* (Austin: Texas Youth Council, May 1964).

54 State Youth Development Council minutes, 19 June 1952; TYC Minutes.

55 *Texas Juvenile Court Statistics for 1958* (Austin: May 1959).

56 Texas State Youth Development Council, *Eighth Annual Report of the State Youth Development Council to the Governor of Texas* (Austin: Texas State Youth Development Council, 1957), 9.

57 "Try 15-Year-Olds, Judge Hunt Says," *Houston Chronicle,* 4 January 1958; "Bigger Reformatories, Tougher Laws Favored," *Houston Chronicle,* 26 January 1958; both in "Juvenile Delinquency" Vertical File, Houston Metropolitan Research Center, Houston Public Library.

58 State Youth Development Council Minutes, 2 August 1956, TYC minutes.

59 "Citizens Panel Draws Blueprint Aimed at Curbing Teen Crime," *Houston Chronicle,* 15 January 1958; Bo Byers, "Bigger Reformatories, Tougher Laws Favored," *Houston Chronicle,* 26 January 1958; "Are Youngsters Coddled by Law?" *Houston Chronicle,* 27 January 1958; both in "Juvenile Delinquency" Vertical File, Houston Metropolitan Research Center, Houston Public Library.

60 "Juvenile Laws Hit by Turman," *Austin Statesman,* 10 March 1958; both in "Texas Youth Council" Vertical File, Barker Center for American History, University of Texas at Austin.

61 Ibid.

62 For a recent analysis of these policies see Alice O'Connor, *Poverty Knowledge: Social Science, Social Policy, and the Poor in Twentieth-Century US History* (Princeton, NJ: Princeton University Press, 2001), 99-136.

63 The following discussion comes from William S. Bush, "Representing the Juvenile Delinquent: Reform, Social Science, and Teenage Troubles in Postwar Texas" (PhD dissertation, University of Texas, 2004), 128-40.

64 This description draws on a script for *The Lonely Ones,* Greater Houston Action for Youth Project Folder, October 11, 1962. Robert Lee Sutherland Papers, Center for American History, University of Texas at Austin. The only known copy of the film itself is in the possession of Richard Evans, the Principal Investigator for the project.

65 For more thorough discussions of Mountain View, see Frank R. Kemerer, *William Wayne Justice: A Judicial Biography* (Austin: University of Texas Press, 1991), 145-81, and Bush, "Representing the Juvenile Delinquent," 166-208.

66 Bush, "Representing the Juvenile Delinquent," 166-208.

5

Nocturnal Disorder and the Curfew Solution: A History of Juvenile Sundown Regulations in Canada

Tamara Myers

In the late spring of 2004, a small former textile town on the periphery of Montreal erupted in a fury over a proposed juvenile curfew. Acts of vandalism and harassment had prompted Huntingdon's mayor, Stéphane Gendron, to take decisive action against young people, mandating their return home at the sound of a 10 p.m. siren. The announcement that Huntingdon's teens would have to observe a curfew – the first in the province since the 1960s – raised more than a few eyebrows. Not surprisingly, the proposal provoked Huntingdon's teenage population: adolescent girls and boys argued against the unfairness of criminalizing their presence on the streets at night and the labelling of their generation "delinquent." Less predictably, joining teens in protest were parents, members of the Quebec Legislative Assembly, and eventually the Quebec Human Rights Commission (QHRC).[1] The combined weight of the opposition to the teen curfew and the accompanying media frenzy caused the mayor to delay implementation.[2] In the meantime, the QHRC argued that the proposed curfew violated the provincial charter of rights and freedoms, which guarantees freedom of movement and of peaceable assembly regardless of age. Yet the mayor persisted, altering his tack by targeting parents: in August, his municipal council voted in favour of a bylaw that required children under sixteen be in the company of parents while outdoors after 10:30 p.m. A first offence would generate a fifty-dollar fine, and repeat parental offenders would to be fined one hundred dollars. Gendron's argument was consistent, he claimed, with Quebec's Civil Code, which states that parents must supervise their children at all times and be responsible for them.[3] In reaction to this change in the bylaw, the QHRC offered to assist any Huntingdon parent who wanted to challenge the bylaw in court, convinced that although the words had changed, the end result was the same attack on children's rights.[4]

Since the 1990s, municipalities across Canada have debated using curfew bylaws as a remedy for bored, actual and potentially violent, and destructive youth, especially during the warmer months of summer.[5] What has triggered a call for curfew most often is vandalism, as in the case of Huntingdon, or acts of shocking violence, such as the murder in October 2006 of a thirty-four-year-old woman on a Winnipeg street in the city's west end. Although the area is known for incidents of extreme violence, children were rarely responsible. Yet, in this case, the city woke to the disturbing news that Audrey Cooper had been slain by two girls and a boy, all under sixteen years of age. A call for a nighttime youth curfew led the public discussions in the days following the murder as politicians, local business owners, and others pointed to the urgent need to curb teen violence. Assumptions about the teens' Aboriginal background and poor home environments permeated debates about the efficacy of sending all children and youth home at a specified hour.[6] As evident in Huntingdon's "curfew summer" and Winnipeg's more recent curfew debate, today, sunset regulations directed at adolescents are at once popular disciplinary measures among municipal authorities and hotly contested solutions to both youth crime and vulnerability.

As Canadians marked the centennial in 2008 of the Juvenile Delinquents Act (now the Youth Criminal Justice Act) and the separate court system for young people, it is worth contemplating why curfew bylaws – which stand outside the juvenile justice system – are deemed necessary. Why have towns and cities sought this extra-judicial measure of policing minors? This action may be indicative of the frustration with the Youth Criminal Justice Act and its impotence in the face of the apparent spread of violence among young people at night;[7] certainly, exasperation with the community's inability to quell youth crime fuelled the decision to call for juvenile curfews in the case of Huntingdon, Winnipeg, and a host of cities across North America.[8] Yet, there are serious problems with curfew law. As the QHRC pointed out, curfew violates the rights of young people, especially to freedom of movement and association.[9] Curfew regulations are too often arbitrarily enforced, with the targets being minority youth.[10] The restriction on youths' movement at night also does nothing to prevent violence and crime outside curfew hours. Notwithstanding these solid arguments against municipal curfews, they remain a popular "suppression" tactic and the choice of city administrations and police forces.

Although historians have thoroughly explored the emergence of coercive strategies and disciplinary measures designed to make parents and children alike behave, one of the most popular but least explored historically is the juvenile nocturnal curfew. This chapter investigates the origins of curfew regulations in Canadian municipalities and the concomitant explanatory discourses of lost children, "night children," and juvenile delinquents. Its purpose is to provide insight into the reasons why a curfew law tradition was forged in modern Canada and elsewhere. Using newspapers and other publications advocating youth curfews, I examine Canadian curfew developments and focus on an era a century ago in which curfew's proponents were highly successful. Like today, curfew had its detractors, people who argued against the law's interference with personal liberty and the anti-modern orientation of the public nighttime control of youth. The chapter ends with an examination of a watershed moment in the history of curfew – the Second World War – when Canada's major urban centres joined smaller centres in calling for an end to nocturnal disorder through the use of the curfew cure.

The Advent of Curfew Law in Canada

Just over a century ago, one of Canada's pre-eminent child savers, J.J. Kelso, advocated reviving the practice of curfew in towns and cities across North America.[11] Kelso was well positioned to take the lead in the campaigns for youth curfew, having in the 1890s been central to the establishment of Canadian Children's Aid Societies (1891) and the Ontario Children's Protection Act (1893). The historical consciousness Kelso demonstrated is related to curfew law, or nocturnal population control, having a rich past. The most famous, and perhaps first, enforcer was William the Conqueror, who allegedly set an 8 p.m. curfew for England in 1068.[12] Beginning in medieval times, curfew referred generally to the practice of clearing the streets at nightfall or, more precisely, to the insistence on the extinguishment of street fires, thus the origins of the word "couvre-feu": to cover the fire.[13] Fortified European towns imposed curfew hours and literally closed down at nightfall. For centuries, night watchmen ensured that the streets were vacated and fires were out. In later centuries, generalized curfews continued, with bells announcing the advance of darkness in pre-industrial Europe.[14] In the seventeenth-century settlement of Ville Marie (now Montreal), a general curfew was implemented as a public safety measure against possible raids by hostile Aboriginal neighbours.[15] In more recent times as strict adherence to curfew regulations waned, emergency measures included generalized curfews, as in the example of Chicago's Great Fire of 1871.[16]

Curfews fell into disuse in the larger European centres through the eighteenth century as a transformation in social and commercial behaviour opened up the urban night to "pleasure and profit," according to night historian A. Roger Ekirch.[17] Aiding the decline in the general curfew was the changing characterization of the night – from sinister to compelling – and the impracticality of general curfews in large urban centres. Yet, as new possibilities for sociability and work transformed cities' nighttime landscape, incidents of crime and nocturnal disorder rose, leading to calls for curfew's rule over certain groups of people, particularly vagrants, prostitutes, and beggars.[18]

Proponents of the curfew in modern times displayed knowledge of the importance, longevity, and centrality of this measure in Western culture. Joining Kelso in advocating for a revival of the curfew in Canadian cities was his child-saver colleague, Beverley Jones, who wrote of the long and venerated tradition of curfew in seventeenth-century England and its arrival on North American soil at the insistence of the Pilgrim Fathers.[19] In 1940s Montreal, implementation debates provoked the *Gazette* to wax historical about its origins lying with William the Conqueror.[20] Of course, opponents were less generous, calling it "a relic of the dark ages."[21]

Yet, Kelso and others did not insist on the broadly directed curfews of centuries past but, rather, sought out implementation of the targeted curfew. In the nineteenth century, it was often specific cohorts of people, particularly minority groups and youth, that fell under curfew's rule, revealing the highly arbitrary and discriminatory character of this social control mechanism. In the antebellum American South, for example, curfews were enacted to keep African Americans off the streets and out of the public realm at night as a measure to maintain control over former slaves.[22] Beyond the South, during the twentieth century, racist policies in what are referred to as "sundown towns" insisted that African Americans, and other people of colour, vacate town boundaries at the sound of a whistle each evening.[23] Outside of general and temporary curfews during emergencies, children and youth have most often been targets of curfew regulations.

The North American juvenile nightfall curfew has its origins in the latter part of the nineteenth century. This is no coincidence; the closing decades of that century gave rise to a moral reform impulse that comprised child rescue and child protection movements, which were facilitated by a transnational dialogue on the state of children and condition of childhood, and which produced separate justice systems for youth and, eventually, a discourse of children's rights.[24] Protecting children from the night presented an opportunity to update a "relic of the dark ages" and transform curfew law – with its attention to time, age categories, and standardization – into a tool of modernity.

At the close of the late nineteenth century, the impetus behind both the child welfare movement and curfew measures was a growing consciousness of the centrality of the street in the lives of working-class, often immigrant, girls and boys.[25] Stories of children on the street after dark abounded in late-nineteenth-century Canada. The author of the *Globe*'s Woman's World column claimed her streets in 1888 were "teeming with little children from the toddler of two years to the vile-tongued youth of almost any age, who defiles the air with his blasphemy and the street with his slimy spit."[26] In advocating a curfew, the writer sought to put an end to the common appearance of dirty, bullying, and pathetic boys on streets at night. "Street-roving" children, according to Beverley Jones, were necessarily corrupted and corrupting; a curfew, therefore, was an "act of humanity."[27] Kelso warned about the rampant spread of a desperate and delinquent child population in his pleas for child-protection legislation in the 1890s that would champion the forced return home of children each night.

Not surprisingly, leading Canada's campaign for the juvenile curfew was Toronto's Kelso. Following the implementation of Ontario's Children's Protection Act in 1893, the province appointed him superintendent of neglected and dependent children, and for decades he worked to create a broad network of Children's Aid Societies across Canada.[28] Juvenile curfews were very much part of this dynamic era of child protection. The 1891 *Report of the Prison and Reformatory System* in Ontario recommended that a curfew be implemented to help prevent and "cure" juvenile delinquency.[29] Two years later, the province's Children's Protection Act provided an enabling clause for municipalities that wished to pass curfew bylaws. As curfews gained in popularity after the passing of the 1893 act, Kelso lent his support to a widely distributed pamphlet reproducing an 1896 curfew speech he gave to the National Conference of Charities and Corrections in Grand Rapids, Michigan.

In 1896, Kelso's main argument for the juvenile nocturnal curfew was predicated on the ostensible fact that children's exposure to nighttime was destructive to themselves and therefore to society. Kelso wrote that "unlimited street-roving after dark" was "destructive of pure instincts"; under the shroud of darkness, children were inculcated with "vicious, soul-destroying thoughts," exposed to "filthy communications and the plottings of street-corner loitering."[30] A year later, in an article in *The Evangelical Churchman,* Jones argued that the curfew bell would "put a stop to sights and sounds that now nightly disgrace the public street corners."[31] The ubiquity of "night children," as Peter C. Baldwin writes about the contemporaneous American experience, was caused by their involvement in both "nightlife and night work," pointing to the place of working-class children in modernizing cities.[32]

Nighttime's negative reputation was well ensconced in nineteenth-century urban culture.[33] Publications such as *Montreal by Gaslight* (1889) highlighted the problem of the ill-lit street, as the darkness allowed for nefarious activities to multiply and for the depraved and indifferent to go unobserved. Anti-night commentators in New York City pointed to the "promiscuous intermingling" across gender and class boundaries.[34] An otherwise respectable citizenry mixed with the so-called low-brow element known to most urban settings, producing under night's blanket an industry of vice and immorality. New York City historian Mark Caldwell writes that between the 1870s and 1890s, "night became a theater of sudden appearances and quick escapes, lonely crowds, wanderers, strollers, and predators – spinoffs of a burgeoning and diversifying population, the proliferation of new things to do after dark and the technologies that invented them, lit them up, and transported their patrons."[35] Canadian social purity activists hoped that their cities would be spared the moral degeneration witnessed in New York City and London and actively sought out prevention controls on the most vulnerable urban souls, such as women and children.[36]

Canadian Evangelical Protestant reformers, including the Woman's Christian Temperance Union (WCTU), pursued the curfew to protect children's bodies and souls from exposure to the devil's playground that was night. Shining a light on these problems was figuratively and literally followed.[37] Cities worked on the technological front to install better lighting systems, while middle-class social reformers such as Kelso and the WCTU tackled the threat posed by moral and spiritual lapses produced in nighttime pursuits. Baldwin writes of New York City and the response to the growth of nineteenth-century nightlife: "Night could not be turned into day anywhere, either in the literal sense of illuminating the street as brightly as sunlight, or in the figurative sense of creating an island of virtue in a sea of moral darkness."[38]

Discursively, children became innocents unable to resist the temptations of nocturnal cultural life. These children were not bad themselves but were too weak in their tender years to avoid being swept into a path of moral descent, sin, vice, and crime. "Darkened young life-histories" began, Kelso warned in *Revival of the Curfew Law,* with the "evil stories and suggestions heard while loitering in the streets after sundown."[39] Although this language is suggestive of the religious scaffolding of reformers' activities, other curfew supporters pointed to the supposedly weak nature of children. Children's nighttime "wanderings" caused "moral injury" producing an "excitable and uncontrollable" temperament.[40] In this state, the child rejects the domestic world, "grows contemptuous of civil authority, and [is] initiated into criminal practices."[41] Reformers argued that for children the night presented an introduction to a vice-ridden, criminal, and sexualized adult world from which return was difficult if not impossible. Unable or unwilling to return home, the child would turn to gangs (referred to at the turn of the nineteenth century as "clubs" or "coteries") for sociability and community. Thus, evenings spent on the streets foreshadowed a future life spent bound by the four walls of the reformatory, prison, or penitentiary.[42] In echoing support for a Toronto curfew, Jones asked rhetorically, "Why build and maintain gaols and refuges, workhouses and reformatories, and at the same time refuse to support a measure that will reduce the necessity for these institutions?"[43]

Both girls and boys were vulnerable, but the threat of the night and the street-corner culture was expressed in gendered terms. In the case of boys, petty crime and an awakened taste for lust and vice held no future alternative than adult criminality: "The evil impress made upon the soul remains indelible, and can seldom if ever be eradicated."[44] Boys were largely the subject of reformers' rants against nighttime effects on childhood, but Kelso also underscored the particular danger facing girls who had fallen for the "allurement of dimly lighted streets and street-made acquaintances."[45] Girls, he claimed, were not "wicked" but, rather, "foolish and giddy" and therefore not equipped to resist the situations arising from these encounters, leading them to their shame.[46] Kelso's musings on the fallen girl and street-corner loitering insist on a close relationship of children's access to the street after dark and the production of depraved and criminal adults. For girls, once shame had befallen them, their only recourse to survival was prostitution. This image of children lost – crime and immorality – inspired his campaign for the juvenile curfew. This argument, largely evocative of the child protection discourse prominent in the 1890s, would persist through the early decades of the twentieth century.

Kelso's secondary argument promoting curfew related to his contention that the state must enter the private realm of familial relations where insufficient parenting was present. An idealized, bourgeois "haven in a heartless world" was the foil to contaminated street life. Kelso believed in the power of the home to inculcate children with values and lessons necessary for model citizenship: a good home provided a child with moral instruction, proper rest, and early sleep.[47] Parents were encouraged to improve the home environment – "make it attractive" – so that children would choose to be there and would "not regard compulsory detention there as a form of imprisonment."[48] When children were absent from home in the evenings, Kelso argued, they accumulated a series of deficiencies that would endanger any prospects for a healthy transition to adulthood.

The process of becoming an adult and a good citizen became much studied and discussed in the early decades of the twentieth century with the birth of adolescence. The popularizing of G. Stanley Hall's 1904 *Adolescence* and Freudian theories meant that discussions about children's health increasingly entered the arguments in favour of curfew.[49] Imperative for ideal maturation was a good night's sleep and freedom from overstimulation of the senses, especially at night (or by those elements associated with the night, such as sensuality). This line of reasoning gained ground through the twentieth century and predominated in the 1940s, as we will see.

Kelso was a child-saver leader in an era when the state and legislation were deemed an intricate part of the solution to modern urban social ills. Canadian age-of-consent laws, for example, had been implemented in the 1880s, passed with the express purpose of protecting young womanhood and criminalizing carnal knowledge of girls under fourteen (later sixteen); this legislation implied that families and communities could not protect girls sufficiently and that the strong arm of the state was necessary to truly do the job.[50] In an 1888 Woman's World column in the *Globe* on the subject of the curfew entitled, "Evils of Street Education," the author rhetorically asked: "Are not all laws moulded and framed with the direct object of making us better people ... and might we not use its [the law's] august arm to supplement the laxity or incapacity of parents?"[51] Similarly, Ontario's assistant superintendent of children wrote to the *Globe* responding to the argument that parents should determine children's curfew hour with the point that "government is but the cooperative act of parents who need to act together in cities and villages ... Where the individual parent does not do his duty it is not only the right but the duty of the municipality as a means of self protection."[52]

The main assumption behind the child protection movement, and its cousin the juvenile justice movement, was a critical role for the state in ensuring the welfare of children. The implicit assumptions in the state acting *in loco parentis* were that parents were negligent, the task of raising the next generation was too important to leave to those substandard parents, and therefore the state had a vested interest in playing public guardian. Evidence of deficient parenting was often anecdotal, and reformers needed only to point to the emergent lamppost youth culture to prove it. Industrial and reform schools originated from this thinking – that in extreme cases the state should replace the parent – but curfew law became popular in the era when institutionalization of children fell into disrepute.

Canada has been given the dubious distinction of being the first country to use curfew against youth. According to Kelso, the juvenile curfew was first implemented in Canada in the 1880s in Waterloo, Ontario. The town council of Waterloo moved and adopted successive resolutions requiring the ringing of a bell at nine o'clock each night, signalling the hour at which children less than fifteen years of age must return home if unaccompanied by a responsible adult.[53] Through the 1890s, city and town councils debated following Waterloo's lead. The popularity of this street-clearing measure spread during the 1890s mainly to other small towns in Ontario and across the country, partly as evidence of a robust child protection movement. Through that decade across Canada, women's Christian organizations and child welfare reformers lobbied local governments for the passage of curfew bylaws.[54] In Ontario, petitions demanded that municipalities act on section 31 of the 1893 Children's Protection Act, which provided for a curfew ordinance (this was effectively enabling legislation for local governments to pass curfew bylaws and/or for local police to enforce them). In 1897, the WCTU Ontario chapter proposed that the government make it compulsory for municipal corporations to pass curfew laws and enforcement mandatory for those that already had such bylaws.[55] Women's efforts were not successful in getting the province to act, though on the local level many towns and cities passed curfew bylaws.

The proliferation of the curfew to as many as fifty towns and villages in that decade sparked debate in municipal councils and in newspapers about child welfare, public order, and individual rights.[56] Most curfews specified that children would be home by 9 or 10 p.m. and set the age requirement at less than sixteen years, though it could be set at twelve years; in some cases, there was a gender differential, with older girls also required to respond to the curfew bell. In Newmarket, Ontario, for example, boys under fourteen and girls under sixteen could not be on the streets after 9 p.m. unless accompanied by a parent.[57] This discrimination against girls was picked up by a reader, who wrote to the editor of the *Globe* to register her dismay – "a girl of sixteen is as mature both in judgment and morals, as a boy of nineteen or twenty, and not one-half as likely to be led into wrong-doing" – and to advocate greater parental control of children.[58]

Skeptics persisted in the face of the widespread endorsement of curfew laws across small-town Canada. In the 1895 electoral race in Toronto, for example, one candidate for alderman rejected the idea of a youth curfew bell on the basis that no one should have the right to legislate for another's children.[59] Another joked that it made more sense to have a curfew for men over thirty-five years of age rather than one for minors.[60] Others argued that if there was in fact "street contamination after dark," the appropriate response would be to target it, rather than all children.[61] Individual freedom was at stake, curfew's detractors argued, and a repressive law served only to make the street more attractive to youth.[62]

By 1906, Kelso publicly admitted that although the curfew campaign had been a success in calling attention to the nightly "Cry of the Children," he was disheartened by the effectiveness of curfew law. Many towns and cities had enacted curfew bylaws, but he noted that the bell and sirens marking the time the children were to return home were "treated with indifference." A more practical goal, Kelso now thought, was to target the "worst cases of street wandering" and have the culprits dealt with by the Children's Aid Societies.[63] This indifference to the curfew hour appears to have spread across towns and cities for, by the 1920s and 1930s, women's groups and other concerned citizens were again asking city councils to either revive old 1890s curfew laws or to implement new ones.[64]

From the 1880s through the early decades of the twentieth century, curfew gained the support of a successful generation of child welfare reformers. Belief that evil lurked at sundown, making society's most vulnerable members powerless against its influence, convinced reformers and townspeople to pass bylaws regulating children's use of the streets. Children were cast as victims or potential victims in need of the state's protective power; denial of the problem of "night children," reformers argued, was at society's peril, for the next generation would certainly consist of criminals and depraved individuals. Not everyone agreed with this legislative innovation; larger Canadian centres such as Toronto and Montreal resisted the calls for curfew, outlining the anti-modern orientation of the curfew and the reluctance to interfere with family prerogative in controlling children.

The Second World War and Curfew's Leap to the Big City

Before the 1940s, the curfew bell was widely accepted outside large urban centres in Canada. The national emergency coupled with the real and apparent rise in juvenile delinquency and latchkey children created the conditions necessary for big-city politicians to embrace this once disdained mechanism of social control. Toronto, Montreal, Ottawa, Edmonton, Vancouver, and many smaller cities used curfew laws to clear the streets of young people in the name of keeping the home front disciplined while fathers served overseas and mothers engaged in war work.

Ontario cities, including Toronto, that had not previously availed themselves of the provisions under the Children's Protection Act regarding enforcement of curfews now asked local police forces to round up youngsters under sixteen.[65] Toronto's juvenile curfew was implemented when, in 1944, the city council requested enforcement of the provisions within the Children's Protection Act. The council instructed the police department, the juvenile court, the Children's Aid Society of Toronto, and the St. Vincent de Paul Children's Aid Society to enforce the curfew provisions of the act. Any child caught "loitering" at night was issued a warning and a one-dollar fine for the first offence. A second offence led to a fine of two dollars; any further breaches of curfew would result in a five-dollar fine.[66] From Nova Scotia to British Columbia, municipalities embraced the curfew as an important anti-delinquency strategy. Thus, curfew became one of the most popular weapons used against the wildly rising delinquency rate.[67]

Montreal's curfew bylaw came into effect in 1942. This city's curfew is notable because of the strong opposition to it before the war and its longevity: it far outlasted the wartime emergency that had given it birth. With an apparent delinquency crisis, curfew proponents gained the upper hand, leading to its successful passage in 1942. However, it was not without controversy.

In the decade before the war, curfew law had attracted child welfare advocates in Montreal and sparked a debate that raged from the provincial legislature to the halls of Montreal schools.[68] A substantial campaign for the curfew was launched by the Comité des oeuvres catholiques de Montréal (representing the Société de Saint-Vincent de Paul, the Association catholique de la jeunesse canadienne, and L'Action catholique), and a petition favouring the curfew was presented to city councillors in 1937. Smaller towns near Montreal, including Sainte-Anne-de-Bellevue, already had curfew laws. Sainte-Anne's police force had used the curfew to resolve a youth loitering problem. The police chief aimed the curfew at twelve- to sixteen-year-olds who were not guilty of any criminal offence but who were "fraternizing, annoying people, and standing on the sidewalks in front of restaurants and theatres." Resistance to the curfew came from adults who called it an infringement on their rights as parents to discipline their children, but according to the police chief, eventually "everyone" got used to it.[69] Montreal city councillors remained unimpressed by the evidence and support for the curfew prior to the war, and resisted it on the basis that it intruded on the privacy of the family.

Montrealers remained immune to the arguments for the curfew until the delinquency panic of the Second World War and the discourse surrounding the troubled family led to the successful passage of the bylaw in 1942. The threat of a full-scale delinquency problem appeared to be nationwide by the early 1940s. The Dominion Bureau of Statistics observed that the first three years of that decade were marked by a serious growth in the number of juvenile delinquents. While delinquency rates in Canada increased by around 45 percent during the war, press accounts of delinquency, according Jeffrey Keshen, increased by 125 percent.[70] Broader policing of youth during wartime helped to swell the numbers, but the delinquency panic was generally caused by the population's willingness to believe that one result of war-stressed families was bad behaviour on the part of children and adolescents. Blacked-out cities had apparently led to youth going bad: boys loitered and looted, whereas girls lost their moral sense. With mothers at work and fathers absent from the home front, a new tack was sought to quell a mounting problem of neglected and delinquent youth.

In an era in which children's *sorties nocturnes* were identified with the "great evils of our time," the curfew law's reputation evolved dramatically. In the context of wartime, it was cast as a way for the state to come to the aid of needy families. No longer deemed a relic of the dark ages, the curfew now became known as a "crime reducer, a child protector, and a home builder."[71]

Continuing from an earlier era were the overtones of religious arguments about the effect of night on children's souls, but generally there was a stronger emphasis on the potential problem of criminality among the young. The juvenile nocturnal curfew was not aimed at the older teenager who was largely responsible for the wartime "crime wave" but at children who might be led astray by older brothers and sisters. Curfew's crime-reducer effect, therefore, was designed to prevent the next generation of mature adolescents from turning into street-savvy punks.

Throughout the Montreal curfew campaign, this municipal regulation was characterized as a measure to protect childhood and reinforce the family, as if this reasoning were new. Whereas the war created family instability, the curfew was conceived of as a remedy or a home builder. As Father R.P. Archambault argued in his 1942 treatise on the curfew, without fathers at home, "Mother ... doesn't have the needed authority to make children obey. The children go out and run [in the streets] at night despite her."[72] The curfew, then, became a welcome support for parents, especially mothers, facing new and difficult circumstances. This sentiment was echoed across the country.[73] From Prince Edward Island, in support of a more stringent curfew law in 1942, Reverend Webster of the Children's Aid Society remarked that "the strong arm of the father is missed" and mothers are grateful for aid in this way.[74]

Implicit in all curfew law is the regulation of parental behaviour. Montreal commentators frequently mentioned how "today's" parents fell short of expectations. Montreal's mayor remarked that "times are difficult ... mothers are working in war factories, and more will follow, especially in working class areas, where children are without surveillance in the evenings."[75] Montreal juvenile court judge J.A. Robillard noticed that in the previous twenty years parents appeared to take less seriously their responsibilities to keep children off the streets at night.[76] The argument for the curfew re-affirmed that the "home was the natural habitat of the young child; without the curfew he misses family life that offers the child a sense of belonging and security."[77] Imbuing the child with a sense of these qualities of home was thought fundamental to producing a well-adjusted teenager.

Increasing stress was placed on the physical and social costs of nighttime indulgence. Judge Nicholson of the juvenile court admitted that a high percentage of children who were brought to court were in the habit of being away from their homes into the late hours of the night. Every day he saw the price Montreal paid for sleep-deprived youth. Quickly dropping his concern that adolescent crime occurred predominately at night, he engaged a different line of argument concerning proper adolescent development. Without a curfew hour imposed on children under fourteen, sleep depriva-tion would wreak havoc with youth. Sleep deprivation had long-term con-sequences for children's physical and mental well-being and especially for their morality: it resulted in poor "brain-muscle coordination," weak "pow-ers of concentration and judgement," and irritability. Athletic and intellectual ability were compromised, Nicholson argued, leading to "feelings of inferior-ity" and poor morale. In turn, these problems exacerbated delinquent acts such as the telling of lies, bullying, and rudeness. Nicholson acknowledged that big-city nightlife offered a world of excitement for young people with "bright lights, gaiety, and movement of people," but this was superficial and by staying out late, the child sacrificed development of such virtues as "calm-ness of thinking, sense of duty, and responsibility." The curfew would save the child from such deterioration and missed opportunity, for if a child was a "building block for society," each one who "develops badly, contributes to the general store of misery and unhappiness." Each child lost to sleep deprivation and the street "lower[ed] the quality of our culture."[78] A curfew, he argued, was the panacea needed to ensure that the generation that came of age after the war would be ready to lead.

Similar arguments were found outside Montreal. The Shelburne, Ontario, town council adopted a 9:30 p.m. curfew to mark "children's bedtime." At a special council meeting in August 1942, the curfew was reinstated after many years as "an aid to physical and intellectual improvement in children."[79]

The argument that the curfew helped protect childhood and build better children was an attempt to relieve the curfew of its repressive and illiberal nature. Montreal mayor Adhémar Raynault defensively argued, "We don't want to put in place a harassment mechanism but rather we want to protect young children from the dangers of the street."[80] Archambault stated simplistically that wartime was a moment of sacrifice; the curfew taught children that, when freedom was in danger, even they must "submit to a spirit of obedience and discipline ... They will only be better citizens, more devoted to their country, more disposed to serve and defend constituted authority."[81]

One of the strongest arguments made against proposed curfew laws in the 1930s and 1940s concerned parental responsibility, rights, and authority. Would the curfew not perform the job of parents? Judge Nicholson argued that such a law did not "unduly interfere with personal liberty and with the exercise of parental authority."[82] For him, children's presence on the street at night was a sign of parental failure. Montreal city councillors were more reticent to intervene in the relationship between parents and children. In September 1942, as city councillors debated the curfew bylaw articles, this issue was front and centre. Two councillors who proposed the curfew bylaw argued "that while this council is in accord with the principle of juveniles being kept from loitering in the streets, parks and public places of the city after nightfall, it is very widely held that this should be a responsibility of the parents and that every effort should be made to avoid bringing the children under the stigma of police action."[83] Although the juvenile court judges did not worry about the criminalizing of children under fourteen, councillors did. City council accepted the proposal that first offenders be taken home to their parents rather than to police stations or courthouses.

Other forceful arguments against curfew bells involved the expense of implementation. Police forces across the country had lost men to the armed forces, and the curfew bylaw appeared to require a significant force of foot patrols. Montreal's police chief admitted to *La Presse* in September 1942 that he had only 150 men on the streets at night and therefore few of the 100,000 children in the city would be subject to policing. Suggestions were made that parish priests and night patrols consisting of responsible citizens could join together in eradicating "night children."[84]

Wartime seemed to mute the opposition to curfew even in large urban centres. The police chief's concerns went unheard and in September 1942 the municipal government of Montreal passed Bylaw 1715.[85] The curfew stipulated that all children under fourteen years of age were forbidden to "circulate in the streets, lanes and public places" between 9 p.m. and 5 a.m. Exceptions were made for children attending night courses or in the company of a parent or guardian. The bylaw required that, with the first infraction, the adult responsible for the child be brought before the juvenile court; a repeat juvenile offender would be brought directly to the court. Besides the ignominy of being brought to court, the child was also subject to a fine or detention in the case that he or she was unable to pay the fine.

Following passage of the bylaw, children were routinely rounded up after the curfew hour. From the records of the Montreal Juvenile Delinquents' Court, it is evident that children aged eleven, twelve, and thirteen were brought to juvenile court for being on the streets at night. Most pleaded guilty and were fined between fifty cents and one dollar. Failure to pay the fine within one week resulted in incarceration in the detention home.[86] The court had used curfew law for decades to regulate specific youth who had been convicted of an offence under the 1908 Juvenile Delinquents Act; these targeted curfews frequently required that the juvenile be at home after 6 p.m. Although this might appear to be a harsh measure, the youth was spared reform school and permitted to return home. The immediate impact of the more generalized curfew was to make delinquent throngs of children whose only offence was not being at home in the evening.

According to the Montreal Police Department's annual reports, the number of children arrested during the war skyrocketed. The curfew law and juvenile delinquency in general became the responsibility of a new corps of officers, the Juvenile Morality Squad. Charged with clearing the streets, parks, and laneways of loitering children and adolescents, this force resulted in the heavy policing of children during the war. This squad comprised just over ten officers at the end of the war, but by 1948 the squad was many times that size. Through the early postwar period, thousands of children were arrested by Montreal police, a legacy of the successful curfew campaign of 1942.[87]

During the Second World War, Montreal city councillors finally embraced the arguments in favour of a juvenile curfew for the city. It had been pushed from the perspective that it would encourage family stability and cohesion at a moment when these seemed unrealistic goals. Not only did curfew clear the streets of children at 9 p.m. but it was also cast as a family stabilizer at a moment of intense familial distress. As well, it was promoted for the health benefits proffered youth: eliminating the tired child would result in a better formed adolescent and future citizen.

Conclusion

Canadians embarked on a mission to save and protect children in the late nineteenth century. A fundamental part of this movement involved using the state and specifically laws to govern the behaviour of children. A strong belief in the need to relieve street-corner culture of its attraction for youth led to widespread calls for criminalizing children's presence in public after sundown. Such coercive strategies to control all children's behaviour were supported by arguments about the dangers of the night and the vulnerability of children to pernicious influences. This mechanism of social control found most favour among women's groups, child savers, and small towns. Women's organizations looked to bolster the family by making sure its members were confined to the home. Child savers' bourgeois understanding of children's use of the streets blinded them to the fact that many children worked at night (or very early in the morning) out of necessity and that "home" for some children was not the haven it "ought" to have been. Small towns and cities of late-nineteenth-century Canada embraced the curfew law in an era when these municipalities were being transformed by immigration and industrialization.

Canadians' initial reaction to juvenile nocturnal curfews was mixed. Most large urban centres, especially Toronto and Montreal, resisted the juvenile curfew as a retrograde and impractical policing innovation. Yet, as the Second World War turned Canadian cities into apparent delinquency factories, curfew's proponents gained ground and virtually all municipalities in the country employed a youth curfew. By the 1940s, arguments about curfew's benefit for children's health and the future of the nation made it more palatable. Ironically, although curfew laws were seen as a wartime expedient, they far outlasted the war. And, although some argued that the curfew infringed on parental rights, absent from the debates was a strong sense that youth's rights were abrogated. In fact, most vulnerable – or lost – in this story were the rights and voices of children and youth whose lives were shaped by this technology of control. This was entirely consistent with early juvenile justice in Canada, which trampled on children's rights; only in the 1960s would a children's rights movement overhaul the system.

Although curfew bells, sirens, and whistles persist today, discussion around children's rights has come to the fore in some areas. In the case of Huntingdon, we have a strongly articulated sense of children's rights. *La Presse's* columnist found that kids at the local high school were not aware of it – and did not read *La Presse*! – but when told were indignant: Natacha said that ten is too early; that she preferred 1 a.m. An incredulous Eric, using a pseudonym, told the reporter, "No one is going to listen to that, fuck off." A girl interviewed on CBC's *The Current* said it is kids over sixteen who are the real problem.[88] In an online discussion board, seventeen-year-old Julie, from Huntingdon, rambled on about the unfairness of the curfew but also about the proposed skate park, which she felt served only boys. Michael Skala, a youthful Canadian blogger and former member of the Americans for a Society Free from Age Restrictions commended MLA André Chenail for challenging the curfew law.

In looking at the history of curfew laws a century ago, we have little sense of how children understood their place in society and how they felt about curfew hours, though we can read their actions and their persistence in loitering, forming street coteries, and taking a place on the street at night. The problems that curfew is meant to address have shifted over time: a century ago, the seeming growth of "night children" who loitered or worked on the streets after sundown and an assumption about the negative effect of night on children's souls and bodies prompted calls for a curfew; more recently, kids hanging out and turning to senseless violence and vandalism informs the curfew call. The protective stance of J.J. Kelso and others suggests an innocent was endangered; in cities such as Winnipeg a racialized discourse on bad kids suggests a need to protect society from them. The lack of academic attention given to historical curfews has assisted the silent spread of such regulation and marks a missed opportunity to inform today's political debate about the much touted rights of children.

Notes

1 The story of Huntingdon's curfew summer began May 2004 and continued through August 2004. Most Montreal newspapers (*La Presse, Le Devoir, The Gazette*) and the visual media (Radio Canada, CBC), as well as national media sources (*Globe and Mail* and Global Television) reported the issues as they unfolded.
2 "Huntingdon suspend l'imposition d'un couvre-feu," *Le Devoir,* 6 July 2004.
3 "Huntingdon By-Law Targets Parents," CBC News Online, http://www.cbc.ca/canada/story/2004/08/05/bylaw_quebec040805.html, 3 August 2004.
4 "Huntingdon Mayor Stands by Convictions," *Globe and Mail,* 4 August 2004.
5 "Curfews: Do You Know Where Your Children Are?" CBC News Online, http://www.cbc.ca/news/background/curfews/, 3 August 2004. According to this report, the Federation of Canadian Municipalities and the Association of Municipalities of Ontario claimed that most municipalities had curfew laws but that they were not generally enforced.
6 Colleen Simard, "Curfews Won't Save Our Kids," *Winnipeg Free Press Live,* http://www.highbeam.com/doc/1P3-1173389421.html, 4 December 2006.
7 The YCJA provides no mechanism for generalized youth-specific curfews.
8 Quint C. Thurman and David G. Mueller, "Beyond Curfews and Crackdowns," in Scott Decker, ed., *Policing Gangs and Youth Violence* (Belmont, CA: Thomson, Wadsworth, 2003), 167-87; William Ruefle and Kenneth Mike Reynolds, "Curfews and Delinquency in Major American Cities," *Crime and Delinquency* 41, 3 (1995): 347-63.
9 On the constitutionality of curfew law in the United States see Craig Hemmens and Katherine Bennett, "Juvenile Curfews and the Court: Judicial Response to a Not-So-New Crime Control Strategy," *Crime and Delinquency* 45, 1 (1999): 99-121.
10 Thurman and Mueller, "Beyond Curfews and Crackdowns," 170.
11 J.J. Kelso, *Revival of the Curfew Law: A Paper Presented for the Twenty-Third National Conference of Charities and Corrections, Held at Grand Rapids, Michigan, June 4-10, 1896* (Toronto: Warwick Bros. and Rutter, 1896).
12 A. Roger Ekirch, *At Day's Close: Night in Times Past* (New York: W.W. Norton, 2005), 63.
13 "Curfew," *Oxford English Dictionary* Online, www.oed.com.
14 Ekirch, *At Day's Close,* 61-63.
15 "Curfew Was Rung in the 17th Century," *Montreal Gazette,* 18 September 1942; "Le Couvre-feu aux débuts de la colonie," *La Patrie,* 13 September 1942. This historical tale was told by the courthouse archivist, E.Z. Massicotte. See also E.Z. Massicotte, "Couvre-Feu et Rondes de Nuit," *Bulletin des Recherches Historiques* 36 (May 1930): 266-69.

16 See Craig M. Johnson, "It's Ten O'Clock: Do You Know Where Your Children Are? *QUTB v. Strauss* and the Constitutionality of Juvenile Curfews," *St. John's Law Review* 69 (1995): 327-63; Hemmens and Bennett, "Juvenile Curfews and the Court."

17 Ekirch, *At Day's Close,* chap. 3 and p. 324.

18 Ibid., 65, 329.

19 Beverley Jones, "The Curfew Bell," *Evangelical Churchman* 22, 8 (1897): 123.

20 "William the Conqueror Ordered General Curfew for England," *Montreal Gazette,* 17 July 1942.

21 Letter to the editor of the *Globe,* signed "A Woman," 11 October 1894; the curfew is referred to as a "dark age proposal" in a letter quoted in Kelso, *Revival of the Curfew Law,* 11.

22 Hemmens and Bennett, "Juvenile Curfews and the Court," 100; Peter C. Baldwin, "'Nocturnal Habits and Dark Wisdom': The American Response to Children in the Streets at Night, 1880-1930," *Journal of Social History* 35, 3 (2002): 593-611, 603.

23 James W. Loewen, *Sundown Towns: A Hidden Dimension of Segregation in America* (New York: New Press, 2005). Thanks to David Roediger for this reference.

24 Neil Sutherland, *Children in English-Canadian Society: Framing the Twentieth-Century Consensus* (Toronto: University of Toronto Press, 1976; Waterloo, ON: Wilfrid Laurier University Press, 2000).

25 On the emergence of child protection movements in Canada see Sutherland, *Children in English-Canadian Society;* Renee Joyal, ed., *L'évolution de la protection de l'enfance au Québec: Des origines à nos jours* (Quebec: Presses de l'Université du Québec), 2000.

26 Woman's World, "Evils of Street Education," *Globe,* 27 April 1888.

27 Jones, "The Curfew Bell," 123.

28 Andrew Jones and Leonard Rutman, *In the Children's Aid: J.J. Kelso and Child Welfare in Ontario* (Toronto: University of Toronto Press, 1981).

29 Ibid., 51.

30 Kelso, *Revival of the Curfew Law,* 3.

31 Jones, "The Curfew Bell," 123.

32 Baldwin, "'Nocturnal Habits and Dark Wisdom,'" 594. See also Philip Davis, *Street-Land: Its Little People and Big Problems* (Boston: S.J. Parkhill and Co., 1915), 62-63, as quoted in Baldwin, "'Nocturnal Habits and Dark Wisdom,'" 593.

33 See Baldwin, "'Nocturnal Habits and Dark Wisdom'"; on the history of the night see A. Roger Ekirch, *At Day's Close,* and Joachim Schor, *Nights in the Big City: Paris, Berlin, London, 1840-1930,* transl. Pierre Gottfried Imhof and Dafydd Rees Roberts (London: Reaktion Books, 1998).

34 See also Mark Caldwell, *New York Night: The Mystique and Its History* (New York: Scribner, 2005).

35 Ibid., 208.

36 Mariana Valverde, *The Age of Light, Soap, and Water: Moral Reform in English Canada, 1885-1925* (Toronto: McClelland and Stewart, 1991), 130-31.

37 Ibid., 131-34, and more generally, chap. 6, "The City as Moral Problem."

38 Baldwin, "'Nocturnal Habits and Dark Wisdom,'" 596.

39 Kelso, *Revival of the Curfew Law,* 3.

40 "Curfews vs. Playgrounds," *Globe,* 28 September 1903.

41 Ibid.

42 Ibid.

43 Jones, "The Curfew Bell," 123.

44 Kelso, *Revival of the Curfew Law,* 4.

45 Ibid., 3-4.

46 Ibid., 3, 4.

47 Ibid., 3.

48 "Curfews vs. Playgrounds," *Globe,* 28 September 1903; 4 August 1904.

49 Baldwin, "'Nocturnal Habits and Dark Wisdom,'" 597.

50 On seduction laws see Constance Backhouse, *Petticoats and Prejudice: Women and the Law in Nineteenth-Century Canada* (Toronto: Women's Press, 1991).

51 Woman's World, "Evils of Street Education," *Globe,* 27 April 1888.

52 "The Curfew Bell," *Globe*, 3 October 1903.
53 Kelso, *Revival of the Curfew Law*, 7; see also "The Curfew," *Globe*, 28 September 1889. In the *Globe* article, the curfew age is set at "under 16."
54 For example, the *Globe* reported WCTU petitions in Ottawa ("The Curfew Bell," 7 July 1896), in British Columbia ("Legislation and Politics," 9 November 1896), and in Brandon and Winnipeg, Manitoba (28 May 1898).
55 "Ontario WCTU Meet, 20th Anniversary," *Globe*, 13 October 1897.
56 Ibid. The newspaper was quoting a report from an Ontario WCTU meeting.
57 "The Curfew for Children," *Globe*, 14 September 1894.
58 "The Curfew By-Law," *Globe*, 11 October 1894.
59 "Ward Three Election," *Globe*, 31 December 1895.
60 Ibid.
61 Kelso, *Revival of the Curfew Law*, 11.
62 Ibid.
63 "Cry of the Children," *Globe*, 19 November 1906.
64 "Calls for the Ringing of the Curfew Bell," *Globe*, 22 April 1913; "Want Curfew to Ring in Kingston Again," *Globe*, 12 May 1914; "Quebec Housewives Doing Large Work," *Globe*, 13 October 1917; "Curfew Is Ringing for Windsor Children, *Globe*, 21 August 1922; "Close Cafes at Midnight and Ring Curfew Bell" (Owen Sound), *Globe*, 16 April 1924; "Curfew Enforcement" (Niagara Falls), *Globe*, 13 April 1934; "London Trustees Urge Curfew Law" (London, ON), *Globe*, 27 April 1934; "St. Thomas Hints Curfew Law," *Globe*, 18 December 1934; "To Enforce Curfew" (Valleyfield, QC), *Globe*, 13 November 1936; "Curfew to Ring in Sudbury Again," *Globe*, 9 October 1937; "Oshawa Parents Offer 9:30 Curfew as Delinquency Curb," *Globe*, 8 January 1938; and "Curfew Wanted" (Halifax), *Globe*, 12 April 1938.
65 In Toronto, for example, the Board of Trade supported Alderman Fishley's proposal for a wartime curfew law. "Memorandum Re: Curfew," 21 November 1944, City of Toronto Archives, Series 100, File 1351, Juvenile Delinquency and Youth Programs, 1944-49, Box 46705, Folio 5.
66 *Globe and Mail*, 5 April 1944 (found in LAC, MG 28, I 10, vol. 49, file 447, Curfew Laws, 1941-44).
67 Jeffrey A. Keshen, *Saints, Sinners, and Soldiers: Canada's Second World War* (Vancouver: UBC Press, 2004), 207.
68 "Pas de couvre-feu pour les enfants de notre ville!" *La Presse*, 6 February 1935; "Curfew Law Issue Discussion Raging," *Montreal Gazette*, 15 February 1935; "Le couvre-feu pour jeunes en notre ville," *La Presse*, 22 February 1936; "Le couvre-feu combattu par des échevins," *La Presse*, 12 March 1937; "Requête en faveur du couvre-feu à Montréal," *La Presse*, 5 March 1937.
69 Library and Archives Canada, Canadian Committee on Social Development, MG 28, I 10, vol. 49, 447, Curfew Laws (1941-44), Letter from Police Chief Lepine.
70 Keshen, *Saints, Sinners, and Soldiers*, 365.
71 R.P. Archambault, *Le Couvre-Feu* (Montreal: L'Oeuvre des Tracts, 1942), 1.
72 Ibid., 2.
73 For example, "Approve Curfew Law, Fredericton," *Toronto Star*, 15 July 1942, 2. Children participated in this positive campaign: "Brampton Girls Are All Set to Obey Nine O'clock Curfew," *Toronto Star*, 19 May 1942.
74 "Curfew Debated," *The Charlottetown Guardian*, 27 November 1942.
75 "Le couvre-feu est nécessaire selon le maire," *La Presse*, 21 August 1942.
76 Archambault, *Le Couvre-Feu*, 4-5; interview with Judge Robillard.
77 Ibid., 7-9; interview with John F. Dalton.
78 J.G. Nicholson, "Curfew Law and Child Delinquency," *Municipal Review of Canada*, September 1942, 7.
79 "Curfew Shall Ring Shelburne Decides," *Toronto Star*, 20 August 1942.
80 "Le couvre-feu est nécessaire selon le maire," *La Presse*, 21 August 1942.
81 Archambault, *Le Couvre-Feu*, 2-3.
82 Nicholson, "Curfew Law and Child Delinquency," 7.
83 "By-Law on Curfew Is Council Feature," *Montreal Gazette*, 2 September 1942.

84 "Le problème insoluble posé par le couvre-feu," *La Presse,* 11 September 1942.
85 Adopted by the executive committee of the municipal government on 18 August 1942 and by the council on 2 September 1942.
86 See, for example, on the eleven children brought in by Sergeant Detective Schaffer on 3 and 4 June 1943 (Archives nationales du Québec à Montréal, Fonds Cour des jeunes délin-quants, Case 4239, 4 June 1943).
87 Archives municipales de la ville de Montréal, Fonds Département de la Police, annual reports, 1939-49.
88 Interview by Anna Maria Tremonti, *The Current,* CBC Radio One, 27 July 2004.

Part 3
In Aid of Small Bodies – Health, Hospitals, and Age in Historical Perspective

Measures to improve public health in industrializing cities at the turn of the nineteenth century dovetailed with related efforts to ensure that children survived infancy, then childhood. Increased professional attention to public health and the reduction of infant mortality spotlighted the health needs of all children in unprecedented ways. Those children assumed to be disadvantaged by their working-class origins, disability, or racialized identity soon became particular targets of intervention.

Across the Western world, the development of pediatrics as a recognized medical specialization spawned separate departments in medical schools, attracted practitioners, inspired new treatment protocols and technologies, and fostered groundbreaking improvements in knowledge regarding infant nutrition, control of contagious diseases, and preventative medicine. These "dividing practices," as Michel Foucault has termed them, at once created and treated the "problem" of small, vulnerable patients. As the chapters in this section demonstrate, however, efforts to help ailing children also had less beneficial, if often unintended, consequences. Children, as Denyse Baillargeon and Mona Gleason suggest, benefited from, but were also often challenged by, professionals' preoccupation with their health.

The two chapters in this section focus our attention on children's health care in the early decades of the twentieth century, how adults cultivated good health, and what this meant for children's relationship to broader national interests for a strong, loyal citizenry. Denyse Baillargeon concentrates on the treatment of youngsters at Sainte-Justine Hospital in Montreal and what this suggests about the interests of the state and the Catholic Church in pre-Quiet Revolution Quebec. Historians such as Annmarie Adams, David Theodore, and Judith Young point out that in many Western nations, middle-class reformers and religious orders, rather than medical professionals, initiated the development of children's hospitals and dedicated wards early in the Victorian period.[1] Beginning with the Montreal General Hospital's thirty-bed children's ward, opened in 1822, medical institutions entirely or partially devoted to children developed in major cities across Canada over the turn of the nineteenth century.[2]

Since hospitalized children often spent many months in care, concentrated efforts were made to ensure their moral, spiritual, and psychological well-being. The meaning of "well-being" was, however, determined by those with social power. Priorities of French-Catholic Quebec, Baillargeon demonstrates, largely determined the kind and tenor of leisure activities encouraged for the patients. Often entirely overlooked as important institutions of socialization for youth, hospitals ensured that the inculcation of sanctioned values would continue throughout treatment and recovery.

In "'Lost Voices, Lost Bodies'?" Mona Gleason interrogates the medical treatment of children over the twentieth century. She analyzes two major sources of information in tandem: the writings of doctors and nurses, and the oral histories of adults who grew up in English Canada in the first half of the twentieth century. Gleason pays particular attention to these encounters' production of relations of power, attitudes toward children, and familial challenges to medical authority. Through the lens of children's medical treatment, both chapters illuminate the importance of youngsters to the interests of the state and the varied responses of girls and boys to these efforts. Concern for children's health, whether on the part of parents, caregivers, professionals, or the state's representatives, shaped national destinies as surely as domestic ones.

Notes

1   Annmarie Adams and David Theodore, "Children's Hospitals in Toronto and Montreal, 1875-2006," *Canadian Bulletin of Medical History* 19, 1 (2002): 201-43; Judith Young, "'Little Sufferers': Sick Children in Late-Nineteenth Century Toronto," *Nursing History Review* 3 (1995): 130.

2   Young, "'Little Sufferers,'" 130. In 1885, a clinic for children was established under the auspices of Les Dormes de la Charité de la Providence in Quebec City. The Montreal Foundling and Baby Hospital appeared in 1892 (later amalgamated into the Children's Memorial Hospital); the Hospital for Sick Children in Toronto in 1875; the Winnipeg Children's Hospital opened in 1909; Halifax Children's Hospital appeared in 1910; the War Memorial Children's Hospital opened in London, Ontario, in 1922. Pediatric admissions to general hospitals, such as the Kingston General Hospital in Kingston, Ontario, occurred in the late 1800s.

6

Learning and Leisure on the Inside: Programs for Sick Children at Sainte-Justine Hospital, 1925-70

Denyse Baillargeon

During much of the twentieth century, patients, particularly young ones, often spent weeks and even months in the hospital. From these circumstances arose the need to organize patients' daily lives, a task that the Sainte-Justine Hospital, a Montreal pediatric institution founded in 1907, undertook very early on. Starting in the 1920s, after it had settled into a preferable location, Sainte-Justine joined a trend embraced by most North American and European hospitals by offering its child patients classes and recreational activities. Unacknowledged by most historians, teaching and leisure activities for young patients that took place within hospitals were another example of the accomplishments of the reform movement that, starting in the twentieth century, advocated in favour of school attendance (compulsory in Quebec only after 1943) and playgrounds. Drawing on the work of historians who have explored the history of children's learning and leisure, this chapter sheds light on the educational and recreational activities offered to Sainte-Justine patients between 1925 and 1970. It examines the hospital's and medical authorities' motivation for instituting such activities and shows that the organization of patients' daily experiences reflected generalized social concerns not only about children's physical development but also about their moral and, eventually, their psychological development. The Sainte-Justine Hospital's annual reports, the board of director's minutes, and the hospital's leisure- and education-related files that form the basis of this analysis illustrate that a major change occurred between the beginning and the end of the period under study. Between 1920 and 1950, classes and games organized for patients relied largely on the initiative of volunteers and targeted as much the reinforcement, or inculcation, of religious and moral values as the children's healing; in the 1960s, the responsibility for hospitalized children's activities was turned over to childcare workers and doctors who drew upon discoveries in psychology to help children better adapt to the hospital environment. However, the professionalization and medicalization of leisure activities did not mean the end of child regulation in the hospital. Indeed, ever increasing intervention by childhood experts in leisure activities in the 1960s was paired with a much more assertive desire to identify so-called problem cases that were then subjected to "corrective" measures that would normalize behaviours deemed deviant or "at risk."

Disciplining Children

During recent decades, studies that focus on the history of schooling and playgrounds have tended to emphasize the objectives that were at the very heart of these reform projects. Many historians acknowledge the humanist and philanthropic impulse of promoters within the parks and playground movement who were concerned with the safety and living conditions of immigrant and poor children, and linked these projects to the larger child-saving movement that spread around the same time to counter infant mortality and improve children's health.[1] From this perspective, the initiatives of playground organizers can be seen as a way to enable children of poor neighbourhoods to enjoy the pleasures of playing in a safe environment, far from the physical dangers of the street. Others also stress that the discoveries of child psychology and the importance these new theories attributed to play contributed to urban reformers' efforts to create supervised space of play for children. The new conception of the child that psychology helped foster suggested that play was the most important feature of childhood, an essential component for the full development of any individual, bringing many urban reformers to argue that all children should have the opportunity to engage in outdoor games and thus have the possibility to experience childhood to the fullest.[2]

If historians recognize that playgrounds were conceived because outdoor activity was good for children and that children need a safe environment in which to play, most of the studies also insist on the educational aims of the movement, especially the formation of character and acquisition of "proper" habits by children. In the 1970s, using the concept of social control, many studies insisted on the middle classes' desire to intervene in the lives of working-class children in order to influence their morals and behaviour; more recently, drawing on the theory of moral regulation put forth by Michel Foucault, others point to the disciplinary technologies used to produce normative behaviour in children.[3] This latter approach, which emphasizes the means employed to make individuals accountable for their own transformation into docile and productive beings, also sheds light on the connections between efforts to control youth and the development of citizenship in liberal societies. For example, in her study of the Montreal Parks and Playground Association, Sarah Schmidt underlines that the organizers considered playgrounds as "the chief Canadianizing influence of the day" and a place "to train boys and girls, that they may grow into useful men and women, and be better citizens."[4] L'Oeuvre des terrains de jeux, an organization founded in 1929 by a Catholic priest in the Quebec area, has not yet been studied; however, a brochure published in 1936 indicates its supporters targeted the same objectives of moral instruction and citizenship training as the organization's counterparts in the Anglo-Protestant movement, only it did so with a Catholic twist. According to the anonymous author of this brochure, play became the "bait" for pursuing spiritual education and a means of "preaching" to children so that they stay far from "sin." "Young people will play sports, but with and in Christ," the author assiduously points out.[5]

As shown in many of these later studies, school and leisure activities take on a particular importance since they represent, along with family and community, the main sites where children were introduced to psychological and behavioural norms and where they confront the processes of surveillance, categorization, exclusion, and integration that ensures their adhesion to these norms.[6] Public health vehicles such as well-baby clinics, medical school inspection programs, and pediatric hospitals were also institutions where children and their parents were under surveillance, labelled, and sanctioned according to medical norms designed to impose a new vision of the healthy child according to society's and the state's needs.[7] Created ostensibly to lower the high infant-mortality rate prevalent at the beginning of the twentieth century, well-baby clinics and other similar services attracted mothers eager to learn how to better take care of their offspring, but their popularity should not obscure the fact that they were conceived as a means to save the nation as much as babies and that they intended to transform motherhood practices.[8] Similarly, schools have been greatly concerned with children's health, partly because of the direct connection drawn between good health, academic success, and the general advancement of society.[9]

More generally, these works also demonstrate that in reformers' minds there was a true synergy between school, medicine, and organized leisure activities and that, each in its own way, these institutions contributed to orienting children's intellectual, physical, and moral development, these three components of infantile subjectivity becoming intrinsically connected. For this reason, it is not surprising that the pediatric hospital became as much a place of teaching and leisure as of medical care. At a time when children incurred long stays in the hospital, it became an obvious place to continue their training. While keeping in mind the complementarity between the three major youth-based institutions, the following pages briefly describe the evolution of Sainte-Justine Hospital and its clientele and infantile illnesses between the 1920s and 1960s, before examining academic and leisure activities established during this period.

Sainte-Justine and Its Patients

Sainte-Justine Hospital was founded in 1907 by a group of middle-class, French-Canadian women as a counterpart to the anglophone community's Children's Memorial Hospital, which had opened three years earlier. The new hospital's purpose was to tackle the "appalling infant mortality" that decimated Montreal's population year after year, which, according to the founders, makes it a "most humanitarian and truly nationalist charitable work."[10] In an era when Quebec's French speakers feared for their survival within Canada, it is not surprising to see these women express their nationalist objectives so overtly.[11] Of course, this desire to make Sainte-Justine a tool for French-Canadian survival did not hinder the charter of incorporation, obtained in the spring of 1908, from specifying that the hospital was committed to "indiscriminately receiving children of all nationalities and religions."[12] However, because of the institution's distinctly francophone and Catholic character, through the 1970s, 90 to 95 percent of the patients treated at Sainte-Justine belonged to this ethno-religious community.[13]

Predominately franco-Catholic, Sainte-Justine's clientele was also mostly male. Indeed, up until the mid-1930s, the hospital welcomed more boys than girls – as many as 40 percent more in 1925. After 1935, annual reports no longer differentiated the young girl patients and the women who came to give birth at the institution, and so the number of female patients surpassed the number of male patients, but we can presume that the over-representation of boys did not come to an abrupt end.[14] In fact, Dr. Claire Laberge-Nadeau, who undertook a study of the hospital's clientele at the beginning of the 1960s, noted that boys always slightly outnumbered girls. This gap is surely in part because of male newborn's increased vulnerability to disease and also because of boys' boldness, which makes them more prone than girls to accidents; it is also highly possible that parents were more inclined to care for their sons – who were valued more – than their daughters, who were taught from a young age not to complain.[15]

Without an exhaustive analysis of patient files, it is difficult to determine the children's socio-economic class, but many indicators suggest that, through the 1950s at least, patients came primarily from the working classes and poorest groups of society. Therefore, for the 1908 to 1920 period, more than 60 percent of the hospital's clientele were needy and not able to pay for the care they received. Another 25 percent paid only part of the cost of their treatments. In the 1930s, administrators estimated that 90 percent of hospitalizations were paid for by public assistance; in 1956, just a few years before Quebec joined the federal hospital insurance program, a little over 55 percent of the hospital's clientele depended on this public program.[16] Better public health programs and economic conditions led to gradual improvements in the standard of living and health conditions of Montrealers throughout the first decades of the twentieth century, which in turn contributed to lowering the proportion of children from destitute and working poor families among Sainte-Justine's clientele, but, at the dawn of the Quiet Revolution, it still made up the majority.

Before the 1940s, a large proportion of patients – nearly one-third – suffered from infectious diseases connected with poverty (diarrhea, peritonitis, pneumonia, pleurisy, ear infections, ophthalmia neonatorum, onchocerciasis or river blindness, impetigo contagiosa, and so on). In 1931, 1946, and 1959, the hospital faced three epidemics of poliomyelitis that left many patients with major muscular damage. There were also congenital deformities (such as cardiac malformations, oral cleft defects, and eversion of the feet) and skeletal afflictions, some of which were a result of rickets, another health problem directly linked with destitution.[17]

Before sulphonamides were introduced in the second half of the 1930s and penicillin made its debut in the 1940s, treatments for the infectious diseases that made up a large part of Sainte-Justine's caseload required long hospitalizations. Orthopaedic cases were also time-consuming endeavours. In 1930, the hospital, which was equipped with 320 beds, admitted 3,600 patients who stayed for an average of twenty-five days, although some children who underwent multiple and successive surgeries stayed at the hospital for several months, even years. The questionable efficacy of treatments or their extreme complexity made the average stay longer than twenty days until 1940.[18]

Through the 1940s, the hospital treated more and more genetic pathologies (hereditary diseases and cancers, for instance), some of which required care and treatment that prolonged patients' hospital stays. All in all, however, there was a decrease in the average number of days of hospitalization from around fifteen days in 1945 to ten days in 1970. During this same period, Sainte-Justine's intake capacity, which had increased steadily through the 1930s, continued to expand, both because of the many additions to the Saint Denis Street building and because of the institution's relocation to a new building on Côte-Sainte-Catherine Road in 1957.[19] From five hundred in 1940, the number of beds increased to just under nine hundred in 1970, while the number of patients went from seven thousand to over twenty-two thousand during these same years.[20]

These few facts about children's conditions and the average length of their stays at Sainte-Justine suggest that from 1920 to 1970 the pediatric hospital was not only an institution of care but also a home for many children who lived there for long periods. Between washing and meals, the tours of doctors and nurses for examinations and administering medicine, and, if necessary, visits to the radiology or physiotherapy services for specialized treatment, there was spare time that needed to be filled in order to keep boredom at bay and, even more importantly, to prevent boredom's counterpart of unruly behaviour. From the nineteenth century on, the first children's hospitals in Paris began countering idleness – the mother of all vices as we are forever reminded – by setting up workshops for older children and classes for younger ones. Starting at this time, hospitals, which by their nature interrupt daily lives, began recreating within their walls a semblance of "normality" as it took charge of children's preparation for adult life, a role that usually falls to the family, or other institutions such as school and church.[21] In the twentieth century, as Western societies bestowed a new importance on play as a means for training children, hospitals endorsed this new mission, as we will see in the case of Sainte-Justine.

Going to School at the Hospital

A photograph dating from 1910, when Sainte-Justine occupied a little house on De Lorimier Avenue, shows two young girls playing in the middle of a room used as a public ward, watched by a third who is confined to her bed (see Figure 6.1). This snapshot suggests that, from the institution's very beginnings, hospital authorities were conscious of distracting children through play. It was only in the 1920s, however, that formal teaching and training programs were progressively put in place, followed by more structured leisure activities. According to the 1933 annual report, these activities, which were run by a volunteer committee, helped calm turbulent children and were held with the goal of "shortening long days by developing children's intellectual and moral sensibilities."[22] In other words, through these pastimes, the hospital intended to equip its patients with knowledge and skills, while also instilling solid values and morals. In the Quebec of this era, this process necessarily meant the transmission of the tenets of Catholicism.

Disabled children who were not hospitalized at Sainte-Justine but who came regularly for treatment were the first to receive formal instruction. Opening in November 1926, thanks to Lucie Lamoureux-Bruneau, one of the hospital's founders, the École des enfants infirmes took on the mission of "teaching religion to the crippled and poor children unable to attend school in their district, and of giving them the necessary medical care and of providing them, according to their aptitudes, with the means of earning a living and becoming useful citizens to their families and to society."[23]

As this statement suggests, the primary objective of the École des enfants infirmes was to aid children who were refused admission to the Commission des écoles catholiques de Montréal (CÉCM) and who "were therefore deprived of instruction or who were turning to the English Protestant system."[24] In the overtly nationalistic context that reigned at the time, this latter situation was deemed unacceptable, since it put in peril the preservation of the French-Canadian nation, strongly associated with the transmission of the French language, and, especially, the Catholic faith. Under these conditions, it is not surprising to learn that religious instruction held "unquestionably the uppermost place" in the program of study, so that children would accept

Figure 6.1   Three young girls hospitalized at Sainte-Justine, 1910
Source: Sainte-Justine Hospital Archives

their "sad fate" and "find life less painful," or, in other words, would resign themselves to the inevitable in a purely Christian way.[25] The importance of religion for moral training and the submission of these children to their destinies were so crucial in the eyes of those in charge that, starting in its second year, the school made sure children attended Sunday Mass by providing them with transportation to and from their homes. Worried that reduced mobility would become an easy excuse for missing church, the École des enfants infirmes quickly took on a parental role in constraining children to respect their religious obligations. During the week, children were also provided with transportation between their homes and Sainte-Justine – a service that certainly facilitated their mobility but that also guaranteed their attendance at school.

Although religion played a paramount role in these young people's moral upbringing, the École des enfants infirmes also sought to develop children's manual abilities so that they might later find work and become good citizens. Organized according to a gender-based view of feminine and masculine roles, technical training occupied an important place in the school curriculum. Accordingly, in 1928, clockmaking classes taught by specialists were available to boys, while girls "learned to use their little hands to make paper flowers and other small, whimsical objects."[26] The annual report of that year

Figure 6.2 Shoe-repair class at the École des enfants infirmes, *ca.* 1930
Source: Sainte-Justine Hospital Archives

candidly revealed that "Madame J.A. Trudeau is providing the necessary materials to teach the art of stringing rosaries in the hope that the young girls will then find employment in the Génin et Trudeau factory."[27] The following year, the technical program was broadened to include drafting (offered to both girls and boys), woodworking, and shoe repair (taught just to boys; see Figure 6.2), and sewing and housekeeping classes (for girls only). Even though it served a clientele with special needs, the École des enfants infirmes thus only offered training that encouraged and maintained the habitual gender-based division of labour: boys learned to be breadwinners despite their handicaps, while girls were taught household sciences, even if the chances of marrying were slim.

Crippled children, as they were called at the time, represented a vulnerable group that was often subjected to economic and social exclusion, which explains the extra attention they received. Especially for boys, a trade provided a minimum of financial autonomy, and, thus, greater dignity and better integration into the community, all of which resulted in a decreased propensity for revolt or delinquency. As for girls, school authorities surely hoped that, in the absence of husbands, these children would remain in the family, where at least they could be useful. Whatever these children's future might be, the religious tenets the children were taught sought to convince them of the necessity of accepting their disability as God's will. Supported by their religious beliefs, these children would be better equipped to face adversity and control any feelings of injustice they might feel. Labelled as different, they were taught to accept and overcome this difference with the help of religion and practical training.

At the beginning of the 1930s, the existence of a school inside the hospital became an issue not only because of its prohibitive cost but also because of the space it took away from hospitalized patients. In 1932, disabled children were thus transferred to the CÉCM, which had agreed to take them on.[28] But this clientele was not the only one to receive instruction at Sainte-Justine, since, starting in 1931, the administration established an educational service for hospitalized children. First offered to patients in the orthopaedics ward, which had the greatest number of long-term patients, from 1937 onward, education was guaranteed for all sick children who had to stay in the hospital for longer treatment or for a long period of convalescence.

In 1932, there was only one teacher, hired by the hospital, but, in 1939, the service was staffed by three teachers, two of whom the CÉCM provided. Nearly two hundred students from grade one through eight benefited from lessons in catechism, French, math, religious and Canadian history, and geography, in accordance with the school board curriculum, which required monthly exams to assess students' progress.[29] Classes were given in a room set up for this use, or at the sides of bedridden patients. Starting in 1941, the CÉCM also provided a teacher for boys' manual work; in 1946, a weekly drawing and painting class was added for both boys and girls.[30] In the 1930s and 1940s, volunteers taught hygiene and safety, among other things, to the young patients so that they might learn to better avoid illness and accidents in the future.

As we can see, Sainte-Justine did not wait for the province to impose compulsory schooling in 1943 to take care of hospitalized children's education. Until 1937, however, it would seem that religious instruction clearly took precedence over other subjects; the annual report of 1951 goes so far as to affirm that until then, catechism lessons to prepare children for their First Communions were, in fact, the only instruction that students received.[31] Although this statement seems a bit exaggerated, it is clear that religious instruction was one of the women administrators' priorities, since, in the 1930s and 1940s, in addition to catechism and religious history classes that were part of children's school instruction, volunteers visited children to prepare them for this sacrament, which, like baptism, sometimes took place at the hospital.[32] The annual reports take special care to highlight the First Communion ceremonies held at the hospital, sometimes in the presence of parents: "Nothing is more touching than this ceremony in the chapel so prettily decorated for the occasion. *Monseigneur* spoke to the little children, making them understand the importance of the sacrament they were receiving and all the advantages they would take home from their forced stay in the hospital. *Monseigneur* also praised the hospital administration for having brought together medical care and the moral comforting these little ones so desperately need."[33] Like with disabled children, religion was seen as sick children's best ally for surmounting the trials of illness and accepting the pain they experienced. In this regard, those in charge of religious instruction freely compared patients to Sainte-Justine, the martyr and patron of sick children after whom the hospital was named. Like the little saint, children were even called upon to offer their suffering to God in a sanctifying act, and to "love Jesus all the more, wanting to suffer for Him, because it is His will."[34] Absolutely indispensable to science, because it taught children to undergo medical treatments without complaining, catechism for First Communion also aimed to avoid "delaying the acceptance of Jesus into these little hearts so pure," especially if death was near.[35]

Preparation for First Communion disappeared at Sainte-Justine in the 1950s at the time when instruction for hospitalized children was growing and the number of patients who took classes rose from 189 in 1940 to 476 in 1949, and to 1,740 in 1959 – the last year these data were published in the annual report. Because of this increase, which was proportionately much higher than that of admissions, by the end of the 1950s the CÉCM were providing four teachers, plus one who specialized in patients with cerebral paralysis.[36] Mandatory school attendance, which came into effect in 1943, thus had a tangible impact on the number of Sainte-Justine students, which quadrupled during the 1950s, even as the average length of stay in the hospital decreased. Starting in the 1960s, the CÉCM offered the services of a male or female teacher only if a patient was hospitalized for more than three weeks, a condition that certainly diminished the number of hospitalized children allowed to follow classes.

Keeping Children Busy and Happy

Starting in 1932, educating the sick was complemented by a host of organized activities supervised by volunteers who came to the hospital each day. According to the nomenclature used in the annual reports, these activities were divided into two distinct categories: on the one hand, there were occupations that served therapeutic ends and, on the other, there was "entertainment" that was intended to take children's minds off their situations. In each case, however, the female administrators and volunteers were careful to choose activities with educational and moral benefits: "We must not ignore the moral perspective that this committee [the Comité d'enseignement, d'occupation et d'amusement] strives for. As these busy little youngsters are distracted and able to forget the inactivity to which they are condemned, their intellectual, spiritual, and physical development is improved."[37]

Once again, it was the children from the orthopaedic service who were targeted first. As the minutes from a board meeting state: "[These] patients, whose treatment sometimes requires long stays at the hospital, need care for their intellects as much as for their poor little bodies, and it would be good to interest them manually or intellectually, and entertain them while they are being treated."[38] In fact, keeping children busy found a new rationalization with the dawn of occupational therapy (today called rehabilitation therapy), a practice intended to improve patients' state through manual work adapted to their conditions. The "therapies" were seen as a way to fill free time while favouring healing, yet the annual reports show that this daily, gender-based work was, in fact, intended to benefit the hospital as much as the children: "Daily tasks consist of leather tanning, woodworking, painting and drawing for boys, and weaving, knitting, embroidery, and sewing for girls. All our children did their part for Dollar Day, by folding brochures. Later, they made four hundred candy dishes and five dozen calendars for Christmas. These calendars were sold to raise money for the hospital. Three times a week, the children made bags for tongue depressors used in the hospital."[39] Starting in 1936 and through the 1960s, patients' needlework and crafts were shown at the annual meetings of the Société de Secours des enfants infirmes and the Société d'Occupation thérapique du Québec and sold to benefit the hospital. As part of these activities, during two consecutive years at the end of the 1930s, young girls made baby clothes for poor mothers in the hospital's maternity ward – a way of teaching them "that it is good to help those worse off than oneself."[40] According to the annual reports, girls and boys, who turned "naturally" to the activities considered "appropriate" for their sex, set themselves as best they could to performing these tasks. Indeed, the volunteers who supervised these activities must have strongly encouraged this attitude, just as they sought to instill values, like perseverance, discipline, a good work ethic, and, for girls, charity.

Encouraged by doctors who considered that "work and distraction are part of the treatment of certain cases," occupational therapies were more a form of learning than of play per se.[41] Hardly giving children an opportunity to play physically or run around, the hospital administrators structured the free time according to a utilitarian and educational view of leisure. Through these manual tasks, children learned to be productive and not waste their time on futile or vain activities but rather to profit from every minute of the day.[42] In this regard, the biggest lesson the hospital sought to teach the children was that even illness did not justify idleness (see Figure 6.3). Although therapeutic occupations did encourage physical strengthening, the concentration on these activities also prepared the children, who were mostly from the working classes, to accept their future as workers and homemakers without letting discomfort or even physical pain interfere with their tasks and responsibilities.

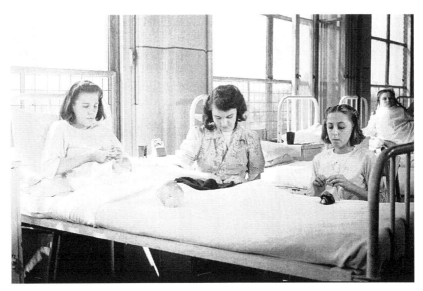

Figure 6.3   Young volunteers and a patient doing needlework, 1946
Source: Bibliothèque et Archives nationales du Québec, Conrad Poirier

Besides handiwork, the patients at Sainte-Justine were also invited to participate in show and tell and games, to watch films, or to read, paint, draw, or sing – activities chosen by adults for their educational value. If sometimes patients participated in outings that, in appearance, had no other goal but entertainment (attending the *Ice Follies* and the *Ice Capades* figure-skating shows, picnics, etc.), the most frequent leisure activities were intended not as pure relaxation but as another opportunity to form children's characters and personalities according to moral imperatives. The creation in 1937 of a Boy Scout troop, called the scouts "allongés" ("reclining scouts"), led by Scouts from the community, may be the best illustration of the desire to take advantage of every opportunity to transmit the most worthy values and, especially, the highest Christian principles. Noticing the "healthy influence" that Scoutism had on patients' moral training, the writers of the 1937 annual report congratulated themselves for the presence of a troop in the hospital, since the Scout pledge these boys took encouraged them to make "a life of honesty, devotion, and purity."[43] For the hospital administrators, the teachings of Scoutism were also "powerful elements for staving off the wave of Communism that is washing over our country," and they hoped that Sainte-Justine's scouts allongés "would remain in the movement even after they left the hospital."[44] Here again, religious teachings were brought to the fore, as the troop leader in charge of activities for the hospital's Scouts expressed in 1941: "Serving, a word that resonates like a sounding trumpet in the heart of pure and ardent youth. 'Serving' is the most beautiful word

Figure 6.4   Art class in the room on the eighth floor, early 1960s
Source: Sainte-Justine Hospital Archives

in the world. It is the expression of a complete devotion to the service of the Great Leader and Humanity."[45] Submission to authority, helping among peers, charitable acts for the less fortunate, and the development of a can-do attitude were among the Scout values that were highly prized, since they prepared young boys to become citizens who were independent, compassionate, and, especially, respectful of hierarchy. As for the Girl Guides, the organization came only one year to Sainte-Justine, in 1936. That year, the annual report proclaimed that the "real goal of these visits" was not so much to "entertain young patients" or even to "develop their intellectual faculties through instructive games" but, rather, to "work to instil the Christian principles that make up the spirit of the Guides."[46]

   The organization of children's free time, divided between schooling, manual tasks, reading, and drawing, remained greatly unchanged until the hospital moved to its Côte-Sainte-Catherine Road location in 1957. The much bigger, new building had a recreation room on the eighth floor, though in the beginning, this room served mainly for a continuation of the crafts classes.[47] At the beginning of the 1960s, however, leisure activities took on a new dimension. The creation in 1958 of the Volunteer Service, directed by a salaried manager, encouraged in effect the reorganization of leisure activities according to new rules and new priorities. Fine arts, which emphasized children's creativity, replaced the crafts classes, while play took on greater importance (see Figure 6.4). In addition, supervision of activities was now entrusted to childhood specialists such as kindergarten teachers and new child experts. In an even more fundamental way, the philosophy that dictated the organization of activities and their objectives changed radically over the course of this decade. While annual reports from the 1950s reiterated the moral, physical, intellectual, and spiritual benefits of leisure, it was the psychological dimension that was increasingly emphasized during the 1960s.

Fernande Robitaille, who took over the direction of the Volunteer Service created in 1958, became the primary advocate of this new orientation. Obviously influenced by the work of American and French psychologists, she was convinced of the necessity of transforming play into a tool for helping children adapt to hospital life.[48] In a speech given in 1963 to nurses, she emphasized that play, necessary for ensuring the full development of children in good health, became a therapy for sick children, since it helped surmount the trauma of hospitalization. Separated from their parents, plunged into a totally different and unknown environment full of strangers who sometimes treated them without sensitivity, children could feel abandoned, even guilty, and experienced their illnesses as a punishment of sorts for their mistakes. Anguished and disoriented, they might resort to temper tantrums or prostration. Labelled "hospitalism," these symptoms could be dealt with through play ("a reassuring language"), which helped children feel at home and enabled personnel to "better understand and help the child."[49] Happy children got better faster, Robitaille also believed. This is why play had to be considered as a therapy and even scheduled into the care and treatments, so as not to prevent children from playing. "We must always keep in mind that we don't just have a sick child to heal, a wound to close, a limb to mend, but a *human being* to bring back to good physical and psychological health," she explained.[50] In this vein, play became a vehicle for children's feelings and encouraged the "moral and social growth that a hospitalization can interrupt, put in check, and shake up for a long time."[51] Group activities were the best way of reaching this objective, since they put children into a less foreign environment and allowed them to recreate social connections. Since play was children's "work," they had to be provided with the right tools, that is, a variety of games and toys adapted to each age group, and the activities had to take place in a space that stimulated and encouraged children to express their creativity.

Associated with children's psychological well-being and mental health, play quickly became a medical affair. Looking to the example of other hospitals for children in North America and Europe, Robitaille insisted throughout the 1960s on the necessity of creating a truly therapeutic environment for the young patients; in her opinion, this required hiring a large number of child specialists. In 1965, to further her ideas, she set up a committee for play-based therapy (Comité de thérapie par le jeu) to which she invited three doctors, one of whom was a psychiatrist. As early as the second meeting of this committee, the members decided that "[the] kindergarten (one per floor) will have the task of establishing a screening program [for children's needs] and of implementing it. Cases presenting problems will be referred to social or psychiatric services, according to their nature and severity. It is understood that the attending physician will participate in analyzing the case and should give his agreement on the proposed program of therapy before it is implemented."[52] During a subsequent meeting, Dr. Albert Royer, one of the most eminent pediatricians of his generation, stated that "children should not go to the play room on the eighth floor, except on orders from their attending physicians" and he suggested that "every nursing station be equipped with prescription forms entitled: Play Therapy, eighth floor, on which the names of children who have obtained permission to go to the eighth floor will be entered as well as the kind of activities they are allowed to do."[53] At the same meeting, the hospital's medical director called for keeping a close watch on the films children were shown, an issue that had never been raised before.[54] Finally, in 1967, when a therapeutic environment service was on the brink of being established, Robitaille specified that the coordinator of the new service, backed by a secretary and a team of seven specialists, should be a person "aware of parent-child separation issues, with knowledge about children, the value of creative activities in their development, and the causes of hospital-related trauma." To reinforce the work of this team, regular meetings with the pediatricians, psychiatrists, nurses, rehabilitation therapists, and social workers were also to be held.[55]

Because of insufficient funding, this service remained in a rather embryonic state. At this same time, Sainte-Justine was becoming an ultra-specialized hospital, which meant that it admitted a more and more severely affected clientele who were less able to play, while less serious cases were treated in shorter and shorter periods. Moreover, the hospital, which had always seriously restricted its access to parents, now opened its doors to families by extending visiting hours from 11 a.m. to 8 p.m. without interruption.[56] Previously considered as undesirable propagators of germs and an obstacle to the proper functioning of hospital routine, parents had become essential partners to the caregiving team. This radical shift could be attributed to widespread acceptance of psychological theories that insisted on children's emotional security. Under these conditions, although leisure activities did not disappear altogether, they lost their importance in a dramatic way. However, throughout the 1960s, there was a marked attempt to medicalize leisure activities – leading to increased doctor participation in the new services (including the Comité de thérapie par le jeu and the Service du milieu thérapeutique), to increased decision-making power that doctors appropriated when it came to children's participation in leisure activities, and, most notably, to a psychology-based rationale that justified the intervention of modern childhood experts.[57]

Conclusion

Most historians agree that a medicalization of hospitals occurred during the second half of the nineteenth century and can be witnessed in part through the increased presence of doctors and nurses. Children's hospitals certainly were not exempt from this phenomenon. But just as hospitals for adults did not abandon their pretensions of caring for the soul as well as the body from one day to the next, the experience at Sainte-Justine shows that during the first half of the twentieth century pediatric institutions also continued to promote objectives other than those of simply treating and healing children, namely to educate and ensure moral training. A public health institution, the pediatric hospital became a tool to normalize children from the working classes. Children from low-income families, who were the most likely patients to end up at the hospital, were taught to become useful citizens, good Christians, productive workers if they were boys, and accomplished homemakers if they were girls. In the hospital, like at school or on the playground, hospitalized children were subjected to a disciplined regime that made them accustomed to respecting authority, to accepting gender-based social roles and responsibilities, to making good use of their time, and to remaining productive, despite their illnesses. Just as important, they were constantly exposed to Catholic discourse that magnified the spiritual values associated with the French-Canadian nation. Similar to what happened in the schools and on the playgrounds run by priests, children hospitalized at Sainte-Justine were immersed in an atmosphere that constantly reminded them that religion was a "natural" component of their identities.

Generally following the transformations in Quebec society during the same period, the objectives of leisure activities took a major turn in the 1960s. Abandoning the moral discourse of the previous decades, the director of Volunteer Services, Fernande Robitaille, used "scientific" language to justify these changes. From then on, under the banner of protecting children from psychological trauma, leisure activities were legitimized and reorganized with professionals leading the operation. But this new rhetoric, which seemed to prioritize children's needs and protect them from psychological problems, was in fact intended to establish a new way of regulating childhood, one in which medicine played a paramount role. Through play, administrators hoped to adapt children to the hospital – rather than the opposite – so that they might experience the situation naturally. They also hoped that children's hospital stays would allow them to observe children's behaviour and, if necessary, to refer them to specialists (psychiatrists, social workers, etc.) to correct any detected "anomalies." In fact, psychological balance, as defined by experts, was becoming the new gauge of normality but, like the religious agenda that had preceded it, this new credo was also intended to form personalities that were adapted to society's expectations. To what extent children benefited from the hospital's academic and leisure activities is a question that deserves further attention. Although interviewing adults about their childhood experiences has its own shortcomings, this approach would nonetheless allow scholars to shed different light on these activities and to see how and to what extent the objectives of these activities were met.

Notes

1 Kevin J. Brehony, "A 'Socially Civilising Influence'? Play and the Urban 'Degenerate,'" *Paedagogica Historica* 39, 1-2 (2003): 87-106; Mark A. Kadzielski, "'As Flower Needs Sunshine': The Origins of Organized Children's Recreation in Philadelphia, 1886-1911," *Journal of Sport History* 4, 2 (1977): 169-88.

2 Dominick Cavallo, *Muscles and Morals: Organized Playgrounds and Urban Reform, 1880-1920* (Philadelphia: University of Pennsylvania Press, 1981); "Social Reform and the Movement to Organize Children's Play during the Progressive Era," *History of Childhood Quarterly* 3, 1 (1975): 509-22.

3 On the playground movement see also Cary Goodman, *Choosing Sides: Playgrounds and Street Life on the Lower East Side* (New York: Schocken Books, 1979). On the movement in Montreal see Sarah Schmidt, "Domesticating Parks and Mastering Playgrounds: Sexuality, Power and Place in Montréal, 1870-1930" (MA thesis, McGill University, 1996), and Catherine Cournoyer, "Les accidents impliquant des enfants et l'attitude envers l'enfance à Montréal (1900-1945)" (MA thesis, Université de Montréal, 1999). For a critique of the social control theory see Gareth Stedman Jones, "Class Expression versus Social Control: A Critique of Recent Trends in the Social History of 'Leisure,'" *History Workshop* 4 (Fall 1977), 162-70. For a critique of the social control approach in the history of the park and playground movement in the United States, see Stephen Hardy and Alan G. Ingham, "Games, Structures, and Agency: Historians on the American Play Movement," *Journal of Social History* 17 (Winter 1983): 285-301. On the history of education see Paul Axelrod, "Historical Writing and Canadian Education from the 1970s to the 1990s," *History of Education Quarterly* 36, 1 (1996): 19-38. For an approach that built on Foucault's work see Bruce Curtis, *Building the Educational State: Canada West, 1836-1871* (Lewes, UK: Falmer Press, 1988), and Mona Gleason, "Disciplining the Student Body: Schooling and the Construction of Canadian Children's Bodies, 1930-1960," *History of Education Quarterly* 41, 2 (2001): 189-215.

4 Cited in Schmidt, "Domesticating Parks and Mastering Playgrounds," 148, 149. See also Margaret Kernan, "Developing Citizenship through Supervised Play: The Civics Institute of Ireland Playgrounds, 1922-1975," *History of Education Quarterly* 34, 6 (2005): 675-87.

5 Anonymous, *L'oeuvre des terrains de jeux* (Montreal: École sociale populaire. 1936), no. 200 (February), 8-9, 6.

6 Michel Foucault, *Surveiller et punir: La naissance de la prison* (Paris: Gallimar, 1979); Mona Gleason, "Disciplining the Student Body," 194.

7 Denyse Baillargeon, "'Une opposition regrettable': L'inspection médicale des écoliers à Montréal, 1920-1960," in *Modernité, citoyenneté, déviances et inégalités: Pour une analyse comparative des difficultés du passage à la modernité citoyenne* (Cordova: forthcoming); Mona Gleason, "Race, Class, and Health: School Medical Inspection and 'Healthy Children' in British Columbia, 1890-1930," *Canadian Bulletin of Medical History* 19, 1 (2002): 95-112; and David Kirk, "Foucault and the Limits of Corporeal Regulation: The Emergence, Consolidation and Decline of School Medical Inspection and Physical Training in Australia, 1909-1930," *International Journal of the History of Sport* 13, 2 (1996): 114-31.

8 Cynthia Comacchio, *Nations Are Built of Babies: Saving Ontario's Mothers and Children 1900-1940* (Montreal and Kingston: McGill-Queen's University Press, 1993); Denyse Baillargeon, *Babies for the Nation: The Medicalization of Motherhood in Quebec, 1910-1970,* trans. W. Donald Wilson (Waterloo, ON: Wilfrid Laurier University Press, 2009).
9 Baillargeon, "'Une opposition regrettable.'"
10 Sainte-Justine Hospital Archives (hereafter cited as SJHA), Sainte-Justine Hospital, annual report (hereafter cited as AR) 1908, 3.
11 On the links between infant mortality and the national question in Quebec, see Baillargeon, *Babies for the Nation.*
12 SJHA, minutes of the annual meeting, 16 June 1914.
13 SJHA, AR 1908-41: Dr. Claire Laberge-Nadeau, "Les caractéristiques de la population hospitalière à l'Hôpital Sainte-Justine" (MA thesis, Université de Montréal, 1963).
14 SJHA, AR, 1908-35.
15 On domestic accidents, see Cournoyer, "Les accidents impliquant des enfants."
16 Desjardins, "L'Hôpital Sainte-Justine Montréal, Québec (1907-1921)" (MA thesis, Université de Montréal, 1989), 82, 85-86; SJHA, AR 1938, 35; SJHA, Newspaper Clippings File, "56,3% des malades de Ste-Justine relèvent de l'Assistance publique," *Montréal-Matin,* 21 February 1957.
17 SJHA, AR 1907-60.
18 Ibid. The average numbers of days of hospitalization included women who gave birth at Sainte-Justine (more than one thousand annually in the 1940s) and who stayed at the hospital for more than ten days.
19 The hospital occupied various buildings during its history. From November 1907 to May 1908, it was located in a small house on Saint Denis Street, near Roy Street. From May 1908 to the summer of 1914, it was on De Lorimier Avenue, in a larger house. From then on, and until its last moving to Côte-Sainte-Catherine Road in 1957, it was situated on Saint Denis Street, to the north, near Bellechasse Street.
20 SJHA, AR, 1930 to 1970, and 1967, 51.
21 Musée de l'Assistance publique-Hôpitaux de Paris, *L'hôpital et l'enfant: L'hôpital autrement?* (Paris: Editions ENSP, 2005), 67-68.
22 Volunteer work held a very large place in the history of Sainte-Justine. In fact, in 1931, a little over 80 percent of the staff was made up of volunteers, 30 percent at the end of the 1950s. Aline Charles, *Travail d'ombre et de lumière: Le bénévolat féminin à l'Hôpital Sainte-Justine 1907-1960* (Quebec: IQRC, 1990) (Coll. Edmond-de-Nevers, no. 9), 53-54. SJHA, AR 1933, 29.
23 SJHA, AR 1928, 82.
24 Ibid., 86, and AR 1932, 31, 90.
25 SJHA, AR 1927, 89, and AR 1928, 87.
26 SJHA, AR 1928, 87.
27 Ibid.
28 SJHA, AR 1929, 29, and AR 1930, 27, and minutes of executive council meeting, 5 March 1930, 14 March 1930, 24 March 1930, 7 April 1930, and 19 May 1930. In all, during the six years the École des enfants infirmes was housed at Sainte-Justine Hospital, 207 children aged seven to sixteen attended classes on a regular basis (SJHA, AR 1932, 31).
29 SJHA, AR 1932, 29, 92; AR 1934, 29; AR 1937, 36, 135; AR 1936, 128-29; AR 1938, 27; AR 1939, 120.
30 SJHA, AR 1941, 21; AR 1946, 179.
31 SJHA, AR 1951, 35.
32 SJHA, AR 1937, 36.
33 SJHA, AR 1936, 128.
34 SJHA, AR 1937, 139.
35 Ibid., 138.
36 SJHA, AR 1940, 95; AR 1949, 103; and AR 1959, 99.
37 SJHA, AR 1935, 28.
38 SJHA, minutes of the weekly meeting of the board of directors, 23 August 1933.

39 Dollar Day was the name given to the annual fundraising drive of Sainte-Justine. SJHA, AR 1935, 68.
40 SJHA, AR 1938, 130.
41 Ibid.
42 It should be noted that playgrounds also organized crafts classes aiming at the same ends.
43 SJHA, AR 1937, 141.
44 SJHA, Dossier 220 Ass.-Insti.-Org. et Soc. 1935-57, Scouts catholiques de Montréal, Letter of Ms. A. St-Jacques d'Artois, secretary of the board of directors to Father Bélanger, Principal of the Collège Jean-de-Bréboeuf, 23 February 1937; AR 1939, 124.
45 SJHA, AR 1941, 138.
46 SJHA, AR 1936, 132.
47 SJHA, AR 1957, 90.
48 On the development of psychology in English Canada see Mona Gleason, *Normalizing the Ideal: Psychology, Schooling, and the Family in Postwar Canada* (Toronto: University of Toronto Press, 1999), and Mary-Louise Adams, *The Trouble with Normal: Postwar Youth and the Making of Heterosexuality* (Toronto: University of Toronto Press, 1997). For Quebec, see Denyse Baillargeon, "We Admire Modern Parents": The École des Parents du Québec and the Post-War Quebec Family, 1940-1959," in Michael Gauvreau and Nancy Christie, eds., *Cultures of Citizenship in Post-War Canada, 1940-1955* (Montreal and Kingston, McGill-Queen's University Press, 2003), 239-76.
49 SJHA, Dossier 25-B, Services auxiliaires-Service des bénévoles, 1962-68, Fernande Robitaille, "Thérapie par le jeu" (paper presented at the "journées d'études de pédiatrie," organized by the Association des Infirmières de la Province de Québec, 30 May 1963), 3. (This paper was also published in the *Bulletin des infirmières catholiques du Canada*, March-April 1964, 65-72.)
50 Ibid., 4 (emphasis in original).
51 Ibid., 5.
52 SJHA, Dossier 164 Service du milieu thérapeutique 1958 à 1972, Minutes of the "Comité de thérapie de Jeux," 7 May 1965, n.p.
53 Ibid., 5 April 1966, n.p.
54 Ibid.
55 SJHA, Dossier 25-B, Bénévoles, 1958-72, Letter of Fernande Robitaille to Gaspard Massue, 14 July 1967.
56 Sainte-Justine's new visiting-hours policy was probably influenced by the work of the British psychiatrist and psychoanalyst John Bowlby, whose work, published in the 1940s, insisted on the importance of the attachment of the child to the mother. The documentary film he made in 1952 with James Robertson, *A Two-Year-Old Goes to the Hospital,* portraying the reaction of a toddler after his admission to the hospital, was instrumental in convincing many children's hospitals to allow parents to visit their offspring more regularly and for longer periods of time. On the work of Bowlby, see J. Holmes, *John Bowlby and Attachment Theory: Makers of Modern Psychotherapy* (London and New York: Routledge, 1993).
57 It is highly possible that pediatricians and psychiatrists did not agree on this question, the former being more reticent to let their patients play because they feared physical harm, and thus insisted on giving medical prescriptions, the latter more inclined to favour participation that would justify their own expertise.

7

"Lost Voices, Lost Bodies"? Doctors and the Embodiment of Children and Youth in English Canada from 1900 to the 1940s

Mona Gleason

In 1915, a story entitled "The Little Brother" appeared in *The Canadian Nurse,* the premier journal of nursing practice in English Canada until well into the 1980s. Dramatizations of nursing care were a regular feature of the journal. The story of "The Little Brother," penned by Vancouver writer Rene Norcross, revolved around the hospitalization of Mah Too, a fourteen-year-old Chinese boy who had arrived in Vancouver a month before. Very early in the short tale, the author makes it clear that the presence of Chinese patients in Vancouver hospitals at the beginning of the twentieth century was not unusual. "Indeed," the narrator suggests, "there was some inclination to regard them as unavoidable nuisances to be dealt with as kindly and patiently as possible."[1] But Mah Too was young and vulnerable and singled out for his "astonishing prettiness." Eventually, Mah Too's condition deteriorated and the young boy requested that he be allowed to return to Vancouver's Chinatown with his brother, Mah Soon. The doctor's response to this request foreshadowed the boy's fate: "Confound it, that means cutting in half what little time he has left ... He'll be put into a six by eight hovel with an atmosphere you could cut with a knife and fork and a jabber like a sawmill going on day and night."[2] The hospital surgeon listening nearby offered a sage response: "Perhaps that's what he misses." Mah Too's request was granted and within a week of returning home, he was dead. The story ends here.

The treatment of Mah Too in "The Little Brother" mirrors many of the complexities and contradictions that accompanied medical encounters between adult experts and young people in English Canada over the course of the twentieth century. Although the explicit message delivered in the story revolved around the tragedy of Mah Too, the implicit subtext suggested a lesson steeped in the racial politics of the day: it reminded readers of the superiority of white Western conceptions of health and well-being. Mah Too's death had little to do with the youngster's bleak health prognosis and much to do with his inability to adapt to the expectations of the dominant culture. Racial inferiority, as surely as pneumonia or tuberculosis, contributed to his demise. From the perspective of the white medical establishment, Mah Too's shortcomings set in motion a tragic journey into darkness, dirt, and death.

If we try to imagine Mah Too's motivations for leaving the hospital with his brother, for these are never made explicit in the story itself, very different kinds of interpretations emerge. Family and home, for example, often occupied a central place for young people of all backgrounds faced with professionalized institutional care. The prospect of facing a serious illness in an unfamiliar setting in which his presence was merely tolerated undoubtedly terrified Mah Too and perhaps made his illness seem unbearable. However circumscribed and modest, the boy's decision to leave the hospital and return to his home in Chinatown marked a kind of "knee high agency" or at least a yearning for cultural safety in the midst of the hegemonic demands, advice, and beliefs, however well intentioned, of white adult experts.[3]

Mindful of the interpretive power represented by the perspectives of young people as historical actors in their own right, this chapter brings into conversation two sources from roughly the first half of the twentieth century: the published writings of doctors, nurses, and educators on the medical treatment of children's bodies, and the oral histories of adults who grew up in English Canada over roughly the same period. I explore how adult experts understood the bodies of children and how adults remember their bodies in childhood, particularly the medical care of their bodies at the hands of adult professionals. I argue that the embodied management of children, particularly marginalized children, and their varied responses to this management, forged, sustained, and challenged hierarchies and social divisions based on class, race, and gender. This management and responses to it on the part of youngsters and their families deepens our understanding of the role of age in the production and contestation of unequal relations of power in the modern nation state.

Adult memories are gleamed from a set of eleven oral history interviews conducted between 2001 and 2004 in which aspects of learning to be healthy, going to a doctor or traditional healer, or familial folk medicine were queried.[4] Historians are well aware of the problems and limitations associated with oral histories. They counsel caution in using memories that can be unreliable and fallible, and that tend to reconstruct rather than recollect a life. Paul Thompson, in particular, warns us about the need to recognize the inevitable concerns of the present embedded in stories about the past.[5] In the absence of a rich reserve of sources that try to reflect, however imperfectly, the perspective of young people on their experiences, however, oral histories remain a valuable source. Despite the dangers inherent in the politics of representation, they nonetheless have the potential to give voice to the traditionally voiceless – to children generally, to girls, to First Nations peoples, and to working-class girls and boys. Historians must use them carefully, with healthy skepticism and in conjunction with other kinds of data. All historical sources, after all, have their own unique flaws.

As quintessential "lost children," youngsters outside the boundaries of white middle-class acceptability also remain largely on the margins of English-Canadian historiography. Much of the foundational scholarship on the history of English-Canadian children's health and welfare over the early decades of the twentieth century has focused on the broad contours of statistical improvements in infant mortality rates and rates of contagious disease infection that occurred over the first four decades of the twentieth century in Canada.[6] Subsequent studies detailed the work of medical professionals, legal and urban reformers, and state-sanctioned social welfare departments and networks in their quest to use modern scientific understandings of health and welfare to shape policy, education, and parenting behaviour.[7] As the state became increasingly dependent on the health of its citizens, improvements in sanitation and public health took aim at families and children judged inadequate. From the point of view of a growing cadre of health and social welfare professionals, bringing families up to socially acceptable standards of domestic life, health, education, and employment ensured a strong national citizenry. As Cynthia Comacchio has argued, however, even though experts believed that "nations were built of babies," the needs and preferences of families, or even their best interests, did not always result from health and welfare interventions.[8]

A number of scholars have laid bare the erroneous notion that all children and youth benefited equally from improvements in medical science and life expectancy in the twentieth century. Mary Ellen Kelm, Tina Moffat, and Ann Herring, for example, have shown how the effects of colonization, settlement, and racism resulted in high rates of infant death in First Nations communities over a period otherwise characterized by the triumph of medical science.[9] In the case of adopted children, Veronica Strong-Boag's recent work in the English Canadian context reminds us that social premiums placed on "perfect, healthy children" stigmatized those outside this ideal as much as it was a goal for all Canadian youngsters regardless of life circumstances.[10] Attuned to the difference that class, religion, gender, and other markers of social identity made, Tamara Myers has documented how increasing medical authority in the juvenile courts in twentieth-century Montreal often made "modern girls" into "delinquent bodies."[11]

As embodied subjects rather than merely objects in this long history of health and welfare intervention, the perspectives of children and youth remain conspicuously absent from sustained historical analysis in the English-Canadian context.[12] In a recent international collection of essays dedicated to historical perspectives on children's health, the editors lament that "young voices and opinions remain for the most part missing ... we very much wished for their inclusion and we deeply regret their ultimate omission."[13] The responses of racialized, working-class, and disabled children suffer particularly from under-representation in historical analysis. Their perspectives on their experiences with health professionals, with illness and recovery, and with their bodies add a complicating layer to historical portraits of the period that offer an uncomplicated narrative of the triumph of medical science over high rates of infant and child mortality. This chapter attempts to find the lost voices and bodies of young people, particularly those youngsters from minority and working-class backgrounds who typically appear in historical narratives as objects of medicalization. By repositioning young people as subjects in this narrative, they emerge as social actors in the production, reproduction, and, in some places, interruption of dominant social relations.

Doctors, Nurses, and the Problem of Small Bodies

Early in the twentieth century, social reformers, in large part white and middle class, worked to reconstitute childhood as a time deserving of special protection. As Veronica Strong-Boag, Neil Sutherland, Robert McIntosh, and others have summarized, ideal childhoods, and consequently ideal children, came to be characterized by vulnerability, dependence, protection, segregation, and delayed responsibility.[14] This "needs" orientation could have unintended consequences; it could be malevolent as well as benevolent and was often characterized by an ambivalence about *which* children deserved attention and *what* form that attention should take. The emerging urban and capitalist social order that unfolded over the course of the twentieth century in English Canada developed in a context of eugenics, potent ideas about white racial supremacy, solidifying class hierarchies, gendered and able-bodied biases, and the dominance of Protestant Christianity as the only true religion. This context had enormous consequences for the increasingly professionalized and public management of children's health and welfare. For their part, youngsters were vitally important to the production and maintenance of hierarchical social relations.

Historians in English Canada, following very much along the lines of explanation offered in other national contexts, suggest that specialized interest in the health and welfare of youngsters was nurtured through the convergence of public health reform and concern about high rates of infant mortality in the early years of the twentieth century.[15] As Neil Sutherland has shown, at the turn of the century, approximately one out of every five to seven babies born died in the first year or two of life. This was a state of affairs largely accepted as tragic but not yet a matter of public concern. "What actually prevailed," Sutherland explains, "was a vague but generally unstated sense of inevitability and resignation."[16] In 1916, prominent Toronto physician Dr. Alan Brown would note "how frequently one hears the assertion that delicate infants should not live ... in fact, some go so far as to state that it interferes with the law of natural selection which is the survival of the fittest."[17]

By the end of the First World War, however, this resignation faced challenge for a complex range of reasons: increased understanding of the need for public health reform, concerted medical effort on the part of dedicated medical professionals to confront and eradicate infant and maternal mortality, and lingering eugenic fears of race suicide. The death toll exacted by the First World War, along with the arrival of large numbers of new immigrants, fostered homegrown anxieties about the health of the white population. Eugenics, the "cultural policing of the country's 'genetic stock,'" lent its support to numerous welfare initiatives to ensure that middle-class standards of health were either adhered to or, at the very least, represented the ultimate goal for families in English Canada.[18] Thus, infant and maternal welfare movements, dominated by white, Protestant, middle-class reformers and professionals, struggled to reduce the abysmal infant mortality rate in the early decades of the twentieth century.[19]

Doctors were central to this growing attention to the health of the nation's babies. With increasing momentum behind pediatrics as a recognized medical specialization over the turn of the nineteenth century, professional medical writing in the form of textbooks and journal articles focused specifically on the needs of young patients. Conditions of the body "peculiar to, chiefly found during, infancy and childhood," as one textbook writer characterized them, were increasingly understood as warranting separate attention.[20]

Textbooks on pediatrics used in Canadian medical schools, such as Kenneth Fenwick's 1889 *Manual of Obstetrics, Gynaecology, and Paediatrics,* clearly show that notions of normalcy and health were not characteristics readily associated with small bodies. Given the high infant mortality rate with which doctors had to contend, anxiety surrounding the preservation of life in the early years was understandable. Notwithstanding this concern, the intensity of assumptions about children's embodied volatility in the writings of medical professionals is striking: children's feeding is highly problematic, they suffer from "nervous complaints" that come on without warning, they are unreliable sources of information about their own health and are not to be trusted by doctors, and they need to be closely monitored for any number of conditions.[21] Fenwick, for example, conveyed the impression that children – based on assumptions about their small, young bodies – were principally medical problems: "In childhood the tissues are softer, more vascular, and more succulent; the glandular, lymphatic and capillary systems are extremely active; the skin and mucous membranes are softer; more delicate and more sensitive; the brain is large, vascular, and almost fluid in consistency; there is excessive nervous excitability due to want of controlling power; and reflex sensibility is excessively acute."[22] Fenwick was certainly not alone in this presentation of young bodies, particularly infant bodies, as inherently pathological. "One should point out," remarked Dr. George Smith, "and emphasize the frailty of the material one is working with. Anatomically the infant lends itself to infection. The organs are small and almost fragile. The distance from the nose to the lung is very short. The physiological and mechanical resistance to oncoming infection is slight."[23] In *Diseases of Child-hood* (1926), Hector Charles Cameron warned, "at the moment of birth there is risk both of trauma and infection."[24] Young children, Cameron states, are born vulnerable to a triad of complications that vex the doctor and parent alike throughout childhood: this triad consists of dietetic disturbances, infections, and severe emotional unrest.[25] "The metabolism of all children, just because they are children," advised Cameron in the *Canadian Medical Association Journal* of 1931, "is less stable than that of later life."[26] Alan Brown, physician-in-chief at Toronto's Hospital for Sick Children, and Frederick Tisdall, his colleague there, advised doctors in *Common Procedures in the Practice of Paediatrics* that "the physical examination of infants and children presents many problems quite distinct from those encountered in the examination of adults."[27] Young patients, they advised, needed thorough inspection from head to toe. Judging the child's cry – its intensity and tenor – was a valuable tool for the diagnosing doctor. Further, "Much information can be obtained by observing the child while the mother is being questioned. If the patient is crying vigorously or taking an interest in its surroundings you know at once that it is not acutely ill. In regard to the character of the cry, with a little practice it is possible to determine whether it is due to the patient being hungry or in pain or whether it is merely the result of fright or temper."[28]

Doctors, it would seem, were right to be very cautious around young, small bodies. Not only were children vulnerable to any number of physical threats, they did not give up their secrets easily. As Fenwick reminded his readers, the diagnosis of medical problems was hard enough in adults, never mind the additional complications that infants and children presented for practitioners: "The task is one which requires patience, good nature, and tact for the helpless silence of the infant, the incorrect answers of the older child, the fright, agitation, or anger produced by your examination, or even mere presence, render it difficult to detect the real aberration of function."[29]

Challenges to the provision of good health posed by small bodies were mitigated by middle-class affluence, according to the advice of doctors. In professional conceptions of good health, minimal standards of housing and cleanliness were solidly middle class. Consider the advice of Dr. A. Grant Fleming, offered in 1929, and typical of the era and beyond: "Individual health depends essentially upon the individual's practice of what we call 'personal hygiene.' Even in our age of organization, we expect that we must consider our bath, our bed-time, and our open bed room window as personal responsibilities. Modern inventions have given us conveniences that greatly assist and make reasonably easy the practice of personal hygiene."[30] Running water, separate bedrooms with windows, new household gadgets, choices about sleep – for all the veneer of scientific objectivity, good health and personal hygiene were thoroughly steeped in middle-class habitus.

That the working class, and in particular the racialized working class, did not participate in such middle-class habitus made them particularly "unhealthy." Professional practitioners tended to conceptualize these "other bodies" as in need not simply of good advice but of significant health salvation and reformation. The story of Mah Too is a stark testimony to the racialization of health status and its recuperation by middle-class white health professionals in early-twentieth-century Canada. Another example is offered in a feature story entitled "In the Children's Ward," written by B.E.A. Philmot for *The Canadian Nurse*'s April 1909 edition. In her account of the various children and families encountered on the ward, intertwined issues of ethnicity and class come to the forefront. Readers learn of the fate of Dennis, a three-year-old boy of working-class Irish descent, early in her observations. According to the nurse, "We undressed him by main force and put him in the tub. He evidently, to judge by his struggles, thought we were going to drown him. Probably he had never seen so much water collected in one place before. Also he dreaded to part with that outer covering of dirt; it had been his own for so long it was well-nigh impossible to take it from him."[31] Although Dennis eventually "learns" to be a proper patient, he cannot simply wash away his ethnic and class identity. Drawing on entrenched stereotypes of Irish-Canadians, the author notes that the boy will likely become "a prizefighter one day for he had just the figure for it!"[32]

Racialized assumptions about the inferiority of Aboriginal peoples on the part of some professional medical practitioners over the course of the century had a direct impact on the care and treatment they received, or did not receive. That Aboriginal children made seemingly ideal specimens for health exhibition and experimentation, particularly during the second half of the twentieth century, was belied by fact that they often suffered for want of medical attention. "There was no doctor at the Indian villages of Klemtu and Kitamaat, and these places were not receiving much in the way of medical attention," reported Florence Moffatt, a nurse at the R.W. Large Memorial Hospital on Campbell Island, in British Columbia, in the 1940s. When Moffatt visited these neglected villages, she struggled, often unsuccessfully, to help keep her patients alive: "I treated more than forty people with penicillin and mild sedatives. One young girl had a severe ear infection following a mastoid operation. I had taken her to the hospital, but the infection had been too severe and too longstanding, and she died shortly afterward."[33]

When medical attention was forthcoming, it could run the risk of reifying racist stereotypes of Aboriginal people at best, and seriously compromising their health status at worst. In the late 1940s, for example, an "Indian Baby

Show," initiated by the Indian Affairs health nurse responsible for overseeing the Coast Salish peoples of British Columbia, sought to respond to the "commonly held white belief that Indian parents neglect their children and that Indian children in particular suffer from poor nutrition, inadequate clothing, and poor hygiene." The resulting baby show displayed several classes of baby contestants, "set up and judged by a doctor and nurse as to which child was the healthiest."[34] Writing about her nursing experiences in the Arctic during the 1930s and 1940s, Margery Hind reported on a study of the "effects of white man's food upon Eskimo children" undertaken by the Toronto-based white nurse stationed there. Each morning, the children "received a bowl of porridge, half a pint of rich milk, a pilot biscuit, a vitamin pill and a spoonful of cod liver oil ... these children are weighed regularly, and a special note is made of their ailments."[35] In a large study of the nutritional status of the First Nations of James Bay published in the prestigious *Canadian Medical Association Journal* in 1948, the authors suggested that "many characteristics, such as shiftlessness, indolence, improvidence, and inertia, so long regarded as inherent or hereditary traits in the Indian race, may at the root be really the manifestation of malnutrition. This is of concern not only to the Indian but to the white population, as any attempt to eradicate tuberculosis in Canada must include the institution of preventative measures for everyone. In addition, from the economic standpoint a group of people in poor health tends to be a liability rather than an asset to the nation."[36]

Such evidence of the "scientific" study of Aboriginal children's health appeared to unfold in tandem with their virtual neglect by professional medical practitioners in other contexts, such as the residential schools.[37] While "science" aided in the discovery of new explanations for Aboriginal peoples' seemingly "natural" characteristics, it did nothing to challenge the racist assumptions that undergirded such thinking.

Small Bodies in Schools

While doctors approached small bodies as problems to be solved, educators in the same period approached the body and health as pedagogical imperatives. More so than professional medical practitioners, educators in schools were uniquely placed to impart specific lessons about good health to children. Compulsory schooling, as historians have documented, represented an unprecedented opportunity to educate children about "proper" standards of morality, industry, cleanliness, and bodily care.[38] State-supported public schooling became a powerful site for the inculcation of citizenship and something of a health laboratory for the treatment and prevention of illness in children. The provision of public schooling for children spread across the country just before the period under study, starting with Ontario by the mid-nineteenth century, Manitoba and New Brunswick in 1871, British Columbia in 1872, Newfoundland and Nova Scotia in 1874, the North-West

Territories in 1901, and Alberta and Saskatchewan in 1905. In Quebec, legislation in 1868 created the Ministry of Public Instruction, which was abolished in 1875. Coexisting with this was the Council of Public Instruction, created in 1856 and divided into two separate denominational committees (Catholic and Protestant), which included both clergy and laypeople.[39]

At the turn of the nineteenth century, the notion of science contained in discussions of germ theory, eugenics, and sanitation in health texts authorized in English-Canadian curricula reflected a dominant social order steeped in Christian moral values and an acceptance of personal responsibility for poor health. Ideas about the primacy of heredity intimated that particular children – those associated with undesirable social characteristics – had to be more vigilant in their personal health habits than those considered more fortunate. Whether through ignorance, wickedness, or wilful disobedience, then, poor health was presented as at least partly a matter of choice. As Dr. A.P. Knight, professor of physiology at Queen's University in Kingston, Ontario, and author of *The Ontario Public School Hygiene* (1910) wrote, "If you have followed the teachings of this book thus far, it must be clear to you now that our lives from birth until old age are shaped largely by two great influences: (1) by what we inherit from our parents, grandparents, or other ancestral relatives, and (2) by our environment, that is, by our surroundings."[40]

Health curriculum was offered as an antidote to ignorance and to unhealthy practices and was presented as a moral and religious duty. Adherence to traditional gender roles was a key avenue to the observance of healthful morality. In *The Essentials of Health: A Text-book on Anatomy, Physiology, and Hygiene* (1909), for example, children learned that

> what every boy and girl should aim to do is put his body under the control of his mind in matters relating to his own health. That is to say, he should so apply his understanding of the uses of the various organs of the human body and the effects of this or that treatment upon them, so that he is able for the most part to avoid those things which will be harmful to his health and cultivate those things which will help to upbuild his physical and mental manhood ... Control of our own bodies, then, based upon a proper understanding of them, is the first step toward the attaining of true manhood or womanhood.[41]

Girls and boys were encouraged to understand abstinence from alcohol, tobacco, and self-abuse as part and parcel of their healthful journey to appropriately gendered adulthood.[42] Girls would be expected to parlay healthful habits into motherhood and marriage, while boys would prepare for public roles of leadership and governance.[43]

In *How to Be Healthy,* a 1911 textbook co-written by Manitoban doctor J. Halpenny and approved for use in elementary and middle schools in British Columbia, Alberta, Saskatchewan, Manitoba, Quebec, Nova Scotia, and Prince Edward Island, good health and vigour were unmistakably moral virtues reserved for those who chose to live "a sensible, normal life." By extension, those who struggled with poor health were cast with the pall of immorality, bad choices, and weak wills. Students were instructed, "when real difficulties come to us, let us meet them manfully, and win or lose, but never hold onto them or brood over them. This is the cause of much ill-health. Our right to be happy must not be interfered with by anything ... Once we begin to brood, our power to do difficult things and our course to face the trouble begins to fail. Thus we weaken ourselves." Failure to meet "real difficulties," particularly on the part of working-class whites, was interpreted as a matter of alterable ignorance.[44] In a paper presented at the Canadian Nurses Association meeting in Toronto in 1918, Dr. W.W. Chipman noted, for example, that unfortunate babies have to "fight from the very start ... Their mothers fought before them – fought in poverty, in ignorance and neglect – to give them birth; and so in poverty, ignorance and neglect the child's life begins."[45]

Scholars have argued that school textbooks, including those used in furthering lessons in health, reflect a great deal about whose knowledge counted as meaningful in the past.[46] Like their medical school counterparts, public school textbooks promoted the ideological priorities of those powerful enough to drive the social agenda.[47] To intervene in the care and treatment of children's bodies – either in the doctor's office or in the classroom – was to inculcate, however imperfectly, moral values judged acceptable.

Bodies and Memory

From the perspective of professionals with the power and inclination to intervene in family life, the modernizing twentieth century rendered children vulnerable to death, disease, and malnutrition, and thus they needed saving, healing, and training. Even though domestic efforts to treat illness and cultivate healthfulness were routinely discouraged by professional medical practitioners, family members and neighbours typically responded first to the health needs of youngsters. In many cases, mothers were often the only source of medical treatment many children had, particularly in isolated or rural parts of the country. Although they occasionally found themselves at odds, both family members, particularly mothers, and professional medical practitioners understood the health needs of children as under their direct purview.

Interviews with adults who grew up in English Canada during the twentieth century deepen, complement, and complicate seemingly straightforward and uncontested constructions of white, middle-class hegemony. Conditions of poverty, for example, could easily compromise straightforward assumptions about healthy living. Such was the experience of a ninety-three-year-old white male interviewee, born in Montreal in 1913 and raised among twelve siblings. He recalled conditions of poverty in a busy urban centre that made acceptable standards of hygiene and freedom from contagion a luxury rather than the norm. "Let's say that you go to the grocery," he remembered when asked about family routines surrounding hygiene, "you buy some rice, you buy some beans, you have to go through everything to remove the – not rats – the mice, all the manure of the mice, you had to clean all that, you have to remove it before you cook it ... Because in the grocery they would have everything in bowls, you know, and so you had all of those visitors."[48] Even the provision of middle-class assistance was often far from the ideal touted by professionals and reformers. A white interviewee recalled receiving city welfare in the form of food aid when her family moved to Toronto in the depths of the Depression. "They sent you a box of food," she recalled, "with what they considered staples, and that had to do you for the week ... you did get milk and you did get bread. And the box of food contained probably flour, and sugar, tea, probably some carrots or cabbage. And then once a week they would give you a package of meat, maybe a roast ... so we were never hungry but we certainly weren't ... I suppose in retrospect it wasn't too bad a diet except for the lack of fresh fruit and fresh vegetables."[49]

While medical professionals and textbook authors warned about the dangers of folk or home remedies, patent medicines, and general "quackery," many interviewees remembered their use in their homes. At school, health curriculum disparaged homespun medicine. In *Health Essentials for Canadian Schools,* for example, authors J. Mace Andress and Elizabeth Breeze warned students that "promises, like many others made by patent-medicine manufacturers[,] are deceptive, and the drugs they sell may be dangerous to health. It is always best to rely on the advice of a reliable physician."[50] Despite professionals' distaste for "domestic doctoring," it was a memorable part of growing up for many children. If Jean Tierney, born in 1906 in Gladstone, Manitoba, had a tummy ache, her mother would tell her to put some salt in her hand and "lick it a little bit at a time ... and that really worked."[51] Born in 1910 in Nova Scotia, another informant remembered wearing a camphor bag around her neck during the Spanish influenza outbreak of 1918. "After that [outbreak of 1918]," she concluded, "every winter almost we wore that little bag of camphor around our necks and we were healthy, we never had colds or anything."[52] In 1915, Dorothea Ingram, born in Vancouver, contracted diphtheria. She was five years old, and she remembered the health officials putting a big red card on the door of her house with the word "Diphtheria" printed on it. In a conversation over the backyard fence, the family's neighbour persuaded Dorothea's mother to allow her to try a home remedy on the child. Clearly breaking the quarantine order, the neighbour paid Dorothea a visit. "She came over and she had a big white feather – a chicken feather like, and a bottle of brandy. And she came over and painted all my tonsils and the inside of my mouth with it. And my mother said it just brought new life to me."[53]

Although the feather and brandy might have made Dorothea's experience unique, that her illness was treated at home by her mother and a neighbour was certainly not. For many adults who grew up in Canada during the twentieth century, mothers and other family members are vividly remembered as providing primary care for their sick and injured bodies during their childhoods. Visits to doctors, and occasionally to hospitals, are also remembered, but they stand out as unusual events, undertaken only when efforts at home proved inadequate or an injury was serious enough to warrant such drastic measures.[54]

Into the 1920s and well beyond, families continued to concoct their own folk remedies to check the spread of diseases. An informant born in the mid-1920s in Toronto remembered vividly her father's painting the outside of her and her siblings' necks with iodine to prevent sore throats. "Now that was a strange one," she recalled, "and, of course, you hated that because you went back to school with this great big brown throat from the iodine."[55] She also remembered that if any of the children had whooping cough, her father would seek out a newly paved road. "Somebody told my father that if we breathed in the tar it would stop the cough, so I remember him trekking us all out there and we had to stand there and breathe in this tar ... and I don't know if it helped or not!"[56] A male interviewee, born just after the Second World War, grew up in Peterborough, Ontario, with his father and grandparents. His grandparents, according to him, "had some strange ideas about home medicine ... [My grandmother] would take a teaspoon of raw ginger powder mixed with sugar and we'd have to eat that before we walked to school ... we'd be spitting half the way!"[57] Another interviewee, born in the late 1940s on the Sugar Cane Reserve in Williams Lake, British Columbia, understood the preparation of medicine as informed by Secwepemc traditions. He recalled that his mother would often prepare remedies when someone got sick: "I think most of the remedies, my mom made them. And some of them were from different plants that she would gather ... Or, she would buy certain things and make things ... there was a hot kinda tonic that she made – I think it had ginger and honey and some other stuff in it."[58] These familial health strategies complicated the admonishments of doctors and official school health curriculum that privileged "science" over "superstition." Despite, or perhaps because of, the centrality of folk health remedies in many adults' childhood, textbooks took great pains to challenge such practices: "Great and unnecessary waste of life, health and vigour has resulted, and still results, from a neglect of scientific principles in regard to common things."[59]

For some children, the space between what health professionals held up as acceptable standards of healthful living and the actual conditions of life produced deeply unequal social relations. The child's experienced body and the adult's idealized body could be far apart indeed. A Métis woman who grew up in Saskatchewan in the 1930s recalled: "The teacher tried to teach us about daily hygiene like brushing your teeth after breakfast and I don't think any of the kids in my school owned a toothbrush – I know I didn't until I was twelve years old ... The teacher's idea of a good lunch was a sandwich, a couple of cookies or a cake, and an orange or an apple which most of us only saw once a year at Christmas time."[60]

First Nations children, in particular, could experience the imposition of white middle-class notions of cleanliness in especially malevolent ways. Growing up on a reserve in Deseronto, Ontario, in the 1930s, a female First Nations interviewee placed the body at the centre of colonial relations. It was on the body that this relationship was made sensible to her and her Aboriginal classmates. She recalled:

> I went to this school and there was this [Aboriginal] boy in the school who was very, very dirty. And you know, I thought [this] the most humiliating thing when I got older – the teacher couldn't stand it so she got a tub of water and we would all take turns washing him – his back and his hair ... Isn't that awful? Oh, he didn't have his clothes off. He had his underwear on, but, kind of ridiculous ... And, ah, I used to think as I got older that that was a really awful thing to do to him – so embarrassing.[61]

The white teacher enforced standards of cleanliness and, in the process, reinforced prejudices about the First Nations peoples as naturally disinclined to keep clean. Our interviewee made no distinction between learning about oppressive colonial relations and learning about the importance of "keeping clean." In her memory, the two were inextricably linked.

Within some families, the experience of illness could mark a time of mediated pleasure for youngsters. Depending on a wide array of factors, adult assumptions about children's vulnerability and incompetence could have positive effects. For one informant, it meant a welcome reprise in an otherwise hard existence. Introduced earlier, our ninety-three-year-old male interviewee from Montreal remembered his time in a quarantine hospital with scarlet fever as a break in an endless cycle of work and poverty. When asked to tell us what he remembered feeling about the experiences, he said, somewhat sheepishly, "You know, it was the best time of your life! You could have good meals ... the nuns were looking after that ... I was there for about forty days ... Yeah, when I was fourteen years old it was easy to make friends, you know."[62]

Being sick occasionally challenged standard hierarchical relationships between adults and children and introduced quite different dimensions into them. Growing up in Winnipeg in the 1920s, Anna Friesen remembered: "Softly Mother's hand felt my fevered cheeks, then rested lightly on my forehead. Then she pulled up my blanket and tucked it gently around me. After pausing motionless beside me awhile, she tiptoed away. I felt as if an angel had visited me, and my illness seemed inconsequential."[63] A female interviewee growing up in Vancouver some thirty years later had a similar tale to tell: "I do recall the times of illness as actually special times when I received my mother's sole attention ... as the last of five kids, I savoured the feeling of closeness it brought ... she (my mother) was always kind and patient when I was ill, and I will never forget the feeling of her small cool hand on my fevered brow!"[64] Ruth Cook, a Tsimthian woman born in 1931 near Prince Rupert, attended residential school and remembered that the experience of illness depended very much on context. At home, she recalled, "You never had to worry if you got sick ... you always had an uncle or an aunt, or the grandparents were there to lend a helping hand."[65] Such memories suggest that, from the point of view of some children in particular circumstances, times of illness were not simply times of unmitigated grief. They could be far more complex, reflecting the centrality of family culture and of sentimentality in influencing children's experiences with health and illness.

Conclusion

From the point of view of those with considerable social power and responsibility, such as doctors, nurses, and teachers, children's bodies over the first half of the twentieth century were conceptualized as vulnerable and susceptible to serious medical problems. To intervene in the care and treatment of children's bodies – either in the doctor's office or in the classroom – was to inculcate not only good health but also acceptable moral values. Through the body, medical practitioners and educators attempted to legitimize and reproduce traditional hierarchies of power. When the discourse of professionals is positioned alongside the memories of adults, the fissures between them are imbued with additional meanings. On and through children's bodies, social acceptability, civilizing and colonizing techniques, interests of the state, and so-called "good health" were written, operationalized, and vied for space. The lived memories of adults who grew up in different communities in English Canada suggest that the family's primacy in the embodied care of children was often downplayed or disparaged even as it was employed for social reproduction.

The central thrust of this chapter is to go beyond our understanding of children merely as objects of health and welfare interventions – of adult interventions – and to query how children's own embodied subjectivity – their voices and their bodies – gives us a deeper understanding of their role in the social production and reproduction of inequality over the first half of the twentieth century. The remembered body, made and remade in adult memories of growing up, "talks back" to objectifying processes, on the part of both twentieth-century health and welfare experts and historians who overlooked or ignored these voices. They show how adults inculcated social inequity through seemingly uncomplicated and positive processes – like health and welfare – and how young people responded to them.

The process of designating particular bodies as healthier, stronger, and more acceptable than others enshrined inequality deep in the flesh, and it began with the very young. Throughout the entrenchment of conventional medicine and the rise of the health professional over the course of the twentieth century, techniques to promote healthy normative bodies, constructed through adult assumptions, can be readily discerned. Through critical engagements with adult memories of childhood, however, we are privy to a more finely tuned accounting of how these unequal relations of power were woven – sometimes seamlessly but also often with great tension – into the process of growing up.

Acknowledgment
I wish to acknowledge the critical comments of members of the Lost Children workshop and the anonymous manuscript reviewers who helped vastly improve this chapter, and the research assistance provided by Natalie Chambers and Lori MacFadyen.

Notes

1 Rene Norcross, "The Little Brother," *Canadian Nurse* 2 (1915): 436-38.
2 It was likely not lost on readers that the young brothers' names together suggested that Mah Too died "Too Soon." Norcross, "The Little Brother," 437.
3 In the workshop version of this chapter, Molly Ladd-Taylor encouraged me to explore more fully Mah Too's "rejection of the hospital cure" and to focus on what this signified about Mah Too's agency. I am grateful for her suggestion.
4 In total, sixty-two oral history interviews were conducted by me and two graduate students, Lori MacFadyen and Natalie Chambers, between 2001 and 2004; eleven of these interviews are used in this chapter. Interviewees were selected primarily through word of mouth and some limited advertising in retirement homes in Vancouver; Penticton, British Columbia; and Montreal. We relied primarily on a snowball effect in which those interviewed told friends and family who in turn contacted us. The interview was intentionally open-ended and asked participants for their childhood recollections of anything to do with health, health care, learning to be healthy, illness, and medical treatment. We asked only that participants be raised in Canada and born before 1960. Interviews were conducted in places suggested by interviewees. Most took place in interviewees' homes or local coffee shops. The vast majority were conducted in person with a handful conducted by telephone. References below to these interviews are cited as "Child Health Interview."
5 See, for example, Neil Sutherland, "When You Listen to the Winds of Childhood, How Much Can You Believe?" *Curriculum Inquiry* 22, 3 (1992): 235-326, and Paul Thompson, "Believe It or Not: Rethinking the Historical Interpretation of Memory," in Jaclyn Jeffrey

and Glenace Edwall, eds., *Memory and History: Essays on Recalling and Interpreting Experience* (Lanham, MD: University Press of America, 1994), 6-7.

6 Neil Sutherland, *Children in English-Canadian Society: Framing the Twentieth Century Consensus* (Toronto: University of Toronto Press, 1976; Waterloo, ON: Wilfrid Laurier University Press, 2000). All subsequent citations are to the 1976 edition.

7 The most pertinent examples are Angus McLaren and Arlene Tigar McLaren, *The Bedroom and the State: The Changing Practices and Politics of Contraception and Abortion in Canada, 1880-1980* (Toronto: McClelland and Stewart, 1986); Angus McLaren, *Our Own Master Race: Eugenics in Canada 1885-1945* (Toronto: McClelland and Stewart, 1990); Jane Ursel, *Private Lives, Public Policy: 100 Years of State Intervention in the Family* (Toronto: Women's Press, 1992); Katherine Arnup, *Education for Motherhood: Advice for Mothers in Twentieth-Century English Canada* (Toronto: University of Toronto Press, 1994); Carolyn Strange and Tina Loo, *Making Good: Law and Moral Regulation in Canada, 1867-1939* (Toronto: University of Toronto Press, 1997); and John McLaren, Robert Menzies, and Dorothy E. Chunn, *Regulating Lives: Historical Essays on the State, Society, the Individual and the Law* (Vancouver: UBC Press, 2002).

8 Cynthia Comacchio, *Nations Are Built of Babies: Saving Ontario's Mothers and Children, 1900-1940* (Montreal and Kingston: McGill-Queen's University Press, 1993).

9 Mary Ellen Kelm, *Colonizing Bodies: Aboriginal Health and Healing in British Columbia* (Vancouver: UBC Press, 1998); Tina Moffat and Ann Herring, "The Historical Roots of High Rates of Infant Deaths in Aboriginal Communities in Canada in the Early Twentieth Century: The Case of Fisher River Manitoba," *Social Science and Medicine* 48 (1999): 1821-32.

10 Veronica Strong-Boag, *Finding Families, Finding Ourselves: English Canada Encounters Adoption from the Nineteenth Century to the 1990s* (Toronto: Oxford University Press, 2006).

11 Tamara Myers, *Caught: Montreal's Modern Girls and the Law, 1869-1945* (Toronto: University of Toronto Press, 2006).

12 Roger Cooter, "In the Name of the Child Beyond," in Marijke Gijswijt-Hofstra and Hilary Marland, eds., *Cultures of Child Health in Britain and the Netherlands in the Twentieth Century* (Amsterdam and New York: Rodopi, 2003), 287-96. As Cooter suggests, what continues to elude historians is "a history of children's own experience of illness and medicine" (290-91).

13 See Cheryl Krasnick Warsh and Veronica Strong-Boag, "Introduction: Spotlight on Children," in Cheryl Krasnick Warsh and Veronica Strong-Boag, eds., *Children's Health Issues in Historical Perspective* (Waterloo, ON: Wilfrid Laurier University Press, 2005), 3.

14 See Patricia Rooke and R.L. Schnell, *Discarding the Asylum: From Child Rescue to the Welfare State in English Canada, 1800-1950* (Lanham, MD: University Press of America, 1983); Sutherland, *Children in English-Canadian Society;* Robert McIntosh, *Boys in the Pits: Child Labour in Coal Mines* (Kingston and Montreal: McGill-Queen's University Press, 2000); and Veronica Strong-Boag, "Getting to Now: Children in Distress in Canada's Past," in Brian Wharf, ed., *Community Work Approaches to Child Welfare* (Peterborough, ON: Broadview, 2002), 29-46.

15 Buford L. Nichols, Angel Ballabriga, and Norman Kretchmer, eds., *History of Pediatrics, 1850-1950* (New York: Raven Press, 1991); see particularly Buford L. Nichols Jr., "The European Roots of American Pediatrics," 49-54; Howard A. Pearson, "Pediatrics in the United States," 55-64; Silvestre Frenk and Ignacio Avila-Cisneros, "Mexican Pediatrics," 65-76. On the connections made between public health and pediatrics see, for example, Chapter 13, "No Baby, No Nation: A History of Pediatrics," in Jacalyn Duffin, *History of Medicine: A Scandalously Short Introduction* (Toronto: University of Toronto Press, 1999); Nichols, Ballabriga, and Kretchmer, *History of Pediatrics;* George Weisz, *Divide and Conquer: A Comparative History of Medical Specialization* (Toronto: Oxford University Press, 2006); and Russell Viner, "Abraham Jacobi and the Origins of Scientific Pediatrics in America," in Alexandra Minna Stern and Howard Markel, eds., *Formative Years: Children's Health in the United States, 1880-2000* (Ann Arbor: University of Michigan Press, 2002).

16 Sutherland, *Children in English-Canadian Society,* 57.

17 As quoted in Nora Moore, "Child Welfare Work," *Canadian Nurse* 12, 11 (1916): 634-35.

18 Sharon L. Snyder and David T. Mitchell, *Cultural Locations of Disability* (Chicago and London: University of Chicago Press, 2006), ix.

19 Sutherland, *Children in English-Canadian Society;* Comacchio, *Nations Are Built of Babies.*
20 Henry Ashby and G.A. Wright, *Diseases of Children, Medical and Surgical* (New York: Long-mans Green, 1897), Preface. This volume was available through "A.P. Watts and Company, Medical Publishers and Booksellers to College St., Toronto."
21 Joseph Race, "Milk Supply in Relation to Tuberculosis in Ontario," *Public Health Journal* 6 (1915): 378-83; Nora Moore, "Child Welfare Work," *Canadian Nurse* 12 (1916): 634-35; Reginald H. Wiggins, "The Management of Posture in Children," *Canadian Medical Association Journal* 27 (1932): 47-51; D.E.S. Wishart, "The Problem of the Deaf Child," *Canadian Medical Association Journal* 38 (1938): and 254-60; O.M. Moore, "Peptic Ulcers in Children," *Canadian Medical Association Journal* 44 (1941): 462-66.
22 Kenneth N. Fenwick, *Manual of Obstetrics, Gynaecology, and Paediatrics* (Kingston, ON: J. Henderson, 1889), 192.
23 George E. Smith, "The Prevention of Infection in Infancy," *Public Health Journal* 17, 8 (1926): 405-6.
24 Hector Charles Cameron, *Diseases of Childhood: A Short Introduction* (London: Oxford University Press, 1926), 6-7. This text was utilized by teaching staff at the University of British Columbia's Faculty of Medicine.
25 Cameron, *Diseases of Childhood,* 6-7.
26 Hector Charles Cameron, "Sleep and Its Disorders in Childhood," *Canadian Medical Association Journal* 24, 2 (1931): 239-44.
27 Alan Brown and Frederick F. Tisdall, *Common Procedures in the Practice of Paediatrics,* 4th ed. (Toronto: McClelland and Stewart, 1949), 7. The first edition of the work appeared in 1929. The fourth edition was revised with the arrival of sulpha drugs and to reflect "a better understanding of the fundamental principles of mineral metabolism" (Preface to 4th edition, n.p.).
28 Brown and Tisdall, *Common Procedures,* 7.
29 Fenwick, *Manual of Obstetrics, Gynaecology, and Pediatrics,* 193.
30 A. Grant Fleming, "The Value of Periodic Health Examinations," *Canadian Nurse* 25, 6 (1929): 284.
31 B.E.A. Philmot, "In the Children's Ward," *Canadian Nurse* 5 (1910): 176-77.
32 Ibid., 176.
33 Florence C. Moffatt "Forgotten Villages of the BC Coast: Hospital Life at Bella Bella," *Raincoast Chronicles* 11 (1987): 52.
34 John Dewhurst, "Coast Salish Summer Festivals: Rituals for Upgrading Social Identity," *Anthropologica* 28 (1976): 258.
35 Margery Hind, *School House in the Arctic* (London: Geoffrey Bles, 1958), 95.
36 R.P. Vivian, Charles McMillan, P.E. Moore, E. Chant Robertson, W.H. Sebrell, F.F. Tisdall, and W.G. McIntosh, "The Nutrition and Health of the James Bay Indian," *Canadian Medical Association Journal* 59, 6 (1948): 505.
37 See Kelm, *Colonizing Bodies.*
38 See Sutherland, *Children in English-Canadian Society,* 40-42.
39 On the history of schooling legislation in Canada, see J.D. Wilson, Robert M. Stamp, and Louis-Phillippe Audet, *Canadian Education: A History* (Scarborough, ON: Prentice-Hall, 1970), and F. Henry Johnson, *A Brief History of Canadian Education* (Toronto: McGraw-Hill, 1968).
40 A.P. Knight, *The Ontario Public School Hygiene* (Toronto: Copp Clark, 1910), 229.
41 Charles H. Stowell, *The Essentials of Health: A Text-book on Anatomy, Physiology, and Hygiene* (Toronto: The Educational Book Company, 1909), 253. This text was "prescribed for use in the Public and High Schools of British Columbia" (Preface, n.p.).
42 On the significance of the temperance movement in Canada see Jan Noel, *Canada Dry: Temperance Crusades before Confederation* (Toronto: University of Toronto Press, 1995), and Sharon Anne Cook, *Through Sunshine and Shadow: The Women's Christian Temperance Union, Evangelicalism, and Reform* (Montreal and Kingston: McGill-Queen's University Press, 1995).
43 Wendy Mitchinson, *The Nature of Their Bodies: Women and Their Doctors in Victorian Canada* (Toronto: University of Toronto Press, 1991); Veronica Strong-Boag, *The New Day Recalled: Lives of Girls and Women in English Canada, 1919-1939* (Toronto: Copp Clark Pitman, 1988).

44 J. Halpenny and Lillian Ireland, *How to Be Healthy* (Toronto and Winnipeg: W.J. Gage, 1911), 54.
45 W.W. Chipman, "The Infant Soldier," *Canadian Nurse* 14, 12 (1918): 1453-63. Chipman's wife was active in another aspect of reform work: she rallied for women police officers in Montreal and reformatories for girls in the period. I am grateful to Tamara Myers for pointing out this connection.
46 Michael W. Apple and Linda Christian-Smith, "The Politics of the Textbook," in Michael W. Apple and Linda Christian-Smith, eds., *The Politics of the Textbook* (New York: Routledge, 1991), 1-21.
47 Bernd Baldus and Meenaz Kassam, "'Make Me Truthful, Good and Mild': Values in Nineteenth-Century Ontario Schoolbooks," *Canadian Journal of Sociology* 12 (1996): 327-58.
48 Child Health Interview, Participant #024, 3 February 2004, transcript, 10. (See note 4 above.)
49 Child Health Interview, Participant #006, 15 April 2004, transcript, 3.
50 J. Mace Andress and Elizabeth Breeze, *Health Essentials for Canadian Schools* (Boston, Montreal, and London: Ginn, 1938), 159. See also the discussion of the dangers of homespun health practices in J.W.S. McCullough, "Chatelaine's Baby Clinic: The Common Diseases," *Chatelaine* June 1934, 54, and Ross A. Campbell, "The Spastic Child," *Canadian Nurse* 42 (1946): 471.
51 Jean Tierney is a pseudonym. Child Health Interview, Participant #014, 9 March 2004, transcript, 12.
52 Child Health Interview, Participant #010, 28 July 2004, transcript, 2.
53 Dorothea Ingram is a pseudonym. Child Health Interview, Participant #024, 3 February 2004, transcript, 7.
54 Socialized health insurance was first introduced in the province of Saskatchewan in 1962 and had spread to the rest of the country by the mid-1960s.
55 Child Health Interview, Participant #006, 15 April 2004, transcript, 6.
56 Ibid.
57 Child Health Interview, Participant #007, 27 April 2004, transcript, 2.
58 Child Health Interview, Participant #002, 26 February 2004, transcript, 6.
59 This message of the superiority of medical science in treating matters of health and illness is conveyed in a number of texts. See, for example, Ontario Provincial Board of Health, *Manual of Hygiene for Schools and Colleges;* J.H. Halpenny and Lillian Ireland, *How to Be Healthy,* 174; and J. Mace Andress and W.A. Evans, *Healthy Citizenship* (Toronto: Ginn, 1935), 63.
60 Child Health Interview, Participant #004, 3 June 2004, transcript, 8.
61 Child Health Interview, Participant #001, 16 January 2001, transcript, 5.
62 Child Health Interview, Participant #012, 2 October 2001, transcript, 4.
63 Anna Friesen, *The Mulberry Tree* (Winnipeg: Queenston, 1985), 14.
64 Child Health Interview, Participant #005, 14 February 2001, transcript, 2.
65 Ruth Cook, "An Interview with Ruth Cook," in Dorothy Haegert, ed., *Children of the First People* (Vancouver: Tillacum Library, 1983), 24.

Part 4
Colliding Visions –
The Politics of Families and Youth

Do children deserve "normal childhoods"? This idea is at once emotionally compelling and politically loaded. The right to normalcy often serves as a rallying cry on behalf of services for children, yet it also implies that certain childhoods are not normal, and, perhaps, by extension, that certain less mainstream families are less deserving of support.

As the three chapters that follow suggest, children have grown up in a wide range of circumstances, many in families deemed unfortunate or less desirable by their detractors: for example, those whose parents receive welfare benefits, whose mothers and fathers have separated, or who are the offspring of gay or lesbian couples. Molly Ladd-Taylor's "What Child Left Behind? US Social Policy and the Hopeless Child" explores twentieth-century American welfare policies, especially as they concern children's rights and economic status. Ladd-Taylor argues that every policy advance has left behind some children, those deemed too "hopeless" and "damaged" to benefit from help: Progressive-Era government programs that established a clear dichotomy between "innocent" children and the eugenically "unfit"; mid-century civil rights school desegregation programs, expanded access to health care, and anti-poverty funding, all of which invoked images of children damaged by cultural or family pathology; and recent welfare reform and rising youth incarceration rates, which evinced sympathy for punitive measures for the "hopeless."

Leslie Paris's "'The Strange Way We Lived': Divorce and American Childhood in the 1970s" explores how American children of the 1970s were affected when divorce became a mainstream American phenomenon. At a time when the "traditional" family ideal (however imperfectly realized in historical practice) was under evident stress, a growing minority of children experienced the separation of their parents (and often new family arrangements involving step-parents and new siblings). Drawing on a range of sources, from legal decisions to the popular film *Kramer vs. Kramer* (1979) to children's own accounts of their parents' divorces, Paris explores some of the implications of the new culture of divorce: not only how it propelled more women and children into poverty, or lessened many fathers' involvement in their children's lives, but also how, in the context of a period of growing acceptance of divorce, children whose parents were separating drew on supportive peer communities to help one another through this difficult process.

Finally, Cindy Baldassi, Susan B. Boyd, and Fiona Kelly's chapter, "Losing the Child in Child-Centred Legal Processes," explores the extent to which the principle of the best interests of the child, especially within child custody law, takes children's interests seriously. The authors explore the indeterminacy of the principle of best interests, and the variability of its application depending on gender, race, class, sexual orientation, and disability. Paying particular attention to child custody law in non-normative families, especially those headed by lesbian parents, the authors contend that the law's emphasis on a child's "right to a father," and its marginalization of non-biological mothers, essentially ignores the child's interests.

These essays share common concerns. What is "normal" childhood, and how has this idea varied historically? How and in what ways have children from families deemed non-normative been protected (or ignored) by the law and their communities? What does it mean to advocate for children's best interests, and who are the adults best able to perform this task? As these chapters collectively suggest, the idea of the "best interests of the child" has shifted over time, as social mores have changed, but it remains an active site of political and familial contestation.

8

What Child Left Behind? US Social Policy and the Hopeless Child

Molly Ladd-Taylor

In 2005, former US Secretary of Education William J. Bennett told a radio audience that "you could abort every black baby in this country, and your crime rate would go down." Although he admitted that such a policy would be "impossible, ridiculous and morally reprehensible," Bennett's remarks set off a storm of controversy. By contrast, there was little objection when, three days after Seung-Hui Cho massacred thirty-two people at Virginia Tech the *New York Times* published an opinion piece that criticized liberals' efforts to seek a social or environmental explanation for the tragedy. Better mental health services or stronger gun laws would not have prevented the killings, Oakland University professor Barbara Oakley insisted, because "mean, sometimes outright evil behavior has a strong genetic component. Some of us, in other words, are truly born bad."[1]

References to "born criminals" may seem like the product of a bygone era, but they are a powerful reminder that not every childhood is seen as a time of innocence and hope. Despite the idealization of what sociologist Viviana Zelizer calls the "economically 'worthless' but emotionally 'priceless' child," the belief that some children are destined to be failures or villains remains strong. Yet, although much has been written about the innocent, fragile child and the social programs established to protect him or her, far less attention has been paid to the opposing image of the "bad" child for whom there is no hope.[2] In fact, twentieth-century children's policies were shaped as much by worries about the "hopeless" child as by the sentimental childhood ideal.[3]

This chapter explores changing notions of hopeless childhood in twentieth-century US social policy. Heeding the call of historian Douglas Baynton, it places disability at the centre of analysis, viewing "hopelessness" through a disability lens. As recent scholars in disability studies have shown, disability is a protean concept that is inherently subjective; variations in human functioning become disabilities only in specific social and historical contexts. Disability, like childhood, is not a straightforward matter of biology but a social construct shaped by culture, politics, industry, and, less audibly, the people themselves. In the United States, modern ideas about both disability and childhood took hold in the late nineteenth century, in tandem with economic modernization and industrialization. Mechanization, compulsory schooling, and new scientific theories about evolution and the stages of child development led to increasingly standardized performance expectations for "normal" bodies and minds. Children whose mental processing, physical abilities, or language skills seemed out of synch with school or industrial norms were stigmatized. At the same time, Baynton observes, the attribution of disability was used to justify discrimination against immigrants, women, and people of colour. "Disability has functioned for all such groups as a sign of and justification for inferiority," and it serves as a "marker of hierarchical relations."[4] Throughout the twentieth century, reformers of all political persuasions have used potent images of disability, damage, defect, and hopelessness to rally support for their social policies.

The shifting understanding of the hopeless child can be seen in three pivotal moments in US children's policy. In the first period, the progressive era of the 1910s, reformers extended social services based on middle-class ideas about children's innate goodness to the working class and most immigrants, but not to children considered inferior on eugenic or racial grounds. In the second stage, which began in 1954 with the famous Supreme Court decision *Brown v. Board of Education,* civil rights and anti-poverty activists established new rights and opportunities – and heightened expectations – for children previously excluded from child welfare guarantees. Despite rejecting the idea of biological racial inferiority, however, academics and policy makers built the case for reform by appealing to fear as well as sympathy for children damaged by racism and poverty. Liberals' reliance on negative damage imagery would come back to haunt them in the 1980s and 1990s when conservatives used images of hopeless childhood to demonize welfare mothers and roll back the social safety net. Even so, the American rhetoric of equality and hope for all children remains strong; why else would George W. Bush name his 2001 education bill No Child Left Behind?[5]

Progressive Child Welfare and the Defective Child

The child welfare system established in the twentieth century was a significant departure from the early years of the republic, when the middle class paid little attention to the emotional or even physical needs of working-class children and slaves. Poor children toiled long hours in factories, fields, and on the streets, and those whose parents could not or would not support them were removed from their families and apprenticed out to work for the lowest bidder, placed in an institution, or left to fend for themselves. By the mid-nineteenth-century, organizations such as the Children's Aid Society attempted to save children – and the nation – by separating young innocents from bad influences, including their own parents, and sending them out west or to orphanages where they could be shaped into virtuous citizens. As historian Steven Mintz explains, "Child-saving was driven by a mixture of hope and fear – by a utopian faith that crime, pauperism, and class division could be solved by redeeming poor children; and a mounting concern over growing cities, burgeoning gangs of idle and unsupervised youths, and swelling immigrant populations."[6]

The principles of a new child-oriented social policy were set out at the 1909 White House Conference on the Care of Dependent Children, hosted by President Theodore Roosevelt. Social workers Florence Kelley and Lillian Wald, novelist Theodore Dreiser, and other reformers extended middle-class ideas about children's malleability, innate goodness, and the need for mother-love to working-class and immigrant youth for the first time. "Home life is the highest and finest product of civilization," delegates resolved; "Children should not be deprived of it except for urgent and compelling reasons ... Except in unusual circumstances, the home should not be broken up for reasons of poverty, but only for considerations of inefficiency or immorality." Scholars have commented insightfully on reformers' fixation with sexual immorality but have had surprisingly little to say about "inefficiency." When it is mentioned at all, inefficiency – like mental defect or feeble-mindedness – is simply assumed to be a signifier for ethnicity or class; the connection with disability is left unexplored.[7]

Child welfare reformers reshaped US social policy in the years following the White House Conference. By 1920, most states outside the South had juvenile courts, compulsory school laws, restrictions on child labour, and mothers' pensions programs (also called Aid to Dependent Children, or welfare).[8] Yet, few of these children's programs were available to all children. This is partly because progressive reformers trying to obtain political support for new public expenditures focused on "deserving" children with promising futures, rather than on those considered mentally defective or racially inferior and unlikely to improve. Aid to Dependent Children, for example, was given only to children in "suitable" homes, in which the mother was judged by social workers to be a good housekeeper, sexually respectable, and capable of controlling her children. Similarly, the case for a separate juvenile court was often made by drawing a contrast between young troublemakers who could be rehabilitated (mostly boys who were mischievous but not really bad) and those considered to be defective delinquents who could not change. Court-ordered intelligence tests and psychological assessments ensured that normal delinquents, who could be saved, were separated from the hopeless cases.[9]

That advances in child welfare often depended on the exclusion of the bad or hopeless child is strikingly evident in Minnesota's highly praised

Children's Code, a package of laws enacted in 1917 to modernize the state's child welfare system. In recommending the statutes, the Child Welfare Commission asserted the state's role as the ultimate guardian of all children whose parents could not adequately provide for them but focused particularly on the needs of "specially handicapped children" who were defective, illegitimate, dependent or neglected, or delinquent.[10]

The different treatment of the four groups is striking. On the one hand, the commission broke with nineteenth-century practice and applied the concept of childhood innocence to destitute and illegitimate children. It sought to remove the "sting" of dependency so that impoverished children could be "adjudged dependent without reflection upon a worthy parent," and it promised to children of unmarried mothers the "nearest possible approximation" to the same support, quality of care, and education that they would have if their parents were married. On the other hand, it characterized "defective" children as unequivocally menacing and evil. "Almost every community in the state furnishes examples of hereditary feeble-mindedness," the commission proclaimed, and "mentally subnormal children" could be a "serious public menace." The commission stopped short of endorsing eugenic sterilization, but the much-celebrated Children's Code included a compulsory commitment bill that permitted probate courts to place feeble-minded and insane persons of all ages under public guardianship. "Defective" wards of the state were rendered permanent children without direct political or civil rights. The state, as legal guardian, could decide whether to institutionalize and how to control them.[11]

At times, improvements in the status of "normal" children came at the expense of the hopeless minority. Take the case of Minnesota's pioneering adoption law, which attempted to ensure the adopted child's full and equal place in his or her new family. With the 1917 passage of the Children's Code, Minnesota became the first state to require a home study to ensure that adoptive parents were suitable and would not exploit or injure the child, and the first state to seal adoption records. The same law also protected parents from adopting a hopeless child. Adoptive parents were permitted to annul an adoption if a youngster developed "feeble-mindedness, epilepsy, insanity, or venereal infection as a result of conditions existing prior to the adoption" within five years.[12] By defining most children as innocent and in need of state protection, but treating others as biologically inferior or defective, the Children's Code widened the gulf between normal children with bright futures and those regarded as the hopelessly defective few.

The bifurcated child welfare structures established in the 1910s were written into the federal welfare programs of Franklin Roosevelt's New Deal, and they continue to influence social policy today. As many scholars have shown, the 1935 Social Security Act established separate tracks for (male) wage earners and caregivers. While industrial workers – mostly white men – received social insurance as a federal labour entitlement, mothers who were un-married, "defective," or worked long hours outside the home were generally denied Aid to Dependent Children (ADC) on the grounds that they could not provide a suitable home. The 1938 Fair Labor Standards Act, too, excluded the neediest children and most blacks: it prohibited "oppressive" child labour in mining and manufacturing but exempted children who worked in agri-culture. Yet, in spite of racial discrimination and the continuing influence of eugenics (eugenic sterilization peaked in the 1930s), many Americans found reason for optimism in New Deal social programs and Roosevelt's support for the common man. The stage was set for a dramatic redrawing of the boundaries of hope.[13]

Civil Rights, the War on Poverty, and the Damaged Child

The ideas about biological racial inferiority and hereditary defect that seemed so compelling to reformers in the 1910s and 1920s largely fell out of favour after the Second World War.[14] For liberals, the juxtaposition of an increas-ingly child-centred, suburban-based culture with the brutality of Southern racism and horrific revelations about the Nazi Holocaust revealed a heart-breaking gap between the protected-childhood ideal and the actual treatment of children. Youth were at the centre of two of the most shocking and highly publicized instances of Southern racism: the incarceration of the Scottsboro Boys on false charges of rape in the 1930s, and the 1955 beating and drown-ing murder of Emmett Till.[15] In 1954, the US Supreme Court issued *Brown v. Board of Education,* its landmark decision that racially segregated schools were unconstitutional. The court overturned the doctrine of "separate but equal" established in *Plessy v. Ferguson* in 1896, and, in a related case, required public schools to desegregate with "all deliberate speed." *Brown* was the product of years of struggle against racist laws, and it opened the door for stronger civil rights statutes and established a legal foundation by which many non-black children, including children with disabilities, would even-tually demand their rights to an equal education.[16]

The *Brown* decision both reflected and furthered the state's growing re-sponsibility for children's well-being. Prior to *Plessy,* Chief Justice Earl Warren explained, taxpayer-funded public education was not clearly established as a right: most blacks and even many Southern whites lacked access to public schools, and it was illegal to educate African Americans in several Southern states. By the mid-twentieth century, however, access to a taxpayer-funded school was considered essential to democratic society and the "very founda-tion of good citizenship." Further, it was "doubtful that any child may reasonably be expected to succeed in life if he is denied the opportunity of an education," Warren wrote. Racially segregated schools were inherently unequal, even when facilities were the same, because separation was based on the erroneous belief that African Americans were intellectually inferior.

Segregation, Warren maintained, affected black children's motivation to learn and retarded their educational and mental development.[17]

The court's decision relied heavily on "The Effects of Segregation," a powerful brief signed by thirty-six social scientists that spelled out the adverse effects of racial segregation on the personality development of the child. Segregation harmed all children, the social scientists explained, but minority-group children were most affected because the implication that they were less intelligent than the majority led to "feelings of inferiority and a sense of personal humiliation" and a confusion about their personal worth. Lower-class blacks often responded with anti-social and delinquent behaviour and middle-class youth could be excessively submissive, but black children of all classes developed a "generally defeatist attitude and a lowering of personal ambitions."[18] Warren wrote in the court's decision, "To separate [children] from others of similar age and qualifications solely because of their race generates a feeling of inferiority as to their status in the community that may affect their hearts and minds in a way unlikely ever to be undone."[19] Racial segregation, in other words, caused fragile children to lose ability as well as hope.

Two aspects of the social science influence on the *Brown* decision are worth emphasizing here. First, Warren's argument about the right to equal education depended on the essential normality of the students. The policy of separating black children from whites solely because of their race was based on the erroneous belief that African Americans were intellectually inferior; it was harmful because it destroyed the self-confidence of children who did in fact have an equal capacity to learn. (Interestingly, the social science brief noted "in passing" that many educators opposed the intellectual segregation of schoolchildren on similar grounds: it generated feelings of inferiority in the below-average child, had undesirable emotional consequences for the gifted, and reduced learning opportunities that could result from the two groups' interaction.) Second, the brief warned that failure to address the effects of segregation could lead to permanent psychological damage that would have consequences in years to come – consequences not only for the individual children but also for society. Racial segregation not only fostered rigid stereotypes and a "distorted sense of social reality," the social scientists argued, it also contributed to the "development of a social climate within which violent outbreaks of racial tensions are likely to occur."[20]

The fear of what might occur if injustice were not righted shaped liberal ideas about poverty as well as racism. Although liberal writers of the 1960s rejected the progressives' hereditarian explanations, they retained much of the earlier view of the hopeless child. Indeed, the influential "culture of poverty" framework devised by anthropologist Oscar Lewis bore an eerie resemblance to the earlier generation's views of hereditary feeble-mindedness and mental defect. Lewis described a culture of poverty that transcended national and urban-rural differences and was passed down from generation to generation. The culture of poverty was perpetuated by children who grew up in it and adopted its values, and absorbed feelings of marginality, helplessness, and inferiority. People living in a culture of poverty, Lewis maintained, were fatalistic: they lacked impulse control, were unable to delay gratification and plan for the future, and had a low level of aspiration.[21] The psychological damage caused by the culture of poverty was almost indistinguishable from hereditary defect; as poverty researcher Mollie Orshansky observed, some children "seemed destined to poverty almost from birth – by their color or by the economic status or occupation of their parents."[22]

Michael Harrington's 1962 bestseller, *The Other America,* took the concept of the culture of poverty to a popular audience, calling hopelessness the most distinguishing mark of poverty in postwar America. In the past, Harrington explained, poverty was common, and poor people shared in the American dream of upward mobility and a better future. In affluent postwar America, by contrast, poor Americans were isolated and invisible. Poverty in the 1960s was characterized by a vicious cycle of deprivation and demoralization: poor children came from uneducated families who cared little about education, they attended inferior schools, failed to get good jobs, had babies when they were young, and perpetuated the cycle of poverty. Poor Americans "feel differently than the rest of the nation," Harrington opined, for "they tend to be hopeless and passive ... To be poor is not simply to be deprived of the material things of the world. It is to enter a fatal, futile universe, an America within America with a twisted spirit." The hopelessness of children who were supposed to be the nation's future was particularly worrisome. Without aspiration and hope, Harrington believed, the children of the other America "may well be the source of a kind of hereditary poverty new to American society."[23]

In emphasizing the particular harm done to children by racism and the culture of poverty, liberal thinkers signalled a dramatic change in American expectations for childhood. Partly a reaction to the hardships of the Depression and war, the increasingly commercialized and child-centred culture of the postwar years was also shaped by the rising hopes for children's health in the era of modern medicine, and the sheer numbers of children in the baby boom. Children were the centre of the family and the future of the nation, but it seemed that many of them were in trouble. Adults' uneasiness often focused on schools. The anxieties generated by the space race and the Cold War, the bitter struggles over school desegregation, and the large numbers of baby boomers entering school at the same time stoked fears that public education was failing many children. Poor blacks seemed particularly disadvantaged. They scored poorly on achievement tests compared with whites and often dropped out before finishing school. One writer worried that the presence of so many alienated and unemployed youth posed a "menace to the social and political health of our communities."[24]

The belief that saving children could be a solution to the problem of poverty in general grew out of a long tradition in American reform. Traditionally, historian Michael Katz has observed, reformers posited two alternative explanations for poverty. One focused on the biological or cultural failings of the individual; the other emphasized the artificial barriers at odds with the American ideals of openness and opportunity. In reality, of course, the two explanations were not divergent but complementary and coexistent. In the Progressive Era, reformers attributed most poverty to economic and environmental barriers, such as low wages or poor housing, but described the unremitting poverty that characterized some families in racial or eugenic terms. Fifty years later, reformers attributed most poverty to legal and environmental barriers, such as discriminatory laws or poor housing, but described the unremitting poverty that characterized some families in terms of culture or psychology. In both eras, powerful images of defect and damage accompanied the liberal emphasis on external barriers to success. Yet, the shift from biology to culture was not inconsequential. Although mental defect was considered permanent and inherited, the damaging effects of segregation and the culture of poverty could presumably be undone.[25]

One way liberals strived to undo the damage and end the culture of poverty was compensatory education. Since poor children often lacked a stable home environment and the family support necessary for academic success, the theory ran, providing them with books, educational toys, and enrichment activities, and reaching out to their parents, would raise their educational aspirations, level the playing field, and help them reach the academic level of the middle class. In contrast to progressive-era reformers who saw "defectives" and racial minorities as lacking the intellectual capacity to benefit from regular programs, postwar liberals thought that even the lowliest child could be helped. Some social scientists even maintained that intelligence was manipulable, and that compensatory education could raise student IQs.[26]

President Lyndon Johnson, a former Texas schoolteacher and director of the National Youth Administration under Roosevelt, was a strong believer in education as a vehicle of upward mobility. "As a son of a tenant farmer," he said, "I know that education is the only valid passport from poverty."[27] Johnson made compensatory education a centrepiece of his War on Poverty. In 1965, he launched the Head Start program to attack poverty where psychologists believed "it hits first and most damagingly – in early childhood," by making funds available to community action groups so they could establish Head Start centres providing nutrition, health care, and enrichment programs for preschoolers. He also secured passage of the Elementary and Secondary Education Act (ESEA), which targeted funds to educationally deprived children in order to "bridge the gap between helplessness and hope."[28] To win support for the bill and defuse the constitutional question of the separation of church and state, Johnson provided ESEA services to Catholic schoolchildren through public school districts and allowed local bureaucrats to allocate funds. Some critics charged that the educational reforms of the War on Poverty were a conservative war on culture that tried to rescue disadvantaged children by replacing the culture of poverty with the culture of the school. This view is not incorrect, but federal intervention also fostered what one historian has called an "embrace of hopefulness" and dramatically raised expectations for schools.[29]

The embrace of hopefulness extended far beyond the traditional civil rights constituency. The first time Eunice Kennedy Shriver wrote publicly about her sister Rosemary's disability, she titled her article, "Hope for Retarded Children." "In this era of atom-splitting and wonder drugs and technological advance," Shriver wrote in 1962, "it is still widely assumed ... that the future for the mentally retarded is hopeless." Such "weary fatalism" was no longer justified. Thanks to scientific research, special-education programs, and public advocacy, "retarded" persons could become useful citizens.[30]

It is interesting that, while African American activists fought the erroneous labelling of black schoolchildren as mentally retarded, disability advocates found inspiration, and a strategy, in the movement for black civil rights. In the early 1970s, civil rights activist and Children's Defense Fund founder Marian Wright Edelman was surprised to find that most of the 750,000 American children excluded from school were not poor Southern blacks but children with disabilities. The strong language of *Brown v. Board of Education* – that public education was a "right that must be provided to all on equal terms" – provided the basis for a series of legal challenges that helped to overturn both the routine placement of African Americans in classes for slow learners and the policies that kept supposedly uneducable children with disabilities out of school.[31]

In 1975, disability activists scored a big victory: the passage of the Education for All Handicapped Children Act guaranteed all children with disabilities a free appropriate public education and services to meet their unique needs. Under the law, now called the Individuals with Disabilities Education Act, students with disabilities had the rights to an Individualized Education Plan designed by a team of professionals (and reviewed by parents) and to instruction in the least restrictive environment. Wherever possible, students with disabilities should be integrated into a regular classroom in the neighbourhood school rather than placed in a separate class or school for the disabled.[32]

The educational reforms won by civil rights, anti-poverty, and disability advocates significantly narrowed the boundaries of hopeless childhood. By the 1970s, in theory, no child was deemed uneducable. In reality, the belief that some children had hopeless futures persisted. To some extent, the problem was one of unrealistic expectations. Many reformers had seen education as a "painless panacea" that promised to end poverty and make Americans more equal without addressing fundamental economic inequalities or the de facto racial segregation in schools. In addition, because ESEA's remedial programs were not well integrated into the regular instructional program, and local officials played a large role in the distribution of funds, education reform did little to challenge the double disadvantage of poor children with disabilities.[33]

As early as 1958, psychiatrist Bruno Bettelheim remarked on the irony that each step toward the racial integration of schools was accompanied by increasingly intense intellectual segregation. Middle-class liberals enthusiastically supported racially integrated schools, he observed, because their own children were already segregated in all-white suburbs, private schools, and special classes for the gifted or university bound. Thus middle-class youth, studying in a stimulating environment, were given an incentive to excel that working-class black and white children in less privileged school programs did not have. In 1966, sociologist James Coleman issued his famous report, "Equality of Educational Opportunity," which cast another shadow on the liberal assumption that compensatory education and increased funding would automatically improve scholastic achievement. Coleman found that students' test scores correlated not to the amount of money spent on schools but to family status, the quality and educational backgrounds of other students in the school, and children's sense of control over (that is, hope for) their futures. Coleman emphasized the positive impact of integrated schools, but many reformers took a different lesson: families affected students' scholastic performances, and increased school funding was money down the drain.[34] As Daniel Patrick Moynihan later put it, "Per-pupil expenditure, books in the library, all that had but little impact. What mattered was family."[35]

Family, of course, was the focus of Moynihan's controversial 1965 report, leaked around the time of the Watts Uprising in Los Angeles. *The Negro Family: The Case for National Action* was an internal planning document that Moynihan hoped would persuade the Johnson administration to focus the next stage of the War on Poverty on the lower-class black family, which he saw as unstable and matriarchal. An entire section was devoted to the "failure of youth." Drawing on research by African American and white social scientists, Moynihan made the unoriginal claim that black youth (meaning boys) were in trouble. They did poorly in school, committed a disproportionate number of crimes, and were incarcerated at an alarming rate. There was "absolutely no question of any genetic differential," Moynihan emphasized; the problem was that many black children raised by single mothers lacked breadwinning fathers to act as role models. Although "white children without fathers at least perceive all about them the pattern of men working," Moynihan wrote, "Negro children without fathers flounder – and fail." Moynihan's depiction of lower-class black culture as a "tangle of pathology" produced a furious reaction. Despite acknowledging Moynihan's liberal credentials, civil rights leaders and white radicals angrily rejected his claim that matriarchal black families left youth psychologically damaged.[36] They repudiated what historian Daryl Michael Scott has described as liberals' willingness to "exchange black dignity for something other than justice, for social policies that reinforced white America's age-old belief in black inferiority."[37] Like Scott, they saw reliance on damage imagery as a major failing of racial liberalism.

What Child Left Behind? Disability and Damage in the War on Welfare

Four years after the Moynihan controversy, psychologist Arthur Jensen provoked another storm of protest when he asserted in the *Harvard Educational Review* that compensatory education had failed because of innate inequality in mental ability – a black IQ deficit.[38] Yet, whereas both the psychological damage and innate inferiority arguments provoked outrage in the 1960s, they found a more sympathetic audience in the 1980s and 1990s war on welfare. Anti-welfare conservatives turned liberal rhetoric about personality damage and cultural deprivation into a blistering attack on the moral bankruptcy of the black "underclass" and the social programs of Lyndon Johnson's Great Society. In his influential 1984 book *Losing Ground,* conservative writer Charles Murray told a grim tale of inner-city welfare dependency, illegitimacy, and crime but insisted that there was "no need to invoke the specters of cultural pathologies or inferior upbringing." The hopeless pathology of the underclass was a rational response to government largesse. A decade later, in *The Bell Curve,* Murray turned to the older idea of intelligence as genetically (and racially) determined. He and co-author Richard Herrnstein disputed the efficacy of anti-poverty programs such as Head Start, which they said raised false hopes among the disadvantaged, thereby furthering their dependency and despair, and called for an end to welfare because it subsidized the births of children at the low end of the intelligence distribution.[39]

In the 1980s and 1990s, conservatives deployed three powerful images of hopeless childhood in their campaign against welfare and women's reproductive rights. The first two images conjured up fears of innocent children permanently damaged by unfit, out-of-control mothers; the third centred on the familiar figure of the black underclass youth. First, the panic over crack babies roused outrage over the allegedly irresponsible parenting of drug-addicted mothers, usually imagined as black. Sensationalist news stories publicized a series of medical studies linking prenatal cocaine use to low birth weight, mental retardation, and irreversible neurological damage. Although later studies modified such alarmist early findings, the crack children of the 1980s bore a striking resemblance to the feeble-minded of sixty years earlier: they were biologically impaired children of defective mothers who were criminally inclined and a drain on the public purse. Crack babies made up a "lost generation," a conservative columnist warned, for they faced a "life of certain suffering, of probable deviance, of permanent inferiority."[40] A second image of childhood hopelessness, caused by fetal alcohol syndrome (FAS) and often stereotyped as Native American, was also attributed to maternal misbehaviour. FAS children, like crack babies and the feeble-minded, were characterized by low IQs, short attention spans, poor coordination, and an inability to understand the consequences of their actions or the difference between right and wrong. While media sympathies focused on the "adoption nightmares" and "wrongful adoption" suits of middle-class parents with FAS children, the frightening images of a biological underclass caused by irresponsible teen mothers led to a surge of political support for harsh policies, including the incarceration of pregnant substance abusers and the termination of their parental rights. In real life, the offspring of substance abusers, some of whom had physical or developmental disabilities, often wound up in foster care or jail. The cycle of policy hopelessness was ensured.[41]

The third image of hopeless childhood centred on inner-city black youth, especially males: the teenage gang members, drug dealers, or petty thieves who had little relationship to the job market and little incentive to go to school. Growing up in the hopeless despair of the inner city, critics maintained, black youth could hardly avoid falling victim to the violent and dysfunctional culture of the street. "The hopelessness and alienation many young inner-city black men and women feel, largely as a result of endemic joblessness and persistent racism, fuels the violence they engage in," sociologist Elijah Anderson wrote in 1994. "This violence serves to confirm the negative feelings ... toward the ghetto poor, further legitimizing the oppositional culture and the code of the streets."[42] Although the culture of poverty had become the code of the street, the imagery of damage and defect was essentially unchanged.

In 1996, President Bill Clinton signed a welfare reform bill that ended direct federal responsibility for poor children and brought "a new day that offers hope, honors responsibility, [and] rewards work." The Personal Responsibility and Work Opportunity Reconciliation Act (PRWORA) ended the Aid to Families with Dependent Children (formerly ADC) program, which had been established in the progressive era and made national during the New Deal, and replaced it with Temporary Assistance for Needy Families (TANF), a new program funded by block grants to the states. Bringing back progressive-era "considerations of inefficiency or immorality," whose importance had diminished in the 1960s, PRWORA instituted strict work requirements for welfare recipients, placed a lifetime limit on federal benefits, and promoted "responsible fatherhood and motherhood" by allocating funds to promote marriage, prevent out-of-wedlock pregnancy, and catch deadbeat dads.[43]

Clinton's goal in signing the bill was to remove welfare – and welfare mothers – from the political arena, where their presence had been a boon for Republicans. From this perspective, the bill was an unqualified success: poor mothers and children left the welfare rolls, went to work, and returned to their previous invisibility. Yet, although some families have done reasonably well – or at least, not worse – under the strict welfare-to-work requirements, welfare reform has done little to alleviate the stresses and burdens of poverty. And for mothers classed as inefficient or immoral – women who are chronically ill, addicted to drugs or alcohol, have physical or mental disabilities, or care for chronically ill children – the end of welfare has been cruel. Welfare reductions were accompanied by an enormous increase in the number of children adjudged neglected or abused and removed from their families. By 2005, more than half a million American children were living in foster care. A disproportionate number were black.[44]

Ironically, the particular vulnerability of sick or disabled TANF recipients coincided with a "quiet revolution" that greatly expanded disability benefits and rights. The expansion of disability benefits through the Supplemental Security Income program, along with the educational entitlements of the Individuals with Disabilities Education Act (IDEA) and the 1990 passage of the Americans with Disabilities Act, has transformed the popular understanding and experience of disability. As the definition of disability was broadened, children with "emotional disturbance" or "specific learning disabilities" were treated as having medical, rather than moral or behavioural, problems, and the stigma of having a disability was reduced. The number of children receiving disability-related benefits increased dramatically: by 2005, about 14 percent of total public school enrolment received IDEA services. Significantly, most of the increase occurred among children with "specific learning disabilities," many of whom would have been classed as feeble-minded ninety years earlier.[45]

The simultaneous expansion of disability benefits and erosion of the welfare-safety net created a paradox for the hopeless child. For one thing, as critics have pointed out, IDEA gave children with disabilities rights that other children did not possess. Students with designated disabilities, but not "normal" children, had the right to an Individualized Education Plan, and until the law was changed in 2004, they could not be given the same punishment as nondisabled students for disruptive behaviour related to their disability.

As well, the vagueness of IDEA's terms "appropriate education" and "least restrictive environment" allowed well-off parents to challenge disciplinary procedures or special-education placements in court.[46] There were growing complaints that disability rights and the cost of special-education programs made it difficult to provide a safe learning environment and an appropriate education for normal children. "A minority of American schoolchildren were being given a financial priority, at the expense of the majority," objected historian Judith Sealander; the disability rights lobby "skewed education policy in an unfair way."[47]

In fact, children with disabilities remained disadvantaged – especially if they were poor, Native American, or black. Racial minorities have been both over-represented in and underserved by special-education programs. A 2002 study by the Civil Rights Project found African Americans disproportionately classified in the most serious (and stigmatized) disability categories of mental retardation and emotional disturbance, and black students with disabilities twice as likely as whites to be removed from general-education classes and schooled in a separate restrictive environment. Significantly, blacks and Native Americans were more likely to be designated mentally retarded if they lived in wealthier school districts. And the designation of hopelessness was self-fulfilling. The researchers found that, within a few years of leaving school, about 75 percent of African American youth with disabilities were unemployed, compared with fewer than half of whites. Forty percent of blacks, but only 27 percent of whites, had been arrested.[48]

On the face of it, George W. Bush's education bill, optimistically titled the No Child Left Behind Act of 2001 (NCLB), tackled such inequities head-on. The bill aimed to "to ensure that all children shall have a fair, equal, and significant opportunity to obtain a high-quality education" and rejected the very concept of the hopeless child. Acknowledging that ESEA failed to achieve educational equity, NCLB held schools responsible for raising the academic proficiency of low-income, minority, and disabled students, and English-language learners. "The fundamental principle of this bill is that every child can learn," President George W. Bush said at the signing ceremony; a second principle was that "we trust parents to make the right decisions for their children." In contrast to the Great Society's emphasis on compensatory education and the culture of poverty, NCLB puts the onus for improvement not on parents or communities but on the schools.[49]

NCLB's accountability provisions are heavily oriented to testing. States are required to measure student progress by annual achievement tests in reading and math, and to place sanctions on low-performing schools. The result, critics argue, is a rigid, test-driven curriculum with little room for recess, the arts, or even subjects, such as history, that are not tested. Testing does not reward, and may even impede, in-depth knowledge or the development of conceptual skills. Moreover, the importance attached to test scores fails to take into account the extraordinary funding disparities in per-pupil expenditures, and the sanctions on underperforming schools actually reinforce these disparities. Contrary to law, children with disabilities and other low achievers are sometimes held back or pushed out of the regular school program.[50]

Unhappily, the No Child Left Behind Act was enacted after decades of cutbacks to welfare and public school funding. Woefully underfunded itself, NCLB rests on top of a horrifically unequal school system: in 2005, the most affluent school districts spent about $907 more per student than the poorest ones, and in 2006-7 some one-third of African Americans and Hispanics, but just 4 percent of whites, attended schools with the highest measure of poverty.[51] Moreover, the racial segregation of schools is increasingly intense. Fifty-two percent of blacks and 57 percent of Hispanics, but just 3 percent of whites, attend schools in which at least 75 percent of the students are racial minorities.[52] More than fifty years after *Brown,* education reformer Jonathan Kozol observes sadly, urban schools named for civil rights luminaries are racially segregated. At Seattle's Thurgood Marshall Elementary School, for example, 95 percent of students are racial minorities, even though the school is in a neighbourhood where half the families are white. This "educational apartheid," and the accompanying erosion of the social safety net, reflect a cruel disinvestment in children that first creates, and then rationalizes the maltreatment of, the hopeless child.[53]

Most critics place racism at the heart of America's flawed children's policy, but contempt and pity for the damaged and disabled also play a role. Throughout the twentieth century, social reformers drew on powerful images of innate defect and psychological damage – images of disability – to build support for (or opposition to) welfare and educational policies, to explain crime and the persistence of poverty in an affluent society, or to rationalize the social exclusion of a hopeless minority. Even today, when American children with disabilities have civil rights protections and theories of innate racial inferiority are no longer mainstream, racialized images of hopelessly damaged or defective underclass youth hold considerable emotional power. The general attribution of disability to poor children and young people of colour is unfair, but it is children who have physical and intellectual disabilities on top of the disabilities of poverty and racism who are the most disadvantaged. Only by confronting society's most basic conceptions of disability, and the economic and structural inequalities that sustain and fuel them, can we truly ensure that no child is left behind.[54]

Notes

1   William J. Bennett quoted in "Bennett under Fire for Remark on Crime and Black Abortions," *Washington Post,* 30 September 2005; Barbara Oakley, "The Killer in the Lecture Hall," *New York Times,* 19 April 2007.

2 This chapter makes liberal use of problematic words such as "hopeless," "defective," "damaged," and "bad," usually without quotation marks. The meanness of the terminology is precisely the point; the words capture a certain way of thinking about the "hopeless" child.

3 Nicole Hahn Rafter, *Creating Born Criminals* (Urbana, IL: University of Illinois Press, 1997); Viviana A. Zelizer, *Pricing the Priceless Child: The Changing Social Value of Children* (Princeton, NJ: Princeton University Press, 1994), 3; Steven Mintz, *Huck's Raft: A History of American Childhood* (Cambridge, MA: Belknap Press, 2004).

4 Douglas C. Baynton, "Disability and the Justification of Inequality in American History," in Paul K. Longmore and Lauri Umansky, eds., *The New Disability History: American Perspectives* (New York: NYU Press, 2001), 34; see also Catherine J. Kudlick, "Disability History: Why We Need Another 'Other,'" *American Historical Review* 108 (June 2003): 763-93.

5 Daryl Michael Scott, *Contempt and Pity: Social Policy and the Image of the Damaged Black Psyche, 1880-1996* (Chapel Hill, NC: University of North Carolina Press, 1997); Judith Sealander, *The Failed Century of the Child: Governing America's Young in the Twentieth Century* (New York: Cambridge University Press, 2003). See also Michael B. Katz, *In the Shadow of the Poorhouse: A Social History of Welfare in America* (New York: Basic Books, 1986); and Molly Ladd-Taylor and Lauri Umansky, eds., *"Bad" Mothers: The Politics of Blame in Twentieth-Century America* (New York: NYU Press, 1998).

6 Mintz, *Huck's Raft*, 157.

7 Quoted in Molly Ladd-Taylor, *Mother-Work: Women, Child Welfare and the State, 1890-1930* (Urbana, IL: University of Illinois Press, 1994), 137. See also Gwendolyn Mink, *The Wages of Motherhood: Inequality in the Welfare State, 1917-1942* (Ithaca, NY: Cornell University Press, 1995).

8 Susan Tiffin, *In Whose Best Interest? Child Welfare Reform in the Progressive Era* (Westport, CT: Greenwood Press, 1982).

9 Edward F. Waite, "The Physical Bases of Crime: From the Standpoint of the Judge of a Juvenile Court," *Bulletin of the American Academy of Medicine* 14 (December 1913): 1-8. See also William Bush, Chapter 4 of this volume, and Michael Willrich, "The Two Percent Solution: Eugenic Jurisprudence and the Socialization of American Law, 1900-1930," *Law and History Review* 16 (Spring 1998): 63-111.

10 Cheuh-Fang Ma, *One Hundred Years of Public Services for Children in Minnesota* (Chicago: University of Chicago Press, 1948), 87.

11 [Minnesota Child Welfare Commission], *Report of the Minnesota Child Welfare Commission* (St. Paul, MN: Office of the Commission, 1917), 14, 13, 11-12.

12 Minnesota Adoption Law, 1917, "The Adoption History Project," http://darkwing.uoregon.edu /~adoption.

13 Linda Gordon, *Pitied but Not Entitled: Single Mothers and the History of Welfare* (New York: Free Press, 1994); Katz, *In the Shadow of the Poorhouse*, 206-45; Molly Ladd-Taylor, "Eugenics and Social Welfare in New Deal Minnesota," in Paul A. Lombardo, ed., *100 Years of Eugenics: From the "Indiana Experiment" to the Human Genome Era* (Bloomington: University of Indiana Press, forthcoming).

14 Of course, the belief in inherited intelligence persisted. See Stephen Jay Gould, *The Mismeasure of Man*, rev. ed. (New York: Norton, 1996), and Carl N. Degler, *In Search of Human Nature: The Decline and Revival of Darwinism in American Social Thought* (New York: Oxford University Press, 1991).

15 Mintz, *Huck's Raft*, 302-3.

16 Richard Kluger, *Simple Justice* (New York: Vintage Books, 1977); James T. Patterson, *Brown v. Board of Education: A Civil Rights Milestone and Its Troubled Legacy* (New York: Oxford University Press, 2001).

17 Warren quotations from Waldo E. Martin Jr., ed., *Brown v. Board of Education: A Brief History with Documents* (Boston: Bedford/St. Martin's, 1998), 173.

18 "The Effects of Segregation and the Consequences of Desegregation: A Social Science Statement," in Martin, *Brown v. Board of Education*, 143, 144.

19 Chief Justice Earl Warren, "Opinion of the Court," in Martin, *Brown v. Board of Education*, 173. See Scott, *Contempt and Pity*, 119-37.

20 "The Effects of Segregation," in Martin, *Brown v. Board of Education*, 145.

21 Oscar Lewis, "The Culture of Poverty," in Daniel P. Moynihan, ed., *On Understanding Poverty: Perspectives from the Social Sciences* (New York: Basic Books, 1969), 187-200. See Alice O'Connor, *Poverty Knowledge: Social Science, Social Policy, and the Poor in Twentieth-Century US History* (Princeton, NJ: Princeton University Press), 99-123.

22 Mollie Orshansky, "Children of the Poor," *Social Security Bulletin*, July 1963: 3-13.

23 Michael Harrington, *The Other America: Poverty in the United States* (Baltimore: Penguin, 1963), 120, 183. See O'Connor, *Poverty Knowledge*, 151.

24 James Conant, quoted in Julie Roy Jeffrey, *Education for Children of the Poor: A Study of the Origins and Implementation of the Elementary and Secondary Education Act of 1965* (Columbus: Ohio State University Press, 1978), 9.

25 Katz, *In the Shadow of the Poorhouse*, 255.

26 Ibid., 17.

27 Lyndon Baines Johnson, "Remarks in Johnson City, Texas, upon Signing the Elementary and Secondary Education Bill April 11, 1965," Lyndon Baines Johnson Library and Museum, http://www.lbjlib.utexas.edu/johnson/archives.hom/speeches.hom/650411.asp.

28 Urie Bronfenbrenner, quoted in Jeffrey, *Education for Children*, 164, and Johnson, "Remarks in Johnson City."

29 Joel Spring, *The Sorting Machine Revisited: National Educational Policy Since 1945* (New York: Longman, 1989), 150; William J. Reese, *America's Public Schools: From the Common School to "No Child Left Behind"* (Baltimore: Johns Hopkins University Press, 2005), 218.

30 Eunice Kennedy Shriver, "Hope for Retarded Children (1962)," reprinted in Steven Noll and James W. Trent Jr., eds., *Mental Retardation in America: A Historical Reader* (New York: NYU Press, 2004), 304, 307.

31 Joseph Shapiro, *No Pity: People with Disabilities Forging a New Civil Rights Movement* (New York: Random House, 1994), 165-66.

32 Quoted phrases from Public Law 94-142 (S. 6); 29 November 1975. See also Thomas Hehir and Thomas Latus, eds., *Special Education at the Century's End* (Cambridge, MA: Harvard Education Press, 1992); Sealander, *Failed Century*, 259-90.

33 Katz, *In the Shadow of the Poorhouse*, 255; Jeffrey, *Education for Children*, 97-142.

34 Bruno Bettelheim, "Sputnik and Segregation: Should the Gifted Be Educated Separately?" *Commentary* 26 (1958): 332-39. See Reese, *America's Public Schools*, 234; Jeffrey, *Education for Children*, 143-78; and Spring, *The Sorting Machine Revisited*, 156-58.

35 Daniel Patrick Moynihan, "James Coleman," APS *Proceedings* 141, 2 (1997): 222-24.

36 Daniel Patrick Moynihan, *The Negro Family: The Case for National Action*, 35, reprinted in Lee Rainwater and William L. Yancy, *The Moynihan Report and the Politics of Controversy* (Cambridge, MA: MIT Press, 1967).

37 Scott, *Contempt and Pity*, 185.

38 Arthur R. Jensen, "How Much Can We Boost I.Q. and Scholastic Achievement?" *Harvard Educational Review* 33 (1969), 1-123. See also Russell Jacoby and Naomi Glauberman, eds., *The Bell Curve Debate* (New York: Times Books, 1995).

39 Charles Murray, *Losing Ground: American Social Policy, 1950-1980* (New York: Basic Books, 1984), 162; Richard Herrnstein and Charles Murray, *The Bell Curve: Intelligence and Class Structure in American Life* (New York: Free Press, 1994).

40 Ana Teresa Ortiz and Laura Briggs, "The Culture of Poverty, Crack Babies, and Welfare Cheats," *Social Text* 76 (Fall 2003): 39-57; Drew Humphries, *Crack Mothers: Pregnancy, Drugs, and the Media* (Columbus: Ohio State University Press, 1999); Mariah Blake, "The Damage Done: Crack Babies Talk Back," *Columbia Journalism Review* 43 (September/October 2004): 10-11.

41 Janice Golden, *Message in a Bottle: The Making of Fetal Alcohol Syndrome* (Cambridge, MA: Harvard University Press, 2005). See also Veronica Strong-Boag, Chapter 2 of this volume, and Dorothy Roberts, *Shattered Bonds: The Color of Child Welfare* (New York: Basic Books, 2002), 154-59.

42 Elijah Anderson, "The Code of the Streets," *Atlantic Monthly* 273 (May 1994): 94.

43 Gwendolyn Mink and Rickie Solinger, eds., *Welfare: A Documentary History of US Policy and Politics* (New York: NYU Press, 2003), 662, 642.

44 See Jason DeParle, *Three Women, Ten Kids, and a Nation's Drive to End Welfare* (New York: Penguin, 2004); Roberts, *Shattered Bonds*; Wendy Chavkin and Paul H. Wise, "The Data Are

In: Health Matters in Welfare Policy," *American Journal of Public Health* 92 (2002): 1392-95; Child Welfare Information Gateway, "Foster Care Statistics: Numbers and Trends," 2007, http://www.childwelfare.gov/pubs/factsheets/foster.cfm.

45 Jennifer L. Erkulwater, *Disability Rights and the American Social Safety Net* (Ithaca, NY: Cornell University Press, 2006); National Center for Education Statistics, "Fast Facts" 2009, http://nces.ed.gov/fastfacts/display.asp?id=64. See also US Department of Education, "Building the Legacy: IDEA 2004," http://idea.ed.gov.

46 See Thomas Hehir and Thomas Latus, eds., *Special Education at the Century's End: Evolution of Theory and Practice Since 1970* (Cambridge, MA: Harvard Education Press, 1990); National Center for Education Statistics, "Participation in Education: Elementary/Secondary Education, Children and Youth with Disabilities (2009)" http://nces.ed.gov/programs/coe/2009/section1/indicator09.asp.

47 Sealander, *Failed Century,* 287, 290.

48 Civil Rights Project, "Racial Inequity in Special Education: Executive Summary for Federal Policy Makers," June 2002, http://www.civilrightsproject.ucla.edu; Daniel J. Losen and Gary Orfield, eds., *Racial Inequity in Special Education* (Cambridge, MA: Harvard Education Press, 2002).

49 "President Signs Landmark No Child Left Behind Education Bill," White House press release, 8 January 2002, http://georgewbush-whitehouse.archives.gov/news/releases/2002/01/20020108-1.html.

50 Deborah Meier and George Wood, eds., *Many Children Left Behind: How the No Child Left Behind Act Is Damaging Our Children and Our Schools* (Boston: Beacon Press, 2004); Jaekyung Lee, *Tracking Achievement Gaps and Assessing the Impact of NCLB on Gaps: An In-depth Look into National and State Reading and Math Outcome Trends* (Cambridge, MA: The Civil Rights Project of Harvard University, 2006), http://www.civilrightsproject.ucla.edu/research/esea/nclb_naep_lee.pdf.

51 Education Trust, "The Funding Gap 2005: Low Income and Minority Students Short-Changed by Most States," Winter 2005, http://www2.edtrust.org/NR/rdonlyres/31D276EF-72E1-458A-8C71-E3D262A4C91E/0/FundingGap2005.pdf. Among elementary and secondary public school students in 2006-7, 33 percent of blacks, 35 percent of Hispanics, 25 percent of Native Americans, and 13 percent of Asians/Pacific Islanders, but only 4 percent of whites, were enrolled in schools where more than 75 percent of students were poor enough to be eligible for free or subsidized lunch. National Center for Educational Statistics, "Contexts of Elementary and Secondary Education, School Characteristics and Climate: Poverty Concentration in Public Schools by Locale and Race/Ethnicity," 2009, http://nces.ed.gov/programs/coe/2009/section4/indicator25.asp.

52 Fifty-two percent of blacks, 57 percent of Hispanics, 33 percent of Asian or Pacific Islanders, and 29 percent of Native Americans, but just 3 percent of whites attended schools in which at least 75 percent of the students were racial minorities. National Center for Education Statistics, "Contexts of Elementary and Secondary Education, School Characteristics and Climate: Concentration of Public School Enrollment by Locale and Race/Ethnicity," 2009, http://nces.ed.gov/programs/coe/2009/section4/indicator26.asp.

53 Jonathan Kozol, "Still Separate, Still Unequal: America's Educational Apartheid," *Harper's Magazine* 311, 1864 (September 2005), 41-54.

54 Scott, *Contempt and Pity,* xi-xvii, 12; Roberts, *Shattered Bonds,* 276.

9
"The Strange Way We Lived": Divorce and American Childhood in the 1970s

Leslie Paris

Picture the scene: a well-to-do New York City family, circa 1979. The father, Ted, is a well-paid advertising executive focused on his career, devoting little time to his wife or to his six-year-old son, Billy. His stay-at-home wife, Joanna, dissatisfied with her inattentive husband and desperate to find herself, surprises Ted by announcing that she is leaving their marriage. By the time she returns, eighteen months later, feeling stronger and now eager to reclaim her child, the father and son have bonded intensely; Ted has made substantive professional compromises and even learned to make a credible batch of French toast for Billy. Although the mother wins their subsequent custody battle, she has a change of heart and ultimately acknowledges that Billy would be better off living with Ted.

This was the plot of Robert Benton's 1979 film *Kramer vs. Kramer,* which won the Academy Award for Best Picture of the Year in 1980, as well as various awards for its two adult leads, Dustin Hoffman and Meryl Streep. At the time of its release, the film was lauded for its relatively even-handed portrayal of the parents, both of whom are shown to love their son dearly, even if the film focuses mainly on the father-son bond. This popular film also struck a chord with audiences contemplating the new challenges couples with children faced when their marriages ended.

A decade after no-fault state divorce laws were first introduced, starting in California in 1970 and sweeping across every state except for Illinois and South Dakota by the end of the decade, divorce had become increasingly mainstream. The national divorce rate doubled between 1966 and 1976, reaching five per thousand married couples yearly. In 1960, there were 393,000 American divorces; by 1974 there were 970,000, far more than would be predicted by population increase. In some areas, applications for divorce were higher than those for marriage licences. One in two contemporary marriages were now expected to fail, and many more children to grow up in what were still sometimes termed "broken homes": approximately a million children per year undergoing the separation of their parents at the time *Kramer vs. Kramer* was released.[1]

Historically, a significant minority of American children have lived outside two-parent family arrangements. Some have lost a parent at home to death, marital separation, or desertion (the latter more common when divorce was more difficult and expensive to procure), others to structural factors in which children and parents were separated: the conditions of slavery prior to the Civil War, patterns of staggered family immigration in the nineteenth and twentieth centuries, the inability of some working-class parents to provide for their children before the introduction of widespread government-funded welfare programs, the forcible attendance of Native Americans at residential schools, or elite parents' support of private boarding schools for adolescents. In every generation, some children have also lived with extended family or other adults in their communities.

However, the sharp rise in divorce rates starting in the mid-1960s created unique and widespread patterns of family disruption. In earlier decades, due to the stress of economic uncertainty, working-class parents ended their marriages significantly more frequently than middle-class parents, making divorce appear mainly to be a problem of poorer Americans and of minorities. In the mid-1960s, however, white, middle-class parents quickly began closing the gap. As American divorce became a mainstream phenomenon, it highlighted the ways in which the institution of the family was troubled across a wide spectrum of American families. There were important variations, however, in children's experience of divorce. Younger children were more likely than their older siblings to see their parents separate before reaching adulthood, simply because the incidence of divorce was rising so rapidly. Meanwhile, in regions of the nation where families were most geographically mobile and risk-taking, and community structures were less stable, divorce was also more common: parents in the Southwest, for instance, were significantly more likely to separate than parents in the more traditional Northeast.[2]

Employing a historical lens, this chapter explores the rising divorce culture in intergenerational terms. The failure of one's parents' marriage, a process that children might at one time have considered odd or even mortifying, was now increasingly commonplace. As new rules for divorce were written, and as the social context within which divorce occurred was reinterpreted, children often remained embarrassed and saddened by their own family circumstances, but the social context of that sadness shifted. Now, as a broader and more diverse cohort of children knew others whose parents were separating, children's culture offered new forms of support to young people finding their way through the challenges of this transition.

Still, parents' freedom from unhappy marriages often came at a considerable emotional and economic cost to their daughters and sons. Divorce did more than pit one adult against another; across an intergenerational divide, children often saw their interests as fundamentally opposed to those of their parents (or at least to the parent initiating the separation). Divorce was a destabilizing process with important economic and psychological repercussions, not only at the moment of parental separation but beyond the divorce, when parents remarried and created new hybrid family arrangements. Adults and children both had to learn new roles, sometimes repeatedly, as they adapted to unexpected revisions of domestic life.

The Normal Family?

What makes family life normal or abnormal? In 1965, Daniel Patrick Moynihan's study *The Negro Family: The Case for National Action* infamously but influentially argued that black families represented a "tangle of pathology." Moynihan pointed to the extended legacy of slavery, enduring economic prejudice, and (most controversially) a distorted family structure marked by black matriarchs and absent fathers as signs of race-based family failure.[3] The Moynihan Report set off a firestorm of debate. Today, scholars have dismissed many of the report's central tenets, from its gendered ideals to its exaggerated claims of African American family breakdown. But the Moynihan Report was prescient in one respect: families of *all* races and backgrounds were undergoing strain. As a result of marital separation (along with rising rates of childbirth outside of marriage), more women would raise children on their own, usually in less secure economic circumstances. Black American parents remained more likely to divorce than their white counterparts, but white, middle-class families were also less stable than they once had been.[4]

For contemporary observers, rising divorce rates represented a litmus test of adult Americans' changing values in the wake of social transformation. In the 1960s, civil rights activism, anti-war protest, the emergence of a youth counterculture, the new feminism, and the beginnings of an activist gay rights movement challenged traditional political assumptions and personal expectations. In the 1970s, the end of a long era of postwar prosperity, the oil crisis, Watergate, and various international crises further unsettled Americans' sense of national direction.[5] On the domestic front, meanwhile, changes in family culture had been building for some time. As traditional institutions such as churches became less powerful, shame and community disapproval around failed marriages lessened significantly.

Changing gender relations also strained many marriages. The nuclear family ideal, which valorized families in which husbands worked for pay outside the home and wives stayed at home raising children, had long been imperfectly realized even at the pinnacle of its mid-twentieth-century popularity. From the war years onward, more mothers of young children entered the paid workforce. By the 1960s, some wives began to express resentment about their status at home and to demand more of their partners; others felt financially stable enough to leave unhappy marriages.

Numerous cultural commentators of the 1970s read rising divorce rates as a symptom of a turn in American culture toward self-centred individualism.[6] *Kramer vs. Kramer* makes this reproach; both Ted Kramer, who is initially too devoted to his career to notice his wife's unhappiness or to participate in raising his son, and Joanna Kramer, the mother who goes off to California (that mythic space of personal growth) to "find herself," are represented as preoccupied with self-actualization at the expense of the family unit and of their son. Historians of the so-called "sexual revolution" have noted that by the 1960s more men and women had higher expectations of the romantic and sexual pleasure, individual happiness, and self-fulfillment they expected to find within marriage. Judged according to these stricter criteria, more marriages failed to satisfy at least one partner.[7]

New no-fault divorce laws of the 1970s reflected the lessening stigma surrounding divorce. But they did not precipitate marital dissolution as much as they reflected and abetted it by making divorce easier to achieve. No longer must one partner claim a "moral" rationale, such as mental cruelty, neglect, alcoholism, or adultery; incompatibility was now enough of a reason to end a marriage. By removing the need for adversarial court proceedings, by simplifying the legal proceedings, and by potentially reducing costs, no-fault laws made divorce available to many Americans who might, in previous generations, either simply have separated without state involvement or else stayed in unhappy marriages.

Now, in an era of increased personal questioning, divorces appeared to give rise to more divorces. As the title of one 1977 *Ladies' Home Journal* article put the matter: "Is Divorce Contagious?" The answer, apparently, was yes: like the measles, as one Iowa State sociologist told the magazine's readers, a single neighbourhood block would experience a sudden cluster of divorces, each one leading other unhappy couples to consider ending their own marriages.[8] Even some of the nation's most famous advice-givers appeared to be unable to sustain happiness (or unwilling to sustain unhappiness) in marriage; both the national advice-columnist Ann Landers and the child expert Dr. Benjamin Spock ended their long-standing marriages of thirty-six and forty-eight years, respectively, during the 1970s.[9] Many such separations involved dependent children. Actor Dustin Hoffman, for instance, was a newly separated father at the time he played Ted in *Kramer vs. Kramer*. While he divided his time between Los Angeles and New York, his children (including a child from his ex-wife's previous marriage whom he had helped to raise) remained with their mother in New York.[10] Such were the increasingly complex grounds on which parents and children renegotiated their family relationships.

The Effects of Divorce on Children

Since the 1970s, a significant social scientific literature has explored the various disruptions associated with divorce for dependent children. These findings remain controversial. As sociologist Paul Amato, co-author of one of the best-known longitudinal studies of divorce and children, has argued, "weaknesses in study methodology mean that many findings are tentative at best."[11] As Amato and others have noted, many studies undertaken during the 1970s had important shortcomings. The majority were based on very small samples, most of them exclusively white and middle-class. Some studies lacked control groups of children from intact homes. Some of the parents who agreed to participate in extensive and time-consuming interviews were likely experiencing more interpersonal stress than average and may have joined the studies in search of professional support or outside counselling, making them less representative of divorcing families overall. Nor did most studies directly address the effects of economic class – a key component, as it turned out, of young people's changing circumstances. Finally, while scholars undertook many studies either on divorce or on stepfamily life, few explored the connections between these states, even though the majority of children of divorce would gain a step-parent (and often a step-sibling) within the next five years.[12]

Despite these methodological shortcomings, scholars have been in substantial accord on numerous points. For one, they argue that divorce is best understood as a process occuring over time, not simply an event. Where parents were fighting at home or appeared discontented, their children's experience of family crisis often began many years before the official separation. Thus, the effects of divorce depended on children's experience of strife in the home before the separation. The more fraught (or even violent) children's home lives had been, the more they exhibited psychological strain, but ultimately separation and divorce often improved their circumstances; indeed, some parental relationships were so obviously fraught with tension, violence, or abuse that children hoped these marriages would end and benefited when they did. Where family relations had been less abusive or contentious, children tended to find the initial period of separation particularly difficult. Overall, most daughters and sons were resilient in the face of their parents' separations, and within a few years most had made significant adjustments. However, there were still measurable differences between their levels of well-being and those of children from intact families.[13]

Many children whose home lives included significant exposure to parental conflict never imagined that their parents would separate. Consider the experience of Alexandra Sheedy, the eldest of three children living in New York City. The author of the 1975 children's novel *She Was Nice to Mice,* she recounted her own story of family rupture in the pages of *Seventeen* magazine in 1977, when she was fourteen. Six years earlier, she explained, her parents had told her that they were separating. They had been fighting, and she had suspected they were not happy, but still their separation came as an unhappy surprise. Like most children in her circumstances, she was at some level aware of her parents' discontents but preferred the marital status quo.[14]

Family crisis generally reached its peak around the moment of separation but continued to reverberate for years afterward. As one member of a "divorced kids" group at a high school in Lexington, Massachusetts, noted in 1979, "People have treated divorce as this big adult tragedy. They'll say, 'The kids are still young, they'll get over it.' But you don't get over it. It goes on the rest of your life."[15] Again, the degree to which the repercussions of divorce were damaging depended on the circumstances: when separated parents continued to fight bitterly over finances or custody issues, or tried to involve children directly in their disputes, or if one parent effectively disappeared, children's stress levels remained high.

Children of different ages experienced different emotional outcomes based on their specific developmental understandings of what had occurred. Many parents were unsure of what to say to their younger sons and daughters, many of whom were, as a result, left in the dark. In one California study, almost 80 percent of preschoolers had been given no explanation at all as to why their parents had separated. Unsurprisingly, given their young age, children of this group exhibited separation anxiety, resulting from significant changes to their sense of security and routines, and often reverted to more "babyish" behaviours.[16] In one 1978 Gallup poll, two-thirds of teenagers endorsed separation on grounds of incompatability.[17] At the same time, however, older children and adolescents were astute enough to see that they themselves did not necessarily benefit from their parents' choices. "The divorce may be better for them, but not for me," noted one twelve-year-old girl.[18]

In the years that followed marital disruption, children continued to reflect on whether divorce had been the right decision, and for whom. According to Judith S. Wallerstein, Sandra Blakeslee, and Joan Berlin Kelly, co-authors of a longitudinal study of children of divorce undertaken in Marin County (a prosperous suburb of San Francisco where divorce rates were among the nation's highest), the majority of children still hoped for reconciliation as late as five years after the divorce: "There is hardly a child of divorce we came to know who did not cling to the fantasy of a magical reconciliation between his separating parents."[19] But not all children shared this feeling. Some were relieved to live calmer lives afterward. As one teenaged girl from the Lexington group contended, the stress of living with her fighting parents made a divorce seem relatively palatable: "I am very much relieved that it's finally come about. Everyone is much happier."[20] If the majority of children who knew their parents were unhappy nevertheless preferred family life as it was to the destabilizing prospect of a divorce, some later reconsidered their positions in light of lessened family strife.

After the Divorce: Mothers, Fathers, and Step-Parents

These general trends were not particular to the 1970s, nor were children's feelings of loss, confusion, disappointment, or even (if their parents had fought long and bitterly) relief. More specific to the historical moment, and where I now turn my attention, were the ways in which this domestic transition influenced American childhood, family, and society more broadly. Perhaps most importantly, as a large number of studies quickly demonstrated, divorce had significant economic implications. Foremost, it was a key contributing factor to what scholars now term "the feminization of poverty," that is to say, the number of women (and dependent offspring) living in poverty. When married couples separated, women usually experienced a sharp financial decline, while men were generally better off. This trend came as somewhat of a surprise to some feminists who had initially supported no-fault divorce on the grounds that it was fairer and less inherently confrontational. Gender equality in no-fault divorce was based on the idea of equality between men and women in marriage and in society at large, but the economic evidence proved that divorce affected men and women quite differently.

Women's generally lower earnings sometimes reflected gender discrimination, but often the discrepancy resulted from earlier choices they had made in the context of their marriages: to remain out of the workforce taking care of young children for years at a time, or to juggle the demands of child care and part-time work while their husbands advanced their careers full time.[21] When these same women had to support themselves and their children after a divorce, they generally began with less-advanced job skills and less paid-work experience than their ex-husbands. Mothers with dependent children at home often found it difficult to focus on career or education and manage their children's day-to-day needs, especially if their daughters and sons were young. The new no-fault divorce laws also deprived many mothers of dependent children of the traditional legal and financial protections they had enjoyed back when dissatisfied husbands had to prove cause to secure a divorce.[22] Alimony payments were now both less generous and more time-limited, anticipating that women would be able to support themselves within a few years of the divorce.[23]

Because 90 percent of all children of divorce remained in the primary custody of their mothers, the feminization of poverty had important implications for dependent children. Living in a mother-led home after a divorce was an important risk factor for child poverty or at least a declining standard of living; fully one-quarter of all American children in mother-headed households (some of which were the products of divorce, others of children born out of wedlock) lived below the poverty line.[24] Even where women with dependent children received alimony or child support, the amounts were often insufficient to maintain their previous standards of living.

In earlier decades of the twentieth century, judges traditionally had awarded custody of young children to mothers on the premise that the "tender years" required maternal care. In the 1970s, many states changed their laws, and judges no longer granted mothers custody as a matter of course.[25] This was especially true in more progressive courts such as those of New York City; a traditional outcome was even less likely in the small minority of cases where women left their children behind at the time of divorce, as does Joanna Kramer in *Kramer vs. Kramer*.[26] However, in actual practice, relatively few fathers fought for primary custody; a small number of men used the demand as a bargaining tactic in adversarial divorces, but more often both parents assumed that children would remain with their mothers. Fathers were more likely to pull back emotionally and financially, whereas most mothers wished to retain primary custody. The story of Ted, Joanna, and Billy Kramer was, in these ways, highly unrepresentative of American divorce culture.[27]

Relations with fathers (generally the non-custodial parents) often became less intimate when parents separated. The weekend visit with one's father was a new American ritual for many children of the 1970s. Even when former spouses remained civil, these visits were often stressful. Some fathers felt pressure to entertain their children in the brief time they shared together. Others, depressed by the relative formality of these visits or engaged in ongoing strife with their ex-wives, retreated emotionally from their children once the natural rhythms of shared daily life were severed. In some cases, fathers chose to become more distant; in others, the distance was a result of mothers discouraging or barring fathers. The frequency of paternal contact was highly correlated to the provision of child support.[28] But some children felt caught in the middle, especially if their mothers asked them to ask their fathers for their child-support cheques.[29]

For a variety of reasons, then, many children experienced increasingly strained relations with their fathers, saw less of them, and mourned the loss of connection.[30] One fourteen-year-old boy recalled of his parents' separation, which had occurred five years previously:

> My father picked up his suitcases one day and walked out, because, as he said, he wanted his "freedom." We thought we were a close-knit family and it was an unexpected shock. I was only nine and my brother was six and a half. It was the death of our family. Today we see him on visitation day, but it is an artificial situation. He doesn't really know what I'm all about. I have actually lived without a real father for five years; perhaps the most important

years of my male life. My luck is that I have a mother who picked up the pieces.[31]

In the 1970s, the majority of non-resident fathers made no child-support payments. Activism around parental child support was still in the tentative stages, and many divorce agreements did not even mention it; only one-quarter of mother-led families received child support six months after the divorce, and after a year, the percentage was even lower.[32] As a result, one-third of separated mothers ended up on welfare, especially the assistance of Aid to Families with Dependent Children (AFDC). The growth of the AFDC program during this period effectively displaced family support from individual fathers onto the state. In the second half of the 1970s, the federal government begin prodding fathers to pay, intervening in child-support cases involving recipients of AFDC. Even so, in the late 1970s, only half of the 3.4 million single parents (generally mothers) entitled by law to child support were receiving it.[33]

Children experienced downward mobility in varied ways. Some moved to less desirable neighbourhoods or attended less prestigious schools. Many saw less of both parents, because their custodial mothers often had to work longer hours to support them. Debby, a girl sharing an apartment in Arlington, Virginia, with her divorced mother, noted with some dismay that her parents' divorce had affected her standard of living. "I'm getting used to it, but our other house was a lot better," she told a newspaper reporter. In contrast, her father, who had remarried and moved to California, appeared to be living rather well: "Dad and Carol live in a house with a swimming pool and two color TVs."[34]

Debby's move from a larger home to a smaller apartment (in a complex filled with single mothers and their children) was not exceptional. In the Marin County cohort, almost two-thirds of the children changed their primary residence within three or four years of the divorce, though most remained within thirty miles of where they started. Often the family home had to be sold after the divorce settlement, or parents relocated to resolve financial issues or to find better jobs or daycare arrangements.[35] Unless or until their mothers remarried, thereby generally improving the children's financial situation, diminished family expectations often still held true years later. For example, middle-class fathers (many of whom had remarried and started new families) were less likely to provide financial support for college educations to children from former marriages. As John, a seventeen-year-old member of the Lexington support group, explained, "There are special problems we kids have – college, for instance. I still don't know what I'm going to get from my father."[36]

Children had to let go of other expectations as well. One girl, who had been only two or three years of age when her parents separated, recalled several years later: "My sister and I, we tried to stop them. We didn't want them to divorce because at Christmas we were used to coming down and seeing what we got for presents." The two daughters, young enough to imagine that they could control the outcome of their parents' friction, seized upon the strategy of interrupting the parents' conversations as a way of impeding family dissolution.[37] Some children of divorce, however, noted that they received more presents from their (perhaps guilty or competing) parents, a partial consolation.[38]

After a divorce, parents' divergent parenting practices often became more obvious. Ken Sommers, the divorced father of three-year-old Stevie, told a *Washington Post* reporter in 1973 that although his ex-wife believed in routine and early bedtimes, "I enjoy a really heavy social schedule. I like to be with a lot of people to socialize and party." Taking care of Stevie on the weekends was no trouble, he related: "Stevie doesn't slow me down at all. The little boy loves to party. He calls my friends the happy hippies." Sommers's attempt to integrate part-time parenting with a hedonistic party lifestyle represented a departure from earlier models of respectable manhood, but the *Post* article depicted this father-and-son pair enjoying a close and loving relationship. Stevie was also clearly distraught at the end of the weekend when he was taken back to his mother's apartment; clutching his father's leg, he begged his father not to go. Stevie was lucky, for despite his parents' divergent values, they were working together to create stability for their son. Still, at a young age the boy understood that his own need for both parents came second to their desire to be apart.[39]

Children's initial adaptation to divorce was thus only the first of several major readjustments that they had to make. When parents found new partners, and most did, a second round of adjustment began. Fathers were somewhat more likely to remarry than were mothers, and younger parents were more likely to remarry than were older ones.[40] By 1980, 3.5 million households included a remarried parent with at least one child from a previous marriage.[41] Perhaps a third of those marriages were unsuccessful, and those with stepchildren tended to be somewhat less stable. Thus, a number of children ended up in a series of different family arrangements, from single-parent to blended families and sometimes back again if parents subsequently divorced their new spouses.[42] "I have eight siblings," reported one girl in a blended family that had undergone several permutations; some were former step-siblings with whom she no longer lived.[43] Another adolescent girl from the Lexington group, whose mother had remarried twice, put it bluntly: "It's very hard adjusting to a new person in the house."[44]

Mothers' remarriages often enhanced children's economic position, but the ambiguity of stepfamily life was itself a source of stress. Such intimate domestic changes generally affected the original family tie as well; if both parents remarried, children were much less likely to have weekly contact with their fathers.[45] In the 1970s, the scripts for blended families were only beginning to be written, and everyone found them baffling at times. For many children, loyalty to birth parents made new connections tentative and unsure. As one sixteen-year-old boy declared, "Our relationship with Sharon [his stepmother] is not tops." His ten-year-old stepsister echoed his feelings: "I don't think of Bob as my Dad. It's hard for me to explain. He's just not like my real father."[46]

Even children who established strong relationships with sympathetic step-parents were often unsure of the appropriate social protocols. Some wondered what to call a step-parent, fearing that to use the term "Mom" or "Dad" would signal disloyalty to a biological parent. Confused about the status of his father's girlfriend, one preschooler settled on "Kathy-Mommy."[47] Parents' new partners also forced children to confront their mothers' and fathers' sexuality. "It's weird," one teen said of her mother's new boyfriend. "They're like high school kids, holding hands and everything. At first I thought, well good, she's found someone. Then I had to decide if I liked him or not."[48] Children's relationships with parents' new partners were perhaps inevitably fraught. This was, after all, complicated emotional terrain. It is not surprising that those step-parents who tried to insist on their new status often met with resistance, nor that as a group step-parents tended to be less engaged, whether as disciplinarians or as nurturers, than were biological parents.[49] Still, the rise of remarriage required more and more children to learn to live with their parents' new partners, and with the practical and emotional issues raised by these family permutations.

Children's Support Networks

In the 1970s, legal and mental health care professionals and child advocates discussed how families might better navigate the stresses of divorce. One legal option widely promoted from the 1970s onward, and designed to keep both parents more actively involved in their children's lives, was joint legal custody. In joint custody arrangements, parents officially maintained shared responsibility for their children's financial and educational choices. This idea was lauded by lawmakers concerned about fathers disinvesting in their children's lives. In practice, however, the efficacy of such shared arrangements often weakened over time. Non-resident fathers tended to become less invested in shared planning. Others, like Debby's father, simply lived too far away ever to be equal parenting partners.

A few parents explored an option that required still more parental co-ordination, shared physical custody. In this instance, either children or their parents regularly shuttled back and forth between two residences. This idea was distinct from weekly formal visits to a non-custodial parent; in joint custody, neither parent would be a child's official primary custodial parent. The Sheedy parents chose this option, so Alexandra and her siblings spent half of the week at each of their parents' New York City apartments. But shared physical custody, while possible in a city with excellent public transportation such as New York, was frequently impractical elsewhere. Many fathers moved out of their family homes into smaller apartments that lacked adequate space to house their children, or else they lived far enough away so that that their daughters and sons could not possibly attend one school while shuttling from home to home.[50]

In addition to these novel legal options, children encountered a new literature designed specifically to address their feelings about parental separation.[51] For example, the self-help literature of psychiatrist Richard A. Gardner provided frank guidance. Gardner challenged children to be clear with their parents about what upset or angered them, and to be realistic about their mothers' and fathers' personal limitations: "If your father hardly ever visits you, this does not mean that there is something wrong with you. The problem is not that you are unlovable. The problem is that your father cannot love. The problem is in him, not in you."[52] Noted juvenile-fiction writer Judy Blume incorporated several mentions of Gardner's *The Boys and Girls Book about Divorce* (1970) in her 1972 novel *It's Not the End of the World,* an example of fiction designed to reflect children's journey through their parents' divorce. Karen, the twelve-year-old narrator, at first cannot believe that her feuding parents are really separating. For much of the novel, she attempts to bring them back together. Only after much struggle does she become reconciled to the fact that her parents will never reunite.

This story, and many others like it, reassured children by representing their feelings as legitimate, if unrealistic. Countless articles in popular magazines, and a spate of new books about divorce written for parents and children, emphasized that children were not responsible for what had happened, nor were they themselves being divorced. Children whose parents remained actively loving and involved likely appreciated such expressions of reassurance and representations of their experience. Those whose experience after marital dissolution was one of lessening parental (usually fatherly) involvement were undoubtedly less reassured.

As divorce rates rose, more children could turn to experienced peers for solace and support. Alexandra Sheedy, for instance, initially experienced her parents' breakup as a source of shame. Like many other children, she imagined that she must somehow have been to blame, and few of her friends were in the same boat: "I dreaded inviting anybody home because I would have to explain the strange way we lived." Later when a close friend of hers found herself in the same predicament, Sheedy offered a wealth of advice and empathy: "I became her understanding confidante."[53] Through her writing in the pages of a national magazine, she offered support to many more. Other children of divorce learned from local cohorts of children in similar circumstances. In Arlington, Debby's best friend in her apartment complex was a girl whose parents had also divorced. The girl's mother noted that "all the kids have sleeping bags and a lot of 'single' mothers who make them feel welcome."[54] In *It's Not the End of the World,* Blume's narrator, twelve-year-old Karen, learns about *The Boys and Girls Book about Divorce* through a new friend, Val, whom she meets at her father's new apartment complex.

Such peer networks offered far more to older children than to younger ones. In the wake of her parents' divorce, Sheedy did not feel that she could confide in her two siblings, perceiving them to be too young to be of any support. Older children were also more likely to have access to adult-led discussion groups. And girls may have been more willing to share the kinds of feelings that allowed them to solicit empathy. The Lexington high school support group, for instance, was founded in 1976 by a school guidance counsellor, himself a divorced father. Local school authorities estimated that 20 percent of the school's nineteen hundred students had divorced parents, but only twenty-five girls and boys joined the group, and most members were girls. As one girl suggested, boys were often ashamed or reluctant to share their feelings.[55] Yet if the group assisted only a small minority of students, its existence provided the possibility of support for those who used it and those who simply knew that it was available.[56]

If this cohort was disappointed in or angry with their parents, they knew that they were at least not alone; the normalization of fractured families provided many opportunities for children to compare notes. As one child from a wealthy New York City suburb attending a support group for children of divorced parents explained, her after-school schedule was busy: "I can't make a date for Monday, that's piano, and Tuesday I have divorce, but Wednesday is O.K."[57] One thirteen-year-old girl living in the Southwest reported that "in school we talk about each other's parents. My friends ask, 'Is your stepfather harder on you than your real father?' 'Does your father not like your mother?' 'What's it like not being with him?'"[58] Hearing their concerns voiced by others, children generally felt less shame about their own family circumstances.

A Tangle of Pathology? Parents and Children of a New Era

In *Kramer vs. Kramer,* both parents are initially compelled by their individual desires. Ultimately, their redemption comes inasmuch as they learn to make choices that prioritize their son, Billy, over themselves. For Ted, this means choosing a less high-powered career. For Joanna, it means allowing Ted to retain primary custody. In point of fact, however, many 1970s parents have found it difficult to work collaboratively with their ex-partners to raise their children. More particularly, fathers' diminished roles after their marriages failed reflected changing expectations about men's obligation to provide for their progeny in American culture. Fathers often found part-time contact fundamentally unsatisfying, took a diminished role in parenting, and suffered few social consequences for doing so. In response, policy makers who might once have been inclined to see the institution of family life as a private matter became increasingly concerned by the public implications of marital breakdown, particularly many fathers' diminishing role in parenting or what was now termed the "deadbeat dad" phenomenon. The Family Support Act of 1988 pushed the states to establish fathers' paternity, mandated that states standardize child-support payments based on fathers' earnings, and allowed the states to garnishee paycheques. These projects represented a new degree of intervention in what was ostensibly the private sphere.[59]

As mothers and fathers forged new ground, they pulled their children along with them, often quite unwillingly, but more as a cohort than ever. American children of the 1970s, the first cohort of American children more likely to lose a parent at home to divorce than to death, experienced an important shift in the meaning of divorce. Some longitudinal studies suggest that children whose parents divorced before the era of no-fault divorce suffered more serious academic impact and psychological adjustment than children whose parents separated afterward; back when the process of obtaining a divorce had been more challenging, children whose parents who did get divorced might well have been exposed to more (and more prolonged) conflict and unhappiness. As divorce became easier to obtain and less stigmatizing, children also gained more peer support.[60] Marital dissolution remains a sad and anxious time for children, but it no longer has the same cultural resonance as once it had; from the 1970s onward, children of divorce were no longer "lost" to the same degree as their predecessors.

Notes

1   Georgia Dullea, "Child Custody: Jurists Weigh Film vs. Life," *New York Times,* 21 December 1979, B6. On the difficulties of interpreting divorce statistics, see Glenda Riley, *Divorce: An American Tradition* (New York: Oxford University Press, 1991), 157-59.

2   Ruth Brandwein, Carol A. Brown, and Elizabeth Maury Fox, "Women and Children Last: The Social Situation of Divorced Mothers and Their Families," *Journal of Marriage and the Family* 36, 3 (1974): 500; Paul C. Glick, "A Demographer Looks at American Families," *Journal of Marriage and the Family* 37, 1 (1975): 22; Larry Bumpass and Ronald R. Rindfuss, "Children's Experience of Marital Disruption," *American Journal of Sociology* 85, 1 (1979): 55.

3   Daniel P. Moynihan, *The Negro Family: The Case for National Action* (Washington, DC: US Department of Labor, Office of Planning and Research, 1965), 29-45.

4   Bumpass and Rindfuss, "Children's Experience of Marital Disruption," 55. Steven Mintz and Susan Kellogg make a similar point about the meaning of the Moynihan Report in *Domestic Revolutions: A Social History of American Family Life* (New York: Free Press, 1988), 213.

5   The relevant historiography includes Peter N. Carroll, *It Seemed Like Nothing Happened: America in the 1970s* (New Brunswick, NJ: Rutgers University Press, 1982, 1990); Peter Braunstein and Michael William Doyle, eds., *Imagine Nation: The American Counterculture of the 1960s and '70s* (New York: Routledge, 2002); Van Gosse and Richard Moser, eds., *The World the Sixties Made: Politics and Culture in Recent America* (Philadelphia: Temple University Press, 2003); and Beth Bailey and David Farber, eds., *America in the 1970s* (Lawrence, KS: University Press of Kansas, 2004).

6   Examples of this criticism include Tom Wolfe's "The Me Decade," originally published in *The New Yorker,* republished in Tom Wolfe, *Mauve Gloves and Madmen, Clutter and Vine, and*

Other Stories, Sketches, and Essays (New York: Farrar, Straus and Giroux, 1976), and Christopher Lasch, *The Culture of Narcissism: American Life in an Age of Diminishing Expectations* (New York: Warner Books, 1979).

7 See, for example, Mintz and Kellogg, *Domestic Revolutions,* 205.

8 Sally Wendkos Olds, "Is Divorce Contagious?" *Ladies' Home Journal* 94, 2 (1977): 81.

9 Ibid., 81, 151-52.

10 Ingrid Groller, "Families: On Being a Parent, It's Dustin vs. Dustin," *Washington Post,* 28 November 1979.

11 Paul R. Amato, "Life-Span Adjustment of Children to Their Parents' Divorce," *The Future of Children* 4, 1 (1994): 144. See also Paul R. Amato and Alan Booth, *A Generation at Risk: Growing Up in an Era of Family Upheaval* (Cambridge, MA: Harvard University Press, 1997).

12 Reviews of the divorce literature from the 1970s onward include Deborah Anna Luepnitz, "Children of Divorce: A Review of the Psychological Literature," *Law and Human Behavior* 2, 2 (1978): 167-79; David H. Demo and Alan C. Acock, "The Impact of Divorce on Children," *Journal of Marriage and the Family* 50, 3 (1988): 619-48; Frank F. Furstenberg Jr., "Divorce and the American Family," *Annual Review of Sociology* 16 (1990): 379-403; Paul R. Amato, "Children's Adjustment to Divorce: Theories, Hypotheses, and Empirical Support," *Journal of Marriage and the Family* 55, 1 (1993): 23-38; Amato, "Life-Span Adjustment"; and Paul R. Amato, "Reconciling Divergent Perspectives: Judith Wallerstein, Quantitative Family Research, and Children of Divorce," *Family Relations* 52, 4 (2003): 332-39.

13 See, for example, the findings of E. Mavis Hetherington and W. Glenn Clingempeel, "Coping with Marital Transitions," *Monographs of the Society for Research in Child Development,* ser. 227, vol. 57, nos. 2-3, 1992.

14 Alexandra Sheedy, "How Can Mom and Dad *Do* This to Me?" *Seventeen,* August 1977, 242. Sheedy is better known today as Ally Sheedy, a popular actress of the 1980s.

15 Brad Owens, "Self-Help Group Offers Forum for 'Divorced' Kids," *Christian Science Monitor,* 9 May 1979.

16 Shirley Streshinsky, "How Divorce Really Affects Children: A Major Report," *Redbook,* September 1976, 136.

17 Carroll, *It Seemed Like Nothing Happened,* 278.

18 Streshinsky, "How Divorce Really Affects Children," 136.

19 See Judith S. Wallerstein and Joan Berlin Kelly, *Surviving the Breakup: How Children and Parents Cope with Divorce* (New York: Basic Books, 1980), and Judith S. Wallerstein and Sandra Blakeslee, *Second Chances: Men, Women, and Children a Decade after Divorce* (New York: Ticknor and Fields, 1989), xvii. The study followed sixty families, most of which were white and, in all but one case, where the mothers had custody of the children and the fathers were living elsewhere.

20 Owens, "Self-Help Group," 15.

21 For an early elaboration of this argument, see Brandwein, Brown, and Fox, "Women and Children Last."

22 Lenore J. Weitzman, *The Divorce Revolution: The Unexpected Social and Economic Consequences for Women and Children in America* (New York: Free Press, 1985), xi. See also Riley, *Divorce,* 165.

23 Charles E. Welch III and Sharon Price-Bonham, "A Decade of No-fault Divorce Revisited: California, Georgia, and Washington," *Journal of Marriage and the Family* 45, 2 (1983): 411-18.

24 Forty percent of children born in the 1970s would spend some time in a single-parent household, 90 percent of which were headed by women, mainly as the result of separation or divorce but also, in a growing minority of cases, as a result of births outside of marriage. Carroll, *It Seemed Like Nothing Happened,* 282. By the early 1980s, about one-third of all American children were not living with both natural parents – an increase of two-thirds over the past decade. V.O. Packard, *Our Endangered Children: Growing Up in a Changing World* (Boston: Little, Brown, 1983), 186, 259.

25 Leon Friedman, "Fathers Don't Make Good Mothers," *New York Times,* 28 January 1973.

26 Groller, "Families."

27 On the effects of father absence after divorce see, for example, Sara McLanahan and Julien Teitler, "The Consequences of Father Absence," and Michael E. Lamb, Kathleen J. Sternberg,

and Ross A. Thompson, "The Effects of Divorce and Custody Arrangements on Children's Behavior, Development, and Adjustment," in Michael E. Lamb, ed., *Parenting and Child Development in "Nontraditional" Families* (Mahwah, NJ: Lawrence Erlbaum Associates, 1999), 83-102, 125-35. On the reasons why fathers might have infrequent contact, see James R. Dudley, "Increasing Our Understanding of Divorced Fathers Who Have Infrequent Contact with Their Children," *Family Relations* 40, 3 (1991): 279-85.

28 Frank F. Furstenberg Jr., Christine Winquist Nord, James L. Peterson, and Nicholas Zill, "The Life Course of Children of Divorce: Marital Disruption and Parental Contact," *American Sociological Review* 48, 5 (1983): 664.

29 See, for instance, Randy Shipp, "Helping Children of Divorce," *Christian Science Monitor*, 11 December 1979.

30 Furstenberg et al., "The Life Course of Children of Divorce," 656-68.

31 Wallerstein and Kelly, *Surviving the Breakup*, 302.

32 Packard, *Our Endangered Children*, 267.

33 Ibid., 268; Kathryn Tolbert, "Fighting for Child Support," *Washington Post*, 20 November 1980.

34 Eloise Taylor Lee, "Single Mothers," *Christian Science Monitor*, 15 August 1978.

35 Wallerstein and Kelly, *Surviving the Breakup*, 183.

36 Shipp, "Helping Children of Divorce." Judith Wallerstein, Julia Lewis, and Sandra Blakeslee, *The Unexpected Legacy of Divorce: A 25 Year Landmark Study* (New York: Hyperion, 2000) also note that divorced fathers were less likely to pay their children's college tuitions. See also Amato, "Life-Span Adjustment," 147.

37 Wallerstein and Kelly, *Surviving the Breakup*, 200.

38 Janice M. Hammond, "Children of Divorce: A Study of Self-Concept, Academic Achievement, and Attitudes," *Elementary School Journal* 80, 2 (1979): 60.

39 William Hoffer, "Sunday's Child," *Washington Post*, 9 December 1973. These names are pseudonyms. See also Wallerstein and Kelly, *Surviving the Breakup*, 3, 10.

40 Wallerstein and Kelly, *Surviving the Breakup*, 183-84. Forty-three percent of the fathers and 33 percent of the mothers had remarried five years after the divorce.

41 Michael Norman, "The New Extended Family," *New York Times Magazine*, 23 November 1980, 44.

42 Furstenberg et al., "The Life Course of Children of Divorce," 661; Riley, *Divorce*, 170.

43 Letter to ZOOM, WGBH archive, Brighton, MA.

44 B.J.O., "Teens from Broken Homes Share Views," *Christian Science Monitor*, 9 May 1979.

45 Furstenberg et al., "The Life Course of Children of Divorce," 666.

46 Norman, "The New Extended Family," 147.

47 Hoffer, "Sunday's Child."

48 B.J.O., "Teens from Broken Homes Share Views," 14.

49 #17, male, 1984, interview by Frederick W. Bozett, "Children of Gay Fathers, 1985," hdl: 1902.1/00874, Murray Research Archive, Harvard University, Cambridge, MA.

50 Furstenberg, "Divorce and the American Family," 385; Amato, "Life-Span Adjustment," 153.

51 See, for example, Beth Goff, *Where Is Daddy: The Story of a Divorce* (Boston: Beacon Press, 1969); Richard A. Gardner, *The Boys and Girls Book about Divorce* (New York: Bantam Books, 1970); Judy Blume, *It's Not the End of the World* (Scarsdale, NY: Bradbury Press, 1972); Linda Sitea, "Zachary's Divorce," in Carole Hart, Letty Cottin Pogrebin, Mary Rodgers, and Marlo Thomas, eds., *Free to Be ... You and Me* (New York: McGraw-Hill, 1974); Jonah Kalb and David Viscott, *What Every Kid Should Know* (Boston: Houghton Mifflin, 1976); Edith Atkin and Estelle Rubin, *Part-Time Father* (New York: Vanguard, 1976); Arlene Richards and Irene Willis, *How to Get It Together When Your Parents Are Coming Apart* (New York: David McKay, 1976); Richard A. Gardner, *The Parents Book about Divorce* (Garden City, NY: Doubleday, 1977); Richard A. Gardner, *The Boys and Girls Book about One-Parent Families* (New York: Putnam, 1978); Patricia Perry and Marietta Lynch, *Mommy and Daddy Are Divorced* (New York: Dial, 1978); and Eda LeShan, *What's Going to Happen to Me?* (New York: Four Winds, 1978).

52 Gardner, *The Boys and Girls Book about One-Parent Families* (New York: Bantam, 1978, 1983), 55.

53 Sheedy, "How Can Mom and Dad *Do* This to Me?" 243, 290.
54 Taylor Lee, "Single Mothers."
55 Owens, "Self-Help Group," 15.
56 Shipp, "Helping Children of Divorce." Similar programs were developed across the country, including a Children of Divorce program at Pennsylvania State University. On a course called "Understanding and Coping with Family Change" in the Minneapolis school system (titled so as not to stigmatize children of divorce but designed primarily with them in mind), see Shirley Holdahl and Paul Caspersen, "Children of Family Change: Who's Helping Them Now?" *The Family Coordinator* 26, 4 (1977): 472-77.
57 Jeanne Clare Feron, "Helping Children Live with Divorce," *New York Times*, 22 May 1977.
58 Norman, "The New Extended Family," 173.
59 Furstenberg, "Divorce and the American Family," 399.
60 See the discussion in Amato, "Life-Span Adjustment," 149.

10

Losing the Child in Child-Centred Legal Processes

Cindy L. Baldassi, Susan B. Boyd, and Fiona Kelly

In many legal fields involving children, a child-centred approach is touted, and decision makers such as judges are directed to give sole or paramount consideration to the best interests of the child. Indeed, the Convention on the Rights of the Child affirms that the best interests of the child shall be a primary consideration in all actions concerning children.[1] This test has been widely embraced as allowing a necessary flexibility in decision making, given the diverse scenarios that can arise. In fact, Canadian judges and lawmakers have made it clear that there should be no starting presumption about what is in a child's best interests in the context of child custody and access decisions.[2] Such presumptions are understood to detract from the "individual justice to which every child is entitled."[3] Rather than applying presumptions, decision makers should be concerned with what arrangement is best for a particular child.

This chapter suggests that social biases influencing the application of the best interests test can produce decisions that miss the relevance of key factors in children's lives. The omission of these factors is often most apparent in the relatively new phenomena of lesbian parenting and parenting through the use of reproductive technologies; however, for some time it has been clear that the modern directive that legal decision makers focus only on a child's best interests raises more questions than it answers. Robert Mnookin famously pointed out in the 1970s that the best interests principle was highly indeterminate.[4] Some scholars have even toyed with the notion that, provided neither parent is unfit, tossing a coin to resolve custody disputes might result in decisions as satisfactory as those that judges make using the principle.[5] Because decision makers are relatively unfettered in their ability to insert their own ideological judgments into the determination of a given child's interests, the perceived value of certain family forms may be overemphasized and important factors in the lives of marginalized children, such as poverty or racism, may be overlooked.

Most pertinent to this volume is the insight that determination of the best interests of the child may vary as a result of factors such as sexism, racism, or class. The extent to which a family deviates from whatever norm is dominant at a particular historical moment may influence the extent and manner of state intervention in the name of children. Determination of a child's best interests is, then, far from objective. Rather, the same social biases that influence other fields, such as social policy, also influence legal decisions. Moreover, the process of determining what is in a child's best interests is intrinsically, and perhaps inevitably, connected with an assessment of the adults in a child's life. Thus, it would be a false exercise to try to study the interests of any child, including marginalized or "lost" kids, without also examining familial contexts within which that child lives or has lived, the race, class, gender, sexual orientation, and/or (dis)ability of associated adults, and the ways in which decision makers frequently assess adults by reference to dominant norms that may have little to do with a child's lived reality.

Child protection provides one example. Although family members sometimes jeopardize children's safety, many cases of apprehension and intervention appear to have at least as much to do with disapproval of diverse parenting styles and failure to appreciate conditions beyond parental control as with protection. Child welfare policies that have removed children from impoverished parents and placed them in state custody or allowed them to be adopted into wealthier households have too often appeared to enforce the subordinate citizenship status of the poor, Aboriginal peoples, and other racialized minorities. The best interests principle has been invoked in state apprehension of Aboriginal children from their Aboriginal caregivers or parents in a manner that effectively precludes systematic consideration of the racism, colonialism, and poverty experienced within Aboriginal communities.[6] The best interests test may also be applied in a manner that fails to take account of parenting practices that vary from the normative nuclear family or that are more community-oriented. Reforms to welfare law and policy in the United States, combined with changes in child welfare law and policy, have created a system that appears to take for granted the benefits of breaking up many African American families.[7] When parents with disabilities are concerned, psychiatric evidence is sometimes deployed uncritically in an effort to determine the best interests of children.[8] The recurrence of diverse prejudices when it comes to legal regulation of parent-child relationships requires constant vigilance from scholars and those interested in justice. Otherwise, the realities of children and their actual needs may be rendered invisible.

This chapter undertakes the problem of assessing just how the "best interests of the child" doctrine is operationalized, first in relation to the highly gendered history of child custody law, then in relation to two new fields involving so-called alternative parenting: lesbian parenting and parenting through the use of reproductive technologies. We ask how the best interests principle is interpreted in these scenarios and highlight the central role of familial ideology in mediating the application of the principle. Our primary focus is Canadian law, but, since legal decisions circulate readily, especially among nations drawing on shared legal traditions, we also draw on developments in other English-speaking countries when Canadian examples are sparse. Judicially determined cases are our main subject, though they constitute a small minority of parentage and custody resolutions, which can be reached by agreement or negotiation and often never become the subject of a court decision. For example, less than 4 percent of divorces involving dependent children in Canada are finalized by contested court hearings.[9] Judicial decisions, while forming the tip of the iceberg, illustrate both the coercive and the ideological power of law, and show that the tenacious nature of patriarchal rights to custody has not served all children well. We suggest that children's interests are undermined if decision makers overemphasize (1) the necessity of a particular family form in a child's life (especially the need for a father figure); and (2) the interests of certain adults (such as those with biogenetic ties to the child) over others (such as social parents). We argue that by overemphasizing family form or the interests of specific adults, what is important to children may well be lost, a deep irony in a legal system that claims to be child-centred. It is, of course, impossible to sever entirely children's interests from those of adults, particularly their caregivers. Our concern is that the legal system prioritizes abstract ties, often grounded in genetic essentialism, over concrete relational ties of care. We argue that in order to prioritize children's interests, a child's *relationships* should be emphasized rather than the abstract allure of biogenetic ties.

"Lost" Kids, Absent Fathers

Over the past two centuries, Anglo-Canadian legal discourse shifted from an explicit emphasis on parental (primarily paternal) rights to a focus on children's interests and welfare. During the nineteenth century, the nearly absolute rights of fathers to guardianship and custody of sons and daughters born within wedlock began to be eroded in the name of the welfare of the child.[10] This change was in part the product of early feminist struggles that challenged the patriarchal rights of fathers over children regardless of a history of maternal care and paternal absence; but the transition to a legal system that recognized children's interests and mothers' rights was agonizingly slow.[11] For quite some time, maternal custody was granted only in exceptional circumstances. Certainly in the nineteenth century, mothers who were awarded custody both conformed to the strict expectations of chaste female behaviour and were contrasted to fathers who made "normal" marital life impossible through their drunkenness or violence.[12] Many judges in the nineteenth, and even the early twentieth, century were concerned that the sanctity of marriage might be diminished should wives be permitted to separate from their husbands *and* receive custody of the children.[13] A mother who failed to provide a judge with an appropriate reason for having left the marital home or her duties as a wife might fail to obtain custody and be abjured to return to the marriage, even if cruelty had been alleged against the husband.[14]

This presumptive paternal right to custody prevailed well into the twentieth century in many jurisdictions. Prince Edward Island, for instance, did not legislatively alter the common law rights of fathers until 1968.[15] In New Brunswick, many judges continued to ignore what appeared to be statutory declarations of parental equality well into the 1980s.[16] The so-called maternal presumption offered by the tender years doctrine did not become established until the mid-twentieth century. Even then, many factors could trump the notion that children of tender years should be cared for by their mothers.[17] A higher standard of sexual morality was expected of mothers, and they bore a greater responsibility for maintaining the nuclear family unit, so that judges applied a more intense scrutiny to mothers' conduct than to fathers.'[18] Mothers who did not adhere to the norms of good wifely behaviour could easily be challenged, regardless of the quality of their parenting or their ties with a child. A mother who left her husband without what a judge considered good reason might be viewed as depriving her daughter or son of the opportunity to live in a "normal" family. In neither the nineteenth nor twentieth century did judges always find proof of abusive conduct by a husband of a wife to be a convincing reason for a wife to leave, because of the presumed advantage of a child growing up with both parents in a family home. Well into the twentieth century a mother might be denied custody because of her refusal to "quit work and devote herself to what is or should be a full-time job as a married woman and mother" or doubts about her reputation as a "model housekeeper and mother."[19] The focus was not so much on the child's interests as on the highly gendered and differentiated expectations of maternal and paternal behaviour. Although these expectations shifted over time, the continuities are striking in terms of the heightened scrutiny of maternal conduct.

In all historical periods, many fathers, of course, have agreed to custody arrangements that recognize the caregiving link between most mothers and children. Canadian custody statistics are frustratingly incomplete but indicate that from the 1970s until the 1990s mothers received sole custody of between 70 and 80 percent of children in divorces, reflecting in large part such agreements.[20] The minority of fathers who chose to disrupt that caregiving link were, however, quite successful, given the continuing predominance of female care for children. Those fathers who took the proactive role of petitioning for divorce (and custody) in the 1970s received custody in 42.6 percent of such cases.[21]

Since the 1970s, parenting laws have become increasingly gender neutral, with distinctions between mothers and fathers diminishing as the emphasis on children's best interests became more firmly entrenched. In Canada, as in most Western countries, shared parenting or joint custody has also become the preferred legal norm for post-separation parenting.[22] Statistics reflect this trend, with maternal custody awards on divorce diminishing in favour of joint custody. By 2002, custody of 49.5 percent of dependents was awarded to the wife, and custody of 41.8 percent was awarded jointly to the husband and wife.[23] Although the women's movement has long advocated for greater participation by fathers in children's care, and change in the sexual division of labour is slowly happening, the joint custody trend also reflects the increasingly global influence of the fathers' rights movement, a socially conservative social movement in the main.[24] Canada does not have a legislative presumption in favour of joint custody, but most commentators agree that, in practice, such a presumption is the starting pointing for many legal determinations. This presumption is based first on a concept of equality between the parents regardless of their parenting histories and, second, on a normative judgment that children fare better when they have a relationship with their fathers. Despite the unclear social science evidence on this point, case law relating to custody and access, as well as birth registration and naming, indicates that preserving father-child relationships is now a key policy emphasis.[25] The result is that a mother who seeks restrictions on paternal contact or decision-making authority must raise clear evidence that joint custody is *not* in a child's best interest, for instance, if the father compromises a child's safety or has not taken appropriate responsibility for a child. In fact, the legal system increasingly grants male parents formal legal rights, regardless of whether they are responsible for a child's care or not. In many joint custody cases, children continue to reside primarily with their mothers, but both parents hold equal decision-making authority.[26] As a result, one could argue that joint custody creates a situation in which mothers have responsibilities whereas fathers have rights.

Although mothers are still more often their children's primary caregivers than are fathers, both before and after marital breakdown, judges are reluctant to make decisions that might diminish the father-child relationship.[27] Even fathers who abuse their partners are awarded some form of custody or access in a large number of cases, reflecting the fact that access is rarely denied outright. Melanie Rosnes studied sixteen Canadian custody cases involving evidence or allegations of physical violence (all by men) from 1992 to 1994. In most cases, the mother received custody and the father *unsupervised* access. Access was terminated in only two cases and ordered to be supervised in only one case.[28] Linda Neilson's later study of court files found that abusive partners obtain not only access but also joint, split, or even full custody of their children in appreciable numbers, ranging from 16 to 26.7 percent of relevant cases.[29] Yet, research indicates that children who witness domestic violence may exhibit a wide variety of symptoms, including post-traumatic stress disorder, and between 30 and 60 percent of those whose mothers experience abuse are themselves likely to be abused.[30] The unwillingness of judges to acknowledge such harm highlights the disproportionate normative power of the two-parent, heterosexual, nuclear family norm in decision makers' minds and unwillingness to acknowledge that abuse can continue or accelerate after parents separate. When coupled with an adherence to formal gender equality or, rather more accurately, gender blindness, the deference to traditional norms becomes very difficult to displace.

Serious questions arise about whether the trend toward equal parental rights benefits children or instead promotes adult interests – primarily those of fathers. Some prominent sociologists have concluded that children's interests take second place within this paradigm.[31] Even putting aside abuse scenarios, social science research indicates that a legal emphasis on greater contact with non-custodial parents and/or joint custody is misplaced. It is the type of parenting the non-custodial parent engages in, not the amount of time spent with children, that is the most significant indicator of children's well-being. Some children may fare worse in joint custody arrangements, particularly those from high-conflict families.[32] Children value quality and flexibility of relationships with parents rather than quantity of time.[33] To the extent that judges are excessively influenced by normative trends affirming the importance of paternal access, then, they may not serve children's interests well.

Losing Children to Heteronormativity

Although most judges take seriously their mandate to determine the best interests of a child, decision making about lesbian parenting is often visibly ideological. An abundant literature identifies how lesbian mothers who have left heterosexual relationships after coming out have encountered difficulty in obtaining custody.[34] The best interests standard has often been interpreted by reference to preferred heterosexual familial norms rather than by reference to the quality of parent-child relationships. Many judges have effectively cautioned lesbian mothers to be discreet about their intimate relationships, with the implicit or sometimes explicit threat that no matter the strength of maternal-child tie, custody may still be lost.[35] Gay fathers have also encountered difficulties in gaining access to their sons and daughters.[36]

The situation is equally prejudicial when it comes to decision making about children conceived through donor insemination and living in lesbian-headed families. These households raise unique challenges for family law because they do not adhere to the heteronormative nuclear model. Some are, in fact, nuclear in form, with two mothers playing parenting roles. Others include three or more possible parents – two mothers, as well as a known sperm donor, who may have a relationship with the child but may or may not be regarded as a social parent. The best interests test should, in theory, be able to meet the challenge of domestic diversity, but given its focus on the individual child in his or her discrete family circumstances, more often than not the heteronormative underpinnings of the principle are exposed as judges apply a one-size-fits-all model. Assumptions about appropriate family structure, the importance of fathers, and the significance of biogenetic connection rise to the surface as judges struggle to treat lesbian-headed families as complete. In many instances, the result is that legal families fail to mirror children's lives.

The potential for conflict over children born into lesbian families, and thus of the application of the best interests principle, arises in two distinct circumstances. The first instance involves conflict between lesbian mothers and a sperm donor, where a court must determine whether it is in the child's best interests to have a legally protected relationship with his or her donor. The second instance involves conflict between lesbian mothers, where a court must determine the legal relationship of each woman to the child. In both situations, the various legal arrangements made by the parties, such as the completion of a second parent adoption, will be relevant, but the best interests of the child remain paramount in determining custody and access.[37]

Disputes between Lesbian Mothers and Sperm Donors

The assumption that ongoing contact with biological fathers is in children's best interests is highlighted in the lesbian family context. The assertion of many lesbian mothers that their children neither have, nor need, a father directly challenges the pro-father and pro-access approach that currently dominates both Canadian and international family law and the best interests test in particular.

Although little Canadian case law exists as yet, the international jurisprudence suggests that judges do not readily move beyond a heteronormative understanding of the best interests principle. Rather than considering how children's interests might be met by maintaining the stability and security of their two-mother households, and despite studies showing no differences in developmental outcomes between those raised in lesbian- or gay-headed families and those in heterosexual households, judges tend to treat the former as deficient. In the absence of a "father," lesbian families are presumed to be "incomplete."[38] Such an approach makes lesbian mothers extremely vulnerable to unplanned and unwanted donor access. Perhaps most significantly, it affects children, who live with the very real possibility that if their households experience conflict, the law's perception of their best interests may usurp their own understandings of family.

Numerous trends emerge from the jurisprudence on the status of donors to lesbian couples, all of which connect best interests and paternal presence. The most obvious trend relates to access. In all but one reported case, donors have successfully petitioned for access, often over the strong objections of lesbian mothers.[39] In fact, in some instances, donors have been awarded access at a level that far exceeds their initial request.[40] Judges seem to assume that access constitutes a child's best interest but rarely discuss why. Rather, access orders often appear as statements of "common sense," justified on the basis that children can only benefit from additional parents. A closer reading of decisions, however, suggests that courts presume that children benefit from parents of *both* sexes.

This judicial perspective is well illustrated by the New Zealand High Court decision in *P. v. K.* and the Australian Family Court decision in *Re Patrick*.[41] In both instances, statutes made it clear that sperm donors were not legal parents. The judges nevertheless expressed dissatisfaction with this outcome and ordered access (and guardianship in the case of *P. v. K.*) at a level that closely resembled what might be awarded to a non-custodial father upon the breakdown of a heterosexual relationship.[42] In fact, in *P. v. K.*, the access awarded dramatically exceeded what the donor had actually requested. Such cases suggest that, despite legislation to the contrary, judges will endeavour to guarantee a "father." The best interests test is applied in such a way that paternal access is the *only* possible outcome, whatever the benefits to the children involved.

In *P. v. K.*, the mothers and donor had agreed before insemination that the donor would be included in the child's life and would have access for not less than fourteen days a year. Unfortunately, the relationship deteriorated and access was denied. The man then applied for custody. The application was ultimately unsuccessful, but he was permitted to bring an appeal to determine whether it was possible for a sperm donor to claim parental rights to a child conceived through his donation. The High Court held that the letter of the law was clear – the method of conception meant that the donor could not be a legal parent – but nevertheless decided that the man could still apply for guardianship and access. Ultimately, the court awarded him guardianship, as well as access for one week per month. At the heart of the decision was the view that having a father trumped any legal provision to the contrary.

The New Zealand High Court made it very clear that it believed denying contact with a genetic father threatened the child's well-being. The father was presumed to offer otherwise unavailable educational, physical, and emotional benefits. In coming to this conclusion, the court distinguished between the best interests of a child born via donor insemination to hetero-sexuals and one born similarly to lesbians. In the first context, the court felt that access by donors should not be favoured because of the importance of protecting the "security of the traditional nuclear family."[43] In contrast, no such principle applied to the mothers because there was "no traditional nuclear family to protect." The court was willing to accept that there "may here be a 'psychological' nuclear family" but also suggested the introduction of a donor into a lesbian family could only benefit children. In other words, children's best interests required a male parent. Lesbian families, because they lack a "father," are thus not entitled to the same protection as their heterosexual counterparts.

The Australian decision of *Re Patrick,* involving a fact scenario very similar to *P. v. K.,* reveals similar presumptions of domestic normalcy. While the judge in *Re Patrick* showed considerably more respect for the two-mother family, he still assumed that paternal presence benefited the child, Patrick. The gendered nature of the judge's reasoning in *Re Patrick* was explicit: the benefits Patrick is expected to enjoy include visits to the Melbourne Cricket Ground to watch sports, assistance with schooling, and sharing in his donor's love of competitive cycling. These examples reveal the extent to which father presence was understood by the judge to produce masculinity. That the "father" in *Re Patrick* was gay did not, when placed in opposition to two (lesbian) women, seem to jeopardize his ability to offer an appropriate mas-culinity. Homosexuality was effectively, if momentarily, negated during the trial by identification as a "father," a role clearly understood as gendered. Although both cases involved statutes that made it clear the donor was not a legal parent, each resulted in courts finding a father in the name of best interests. Lesbian families were effectively viewed as disordered with a gen-dered gap that needed to be filled. Legal recognition of the realities of par-enting took an inevitable second place.

At present, very little similar case law or legislation exists in Canada, mak-ing it difficult to predict judicial outcomes. The only cases to directly address the issue of whether a sperm donor is a legal parent emanate from Quebec, which has unique statutory language in Article 538.2 of the Civil Code. The article refers directly to children conceived via the donation of third-party gametes, and parentage is determined on the basis of who is understood to be party to the "parental project."[44] In one interim decision in 2004, the court refused to find that such a project existed between the two mothers, who had entered into a civil union and raised their child since birth. Instead, the court held that the biological mother had actually planned to parent with the donor and that the two women therefore did not meet the require-ments of the Civil Code provision.[45] In a more recent decision, the court decided otherwise: the parental project existed between the two lesbian mothers and the donor was simply a third-party gamete provider.[46] Thus, the question remains, both in Quebec and beyond, whether judges will be influenced by international trends in lesbian-parenting litigation or even Canadian cases outside the lesbian-parenting context, where the importance of finding a father for a child has resulted in biological fathers being given parental rights against the wishes of single mothers.[47] Although the existing trends have attracted criticism, they are unlikely to be displaced in the immediate future.

Disputes between Lesbian Mothers

Disputes between lesbian mothers over the custody and access of their children further expose the deeply ingrained ideological content of the best interests test. Outcomes are often linked to assumptions about the value of biogenetic rather than of social relationships.

The first Canadian case to consider a dispute between two lesbian mothers was the hotly contested *Buist v. Greaves,* in which an Ontario court refused to declare a non-biological mother a legal parent.[48] The non-biological mother, Buist, had planned the conception and birth with the biological mother, Greaves, and had parented the child, Simon, from birth. When they separated, Greaves refused to recognize Buist's parental status and planned to move from Ontario to Vancouver. In response, Buist sought an order recognizing her as Simon's mother, giving her sole or joint custody, and prohibiting the move. In asserting legal parentage, Buist effectively asked the court to recognize that Simon had two legal mothers, pointing to Ontario's second-parent adoption law, which permits a child to have two parents of the same sex. In rejecting her application, the court stated that even if it had been possible for it to make such a declaration, Buist had not proved that a mother-child relationship existed. The court purported to take Simon's perspective. Despite Buist's heavy involvement in care, it found that a mother-child relationship did not exist because Simon referred to Buist as "Gaga" whereas he called Greaves "Mama" and became upset when left alone with Buist for extended periods. In concluding that Buist was not a legal parent, the court made no reference to Simon's best interests other than to state that Buist was more interested in her own rights. The best interests test *was* applied to the custody, access, and mobility questions, with the court concluding that it was in Simon's best interests to move with Greaves to Vancouver. Buist was awarded access to Simon, though at a level significantly less than she had previously enjoyed. The court found that any loss to Simon flowing from having less access with Buist was offset by the benefits of moving with his mother.

Similarly, in the more recent decision of *K.G.T. v P.D.*, a BC court refused to declare the non-biological mother a legal parent, despite finding that the two women had intended to co-parent and had done so for over five years.[49] The parties in *K.G.T.* lived together for seven and half years, during which P.D. gave birth to a child. The child's non-biological mother, K.G.T., was involved in planning, and participated in, the insemination process at the fertility clinic. The child took K.G.T.'s surname as a middle name. The parties separated amicably. The dispute arose when P.D. indicated that she wished her new partner to adopt the little girl. K.G.T. opposed the adoption and filed her own adoption application. Evidence was provided indicating that both women, the child, family, and friends regarded K.G.T. as a "mom." She had a close relationship with the child and continued to exercise regular access after separation. The court nevertheless refused to declare K.G.T. a legal parent or allow her to adopt without the birth mother's consent, stating that any anticipated benefits for the child were nebulous. K.G.T. *was* awarded joint guardianship and her pre-separation access rights on the basis that both were in the child's best interests. P.D. retained sole custody, and her new partner was barred from adopting. Although this final outcome gave K.G.T. some legal recognition, it required that she go to court to achieve what heterosexual parents are automatically guaranteed. Furthermore, by failing to grant K.G.T. parental status, the court prevented both her and her daughter from realizing the security of a legally recognized parental relationship.

Both the *Buist* and *K.G.T.* cases suggest that children's best interests are met by prioritizing biogenetic over social relationships, typically in a way that fails to acknowledge the intentional family practices of lesbian mothers and their children's lived reality.[50] In situations of conflict, judges often reshape children's families in ways that jeopardize the maintenance of ties with social parents. Whether the outcomes in these cases were in the best interests of the individual kids involved is less the point than whether there is any scope within the best interests test for the result to be different. The refusal of the court to recognize Buist's relationship as that of a "mother," which, in turn, resulted in permission for Greaves to take Simon to Vancouver, appears to apply the best interests test differently from its application in a heterosexual context. Non-biological mothers seem held to far higher standards than biological fathers, and this devaluing of social parenthood finds its way into the best interests analysis. Whereas it is almost always deemed to be in the interests of children to have biological fathers recognized as "parents" (even absent a social relationship), non-biological mothers who have significant social relationships have no equivalent advantage.

Lost Kids and Reproductive Technologies
Reproductive technologies (RTs) such as in vitro fertilization (IVF), intracytoplasmic sperm injection (ICSI), donor insemination (DI), and surrogacy are about creating children, yet RT laws in Canada and internationally pay

little to no attention to the principle of the best interests or rights of the offspring.[51] In jurisdictions that do provide specific rights to donor offspring, most do not accrue directly to the child until maturity, and these largely concern access to background information, including the identity of the donors. Most of the time, the individual circumstances of the "children" are not objectively evaluated by anyone but their parents, who may have a serious conflict of interest if they wish to hide their infertility or their non-genetic kin status. The result is adult-driven and often particularly responsive to genetic ties at the expense of caregiving roles, including gestation. The main exception involves intentional fathers of DI-conceived children who, despite lacking the genetic link, demand parental rights to a child born using RTs. In these cases, courts seem content to uphold prior agreements about parentage arrangements as long as they produce the heteronormative family (even if no longer intact).[52] The lack of legislation requiring consideration of best interests in these situations is far more common than any express application of the best interests test.

Conception and Birth Planning?

Pre-birth decisions do not involve the application of the legal best interests test in most jurisdictions, including Canada, because no child yet exists. RT litigation therefore tends to be about ambiguities in legal parentage, as discussed below. But even when no third parties are involved to create the possibility of multiple parents, some people question whether conception through IVF and ICSI is in the offspring's best interest. For example, both procedures create a higher risk of premature birth and birth defects, such as chromosomal damage, than non-assisted reproduction.[53] Many commentators address this and similar concerns with the argument that it is better to be alive than to not exist at all.[54] In some advocates' minds, even a serious disability might not outweigh this family-creation method.[55] One exception to this perspective comes from people with excess embryos after IVF or ICSI who refuse to donate them to other women who wish to become pregnant. These embryo creators often believe their genetic offspring's future will be compromised by birth to others and that it is therefore in the potential child's best interest *not* to be born.[56]

Unlike adoption but similar to non-assisted procreation, most prospective parents who wish to use RTs, surrogacy, and donor gametes are not pre-screened for parenting skills or criminal backgrounds. The general assumption is that it is sufficient for at least one intended parent to have a genetic or gestational connection with the embryo.[57] However, individual clinics often apply their own standards in choosing clients, and self-regulatory bodies sometimes set up guidelines.[58] These rules may replicate commonplace biases as clinic staff make decisions as to acceptability. Age, wealth, education, family status, and lifestyle all play a factor, usually without any discussion about exactly how such characteristics relate to adequate parent-hood. Some jurisdictions have attempted to constrain this free market. In the United Kingdom, legislation requires that clinics offering treatment first consider the welfare of resulting children, "including a child's need for a father."[59] Such a provision codifies existing biases in a number of ways, in-cluding discrimination against single and lesbian women.[60] No equivalent Canadian laws and regulations restrict RT users; even the Assisted Human Reproduction Act,[61] which contains provisions criminalizing such things as human cloning and payment for gamete donation, says little about who can use RTs. Minor controls on donation exist through general Canadian health legislation, but most focus as much on transmission of disease to recipient adults as on the health or well-being of the future child.[62]

Determinations of Parentage

Much of the media coverage of RT involves cases of disputed parentage, such as surrogacy (dis)agreements and the sperm donor-lesbian mother cases discussed above. In Canada, the most common disputes are not between potential parents but instead between the legal authorities and the adults involved, with the latter reaching an agreement and seeking legal recogni-tion of it. Certain commentators have recommended the use of the best interests of the child standard when adjudicating all parentage disputes.[63] Other authors have promoted the principle in cases of multiple maternity by explicitly basing the standard on the gestational relationship developed during pregnancy, meaning the gestational mother would almost always become the legal mother, especially in cases of a mix-up at the clinic, where the wrong gametes are implanted.[64] But few courts or legislatures have ex-plicitly adopted the best interests approach when deciding parentage cases. One American exception is the famed surrogacy case *In the Matter of Baby M,* arising when the surrogate mother refused to relinquish the baby.[65] The trial court's award of the child to the commissioning (genetic) father and his wife based on a best interests analysis, and its termination of the sur-rogate mother's parentage, were reversed by the Supreme Court of New Jersey. Yet, this court also referred to the child's best interests when stating that upholding surrogacy contracts was against public policy, in part because the contact contained no consideration of parental fitness. The dissenting judge in the equally famous gestational surrogacy case *Johnson v. Calvert* also thought that the best interests standard should apply.[66] However, the major-ity granted legal parentage to the commissioning genetic parents, who in-tended, before the pregnancy occurred, to act as parents. The majority, in a scant footnote, dismissed the best interests test as (1) unjustifiable state interference in private acts, (2) being about custody, not parentage, and (3) creating instability because it is not a completely objective test that gives clear and predictable results, thereby potentially leaving children parentless for lengthy periods. They further noted that it might split custody between two households, which is unlikely to be good for the child, and that the gestational mother had initially contracted away her right to mother, conceding that it was not in the baby's best interest to be left with her. Arguably, their perception of this child's interests influenced their decision, even when they refused to apply the test explicitly.

In Canadian law, many RT parentage determinations take place under statutory provisions that do not expressly incorporate best interests tests. There appear to be two reasons for the absence of such tests: most provinces have not revised their statutes to take account of RTs, and existing laws reflect the idea that parentage is a "natural" event, involving only a factual determination by the courts. Traditionally, the best interests criteria are usually directly applied only in situations deemed somehow "unnatural," such as relinquishing offspring for adoption, the state removal of youngsters from their parents, and even divorce or separation of parents. In effect then, today's courts make many parentage decisions without needing to consider the best interests test.

The most common RT example arises under vital statistics legislation, when prospective legal parents attempt, usually successfully, to add their names to the birth registration after using surrogate mothers, whose names are excluded.[67] As well, several Canadian cases have awarded lesbian co-mothers the right to be named a legal mother – some under human rights legislation and others through Charter challenges.[68] This litigation focuses on discrimination against lesbian couples rather than family law principles; hence, the best interests of the child test is not technically applied. Courts have also relied on general declaration-of-parentage provisions in statutes to award legal fatherhood to men whose wives conceived using DI before the marriages broke down.[69]

Judges do not, however, have to limit application of the best interests test to statutorily mandated situations. They can resort to the court's *parens patriae* jurisdiction , which allows the court to stand in the place of a parent when a child is in danger or when a legislative gap exists.[70] One Ontario court did so in the unusual circumstances of a single man wanting to be the only parent on the birth registration.[71] This gay man had used an anonymous egg donor and a gestational surrogate along with his own sperm; the gestational mother did not contest being omitted from the birth registration. The provincial government did not officially oppose his application, but the Vital Statistics Act had no provision for such a situation. The judge held this was a legislative gap that required remediation when "it is in the best interests of the child to do so" and permitted registration based on evidence that the child was best served with one father and no legal mother.

A further case in Ontario, *A.A. v. B.B.,* involved a lesbian couple that chose a donor who also functioned as a father. They wished the child to have three legal parents – both co-mothers and the donor father, who was the second parent on the birth registration.[72] Although the trial judge refused to resort to *parens patriae,* the Ontario Court of Appeal overturned that decision, declaring that *parens patriae* was indeed available to answer the need for three legal parents in the particular circumstances of this case.[73] The court noted that one of the key statutes that permitted only two legal parents was originally designed for another purpose – to eliminate the disadvantages of illegitimacy. So the legislature had never turned its mind to the question of three legal parents. With the passage of time, "advances in our appreciation of the value of other types of relationships and in the science of reproductive technology have created gaps in the [statute's] legislative scheme," gaps that can be filled by the *parens patriae* jurisdiction.[74] The trial judge found that having three parents was in the best interests of this particular child, so the Court of Appeal granted the order. In this type of decision at least, a few of the legal system's lost children may see their best interests followed after all.

Another Ontario decision subsequently relied on the Court of Appeal's reasons in *A.A. v. B.B.* to justify the use of *parens patriae* to terminate legal parental ties, not create them.[75] *M.D. v. L.L.* involved a gestational surrogacy agreement where the surrogate mother carried the genetic embryo of the intended parents and fully consented to having her parental rights terminated. The judge decided there was no statutory method to sever the maternal tie conferred by the Vital Statistics Act.[76] Given this "indirect" gap in the legislative scheme, the judge found it would be in the best interests of this child to "issue a declaration that the child's surrogate mother, who is without a genetic link to the child, is not that child's mother ... to remove any ambiguity about who the child's mother is."[77] Unlike *A.A. v. B.B.,* however, there was no evidence before the court that the child's interests were well served by this parental arrangement, that is, having only one mother. Since there is almost no research on children born from surrogacy arrangements, this decision appears to be nothing better than a best guess that the adults' intention that the genetic parents raise the child as legal parents was in the child's best interests.

At least two other Canadian RT cases have mentioned the best interests tests in their reasons, although the judges did not expressly decide the cases on this point. In *J.R. v. L.H.,* an uncontested gestational surrogacy case from Ontario, the decision notes that although the other Canadian gestational carrier decisions (at the time) did not refer to the best interests test, granting a parentage order for the genetic parents did meet the best interests of the child, who has been well served by the "thoughtful, responsible persons" who participated in the contract.[78]

In a preliminary motion in a contested traditional surrogacy case from British Columbia, *H.L.W. and T.H.W.,* the adjudicator stated that the applicable legal principle is clearly the best interests of the child, but left it unclear whether he was referring to the entire action regarding legal parenthood and custody or just interim custody and access.[79] Since the surrogate mother refused to consent to the intended mother adopting the child, he may simply have meant that the whole case was about custody (which then requires application of the best interests test), and that he felt legal parentage was not in dispute. This seems unlikely, however, since the commissioning couple was seeking to uphold the oral contract and the adjudicator denied the surrogate and her family access until the trial finished. He concluded that the expert testimony demonstrated that the child would *not* be harmed by lack of contact with his biological mother over the next few months, and he affirmed the status quo. Furthermore, he expressed concern that reintroducing the baby into the birth family, even for short access visits, might be disturbing for the other youngsters in the home. He had no evidence on that point, however, meaning that their actual best interests, though purportedly considered, had no real impact.

Once legal parentage is settled, the best interests test does apply in the remaining custody and access disputes, though Canada has had few such cases arising in the RT context, outside of the lesbian mother cases. In one failed traditional surrogacy case where the mother revoked her consent to the adoption and the intended parents then dropped their application to have the surrogacy contract upheld, the court went on to apply the best interests test for custody and access.[80] However, the judge clearly disapproved of the intended parents' conduct in setting up the surrogacy arrangement, and these factors greatly influenced the decision to award custody to the birth mother.

In summary, while most analysts agree that the best interests test is not generally applied in North American RT law, and some agree with the majority in *Johnson v. Calvert* that it should apply only to custody, other courts are beginning to consider the principle, if only unofficially in some circumstances.[81] However, they may display the same sort of bias toward a heteronormative nuclear (and often genetic) family as described earlier in relation to lesbian parenting.[82] No one demonstrated that the infant in *M.D. v. L.L.* is truly best served by having legal ties to only one mother; it was the adults involved who decided that the heterosexual couple who provided the genes could meet all of the child's parenting needs. When a genetic parent is known and undisputed (e.g., through written contracts and fertility clinic forms), their initial written intent is generally sufficient to displace contrary claims. In such cases, judges typically neither consider what might actually be best for any particular child, nor state that the child's best interests are not legally determinant. But, as evidenced by the Ontario Court of Appeal's decision in *A.A. v. B.B.*, there is arguably an emerging Canadian tendency to recognize some truly alternative families, at least in circumstances where all possible parents are in agreement. Given that the children are usually already resident in these settings, this trend seems to place their best interests at the centre. What will occur when disputes arise among various potential legal parents remains, however, unclear, and the risk continues that children's interests will be lost in favour of those of adults, and of adult biases.

Conclusion

We have shown that despite the legal system's ostensible emphasis on the best interests of children – which can provide openings for innovative decisions – legal decision making too often continues to place significant weight on the abstract interests of certain *adults,* often at the expense of the children involved. For example, the law's increasing emphasis on the child's need for paternal role models produces decision making that reinforces a heteronormative family form, undervalues actual caregiving relationships, and underrates the impact of domestic abuse. At the same time, an excessive focus on biogenetic connection has undermined some children's ties with social parents, or even gestational mothers. Finally, to the extent that decision makers view families through a lens grounded in what are arguably classed, raced, and gendered assumptions about how adults should behave and households be constructed, the potential to "do" kin differently is greatly diminished. For children being raised in so-called alternative families, the consequences of a lack of recognition can be dire. In fact, these examples highlight the ways in which the current application of the best interests principle fails to acknowledge the *child's* sense of who makes up his or her family. These children will remain the "lost" kids of the legal system unless efforts are made to move away from dominant familial ideology and toward the sort of analysis offered in *A.A. v. B.B.,* which found that declaring three adults to be the child's legal parents was the right approach for the particular child in the circumstances of that case.

It is not our intention to discard the best interests test, which offers the flexibility needed to deal with diverse circumstances but, rather, to free it from problematic ideological entanglements that may compromise children's well-being. In considering how to remedy the test's indeterminacy, some scholars have argued for guidelines or even presumptions that might better direct decision making in the best interests of children. For instance, a consideration of the specific history of caregiving might well be appropriate when determining a dispute over which parent should have custody of a child, just as a focus on the cultural identity of an Aboriginal child is a necessary concern in adoption and child-protection law.[83] How to balance the necessary flexibility of the best interests test with guidelines that seek to eliminate bias that compromises children's interests will challenge lawmakers in years to come. Although law has a tendency to reinscribe conservative or traditional ideologies, it also holds promise as a site in the struggle against the normative power of the heterosexual nuclear family and biogenetic ties.

This struggle will, we hope, ultimately promote decisions that reflect meaningful relationships rather than ideological beliefs about what is best for children.

Notes

1 United Nations Convention on the Rights of the Child, G.A. Res. 44/25, annex, 44 U.N. GAOR Supp. (No. 49) at 167, U.N. Doc. A/44/49 (1989), entered into force 2 September 1990, Article 3.
2 *Young v. Young*, [1993] 4 S.C.R. 3; Helen Rhoades and Susan B. Boyd, "Reforming Custody Laws: A Comparative Study," *International Journal of Law, Policy and the Family* 18 (2004): 119.
3 *Claybrook v. Claybrook*, [1999] B.C.J. No. 1083 (B.C.S.C.) (QL) at paras. 12-16.
4 R.H. Mnookin, "Child-Custody Adjudication: Judicial Functions in the Face of Indeterminacy," *Law and Contemporary Problems* 39, 3 (1975): 226.
5 Jon Elster, "Solomonic Judgments: Against the Best Interest of the Child," *University of Chicago Law Review* 54 (1987): 1 at 40-45; Joseph Goldstein, Anna Freud, and Albert J. Solnit, *Beyond the Best Interests of the Child,* rev. ed. (New York: Free Press, 1979), 175n12.
6 Marlee Kline, "Child Welfare Law, 'Best Interests of the Child,'" Ideology, and First Nations," *Osgoode Hall Law Journal* 30, 2 (1992): 375.
7 Dorothy Roberts, *Shattered Bonds: The Color of Child Welfare* (New York: Basic Books, 2001), 174.
8 Judith Mosoff, "'A Jury Dressed in Medical White and Juridical Black': Mothers with Mental Health Histories in Child Welfare and Custody," in Susan B. Boyd, ed., *Challenging the Public/Private Divide: Feminism, Law and Public Policy* (Toronto: University of Toronto Press, 1997), 227.
9 Canada, Department of Justice, *Evaluation of the Divorce Act Phase II: Monitoring and Evaluation* (Ottawa: Canadian Department of Justice Bureau of Review, 1990), 47.
10 The children of unmarried mothers were of much less interest to both fathers and the legal system, which was concerned with inheritance systems and wealth transference related to marriage. This fact alone illustrates the legal system's focus on certain powerful adults rather than on children's interests. Constance B. Backhouse, "Shifting Patterns in 19th-Century Canadian Custody Law," in David H. Flahert, ed., *Essays in the History of Canadian Law* (Toronto: Osgoode Society, 1981), 1:212-48; Susan B. Boyd, *Child Custody, Law, and Women's Work* (Don Mills, ON: Oxford University Press, 2003), 20-40.
11 On paternal absence even in intact families see Richard Collier, "'Waiting Till Father Gets Home': The Reconstruction of Fatherhood in Family Law," *Social and Legal Studies* 4 (1995): 5-30.
12 Backhouse, "Shifting Patterns," 235-36.
13 Boyd, *Child Custody,* 54-59.
14 Backhouse, "Shifting Patterns," 220-26.
15 *An Act to Amend the Children's Act,* S.P.E.I. 1968, c. 5.
16 *Oakes v. Oakes* (1975), 11 N.B.R. (2d) 170 (N.B.C.A.); Boyd, *Child Custody,* 83-84.
17 Boyd, *Child Custody,* 41-72.
18 Karina Winton, "'The Spoilt Darling of the Law': Women and Canadian Child Custody Law in the Postwar Period (1945-1960)," *Canadian Journal of Family Law* 19 (2002): 193-236.
19 *Re Moillet* (1965), 54 W.W.R. 111 (B.C.S.C.) at 114; *Dewar v. Dewar,* [1950] O.W.N. 1.
20 The most commonly cited statistics include only cases decided by divorce courts or where custody agreements are affirmed or rubber-stamped by courts. They do not include cases where parents make arrangements without involving a court. Nor do the divorce statistics include custody determinations involving unmarried parents. We do know that when unmarried relationships break down, children are more likely to remain in the custody of mothers: Nicole Marcil-Gratton and Céline Le Bourdais, *Custody, Access and Child Support: Findings from the National Longitudinal Survey of Children and Youth* (Ottawa: Department of Justice, 1999), 19.
21 Statistics Canada, *Divorce: Law and the Family in Canada* (Ottawa: Minister of Supply and Services Canada, 1983), 205, 211.

22   Helen Rhoades, "The Rise and Rise of Shared Parenting Laws – A Critical Reflection," *Canadian Journal of Family Law* 19 (2002): 75; Kirsti Kurki-Suonio, "Joint Custody as an Interpretation of the Best Interests of the Child in Critical and Comparative Perspective," *International Journal of Law, Policy and the Family* 14 (2000): 183.

23   Statistics Canada, *The Daily,* 4 May 2004.

24   Richard Collier and Sally Sheldon, eds., *Fathers' Rights Activism and Law Reform in Comparative Perspective* (Oxford and Portland, OR: Hart, 2006).

25   See Martha Shaffer, "Joint Custody, Parental Conflict and Children's Adjustment to Divorce: What the Social Science Literature Does and Does Not Tell Us," *Canadian Family Law Quarterly* 26 (2007): 286. *Trociuk v. British Columbia,* [2003] 1 S.C.R. 835 [*Trociuk* S.C.C.]; Hester Lessard, "Mothers, Fathers, and Naming: Reflections on the Law Equality Framework and *Trociuk v. British Columbia (Attorney General),*" *Canadian Journal of Women and the Law* 16 (2004): 168.

26   Marcil-Gratton and Le Bourdais, *Custody, Access and Child Support,* 20-21.

27   In 1998, even women dual-earners aged twenty to forty-four with young children spent more time than men caring for their children on an average day (147 minutes versus 85 minutes). This resulted in an index of 1.72, indicating that women dual-earners spent an estimated 72 percent more time on child care than men dual-earners: Status of Women Canada, *Economic Gender Equality Indicators 2000,* Catalogue 11-008-XPE (Ottawa: Status of Women Canada, 2000), 6.

28   Melanie Rosnes, "The Invisibility of Male Violence in Canadian Child Custody and Access Decision-Making," *Canadian Journal of Family Law* 14 (1997): 31.

29   Linda C. Neilson, "Comparative Analysis of Law in Theory and Law in Action in Partner Abuse Cases: What Do the Data Tell Us?" *Studies in Law, Politics, and Society* 26 (2002): 151. Alarmingly, these results were often obtained not as the result of judicial decision but through agreement by the abused partner after she was awarded custody, raising questions about the pervasive influence of the notion that children must have contact with both parents, as well as about the dismissal of evidence of abuse.

30   Peter Jaffe, Nancy K.D. Lemon, and Samantha E. Poisson, *Child Custody and Domestic Violence* (Thousand Oaks, CA: Sage, 2003), chap. 1.

31   Carol Smart, "Equal Shares: Rights for Fathers or Recognition for Children?" *Critical Social Policy* 24, 4 (2004): 484.

32   Shaffer, "Joint Custody," 287.

33   Carol Smart, Bren Neale, and Amanda Wade, *The Changing Experiences of Childhood: Families and Divorce* (Cambridge, UK: Polity Press, 2001).

34   For an early Canadian example, see Katherine Arnup, "Lesbian Mothers and Child Custody," *Atkinson Review of Canadian Studies* 1, 2 (1984): 35. See also Jenni Millbank, "Lesbians, Child Custody, and the Long Lingering Gaze of the Law," in Boyd, *Challenging the Public/Private Divide,* 280.

35   See, for example, *K. v. K.* (1975), 23 R.F.L. 58 (Alta. Prov. Ct.), and *Bezaire v. Bezaire* (1980), 20 R.F.L. (2d) 358 (Ont. C.A.). Even in the more recent decision of *N. v. N.,* [1992] B.C.J. No. 1507 (S.C.) (QL), the success of the mother was to some degree premised on the fact that her lesbian relationship was not in any way "notorious in the community or in the school. In *S. v. S.,* [1992] B.C.J. No. 1579 (B.C.S.C.) (QL), a mother who left her husband when she came out as a lesbian was told by the judge that her "adventure" was not one that the children should be part of at that point in time.

36   See, for example, *D. v. D.* (1978), 3 R.F.L. (2d) 327 (Ont. Co. Ct.) at 333.

37   However, that a donor or a non-biological mother is not a legal parent does not usually prevent them from applying for a custody or access order in relation to a child. In most provinces, as well as under the federal Divorce Act, "any person" can apply for a custody or access order if granted leave to do so by the court. See *Divorce Act,* R.S.C. 1985, c. 3, s. 16(1); *Children's Law Reform Act,* R.S.O. 1990, c. 12, s. 21; *Children's Law Act,* S.S. 2002, c. 8.1, s. 6(1); *Children's Act,* R.S.Y.T. 2002, c. 31, s. 33(1); *Children's Law Act,* R.S.N.L. 1990, c. C-13, s. 27. Whether they will succeed depends on how the judge applies the best interests test.

38   Judith Stacey and Timothy Biblarz, "(How) Does the Sexual Orientation of Parents Matter," *American Sociological Review* 66, 2 (2001): 159.

39 The only reported case in which a donor has been unsuccessful in his access application is from Quebec, *L.O. v. S.J.* (2006), J.Q. No. 450, in which Quebec's newly reformed filiation provisions were applied. Quebec is the only Canadian province to have enacted legislation specifically designed to assign legal parentage to the non-biological co-parent, whether heterosexual or homosexual, in situations where the child has been conceived using third-party gametes. In *L.O.*, the court applied the legislation and found that the donor was not a party to the "parental project" and thus not a legal parent.
40 See, for example, *P. v. K.*, [2003] 2 N.Z.L.R. 787; *Re Patrick (An Application Concerning Contact)* (2002), 28 Fam. L.R. 579, [2002] F.L.C. 93-096.
41 Ibid.
42 *P. v. K.*, at para. 190; *Re Patrick*, at 88, 923.
43 *P. v. K.*, at para. 26.
44 *Civil Code of Québec*, S.Q. 1991, c. 64, art. 538.2: "The contribution of genetic material for the purposes of a third-party parental project does not create any bond of filiation between the contributor and the child born of the parental project."
45 *S.G. v. L.C.*, [2004] Q.J. No. 6915 (Qc. Sup. Ct.) (QL).
46 *L.O. v. S.J.*, [2006] J.Q. No. 450 (Qc. Sup. Ct.) (QL). The Quebec Court of Appeal recently upheld this decision: [2007] J.Q. No. 1895 (Q.C.A.) (QL).
47 *Trociuk S.C.C.*; *Johnson-Steeves v. Lee* (1997), 50 Alta. L.R. (3d) 340 (Q.B.), aff'd 54 Alta. L.R. (3d) 218 (C.A.).
48 *Buist v. Greaves*, [1997] O.J. No. 2646 (Ont. Ct. Gen. Div.) (QL).
49 *K.G.T. v. P.D.*, [2005] B.C.J. No. 2935 (S.C.) (QL).
50 Fiona Kelly, "(Re)forming Parenthood: The Assignment of Legal Parentage within Planned Lesbian Families," *Ottawa Law Review* 40, 2 (2009): 117.
51 Literature on RTs often includes donor insemination and all types of surrogacy arrangements (despite that neither requires medical professionals and their technical expertise), as well as actual technologies. Therefore, all of the above will be considered here.
52 See the DI cases below at note 73 and accompanying text.
53 Robert G. Edwards and Michael Ludwig, "Are Major Defects in Children Conceived *In Vitro* Due to Innate Problems in Patients or to Induced Genetic Damage?" *Reproductive Biomedicine Online* 7 (2003): 131; Dorothy E. Roberts, "Privatization and Punishment in the New Age of Reprogenetics," *Emory Law Journal* 54 (2005): 1343.
54 John A. Robertson, *Children of Choice: Freedom and the New Reproductive Technologies* (Princeton, NJ: Princeton University Press, 1994).
55 Sheryl de Lacey and R.J. Norman, "What Should We Do with Donated Embryos That May Be Genetically Affected?" *Human Reproduction* 19 (2004): 1065.
56 Sheryl de Lacey, "Decisions for the Fate of Frozen Embryos: Fresh Insights into Patients' Thinking and Their Rationales for Donating or Discarding Embryos," *Human Reproduction* 22 (2007): 1751; Cindy Baldassi, "Babies or Blastocysts, Parents or Progenitors? Embryo Donation and the Concept of Adoption" (LLM thesis, University of British Columbia, 2006).
57 Lori B. Andrews, "Surrogate Motherhood: Should the Adoption Model Apply?" *Children's Legal Rights Journal* 7 (1986): 13.
58 See discussion of Canadian guidelines, voluntary moratoriums, and the potential for clinics to have discriminatory practices in Eric Monpetit, "Policy Networks, Federalism and Managerial Ideas: How ART Non-Decision in Canada Safeguards the Autonomy of the Medical Profession," in Ivar Bleiklie, Malcolm L. Goggin, and Christine Rothmayr, eds., *Comparative Biomedical Policy: Governing Assisted Reproductive Technologies* (London and New York: Routledge, 2004), 64.
59 *Human Fertilisation and Embryology Act 1990* (c. 37) (U.K.), s. 25(2), though that problematic provision may be on the way out: BBC News, "MPs Reject Need for Father in IVF," 22 May 2008, http://news.bbc.co.uk/2/hi/uk_news/politics/7410934.stm. These changes are scheduled to come into effect in October 2009: Human Fertilisation and Embryology Authority, "HFEA Chair welcomes Royal Assent for HFE Act," 13 Nov 2008, http://www.hfea.gov.uk/371.html.
60 Davina Cooper and Didi Herman, "Getting 'The Family Right': Legislating Heterosexuality in Britain, 1986-1991," *Canadian Journal of Family Law* 10 (1991): 41.

61 S.C. 2004, c. 2.

62 Roxanne Mykitiuk and Albert Wallrap, "Regulating Reproductive Technologies in Canada," in Jocelyn Downie, Timothy Caulfield, and Colleen Flood, eds., *Canadian Health Law and Policy*, 2nd ed. (Markham, ON: Butterworths Canada, 2002), 367.

63 Paula J. Manning, "Baby Needs a New Set of Rules: Using Adoption Doctrine to Regulate Embryo Donation," *Georgetown Journal of Gender and Law* 5 (2004): 677; Ilana Hurwitz, "Collaborative Reproduction: Finding the Child in the Legal Maze of Motherhood," *Connecticut Law Review* 33 (2000): 127.

64 Leslie Bender, "Genes, Parents, and Assisted Reproductive Technologies: ARTs, Mistakes, Sex, Race, and Law," *Columbia Journal of Gender and Law* 12 (2003): 1; Alice M. Noble-Allgire, "Switched at the Fertility Clinic: Determining Maternal Rights When a Child Is Born from Stolen or Misdelivered Genetic Material," *Missouri Law Review* 64 (1999): 517.

65 *In the Matter of Baby M*, 217 N.J. Super. 313 (1987), *aff'd in part and rev'd in part*, 109 N.J. 396 (1988).

66 *Johnson v. Calvert*, 851 P.2d 776 (Cal. Sup. Ct. 20 May 1993), aff'g 12 Cal. App. 4th 977 (8 October 1991), aff'g X-663190, Sup. Ct. Orange County, 22 October 1990.

67 *Rypkema v. British Columbia* (2003), 233 D.L.R. (4th) 760 (B.C.S.C.); *J.C. v. Manitoba* (2000), 12 R.F.L. (5th) 274 (Q.B.); *L. v. P.* (No. 0101-22025, Alta. Q.B., 15 February 2002); *J.R. v. L.H.*, [2002] O.T.C. 764 (Ont. Sup. Ct.).

68 *Gill v. Murray*, 2001 BCHRT 34; *A.A. v. New Brunswick (Department of Family and Community Services)*, [2004] N.B.H.R.B.I.D No. 4.; *Fraess v. Alberta (Minister of Justice and Attorney General)*, 2005 ABQB 889; *M.D.R. v. Ontario (Deputy Registrar General)* (2006), 270 D.L.R. (4th) 90 (Ont. Sup. Ct.).

69 *Low v. Low* (1994), 4 R.F.L. (4th) 103 (Ont. Gen. Div.); *Zegota v. Zegota-Rzegocinski*, [1995] O.J. No. 204 (C.J. - Gen. Div.). The orders were made under the Children's Law Reform Act, 1990. One can read these cases as another example of courts wanting a father in the child's life.

70 A history is given in *A.A. v. B.B.*, 2007 ONCA 2 at paras. 27-30.

71 *K.G.D. v. C.A.P,* [2004] O.J. No. 3508 (Sup. Ct.) (QL).

72 *A.(A.) v. B.(B.)* (2003), 225 D.L.R. (4th) 371 (Ont. Sup. Ct., Fam. Ct.).

73 *A.A. v. B.B.*, 2007.

74 Ibid., at para. 35.

75 *M.D. v. L.L.* (2008), 90 O.R. (3d) 127 (Sup. Ct. J.).

76 R.S.O. 1990, c. V.4, s. 1.

77 *M.D. v. L.L.* at para. 67.

78 *J.R. v. L.H.* at para. 20.

79 *H.L.W. and T.H.W.*, 2005 B.C.S.C. 1679.

80 *V.V.H. and P.B.H. v. W.L.P.* (1997), 188 N.B.R. (2d) 130 (Q.B.).

81 Madelyn Freundlich, *Adoption and Assisted Reproduction* (Washington, DC: Child Welfare League of America, 2001); Joan Mahoney, "Adoption as a Feminist Alternative to Reproductive Technology," in Joan C. Callahan, ed., *Reproduction, Ethics, and the Law: Feminist Perspectives* (Bloomington, IN: Indiana University Press, 1995), 35; Larry I. Palmer, "Who Are the Parents of Biotechnological Children?" *Jurimetrics* 35 (1994): 17; and Manning, "Baby Needs a New Set of Rules."

82 Janet L. Dolgin, *Defining the Family: Law, Technology and Reproduction in an Uneasy Age* (New York: NYU Press, 1997).

83 For example, Juliet Behrens, "The Form and Substance of Australian Legislation on Parenting Orders: A Case for the Principles of Care and Diversity and Presumptions Based on Them," *Journal of Social Welfare and Family Law* 24, 2 (2002): 401; Carol Smart and Selma Sevenhuijsen, *Child Custody and the Politics of Gender* (London: Routledge, 1989); Fiona Kelly, "(Mis)placed Justice: Justice, Care and Reforming the 'Best Interests of the Child' Principle in Canadian Child Custody and Access Law," in Law Commission of Canada, ed., *The "Place" of Justice* (Winnipeg: Fernwood, 2006), 44. *Adoption Act*, R.S.B.C. 1996, c. 5, s. 3; *Child, Family and Community Service Act*, R.S.B.C. 1996, c. 46, s. 4.

Part 5
Access and Opportunity at the Beginning of the Twenty-First Century – Equality Delayed

In 2001, George W. Bush, then president of the United States, signed into law a "no child left behind" policy that promised to improve American children's educational opportunities. This law has not had its desired effect; in one of the richest countries in the world, children still do not enjoy equality of education. This differential tells part of a larger North American story. Economically vulnerable populations still spend fewer hours in schools, cope with poorer buildings and equipment, and remain susceptible to streaming directing them to low-wage occupations. Access to health care and recreation has been similarly inequitable. Some children experience the advantages of health and play; others struggle with illness or uncertain finances. In 2005, the United States ranked thirty-fourth in the world in infant mortality and had the highest proportion of children living in poverty in the world's thirty richest nations.[1] In 2007, by one ranking, Canada placed just below the median of better-off nations in terms of the health and safety of children and youth.[2]

Children are not fully enfranchised as citizens. But as the chapters by Wendy Frisby, Ted Alexander, and Janna Taylor and by Stephen McBride and John Irwin suggest, governments make a tremendous difference to young people's quality of life. Wendy Frisby, Ted Alexander, and Janna Taylor explore how Canada's traditional commitment to providing organized play and other types of recreation for underserved youth has been compromised: public recreation increasingly mirrors the private sector in its preoccupation with autonomous individuals, profitable markets, and cost recovery strategies. Such policies, she argues, render marginalized youth invisible as appropriate and worthy participants in publicly funded leisure. Stephen McBride and John Irwin explore youth labour protection in contemporary British Columbia. As McBride and Irwin argue, the provincial government's deregulatory posture, which allows children as young as twelve to work for pay, may harm adolescents by exposing them to dangerous or inappropriate work. The transition from school to jobs, the authors suggest, should be better regulated to protect a vulnerable population from possible abuse. In recent years, conservative administrations in both the United States and Canada have deepened the gaps between the rich and poor. The spread of social services, public education, and health care systems nevertheless represents a vital source of support for children and their parents.

Notes

1 Patrick Martin, "'Measure of America' Report Documents Social Decay of the United States," Centre for Research on Globalization, 9 August 2008, http://www.globalresearch.ca.
2 K. Kellie Leitch, *Reaching for the Top: A Report by the Advisor on Health Children and Youth* (Ottawa: Health Canada, 2007), http://www.hc-sc.gc.ca, and UNICEF Innocenti Research Centre, *An Overview of Child Well-Being in Rich Countries* (Florence: UNICEF Innocenti Research Centre, 2007), 6.

11
Play Is Not a Frill: Poor Youth Facing the Past, Present, and Future of Public Recreation in Canada

Wendy Frisby, Ted Alexander, and Janna Taylor

Although there are rising public panics about childhood obesity, sedentary lifestyles, and the problems of "youth at-risk," the shift from a social welfare to a neo-liberal logic in local government is resulting in the further exclusion of poor children and youth from health-promoting forms of public recreation. Parks, local sports leagues, physical activity programs, music, and art that are provided, in part, by local tax-based dollars make up the public recreation sector. Historically, in Canada, it has focused on youth whose families could not otherwise afford to participate in organized play and other types of privatized recreation. That commitment has been compromised as public recreation increasingly mirrors the private sector with its preoccupation with autonomous individuals, profitable markets, and cost recovery strategies. As public recreation programs shift their efforts toward wealthier citizens who can better contribute to financial imperatives, marginalized youth readily become invisible as appropriate and worthy participants.[1]

In Canada, both the leadership of and participation in local public recreation reflect power relations underpinning the existing social order where norms evoking whiteness, masculinity, physical prowess, classism, able-bodiedness, and heterosexuality dominant public spaces.[2] Although there have been numerous critiques about state control over recreation services, some of which are summarized in this chapter, our previous research demonstrates that male and female youth of different ethnic backgrounds from low-income families nevertheless see significant benefits to participation. That is, they would like to be included but remain for the most part on the margins.[3] Local governments need to return to historic commitments to accessibility and public recreation as spaces for democratization, inclusion, and health promotion for all children and youth. The much observed decline in physical education, music, art, and extracurricular offerings in the Canadian school system make this all the more urgent.

Achieving such goals is especially challenging in a neo-liberal era of governance where values associated with social equality are in retreat.[4] Research on the evolution of public recreation policy, especially that drawing on meaningful input from commonly excluded children and youth, is the first step in reinventing a system that, for all its flaws, has historically embraced a mandate inclusive of rich and poor.[5]

To contextualize our analysis in this chapter, we provide a snapshot of childhood poverty in Canada and discuss how impoverished living conditions are tied to both poor health and a lack of organized recreational opportunities. A brief history of public recreation provision in Canada that illustrates how services for youth have been conceptualized and rationalized follows. Finally, drawing on our own report that was commissioned by the Canadian Parks and Recreation Association and the Public Health Agency of Canada, we include samples of young voices and comments from parents of low-income families to illustrate the factors that undermine equal opportunity and their suggestions for improvement.[6]

Child Poverty and Health

Despite federal government claims to be working toward the eradication of child poverty, a daunting portrait of disadvantage continues into the twenty-first century:

- 1.2 million children live in poverty (one out of every six children);
- child poverty rates for families headed by lone-parent mothers are 52.5 percent;
- poverty rates for Aboriginal, immigrant, and children from visible minority families are more than double the average for all children; and
- 27.7 percent of children with disabilities live in poverty.[7]

These statistics illustrate how childhood poverty is embodied, gendered, and racialized: the victims are disproportionately those who are disabled or are in mother-headed families, Aboriginals, immigrants, or visible minorities. Anchoring poor parents in waged labour, however ill-paid, is the dominant solution of federal and provincial governments to the spectra of child poverty, but this ignores both the cost of raising children and, more particularly, that of child care. The skills of immigrants are often devalued and they, like other marginalized though native-born populations, face a range of prejudices that undermine economic options. State preoccupations with immediate employment also largely ignore the valuable unpaid work and non-work activities (e.g., play, volunteering, recreation, physical activity) that parents on low income engage in within their households and communities on behalf of their offspring and other children.[8]

Compromised health continues the commonplace tale of disadvantage. Compared with national averages, the infant mortality rate is twice as high and deaths from infectious diseases are 2.5 times more common among the daughters and sons of low-income families than they are among the middle and upper classes.[9] Growing evidence ties health directly to neighbourhood conditions; Sally MacIntyre, for example, found that residents of poorer neighbourhoods suffer more ailments and have fewer and lower quality recreation facilities and urban parks available to them.[10] In another study, Colleen Reid showed how women on low income commonly experience social isolation, which produces poor physical and mental health.[11] This same group believed that community development approaches to recreation based on their input and active involvement could improve life for them and their offspring.[12] Research confirms their conviction, as physical activity and recreation have been shown to help prevent illness and spur recovery from many biomedical conditions, including cardiovascular disease, diabetes, cancer, osteoporosis, and depression.[13] Yet, for all the ample evidence, one of the most consistent research findings concludes that the lower one's social class, the lower is the rate of participation in sport and recreation.[14]

Given Canada's fragmented social service system, city councils and managers may be unaware of the extent of poverty in their own communities, may assume that recreation is a frill, and may underestimate the health-promoting potential of recreation for the most vulnerable of citizens.[15] At the same time, the dominant medical model of community health, where public recreation is seldom seen as a relevant partner in disease prevention and health promotion for low-income populations, supports the generally disengaged orientation of planners adopting neo-liberal ideologies and business practices in Canada's parks and recreation system.[16]

A Brief History of Public Recreation for Youth in Canada

Caroline Andrew, Jean Harvey, and Don Dawson argue that the history of public recreation policy can be best understood within a broader framework of the welfare state in Canada.[17] This section briefly outlines how meanings of public recreation have shifted over time and how local governments have conceptualized their roles in meeting citizen needs.

The very concept of recreation is closely tied to the emergence of the first industrial revolution. In the sixteenth and seventeenth centuries, recreation offered an antidote to the stresses associated with adult men's paid work by "providing opportunities for physical and psychological refreshment from the day's labour."[18] Over time, additional meanings, beyond its restorative functions, became associated with the term. Mark Searle and Russell Brayley contend that recreation eventually emerged as an instrument of social public policy in postwar Canada.[19] At various times, all levels of government experimented with initiatives to reduce youth crime, promote community cohesion, and reduce social inequalities. Integrated recreation programs for persons with disabilities, parent-participation play groups, and neighbourhood summer day camps were typical of important efforts at greater inclusion.

At the beginning the twentieth century, the social welfare role of play was associated with the playground movement, with its attention to both physical and character development and the need to address idleness. Middle-class activists, such as those associated with the National Council of Women of Canada, helped convince community leaders to view playgrounds as a basic public service.[20] Critics, especially in the 1930s, linked recreation to hopes for the expansion of democracy, a means for enabling "the less powerful to find their strength as citizens through social action."[21] Athletic and cultural initiatives also promised therapy for morally endangered groups, such as the unemployed and their families, and were increasingly positioned as remedies for juvenile delinquency. They would, when parents failed, keep kids off the streets and out of the criminal justice system. Yet, continuing concerns about intruding into the private sphere meant that volunteerism emerged as an important component of recreation program delivery. Those with the social, financial, and cultural capital required to assume volunteer leadership positions often saw themselves as "doing good for the less fortunate" and may have unwittingly contributed to the very class and racial divisions that public recreation sought to lessen.[22]

During the Second World War, unfit young men reporting for service provided another justification for state intervention.[23] After the conflict, the problems of integrating racial and ethnic strangers into the nation provided further cause for alarm, though girls and women were rarely the targets for such concerns. Organized recreation remained especially valued for preparing young men for work or the military or for integrating male newcomers into Canadian society. Women could assist as mothers but rarely joined as participants.[24] Girls' participation was restricted because of concerns over damage to their reproductive health, thus emphasizing their projected roles as wives and mothers.[25] M. Ann Hall explains how gendered disparities in sport, one avenue for achieving fitness, were both constructed and resisted over time: "As lesser athletes, they [females] could never expect an equal slice of the athletic pie in terms of facilities, resources, coaching, training, and sponsorships, all of which provoked legal, ethical and strategic challenges to these inequalities. More recently, increasing numbers of women have gained greater access to traditionally male sports like rugby, soccer, weight-lifting, body-building, and the martial arts, further challenging the gender boundaries of sport."[26]

Despite explicit public policy goals of social cohesion and integration, many recreation initiatives were organized specifically by gender and along class and racial lines. As Vicky Paraschak's historical research with First Nations youth in Canada illustrates, participation naturalizes dominant understandings of what it means to be male or female.[27] Native boys and men favoured masculine competitive activities associated with status-seeking and physical prowess, and excluded girls and women, who were expected to fulfill culturally defined domestic duties. Yet, Paraschak also found numerous examples of Native women's participation in sport and recreation in both Euro-American and Native contexts, though both male and female Native athletes encountered racism and only partial acceptance in mainstream activities. Racial hierarchies were particularly apparent in the media, where Native male youth were constructed as less civilized and inherently more violent than white male athletes in sports such as lacrosse. In contrast, public narratives of Native women's participation were noticeably absent.[28] Colonialism has been especially apparent during international sporting events such as the Olympic Games, where Natives are invited to perform traditional dances in opening and closing ceremonies but are seldom seen as athletes, coaches, organizers, or spectators.

Shirley Tillotson's analysis of Canadian public recreation from 1945 to 1961 revealed democratic narratives focusing on the rights and freedoms of citizens combined with liberal values of transcending racial prejudices.[29] Both inspirations were, however, ultimately largely subverted by the rise of local bureaucracies where non-elected professionals became responsible for recreation services. This shift to management by predominately white male middle-class experts who rarely lived in low-income neighbourhoods undermined opportunities for poor children and youth and their families when they developed programs with people similar to themselves in mind.

One solution came in the 1950s with the enthusiasm for recreation drop-in centres with less structured and adult-intrusive environments. By the end of the century, Brian Wilson and Philip White's ethnography of a drop-in centre in a low-income area in urban southern Ontario showed youth negotiating their own non-violence rules that allowed diverse groups to coexist in a limited but highly charged social space.[30] Interestingly, youth subcultures within the centre did not organize along racial lines, though a strong masculinist sport culture marginalized most of the female youth.[31] Both male and female inner-city youngsters nevertheless identified their drop-in centre as a place to develop negotiation and leadership skills, cultural awareness, increased self-esteem and confidence, and volunteer opportunities. Youth centres address commonplace barriers to participation, including high membership costs, poor locations, a lack of equipment and transportation, and adult supervision.

During the 1960s, concerns about poor fitness levels and Canada's dismal performance in international sporting competitions resurfaced with public recreation being interpreted as a "feeder system" that could contribute to patriotic and nationalistic ideals.[32] This assumption produced an explosion in facilities (e.g., swimming pools, gymnasiums, sports fields, ice arenas) for structured recreation programs and further bureaucratization through the hiring of more professionalized managers and staff.[33] Because funding was primarily tax-based, more facilities were built in wealthy urban neighbourhoods, creating further transportation barriers for citizens living in low-income areas.

This trend to expansion slowed in the 1970s, an era of fiscal restraint. High operating costs renewed calls for community development approaches and less direct recreation program provision.[34] Some cynics charged that this was simply a way for local governments to privatize and off-load responsibility to individuals and community groups with limited resources; nothing more, in other words, than a capitulation to neo-liberal governance.[35] Despite such very real dangers, by this time recreation had become a part of the social contract that many Canadians took for granted as a proper role for public authorities. For all the financial bottom-line dogma, many still consider state support for recreation to be a right of citizenship.[36]

By the 1980s, the Canadian government, increasingly concerned about rising health care costs, placed greater emphasis on health promotion as a disease prevention strategy. State initiatives such as ParticipACTION revealed ongoing concerns about the health risks of sedentary lifestyles.[37] Yet, as Alan Ingham wryly noted decades ago, such social marketing efforts "conveniently ignored the fact that millions of people who hover around and below the poverty line cannot afford ten-speeds [bikes], tennis racquets and memberships in health fitness centres. And, as an active rather than passive lifestyle, it exhorts us to burn off calories while denying state dependents the food they need to survive."[38]

The connection to the real world of the disadvantaged was not, however, completely ignored. By the 1990s, public recreation provision was associated with the "social problems industry," especially in the United States, and received renewed attention as a strategy for successfully dealing with at-risk urban youth, poverty, unemployment, crime, substance abuse, teenage pregnancy, and delinquency, all under the guise of preserving public safety.[39] Once again, a key assumption was that such programs alone could channel youth into productive activities, first presumably as recreation participants and then eventually as paid workers. According to Douglas Hartmann, distinctive features of youth risk prevention during this decade were the rise in public-private sector partnerships and the targeting of poor inner-city young men of colour. In one of the more high-profile initiatives, Nike joined with nonprofit and public organizations to launch the PLAY initiative (short for "participate in the lives of America's youth") that was built around discourses of "every child's right to play."[40] It was a campaign that helped counter criticisms of Nike's human rights practices in Asian factories. Ironically, the initiative perpetuated stereotypes about who was considered at-risk – the very population least likely to be able to afford expensive Nike products.[41]

The return to youth risk prevention programs and the further shift away from the "sport and recreation for all" ethos of the 1960s occurred at another time of dramatic budget cuts. Just as in the past, character building and self-discipline regimes were championed as the elixir for producing virtuous hard-working young men. This strategy promised to integrate racial minorities into the mainstream, as "sport and recreation providers found it expedient to adopt the social problems rhetoric to secure scarce program resources."[42] At the same time, ironically, market-driven sport and recreation programs for fitness and athletic achievement were growing at breakneck speed, further reinforcing the social and racial divisions the problems-based recreation initiatives were attempting to address.[43]

Apart from a continued lower rate of female participation, gender differences in the meaning of sport and recreation were less pronounced at this time among the middle and upper classes, as many connected healthy exercise with demonstrating status, for example, through the sculpting of the ideal body type.[44] Ultimately, however, participation, with its recurring affirmation of masculine heterosexuality, dominance, risk-taking, and pain tolerance, remained far more meaningful for young men than young women.[45]

Why Recreation Needs to Remain the Responsibility of Local Government

Although other non-profit organizations such as the YMCA, the YWCA, Boy's and Girls' Clubs, Brownies and Guides, Cubs and Scouts, camps, and sports leagues offer recreation, public recreation departments in local governments retain essential responsibilities because of their tax base, existing infrastructures, and democratic mandates. Furthermore, a growing body of research identifies disadvantaged youth as prime supporters of public recreation as a relevant site for their well-being and development.[46]

Clear evidence of this appears in our study commissioned by the Canadian Parks and Recreation Association (CPRA) following a report by the Canadian Council on Social Development (CCSD) in 2001. The CCSD report identified the need for research to uncover the voices of youth and parents of children living in poverty so as to inform recreation policy and program reform. The CPRA drew on the CCSD report, our findings, and other input to develop Everyone Gets to Play, a Canada-wide initiative designed to improve the quality of life of children and youth from low-income families by making public recreation more accessible and appropriate. Although it remains to be seen whether municipalities across the country will take up this initiative, it counters the shift to neo-liberalism and business-oriented practices that cater to middle- and upper-class citizens.

Our study for CPRA involved separate focus groups with male and female youth (twelve to eighteen years of age) of different self-identified ethnic backgrounds from low-income families in three urban centres.[47] They were non-participants in public recreation but had a considerable amount to say about its benefits, barriers, and the desire for change. Separate focus groups were also conducted with low-income parents of offspring less than twelve years of age and public recreation staff in the same cities. The sample was small enough (e.g., six to eight per focus group) to encourage dialogue with a "hard to reach" population. Although this does not lend itself to making generalizations based on ethnicity, gender, or geographic location, the data surfaced voices that are rarely heard when public recreation policy and programs are developed.

All youth in the focus groups saw numerous benefits to recreation participation, including gaining a sense of belonging, releasing stress and anger, developing positive identities, improved fitness, self-improvement, escaping adult rules, and discovering new options for fun, paid and volunteer work, and socializing. Some proudly pointed to volunteer activities outside the formal public recreation system that challenged racialized, ageist, and gendered assumptions about their capabilities. For example, an Aboriginal male youth said: "We did activities with eight patients at a hospital for elders. We did skits and games like shuffleboard so they would not lose their memories." Such comments suggest a willingness to assume responsibility for the well-being of others that state planners rarely consider when delivering direct recreation programs to passive consumers. Overall, male respondents were more interested in sports, computers, music, and high-risk activities, but a few exhibited an ethic of care, such as that revealed in the above remark. Female youth focused more on hanging out with friends, movies, and outdoor activities. They found public recreation spaces generally unappealing and preferred going to malls. As a Jamaican female adolescent explained: "I go to the mall to take a break from the stress of school and anything that has to do with adults. It's important to have that time to yourself to think about things."

All the focus group participants identified barriers to accessibility, including costly program fees and equipment, distant program locations, a lack of transportation, inflexible and uninviting program structures, and poor attitudes of some participants and staff. As a Filipino male teen said: "I think everything at the community centre is there, it's just that some of the things I want to do, I can't afford it. And also the age limit. I already know that I would like to do break dancing or something, but you have to be thirteen."

In the course of the focus groups, low-income parents conveyed their desire for the same opportunities as wealthier families for their daughters and sons and worried about the health risks associated with inactive lifestyles tied to computers and television viewing. At the same time, parents also identified unsafe neighbourhoods, a lack of discretionary income, offspring with special needs, unfamiliarity with fee-subsidy policies, and their limited trust of recreation leaders as major impediments. In one heated exchange between focus group participants, a mother who identified herself as black (Mother 1) and another who described herself as Canadian (Mother 2), discussed how racism figures in:

Mother 1: A lot of parents don't want their kids to participate with other ethnic backgrounds.

Mother 2: Because that is like the way of life here, it is like the cesspool of all diversity.

Mother 1: But the problem is you are not black, you don't see it.

Mother 2: Well, I have a lot of friends that are black and they don't think that way.

Mother 1: But, trust me, they do, they might not tell you.

Mother 2: But I am not like that.

Mother 1: I know. But my youngest boy is Jewish and Italian, he is my baby, and my second oldest is German and English. I know, every time I tell people, yeah, but my oldest boy is Black, and ah and trouble with certain kind of people, they call him the black word, the one.

Mother 2: The what?

Mother 1: The "N" word, and this word and you're this and that or whatever.

Mother 2: Yeah, but people who are aware, they do the same things. They get into the same problems though.

Mother 1: You don't understand what I am saying. I am saying that certain children and certain people will not have anything to do with them. Do you guys understand what I am saying? They will not have anything to do with a certain ethnic background, a certain kind of people.

The few studies exploring marginalized youth experiences with public recreation confirm the concerns of this parent with their children's exclusion. Despite barriers, however, interest persists, a testament to the enduring faith that full citizenship involves rights to state-supported athletic and cultural programs.[48] For example, Alison Doherty and Tracy Taylor observed that Canada's immigrant youth anticipated fun, good health, and improved language skills.[49] At least as important was the hope that participation would offer a positive orientation to the mainstream culture, which was deemed particularly relevant given the dual pressures of adolescence and cultural transition. More female than male immigrant youth reported feeling excluded because of language difficulties, unfamiliarity with mainstream sports, and peer prejudice.[50] In another study, Susan Tirone also found South Asian

Canadian teens were seeking social relationships outside their ethnic communities but were encountering racism from other participants and an apparent lack of concern by recreation leaders.[51] The teens were further deterred when they were met with indifference to their cultures and recreation traditions from their white friends and peers.[52]

As Monika Stodolska and Gordon Walker have documented, providers of public recreation continue to struggle with how best to serve Aboriginal and immigrant youngsters.[53] There is growing awareness that treating them all as one stable homogenous group to be assimilated into the mainstream culture is highly problematic. At least three paths, which may sometimes meet resistance from families anxious to maintain ethnic identities, are becoming more common in recreation. These include acculturation into the white-dominated mainstream, assimilation into a subculture within the original ethnic community, and preservation of original ethnic identities.[54] However, Tirone found that teens in her study enjoyed aspects of both the dominant Canadian culture and their traditional South Asian heritage.[55] She concluded that theories and practices of recreational programming that attribute differences in participation to distinct cultural norms, values, and social patterns ignore the complex dynamics involved in drawing, sometimes simultaneously, on both traditional and dominant cultures.

Some of the youth who participated in our study for CPRA expressed interest in developing recreation policies and programs for themselves and their friends. This suggests that a community development approach is more appropriate than one emphasizing an adult-oriented, top-down approach to policy and program delivery. As an Aboriginal female youth explained, policies need to take financial circumstances into account because fees are increasingly being charged for public recreation activities: "A lot of people cannot afford things. People are on assistance. They might be interested in programs and so they need a way to pay for things." Yet, some youngsters remained cynical about the commitment of recreation departments to letting their families know about fee subsidies, and some questioned if they even exist. One Irish-German teen exemplified this perspective in his blunt assessment: "The reason they do not advertise [the fee-subsidy policy] is because they don't want people to ask for it." A Chinese-Canadian male recreation staff member justified such suspicions by confessing, "There is no willingness to advertise [the policy] because of the fear of abuse."

The pervasive fee-subsidy model in Canadian public recreation requires proving poverty (e.g., by bringing in social assistance records to be reviewed by staff) in order to qualify, even though the process can be humiliating. And even when they do qualify, low-income youth and families often have no discretionary income to cover even reduced fees.[56] Comments from youth, parents, and staff illustrate that, whatever the intent, fee subsidies ultimately offer only an unsatisfactory answer to the problem of disentitled community members. What emerges much more clearly is what Searle and Brayley call the "market equity model" whereby those who provide the most taxes and fees are deemed to have greater rights to services.[57] Driven increasingly by market principles of demand and ability to pay, so-called public programs mirror recreation services delivered by the burgeoning private sector.[58] The neo-liberal orientation has largely supplanted approaches that promise an equal opportunity model where each person receives approximately equal services irrespective of need or the amount of taxes paid, or a compensatory equity model where citizens with the greatest needs are targeted for public services.[59]

Neo-liberalism downplays expending public funds to promote social well-being and equity agendas, because governments have been fashioning themselves as market players since the 1980s and turning a blind eye to the daily lived realities creating social inequalities.[60] Emphasizing individualism constructs the poor as responsible for their own plights because of wilful skill and motivational deficiencies.[61] This logic demands that individuals demonstrate their entitlement by having the capacity to pay full or close to full market rates. As a result, youth and their parents on low income are expected to locate information about recreation programs and fee-subsidy policies through computer technology that is not readily accessible to them. Additionally, they are offered few collective opportunities for public support in the design and location of preferred activities.[62] The result is a two-tiered recreation system of haves and have-nots that reinforces an entrenched pattern that sets up additional structural barriers to participation for those on low income.[63]

Conclusion

Many compelling critiques target the failure of the state to include marginalized youth, yet to simply write off the traditions of public recreation has significant consequences. In particular, it may permit local authorities to absolve themselves of responsibility for offering democratic sites for diverse youth participation. There are far better alternatives. Although public recreation programs and policies are typically developed and delivered in a top-down fashion, rarely taking the overall living conditions of low-income young people into account, we, other scholars, and some recreation programmers suggest that giving marginalized youth more decision-making control in sites close to home will promote a politics of social inclusion and, ultimately, greater social justice.[64]

To do this, staff and managers around the country must revisit what recreation means to diverse groups of young people, be more sensitive to how public recreation reproduces social divisions, and involve youth more directly in programming and policy development. Alliances with youth, likeminded politicians, recreation staff, voters, and community partners would do much to offset the socially destructive consequences of neo-liberalism. Such a shift is possible, as the experience of at least one Canadian city has demonstrated. The city of Winnipeg has reinvested revenues from recreation programs into a wide range of free offerings in low-income neighbourhoods. Such a coexistence of market and non-market programming may be uncomfortable to some in our neo-liberal times, but it promises to assist those who might well do without otherwise. In one of the city's unique programs called SPIN, children and youth in inner-city neighbourhoods participate in sport programs where they learn basic skill development, teamwork, leadership, and fair play in a non-competitive environment. Through sponsorships with a number of government agencies and community groups, the SPIN program tackles barriers by providing transportation, financial assistance, equipment, leadership, and volunteer support. In addition, recreation centres in the downtown area provide space to other social service providers so that more integrated services can be offered close to home to children, youth, and families.[65]

In the future, low-income children and youth should not be viewed as those whom the state needs to discipline and reform through marketplace strategies. Such youngsters are citizens whose rights should include meaningful access and input into public recreation, if they so choose.[66] They require, and we recommend, a compensatory equity model of delivery that uses a community development approach targeting them for assistance and active involvement in policy and recreation programming.[67] Since many of the youth we have talked with see the potential for public recreation to provide spaces of opportunity and inclusion, there is a democratic momentum. Young Canadians who are wrestling with multiple disadvantages can, with support, design the community initiatives that will make a difference in their lives, their communities, and ultimately the nation. If we heed the voices that surfaced in our study for CPRA, the needs and desires of so many youngsters for community-supported recreation will no longer go unheard. A responsible community and nation should ensure that no one, child or adult, stands outside such a circle of care and opportunity.

Notes

1 Wendy Frisby, S. Crawford, and T. Dorer, "Reflections on Participatory Action Research: The Case of Low-Income Women Accessing Local Physical Activity Services," *Journal of Sport Management* 11, 1 (1997): 8-28.

2 M.G. McDonald, "Mapping Whiteness and Sport," *Sociology of Sport Journal* 22, 3 (2005): 245-55.

3 Wendy Frisby, Ted Alexander, Janna Taylor, Susan Tirone, C. Watson, Jean Harvey, and D. Laplante, *Bridging the Recreation Divide: Listening to Youth and Parents from Low-Income Families across Canada* (Ottawa: Canadian Parks and Recreation Association, 2005). The CPRA report was a collaboration by researchers from three universities (University of British Columbia, University of Ottawa, and Dalhousie University). For this paper, only data collected by the University of British Columbia researchers in three of the five cities were used.

4 J. Brodie, "The Great Undoing: State Formation, Gender Politics, and Social Policy in Canada," in B.A. Crow and L. Gotell, eds., *Open Boundaries: A Canadian Women's Studies Reader* (Toronto: Prentice Hall, 2005), 87-96; L. Thibault, L. Kikulis, and Wendy Frisby, "Partnerships between Local Government Sport and Leisure Departments and the Commercial Sector: Changes, Complexities, and Consequences," in T. Slack, ed., *The Commercialisation of Sport* (London: Frank Cass, 2004), 119-40.

5 Mark S. Searle and Russell E. Brayley, *Leisure Services in Canada* (State College, PA: Venture, 2000).

6 Frisby et al., *Bridging the Recreation Divide*.

7 Campaign 2000, "Decision Time for Canada: Let's Make Poverty History; 2005 Report Card on Child Poverty in Canada," 2005. http://www.campaign2000.ca/rc/rc05/05NationalReportCard.pdf.

8 S. Fuller, P. Kershaw, and J. Pulkingham, "Constructing 'Active Citizenship': Single Mothers, Welfare, and the Logics of Voluntarism," *Citizenship Studies* 12, 2 (2008): 157-76; Donald G. Reid and B.L. Golden, "Non-Work and Leisure Activity and Socially Marginalized Women: The Issue of Integration," *Canadian Review of Social Policy* 55 (2005): 39-65.

9 C.P. Shah, M. Kahan, and J. Krauser, "The Health of Children of Low-Income Families," *Canadian Medical Association Journal* 137 (1987): 485-89.

10 Sally MacIntyre, "The Social Patterning of Exercise Behaviours: The Role of Personal and Local Resources," *British Journal of Sport Medicine* 34, 1 (2000): 6.

11 Colleen Reid, *The Wounds of Exclusion: Poverty, Women's Health and Social Justice* (Edmonton: Qualitative Institute Press, 2004).

12 Wendy Frisby, Colleen Reid, and P. Ponic, "Levelling the Playing Field: Promoting the Health of Poor Women through a Community Development Approach to Recreation," in Philip White and K. Young, eds., *Sport and Gender in Canada* (Don Mills, ON: Oxford University Press, 2007), 120-36.

13 J.F. Sallis and N. Owen, *Physical Activity and Behavioral Medicine* (Thousand Oaks, CA: Sage, 1999).

14 Canadian Council on Social Development, *Recreation and Children and Youth Living in Poverty: Barriers, Benefits and Success Stories* (Ottawa: Canadian Parks and Recreation Association, 2001).

15 Frisby, Reid, and Ponic, "Levelling the Playing Field."

16 C.P. Shah, *Public Health and Preventive Medicine in Canada* (Toronto: University of Toronto Press, 1998).

17 Caroline Andrew, Jean Harvey, and Don Dawson, "Evolution of Local State Activity: Recreation Policy in Toronto," *Leisure Studies* 1 (1994): 1.

18 Searle and Brayley, *Leisure Services in Canada,* 40.

19 Ibid.

20 S.E. Markham, "Mabel Peters," *Dictionary of Canadian Biography* (Toronto: University of Toronto Press, 1994), 4.

21 Shirley Tillotson, *The Public at Play: Gender and the Politics of Recreation in Post-War Ontario* (Toronto: University of Toronto Press, 2000), 14.

22 Ibid., 17.

23 Searle and Brayley, *Leisure Services in Canada*.

24 Tillotson, *The Public at Play*.

25 P. Vertinsky, *The Eternally Wounded Woman: Women, Exercise and Doctors* (Urbana, IL: University of Illinois Press, 1994).

26 M. Ann Hall, "Cultural Struggle and Resistance: Gender, History and Canadian Sport," in Young and White, *Sport and Gender in Canada,* 57.

27 Vicky Paraschak, "Doing Race, Doing Gender: First Nations, 'Sport,' and Gender Relations," in Young and White, *Sport and Gender in Canada*.

28 Ibid.

29 Tillotson, *The Public at Play*.

30 Brian Wilson and Philip White, "Tolerance Rules: Identity, Resistance, and Negotiation in an Inner City Recreation/Drop-in Centre," *Journal of Sport and Social Issues* 25, 1 (2001): 73-103.

31 Brian Wilson, Philip White, and K. Fisher, "Multiple Identities in a Marginalized Culture: Female Youth in an 'Inner-City' Recreation/Drop-in Centre," *Journal of Sport and Social Issues* 25, 3 (2001): 373-412.

32 Searle and Brayley, *Leisure Services in Canada.*

33 D. Reid, *Work and Leisure in the 21st Century: From Production to Citizenship* (Toronto: Wall and Emerson, 1995).

34 Searle and Brayley, *Leisure Services in Canada.*

35 Brodie, "The Great Undoing"; Wendy Frisby and S. Millar, "The Actualities of Doing Community Development to Promote the Inclusion of Low-Income Populations in Local Sport and Recreation," *European Sport Management Quarterly* 3 (2002): 209-33; Reid, *Work and Leisure in the 21st Century.*

36 Jean Harvey, "The Role of Sport and Recreation Policy in Fostering Citizenship: The Canadian Experience," in J. Jenson, Jean Harvey, W. Kimlicka, A. Maoni, E. Schragge, P. Greafe, and J.M. Fontan, eds., Discussion Paper No. F/17 (Ottawa: Canadian Policy Research Networks, 2001).

37 P. Donnelly and Jean Harvey, "Social Class and Gender: Intersections in Sport and Physical Activity," in Young and White, *Sport and Gender in Canada.*

38 Alan Ingham, "From Public Issue to Personal Trouble: Well-Being and the Fiscal Crisis of the State," *Sociology of Sport Journal* 2, 1 (1985): 50.

39 Douglas Hartmann, "Notes on Midnight Basketball and the Cultural Politics of Recreation, Race, and At-Risk Urban Youth," *Journal of Sport and Social Issues* 25, 4 (2001): 339-71.

40 C.L. Cole, "American Jordan: P.L.A.Y., Consensus and Punishment," *Sociology of Sport Journal* 13 (1996): 366-97.

41 Ibid.

42 Hartmann, "Notes on Midnight Basketball," 346.

43 R. Pitter and D.L. Andrews, "Serving America's Underserved Youth: Reflections on Sport and Recreation in an Emerging Social Problems Industry," *Quest* 49 (1997): 85-99; Reid, *Work and Leisure in the 21st Century.*

44 Donnelly and Harvey, "Social Class and Gender."

45 Ibid., 104.

46 Frisby et al., *Bridging the Recreation Divide;* Susan Tirone, "Evening the Playing Field: Recreation in a Low-Income Canadian Community," *Leisure/Loisir* 28, 1-2 (2003-4): 155-74; Paraschak, "Doing Race, Doing Gender."

47 See Frisby et al., *Bridging the Recreation Divide.*

48 Harvey, "The Role of Sport and Recreation Policy."

49 Alison Doherty and Tracy Taylor, "Sport and Physical Recreation in the Settlement of Immigrant Youth," *Leisure/Loisir* 31, 1 (2007): 27-55.

50 Ibid.

51 Susan Tirone, "Racism, Indifference and the Leisure Experiences of South Asian Canadian Teens," *Leisure/Loisir* 24, 1-2 (1999-2000): 89-114.

52 Ibid.

53 Monika Stodolska and Gordon J. Walker, "Ethnicity and Leisure: Historical Development, Current Status, and Future Directions," *Leisure/Loisir* 31, 1 (2007): 19.

54 Ibid.

55 Tirone, "Racism, Indifference and the Leisure Experiences."

56 Frisby, Reid, and Ponic, "Levelling the Playing Field"; Frisby et al., *Bridging the Recreation Divide.*

57 Searle and Brayley, *Leisure Services in Canada,* 249.

58 Thibault, Kikulis, and Frisby, "Partnerships."

59 Searle and Brayley, *Leisure Services in Canada.*

60 Brodie, "The Great Undoing"; Harvey, "The Role of Sport and Recreation Policy."

61 Reid, *The Wounds of Exclusion.*

62 Tirone, "Racism, Indifference and the Leisure Experiences"; Wilson and White, "Tolerance Rules"; Wilson, White, and Fisher, "Multiple Identities in a Marginalized Culture."

63 Canadian Council on Social Development, *Recreation and Children and Youth Living in Poverty;* Colleen Reid, Wendy Frisby, and P. Ponic, "Confronting Two-Tiered Community Recreation

and Poor Women's Exclusion: Promoting Inclusion, Health, and Social Justice," *Canadian Women's Studies* 21, 3 (2002): 88-94.

64 Frisby, Reid, and Ponic, "Levelling the Playing Field"; Donnelly and Harvey, "Social Class and Gender"; Tirone, "Racism, Indifference and the Leisure Experiences"; Wilson and White, "Tolerance Rules."

65 T. Fergus, pers. comm., telephone conversation, 28 September 2008.

66 Harvey, "The Role of Sport and Recreation Policy."

67 Searle and Brayley, *Leisure Services in Canada*.

12
Deregulating Child Labour in British Columbia
Stephen McBride and John Irwin

Labour market conditions for young people in Canada deteriorated over the 1980s, 1990s, and early 2000s.[1] This trend can be viewed as a microcosm of broader pressures within the labour market, resulting from increasingly internationalized production that confers on firms the capacity to purchase an optimum blend of more expensive high-skilled and cheaper low-skilled labour.[2] In this situation of increased flexibility, labour rights have been "increasingly perceived as costs of production to be avoided in the interest of enhancing or maintaining 'national competitiveness.'"[3] Working young-sters become near invisible figures in an economic calculation that largely ignores the price paid by them and society more generally.

In this chapter we are concerned with recent regulatory changes in British Columbia that pertain directly to children and youth and have the potential to adversely affect young people, either by discriminating against them or by exposing them to unnecessary danger or harm. In 2000, the election of a new Liberal provincial government introduced a significant reorganization of labour relations. We consider the implications of previous and current legislation and regulations and compare the province's policies on child and youth employment to those of other jurisdictions in Canada and abroad, as well as to international norms as expressed in various international conventions and agreements. The comparison establishes that British Columbia's deregulatory posture is unusual in the lack of protection it affords young workers. There are reasonable grounds to be apprehensive that the legislation may be harmful and discriminatory. Finally, we consider the results of an online survey of twelve- to eighteen-year-old students.[4] The total sample of 624 yielded a good representation of ages, with the exception of the eighteen-year-old category (many in this age group may already have graduated from or left high school). There were 290 girls and 334 boys. We believe our survey is unique in that it includes youth aged twelve to fourteen years. Of these, we focused on the 114 respondents who were currently working (54 girls and 60 boys). These were clustered into two age ranges: twelve to fourteen

(44.1 percent) and fifteen to eighteen (55.9 percent). This way of organizing the respondents reflects changes to British Columbia's Employment Standards Act, which apply to the twelve- to fourteen-year-old cohort, while the fifteen-to-eighteen age category captures the period in life when youth have traditionally begun to make the transition into paid employment.

Youth labour policy forms part of a broader strategy of workplace flexibility. Part-time, temporary, casual, and contract work has been described as a response to the economic crises of the 1970s, the recessions in the 1980s and 1990s, and increased international competition.[5] The costs and benefits have been summarized by the International Labour Organization (ILO). Benefits include rising productivity and reduced wage costs. Greater job instability, increased part-time employment, reduced overtime pay, and greater assignment of work in "unsocial" hours are among the costs borne by workers.[6]

There seem, in fact, to be at least two models of workplace flexibility. The first is flexibility within a high-skill, high-wage, advanced technology economy where well-trained individuals with in-demand skills see change as opportunity. The second flexible labour market involves the unemployed, low-waged workers generally, and all those who have insecure jobs in the low-wage, low-skill sector. These are people "who are neither born flexible nor achieve flexibility but have flexibility thrust upon them."[7]

Similarly, the Organisation for Economic Co-operation and Development's 1994 Jobs Study identified two routes for dealing with problems of youth unemployment.[8] The first focused on skills development and investment in human capital as a route to high-wage, high-value added production. The second was designed to encourage low-waged employment.[9] Far from being competing strategies, they were, in fact, complementary.[10]

In 2001, British Columbia's newly elected Liberal government charted a deregulatory "flexibility" approach to labour relations and employment standards.[11] In combination, its choice of measures could be predicted to reduce trade union effectiveness, adversely impact working conditions, and alter legal statuses (especially as far as the availability of child labour is concerned). These regulatory changes were supplemented by aggressive ad hoc legislation to end strikes, reshape contracts, and impose wage cuts and job losses. After taking office, the BC Liberals enacted back-to-work legislation and imposed settlements on teachers, nurses, hospital workers, ferry employees, and transit workers. The Health and Social Services Delivery Improvement Act was, for example, explicitly designed to increase workplace flexibility, expedite restructuring activities, and provide legislative approval for open tendering of health services.[12] In 2001, the province also introduced legislation imposing essential-service designation on BC teachers, which the ILO subsequently called on the province to repeal.[13] Then, forty-three thousand health care workers from the Hospital Employees' Union were legislated back to work, with the provincial government imposing a 15 percent wage rollback, permitting employers to contract out union jobs, and extending the sector's workweek.

The Labour Relations Code, the provincial statute that governs relations among employers, employees, and unions, has been subject to extensive revisions since the BC Liberals came to power. The Employment Standards Amendment Act, 2002, transformed the province's previous labour standards practices. The Ministry Backgrounder to the legislation used a version of the word "flexibility" six times in its first two pages. It was a fair description of the legislative changes. Rather than have the Employment Standards Branch investigate labour complaints, the burden of responsibility was shifted to the employee. For instance, an employee wishing to file a grievance concerning wage disputes or working conditions is required to complete an Employment Standards Self-Help Kit and provide all evidence related to the complaint prior to the initiation of any investigation. Other significant changes include the termination of fair overtime wages and the repeal of double-time premiums (section 19) and an averaging arrangement in which employees may be asked to enter into flexibility agreements with implications for overtime wages (section 37(1-14)). The minimum length of an employee's shift (call-out) was reduced to two hours from four (section 34(1)). Adults were not the only workers to suffer with legislative changes: one further amendment ensured that employment of children under the age of fifteen no longer required the permission of the director of employment standards but was instead left to parental discretion.

For all provincially – regulated, non-unionized employees in British Columbia, the Employment Standards Act is the most important protection mechanism available, with the sole purpose of stipulating legal rights and responsibilities of both employers and employees and providing protection in the context of the employment relationship. To date, the provincial Liberals have introduced extensive amendments to the Employment Standards Act and reduced state involvement in the protection of non-unionized workers. Thus, significant changes to industrial relations and employment standards law and regulation put British Columbia in the forefront of jurisdictions pursuing a flexibility strategy toward their labour forces.

Children in British Columbia aged twelve to fourteen are able to work with the consent of one parent or guardian. Previously, such children could not work unless the director of employment standards granted a permit. This age threshold is among the lowest in Canada for employment without permission of employment standards officers or school authorities. A permit continues to be required for employment of children under twelve years. Lax regulations (children are allowed to work up to thirty-five hours per week in school boards where school is in session for four days per week, twenty hours in boards where school is in session for five days) may have detrimental effects on school performance. No mechanism, other than the approval of one parent, now exists to ascertain academic standing before granting permission to work. Concerns have also been expressed that very young workers may find themselves exposed to dangerous or inappropriate conditions.[14]

Children and youth are subject to discrimination by way of a reduced minimum wage of six dollars per hour (two dollars per hour less than British Columbia's statutory minimum wage) that can be applied to the first five hundred hours of an individual's working life. Officially, the lower minimum wage is described as a "first job" or "entry" wage. Colloquially, it is called the "training" wage, though no training need occur. We reflect common usage and adopt the "training wage" terminology. The training wage is not explicitly based on age criteria but is discriminatory in its effect, since youth are most likely to lack labour force experience. Other provinces have reduced minimum wages for some categories of workers, but the two-dollars-per-hour gap in British Columbia is substantially greater than elsewhere in Canada. The extension of the "flexibility" agenda to very young workers runs counter to a long-standing emphasis, in Canada and in international organizations, to protect young workers from many of the hazards that might be involved in the employment relationship.[15]

Since federal jurisdiction covers only about 10 percent of the workforce, the most significant legislation is that of the provinces, a major constraint on bringing Canada up to international labour standards, as the recent report of the Senate Standing Committee on Human Rights noted.[16] The gap between wages paid to new employees (typically but not exclusively the young) when compared with the regular minimum wage is greater than any other differential minimum wage in Canada. Moreover, even if a differential were justified, to allow it for five hundred hours, given the skill level required in most entry-level jobs, is unjustified and operates, in effect, as a wage subsidy to low-end employers, including large multinationals operating in the fast-food and retail sectors.

In comparison with the United States, the European Union, and the norms of international organizations, British Columbia's flexible approach to child labour is substandard.

Although the United States deservedly enjoys a reputation for deregulation, child employment is actually more tightly regulated there than in Canada.[17] In the United States, jurisdiction is split, with federal law and regulations covering businesses with an annual volume of fifty thousand dollars or more and state rules covering the smaller enterprises. Given the variety of state-level legislation, no general synthesis can be presented. However, federal legislation, which is relatively far more important than in Canada, sets a minimum age for non-agricultural employment at fourteen, with a few minor exceptions; limits the employment of schoolchildren to three hours a day and eighteen hours a week when school is in session; prevents fourteen- and fifteen-year-olds from working at nights; and prohibits youth under eighteen from performing a wide variety of jobs, with additional restricted occupations for the youngest workers. In Washington State, adjacent to British Columbia, the minimum employment age is fourteen, employment is restricted to three hours a day for a maximum of sixteen hours per week, and nighttime employment is prohibited. Clearly, young workers are more protected south of the border than in British Columbia.

The European Union has developed legislation on labour standards that applies to all member states, even those that have not introduced similar domestic legislation.[18] The 2000 Charter of Fundamental Rights of the European Union limits the employment of children below school-leaving age and requires that workplaces are safe, non-exploitative, and compatible with schooling.[19] In addition, the European Union 1994 directive on the protection of young people at work states that "member states shall take the necessary measures to prohibit work by children under fifteen and regulate work by adolescents aged fifteen to eighteen years of age ... with light work permitted from the age of thirteen."[20] The focus of many European countries is to provide school-to-work training programs to older adolescents in order to address unemployment rates for young adults. The focus for younger children and youth is not on employment but on attaining an education and staying in school.

The United Nations and the ILO have developed global agreements addressing child labour practices. In 1989, the Convention on the Rights of the Child was adopted by the General Assembly of the United Nations. Article 32 of the convention provides that states should recognize the right of the child to be protected from economic exploitation and from performing any work that is likely to interfere with education, or to harm health or physical, mental, spiritual, moral, or social development, and should take legislative, administrative, social, and educational measures to ensure protection.[21]

Employment standards for children in British Columbia contravene the ILO's Convention Concerning Minimum Age for Admission to Employment (1973), which declares that states must set a minimum age for entry into employment that should not be lower than the age of completion of compulsory education, and never lower than fifteen. The convention does allow for exceptions to the fifteen-year-old rule (Article 2.4), but only under special circumstances, such as "a Member whose economy and educational facilities are insufficiently developed." This hardly fits British Columbia, which has a well-developed public school system and an economy that does not require child labour in order to function. The ILO also states that "national laws or regulations may permit the employment or work of persons thirteen to fifteen years of age on light work which is – (a) not likely to be harmful to their health or development; and (b) not such as to prejudice their attendance at school."[22] But the employment of children as young as twelve years of age is clearly not supported.

The ILO has also set standards outlining the appropriate use of minimum age and wage legislation in member countries. These standards are guided by the principle of "equal remuneration for work of equal value."[23] In particular, the Minimum Age Recommendation (No. 146) stipulates that "special attention should be given to the provision of fair remuneration to young people, bearing in mind the principle of equal pay for equal work."[24] Although the ILO does not explicitly forbid the fixing of different rates on the basis of age, legislating a lower minimum wage for young workers does contravene general ILO principles if their work is of equal value. The ILO does recognize a difference between youth who perform the same work as their adult counterparts and those whose work includes formal training, such as apprentices. A lower wage for youth performing the same work as adults and without training is unjustifiable.[25] However, this is exactly what has occurred in British Columbia.

Using an online survey of high school students, we evaluated the experience of young workers under the new child labour regime.[26] It was clear that most working children and youth do get satisfaction from working. This tends to confirm other findings that a moderate amount of work can productively be combined with schooling. Most reported that they worked for their own personal spending; foreign-born children were somewhat more likely to report working to help their families or for a combination of own spending and family assistance than were Canadian-born respondents.

Many children and youth continue, as in the past, to begin their histories of employment in association with family and kin. About 25 percent of today's working children and youth work alongside their parents in the early morning or evening. These young workers are likely employed in their parents' small businesses, or may, given a lack of child care, accompany their parents to work sites. This raises concerns about children from economically marginalized families being pressed to work, potentially for unacceptable hours or under questionable conditions. It also implies that the new regulations, requiring only parental consent, may be putting some parents in a conflict of interest. These issues are eerily reminiscent of findings that provoked the first child labour legislation in nineteenth-century Canada, Britain, and the United States.

Survey results indicated that students work in a wide variety of jobs, with food service and retail being by far the most common. Students were asked how many hours they worked during the following time frames: during the school week, on weekends, and over the summer holidays. The mean number of weekly hours that twelve- to fourteen-year-olds reported working during each time frame is 3.68, 2.90, and 8.97, respectively. The fifteen- to seventeen-year-olds report working two to three times more, at 7.98, 8.56, and 23.14 hours, respectively. These findings reflect the fact that school, when it is in session, is the main focus for most children and youth. As many as 23 percent of all youth and 31 percent of twelve- to fourteen-year-olds indicated that they worked less than two hours per week; this in itself flags a violation of the Employment Standards Act, since few of these cases were in excluded jobs, such as newspaper delivery and babysitting and, for the rest, the minimum two-hour call-out is mandated under the act.

A minority of youth aged fifteen to eighteen (around 3 percent) worked more than twenty hours each week while school is in session but outside of school hours. Thus, these students were working in excess of the legal maximum. Some respondents who noted difficulty with school-job balance worked longer hours. Too many hours of work can impact on school performance. Some literature indicates that students who work twenty hours per week or more experience difficulty with their schoolwork, while those working under twenty hours generally do not report such negative impacts.[27] Our study did find a minority who reported a negative impact on school grades, including cases where fewer than twenty hours were worked. Nine of ninety-eight respondents replied that their grades had declined since they started working. Fifty-eight reported that their marks stayed the same, and fifteen noted improvement (sixteen were not sure if there was an effect). Given that most of the study's participants work ten hours or less each week, it is not surprising that the majority noted no impact on school performance. That around 16 percent replied that their grades improved underlines that a reasonable amount of time spent at work can be positive. Still, 17.7 percent noted that they lacked time to do their homework. Of these, the great majority worked less than twenty hours a week and most worked less than ten, suggesting that some youngsters feel the effects of employment more than others, and the effect is not confined to those working long hours. These mixed findings highlight the benefits of giving school authorities a chance to intervene so that those experiencing difficulty mixing school and work could be required to reduce their work hours.

Some working participants noted a significant impact on their extracurricular and recreational lives – almost 50 percent indicated that they had to give up, or were missing out on sports, music, or other activities. These may very well be the especially disadvantaged young people whom Wendy Frisby, Ted Alexander, and Janna Taylor identify in Chapter 11 of this volume as being otherwise badly served by public recreation programs. The impact of work on student's social lives and their level of fitness nevertheless seems relatively benign. Very few noted any deterioration, and a sizable number indicate that their social life and physical fitness have improved. However, some students (12.4 percent of those aged twelve to fourteen and 13.4 percent of the older group) reported that work negatively affected their social lives and physical fitness. Students were somewhat more likely to report missing out on social life or recreation the more hours they worked. A well-crafted and responsible employment standards regime should rightly be concerned about these children and youth.

Lost opportunities are sometimes accompanied by present dangers. Many respondents are currently employed in the food services sector, and just over 30 percent report they operate stoves, ovens, and other restaurant equipment. Because of their age, relatively few work with heavy equipment, but there are exceptions. Some students reported operating bulldozers, diggers, or tractors. Although this is a very small proportion (3.6 percent), some very young employees handle potentially dangerous machinery.

Over one in five working children and youth report that they have been injured on the job. Many injuries were burns. This probably reflects employment around stoves, ovens, and restaurant equipment, although, surprisingly, retail cashiers also reported this injury. Most respondents were treated either on the job or at home for their burns. Of those injured, 31.6 percent reported being treated in a hospital or by a physician and 5 percent received treatment at a clinic, suggesting more serious accidents.

Almost 30 percent of working respondents indicated that they felt unsafe at work. Foreign-born children were more likely than the Canadian-born to report this (36.8 percent compared with 28 percent). Our survey did not probe the kind of insecurity felt by these young people. They may feel unsafe, in addition to the possibility of physical accidents, because they are required to work alone, or feel vulnerable to harassment, abuse, or violence. As inexperienced workers, already subordinated by reason of age, they may well not identify problems accurately or feel able to complain. Naïveté or overconfidence may also undermine their abilities to estimate threats to their well-being.

Working respondents were asked whether they received any on-the-job health and safety training. Quite a high number reported no training – 40.9 percent – indicating that health and safety are not being thoroughly dealt with by employers. Foreign-born children are significantly less likely to have received health and safety training than their Canadian counterparts. Just as in the past, young foreign-born workers, much like their elders, are likely to experience the least protection and the greatest danger.

Regardless of the age of the young workers in the study, few report that their parents have asked their prospective employers about workplace safety. For all age groups, 72.6 percent report that their parents did not ask about health and safety; for the twelve-to-fourteen age group, the figure was 48.1 percent. The survey did not ask why parents were so reticent, but past experience suggests that silence may well reflect impoverished households' need for child labour in order to survive. The rising cost of living, especially in Canadian urban centres in the last quarter of the twentieth century, only adds to the urgency of this calculation.

In terms of supervision, 9.6 percent of all students reported working without adult supervision, 33 percent reported some supervision, and 57.4 percent indicated that they were supervised all or most of the time. A disturbing picture of unsupervised labour among twelve- to fourteen-year-olds was revealed: 22.2 percent (six respondents) working without adult supervision, 48.1 percent (thirteen respondents) supervised only some of the time, and only 29.7 percent (nine respondents) supervised all or most of the time. In fact, the ESA requires the constant supervision of workers aged fourteen and younger by an adult (defined as some responsible person at least nineteen years old). This raises questions about the value of self-regulation under the current Employment Standards Act. The new employment standards regime relies on the parents to monitor the health and safety of their children's workplaces and requires adult supervision. However, our results indicate that a large proportion of parents may not be monitoring their children's health and safety in the workplace, and many employers seem lax regarding statutory requirements.

The proportion of young workers who reported that their employers did not receive written parental consent is also very high (60.9 percent of students). Of course, many in the upper age group would not require this. However, most students in the twelve-to-fourteen group (58.3 percent) reported employers who did not get parental consent – a clear violation of the act.

Many young workers reported they received the training wage. Forty-four percent of the employed youth indicated that they had been paid less than $8.00 per hour at some time; the remaining 56 percent were never paid less than $8.00 per hour – British Columbia's regular minimum wage. Gender differences in average (or mean) wages were noticeable; for males the mean is $9.42 per hour, for females $8.22. Of those getting paid more than $8.00, males reported a mean hourly wage of $12.70, females $8.66 – again a statistically significant difference. Of those young workers who completed five hundred hours on the training wage, 11.7 percent indicated that they either lost their job or continued to work at $6.00 an hour. Already disadvantaged by the training wage, they then had their right to the general minimum wage abrogated because their employers were unwilling to pay the statutory minimum.

A slight majority (52.2 percent) of all respondents in the survey found the training wage to be unfair. However, that figure rose dramatically among those students who were actually working: 71 percent thought it unfair. There is a statistically significant relationship between students' feelings about the wage and whether or not they had ever held a job. Students with actual work experience (who have a better understanding of the minimal skills and training required for most minimum-wage jobs) are more likely to find the training wage unfair.

Young workers who participated in the study were seldom trained while on the training wage. Of course, there is no legal obligation for employers to provide training. However, the idea that lack of experience warrants lower pay is implicit in the statute and the official designation of this wage as a "first job" or "entry" wage. One justification for the reduced wage could be that new workers require considerable supervision and are less efficient in their jobs than are more experienced workers. The implication is that training will occur, whether formal or on-the-job, over a period of five hundred hours, to remedy alleged deficiencies. This perception explains why the reduced minimum wage has become known as the "training wage." However, our survey indicates that although some young people receive supervision and training, many do not. A sizable proportion of respondents indicated that they were trained only at the start (28.2 percent), or just a few times (21.2 percent). The largest proportion (35.3 percent) indicated that they were not trained at all. The remaining 15.3 percent were trained several times or many times.

The ILO sets out general principles that allow for differential rates of pay when training is required (such as in apprenticeship programs); otherwise, a lower wage is unjustifiable. However, the BC legislation requires no training, and most working children and youth in our sample have jobs requiring limited training. Thus, the reduced minimum or training wage explicitly violates the notion of equal pay for work of equal value and discriminates against the youth paid this rate.

In British Columbia, children as young as twelve years old are allowed to work and for longer hours than in any other province.[28] The relationship between working and school performance is complex. Research has shown that working less than twenty hours a week is not detrimental to schoolwork but that working more than twenty hours a week can be. In general, students who work spend less time on homework are more likely to skip class and have a negative attitude toward school. Studies in Ontario and Quebec show that students who work fifteen hours or less tend to perform well academically. Other studies show that students who work a small to moderate amount (less than nineteen hours a week) are less likely to drop out of school than those who do not work at all.[29]

Under the new regulations, the parent granting their consent to employers of twelve- to fourteen-year-olds "must determine that the employment situation meets the best interest of the child and will not adversely affect the child's social, physical or educational needs."[30] However, this role may not be widely understood by parents, especially those with limited English-language skills or experience with Canadian urban settings, quite apart from the issue of whether they have the necessary expertise to make such judgments. The Workers' Compensation Board of BC believes that parents usually assume that employers provide proper safety training, equipment, and supervision. Many parents believe they have no role to play in this area and, indeed, the act provides no specific direction. As a result, it is likely that many parents are consenting to employment without an idea of the real risks.[31] Without the supervision of the Employment Standards Branch or some other form of regulation, parents might be unwittingly placing youngsters at risk of injury.

The Workers' Compensation Board does not provide statistics on the rate of injury for children under the age of fifteen. Nor were these statistics available for other provinces. As Veronica Strong-Boag establishes in Chapter 2 of this volume, useful data, longitudinal or otherwise, on children's disabilities of any sort are chronically in short supply. However, statistics from the United States indicate that children under fifteen are at serious risk for injury and death. The US National Institute for Occupational Safety and Health states that for children fourteen and under, workplace injuries and fatalities are a significant concern.[32] Canadians should be especially concerned about recent changes to the Employment Standards Act that allow younger children to work in industries such as farming. Indeed, Canadian agriculture has a long history of relying on young workers, including Britain's most vulnerable child emigrants, such as those from the Barnardo's homes.[33] British Columbia's recent legislative changes, coupled with ongoing demand for more farm workers, may encourage more children to seek employment in this industry.[34] For example, the BC Fruit Growers' Association supported changes to employment standards for youth in the hopes of streamlining paperwork for hiring low-wage, low-skill labour to pick fruit and garden vegetables.[35] US studies demonstrate that this industry is inappropriate for children, especially of a young age.[36]

Work in agriculture supplies myriad dangers. Children and youth are generally inexperienced and without the skills needed to operate farm equipment safely: the consequences can be fatal.[37] For example, in the summer of 2002, a fourteen-year-old was killed in the Okanagan when the tractor he was operating on a slope rolled over.[38] Changes to the BC Employment Standards Act, resulting in reduced inspections on farms and cutbacks on regulations, have made farm work "much closer to third world conditions than would be acceptable in BC."[39] Children as young as twelve years of age can now perform agricultural labour with the approval of only one parent. Unfortunately, with one exception, all the rural school districts approached to participate in this study refused. The one rural school district that did approve, however, had no teachers come forward to allow their students to participate. We are thus left to speculate on what exactly is happening in rural British Columbia, albeit on the rather certain basis of repeated historical and international evidence confirming the special disadvantage of girls and boys in agricultural districts.[40]

However inadequate the regulatory framework that governs child and youth employment standards, most citizens would agree that it should be properly enforced and monitored. Yet, the system of self-regulation established by the new legislation and regulations does not appear to achieve consistent enforcement. Young workers ought to experience a fair, smooth, and safe transition into the paid workplace. Parental involvement is a necessary but insufficient condition for making this happen. It needs to be supplemented by the expertise of those trained to evaluate employment conditions. Moreover, minimum criteria for obtaining parental consent should be established such that parents acquire sufficient information about the job and workplace to make their consent informed rather than pro-forma.

That youth are the most likely group to be paid a first job or training rate makes this pay rate discriminatory on the basis of age. In order for society to have a healthy and stable workforce in the future, the transition from school to work should be a well-regulated process that protects a vulnerable population such as children and youth from possible abuse. The formative years for children and youth aged twelve to eighteen are vital for their education and experience. Paid employment can be an important part of the growth and development of children. But society owes its young acceptable standards. Under the existing provincial regime, protection of the most vulnerable workers has been sacrificed for flexibility for low-wage employers. This priority undermines the present and the future of today's young people and returns society to a dangerous past. The losses of and for children and youth need to be counted when neo-liberal regimes trumpet the benefits of global competitiveness.

Notes

1 S. McBride, "Towards Perfect Flexibility: Youth as an Industrial Reserve Army for the New Economy," in Jim Stanford and Leah F. Vosko, eds., *Challenging the Market: The Struggle to Regulate Work and Income* (Montreal and Kingston: McGill-Queens University Press, 2004).
2 R. Chaykowski and A. Giles, "Globalization, Work and Industrial Relations," *Relations Industrielles/Industrial Relations* 53, 1 (1998): 6.
3 Guy Standing, "Global Feminization through Flexible Labour: A Theme Revisited," *World Development* 27, 3 (1999): 584.
4 This study used on an online survey based on a purposive sample of public school students in British Columbia, aged twelve to eighteen years. Non-probability sampling methods were used. Given the challenges of recruiting working youth, random sampling methods were unrealistic. A high target was chosen for the sample (1,000 participants). A total of 629 students completed the survey, with over 100 working youth, who are the primary focus here.

British Columbia has sixty public school districts. Of these, fourteen were contacted for permission to include their students. Selected districts represented various regions in the province in an attempt to obtain a sample from both urban and rural communities. Five districts agreed to participate: Boundary School District, in rural British Columbia; Burnaby School District, an urban board in the Greater Vancouver Regional District, or GVRD;

Langley School District (GVRD); Richmond School District (GVRD); and Vancouver School District. Both Langley and Richmond have agricultural areas.

These districts granted permission to contact principals of secondary, middle, and elementary schools with an information package. School principals who approved either presented the survey to teachers or provided permission for contact by the researchers. The survey was administered to students in participating classes. The Burnaby school district preferred to approach principals and teachers directly and then presented us with information about participating. School districts determined the consent needed to survey students. Some had specific consent requirements, such as signed parental approval. The Simon Fraser University Research Ethics Board required that parents of twelve- and thirteen-year-olds receive a letter describing participation and allowed fourteen- to eighteen-year-olds to participate without parental consent, unless required by their school district. Parents who refused permission were asked to notify the school and the student would not participate. Surveys were completely anonymous. The only identifier was the school's name.

5 I. Zehtinoglu and J. Muteshi, "A Critical Review of Flexible Labour: Gender, Race and Class Dimensions of Economic Restructuring," *Resources for Feminist Research* 27 (Fall 1999/Winter 2000): 97-120.
6 International Labour Organization, "Flexibility Boosts Productivity, Poses Challenges," *Worklife Report* 11 (1998): 10-11.
7 Tony Uden, "Flexible Labour Markets and the Adult Learner," *Adults Learning* 6, 9 (1995): 269.
8 For a critical review of its impact see S. McBride and R. Williams, "Globalization, the Restructuring of Labour Markets and Policy Convergence: The OECD Jobs Strategy," *Global Social Policy* 1, 3 (2001): 281-309.
9 As Richard Marquardt, *Enter at Your Own Risk: Canadian Youth and the Labour Market* (Toronto: Between the Lines, 1998), 133, observes, these designations are equivalent to the distinction between "progressive competitiveness" and "competitive austerity" drawn by Gregory Albo, "'Competitive Austerity' and the Impasse of Capitalist Employment Policy," *Socialist Register* 30 (1994): 144-70.
10 Marquardt, *Enter at Your Own Risk,* 109-36.
11 S. McBride and K. McNutt, "Devolution and Neoliberalism in the Canadian Welfare State: Ideology, National and International Conditioning Frameworks, and Policy Change in British Columbia," *Global Social Policy,* 7, 2 (2007): 177-201.
12 British Columbia, *Speech from the Throne,* 2002. Parts of this legislation were ruled invalid by the Supreme Court of Canada in June 2007 (see *Health Services and Support: Facilities Subsector Bargaining Assn. v. British Columbia,* 2007 SCC 27).
13 BC Teachers Federation, "Education Funding Success for Every Student: Funding BC's Future," http:// bctf.ca.
14 H. Luke and G. Moore, *Who's Looking Out for Our Kids? Deregulating Child Labour Law in British Columbia* (Vancouver: Canadian Centre for Policy Alternatives, 2004).
15 See J. Irwin, S. McBride, and T. Strubin, *Child and Youth Employment Standards: The Experience of Young Workers under British Columbia's New Policy Regime* (Vancouver: Canadian Centre for Policy Alternatives, BC Office, 2005).
16 Senate Standing Committee on Human Rights (the Honourable Raynell Andreychuk, chair), final report, *Children: The Silenced Citizens* (Ottawa, April 2007).
17 This section is based on Luke and Moore, *Who's Looking Out for Our Kids?* 16.
18 Federation of European Employers, "An Introduction to European Labour Law," http:// www.fedee.com/eulablaw.html.
19 European Union, "Charter of Fundamental Rights of the European Union," 2000, http:// www.europarl.europa.eu/charter/default_en.htm.
20 Organisation for Economic Co-operation and Development, *Combating Child Labour: A Review of Policies* (France: OECD, 2003), 116. In this context, light work refers to babysitting and other duties considered to be informal in nature, as opposed to the regulation of more formal jobs at age fifteen.
21 Unless otherwise stated, all paraphrasing based on, and all quotes taken from, the original text of the convention, found at http://www.unhchr.ch/html/menu3/b/k2crc.htm.

22 This and preceding quotation from International Labour Organization, "Convention Concerning Minimum Age for Admission to Employment," http://www.ilo.org/ilolex/cgi-lex/convde.pl?C138.
23 N. O'Higgins, *Youth Unemployment and Employment Policy: A Global Perspective* (Geneva: International Labour Office, 2001).
24 Ibid., 87.
25 Ibid.
26 Full details can be found in Irwin, McBride, and Strubin, *Child and Youth Employment Standards*.
27 Canadian Council on Social Development, *Youth at Work in Canada: A Research Report* (Ottawa: Canadian Council on Social Development, 1989).
28 *Canadian Master Labour Guide,* 17th ed. (Toronto: CCH Canadian, 2003); Canada, Human Resources and Skills Development Canada, Labour Program, *Labour Law Analysis* (Ottawa: Human Resources and Skills Development Canada, 2004).
29 Canadian Council on Social Development, *Youth at Work in Canada.*
30 British Columbia, Ministry of Skills Development and Labour, "General Employment of Young People Fact Sheet," http://www.labour.gov.bc.ca/esb/facshts/youth_general.htm.
31 Workers' Compensation Board of BC, Prevention Division, Strategic Initiatives, *Parent Focus Groups: Results and Analysis* (n.p.: Workers' Compensation Board of BC, 2003).
32 National Institute for Occupational Safety and Health, *Preventing Deaths, Injuries and Illnesses of Young Workers* (Morgantown, WV: NIOSH, 2003).
33 See Joy Parr, *Labouring Children: British Immigrant Apprentices to Canada, 1869-1924* (Toronto: University of Toronto Press, 1994), and V. Strong-Boag, *Finding Families, Finding Ourselves: Canadians Confront Adoption from the 19th Century to the 1990s* (Toronto: Oxford University Press, 2006).
34 BC Fruit Growers' Association, *High Risk Time in Farming* (Kelowna: BC Fruit Growers' Association, 16 August 2002) (bulletin).
35 BC Fruit Growers' Association, *Children (Aged 12-14) Working on Farms* (Kelowna: BC Fruit Growers' Association, 19 December 2002) (bulletin).
36 Human Rights Watch, *Fingers to the Bone: United States Failure to Protect Child Farmworkers* (New York: Human Rights Watch, 2000).
37 William Pickett, Robert J. Brison, and John R. Hoey, "Fatal and Hospitalized: Agricultural Machinery Injuries to Children in Ontario, Canada," *Injury Prevention* 1 (1995): 97-102.
38 BC Fruit Growers' Association, *High Risk Time in Farming.*
39 Ian Bailey, "Pickers Face 'Third World Conditions,'" *Vancouver Province,* 24 September 2004.
40 See, for example, the exploitation of child agricultural labourers reported by Parr, *Labouring Children*.

Postscript
Neil Sutherland

Both the Introduction and the chapters in this book speak for themselves; they need neither summary nor comment. To say this, however, does not mean that nothing more can be said about "lost" children. Indeed, I want, very briefly, to suggest two sorts of follow-ups to these chapters. First, I want to emphasize how important it is that those creating and implementing policies for the health and welfare of children subject the chapters to intensive scrutiny. Second, I want to urge that these investigations stimulate examination of the lives of other "lost" children.

Unlike many histories, this book points to no real villains. On the other hand, it contains the stories of many ill-treated, ill-served youngsters that emphasize that good intentions are never enough. Most of those who work in agencies caring for children believe – and it's an honest if often naive belief – that they look upon and treat their clients as closely as they can in accordance with the best in modern liberal thought and the best of contemporary practice. This attitude is an understandable one in front-line workers facing often less than the best of working conditions. In fact, however, what agencies actually do with and to their clients do not exist in a neutral vacuum but reflect underlying assumptions about how gender, class, race, and physical and mental ability govern the growth and development of children. In turn, acting on these assumptions can lead to a lack of sensitivity to the feelings of children.

It is for this reason that a careful reading of these chapters will reward those working for children, and especially those who set policies and mandate practices. They should be read not as negative examples but as case studies that provide an opportunity to re-examine their own policies and practices, and especially to probe their underlying assumptions.

Most of the sorts of children discussed in these chapters – the sick, the neglected, the delinquent, the abused, the victims of racist or sexist treatment – had counterparts throughout the twentieth century and even in earlier times. Over the twentieth century, however, some new sorts of lost children appeared, some of whom were in many ways a product of the technological development of the century itself. Let me cite two very different examples.

In a survey I made of the transformation of child health in the twentieth century, I noted that improving infant health seems to have been particularly effective in saving the lives of premature and physically and mentally handicapped infants and children.[1] Until the twentieth century, the vast majority of severely handicapped youngsters perished in infancy or early childhood. When improvement in their chances for survival came, however, it was two-dimensional. As American historian Philip Ferguson explains, there is "not simply a one-directional consideration under which improvements in medical care and general public health mean only that fewer organically impaired babies are born today and fewer children are left impaired from childhood diseases that are now controlled." In fact, Ferguson continues, the "same general improvements in health care mean that severely retarded children survive infancy and childhood today who would have quickly perished in earlier years. The example of Trisomy 21 and neural tube defects like spina bifida come quickly to mind."[2]

The closing paragraph of Veronica Strong-Boag's chapter mentions a recent Canadian example of children who, although preserved by modern medicine, face problems beyond those raised by their disabilities. It seems to me that her work, taken together with that of Ferguson and that of Jeffrey Baker, suggests a need for a thorough history of recent work in neonatal medicine and of the practice of prenatal screening, with special attention to the actual lives of the children involved.[3]

The latter part of twentieth century brought an enormous increase in the number of orphan, homeless children. Some are the unfortunate product of diseases, and especially AIDS, pruning the population of parents. The changing technology of war has produced others. In his book *The Shadow of the Sun,* Polish journalist Ryszard Kapuscinski notes that in Africa "bloody chaos ... has spawned tens of thousands of orphans, hungry and homeless ... They gravitate to where troops are garrisoned. They help out, work, become part of the army ... They are given weapons and quickly undergo a baptism by fire ... These armed encounters between youngsters are particularly fierce and bloody because a child does not have the instinct for self-preservation, does not feel dread or comprehend death, does not experience the fear that only maturity will evoke."[4] Certainly, youngsters have always played a relatively minor role in war; what has changed, Kapuscinski explains, is that unlike earlier firearms, the "dimensions of weapons are now perfectly suited to a boy's physique."[5]

Over the twentieth century, well-meaning people established national and international agencies to care for children afflicted by war, by disease, or by extreme poverty. Some employ a strategy that emphasizes helping families and communities address underlying conditions that produce distressed youngsters. Other agencies work more directly with individual children in their families or in childcare institutions. Some agencies employ both strategies.[6]

It seems to me that all these agencies warrant the sort of external assessment that the essays in this book applied to their subjects. What assumptions underlie their policies and practices? How do their marketing strategies portray children?[7] How successful are they in improving the lives of children? Since they are international organizations with branches in many countries, the Christian Children's Fund and Save the Children are prime examples of the sort of agencies I have in mind. The latter is of particular interest because it "firmly believes that children and young people must be active participants in the design and implementation of programs and policies that impact on their lives."[8] Of each of these agencies – and all the others – one can ask, echoing the Introduction, whether their clients "have carved out satisfying lives in spite of their difficult childhoods." All children, lost or not, deserve nothing less.

Notes

1 Neil Sutherland, "North American Perspectives on the Historiography of Child Health in the Twentieth Century," in Cynthia Comacchio, Janet Golden, and George Weisz, eds., *Healing the World's Children: Child Health in International and Interdisciplinary Perspective* (Montreal and Kingston: McGill-Queen's University Press, 2008).
2 Philip M. Ferguson, *Abandoned to Their Fate: Social Policy and Practice toward Severely Retarded People in America, 1820-1920* (Philadelphia: Temple University Press 1994), 13.
3 Jeffrey P. Baker, *The Machine in the Nursery: Incubator Technology and the Origins of Newborn Intensive Care* (Baltimore: Johns Hopkins University Press, 1996).
4 Ryszard Kapschinski, *The Shadow of the Sun,* trans. Klara Glowczewska (New York: Knopf, 2001), 148.
5 Ibid., 149.
6 One agency working, seemingly effectively, with child soldiers is Childsoldiers.net; see http://www.childsoldiers.net.
7 See, for example, Laurie Block, "Selling Disability: Tools of the Trade," in Comacchio, Golden, and Weisz, *Healing the World's Children*.
8 http://www.savethechildren.ca.

Contributors

Ted Alexander is a doctoral candidate in the School of Human Kinetics at the University of British Columbia. His research concerns social justice issues around the inclusion of youth through public recreation programs.

Denyse Baillargeon is full professor of history at the Université de Montréal. She is the author of *Making Do: Women, Family and Home in Montreal during the Great Depression* (Wilfrid Laurier University Press, 1999), *Un Québec en mal d'enfants: La médicalisation de la maternité, 1910-1970* (Remue-ménage, 2004), and *Naître, vivre, grandir, Sainte-Justine, 1907-2007* (Boréal, 2007). She is currently working on the relationship between school and family in Quebec between 1910 and 1960 and on the fundraising drives of pediatric hospitals.

Cindy L. Baldassi is a PhD student in the Faculty of Law at the University of British Columbia, working mainly on adoption, reproductive technologies, and the legal consequences of genetic ties. After finishing her LLB at Osgoode Hall, she clerked at the Federal Court of Canada and then completed an LLM at the University of British Columbia, where her thesis focused on the question of treating embryo donations as if they were adoptions.

Susan B. Boyd is a professor of law and holds the Chair in Feminist Legal Studies at the University of British Columbia. She researches gender and sexuality issues in the fields of parenthood and family law. Her latest book is *Reaction and Resistance: Feminism, Law, and Social Change* (UBC Press, 2007).

William Bush is Assistant Professor of History at Texas A&M University at San Antonio. His book *The Origins of the Super-Predator: Race and Juvenile Delinquency in Twentieth-Century Texas* will be published by the University of Georgia Press.

Cynthia Comacchio teaches in the History Department at Wilfrid Laurier University. Her particular interests are childhood, adolescence, and familial and generational relations in Canada, especially as these were shaped by modernity.

Karen Dubinsky is a Professor in the History Department at Queen's University. This chapter emerges from her book about transracial and transnational adoption in Canada, Cuba, and Guatemala, titled *Babies without Borders: Adoption and the Symbolic Child in an Era of Globalization.*

Wendy Frisby is the Chair of Women's and Gender Studies and a professor in the School of Human Kinetics at the University of British Columbia. She has written extensively on community-based health promotion for those living in poverty and feminist participatory action research.

Mona Gleason is an associate professor in the Department of Educational Studies at the University of British Columbia. She is the author of *Normalizing the Ideal: Psychology, Schooling, and the Family in Postwar Canada* (University of Toronto Press, 1999) and is completing a manuscript entitled *Embodying Difference: Children in Sickness and Health in English Canada, 1900-1960.*

John Irwin completed a PhD in Resource Management and Environmental Studies at the University of British Columbia in 2004. His doctoral thesis is a case study of the Southeast False Creek sustainable development process, which deals with many issues (ecological, economic, and social) surrounding planning for sustainable community development. He teaches Resource and Environmental Management, as well as Geography, at Simon Fraser University. He has a background in social policy, housing, transportation, and water resource management planning and research.

Fiona Kelly is an assistant professor in the Faculty of Law at the University of British Columbia. Her teaching and research focus on family law, children and the law, sexuality and the law, and feminist legal theory. She recently completed her PhD dissertation on the legal recognition of planned lesbian families.

Molly Ladd-Taylor is an associate professor of history at York University in Toronto. Her publications include *"Bad" Mothers: The Politics of Blame in Twentieth-Century America* and *Mother-Work: Women, Child Welfare, and the State.* Her current project is a history of eugenic sterilization and the child welfare system in Minnesota.

Stephen McBride is professor and director of the Centre for Global Political Economy at Simon Fraser University and is a research associate with the Canadian Centre for Policy Alternatives, British Columbia.

Tamara Myers is an associate professor in the History Department at the University of British Columbia and member of the Montreal History Group, based at McGill University. She is the author of *Caught: Montreal's Modern Girls and the Law, 1869-1945* (University of Toronto Press, 2006).

Leslie Paris is an assistant professor of history at the University of British Columbia. Her research concerns childhood, gender, and culture in modern American history. She is the author of *Children's Nature: The Rise of the American Summer Camp* (NYU Press, 2008).

Veronica Strong-Boag is Professor of Women's Studies and Educational Studies at the University of British Columbia, past president of the Canadian Historical Association, a Fellow of the Royal Society of Canada, winner of the John A. Macdonald Prize in Canadian History (1988) and the Raymond Klibansky Prize in the Humanities (2000), and author and editor of many works on women and children in Canada.

Neil Sutherland, an Emeritus Professor of the University of British Columbia and pioneer in the field of childhood studies and the history of children, has written extensively on the subject, including *Growing Up: Childhood in English Canada from the Great War to the Age of Television* (1997).

Janna Taylor is a part-time instructor in the School of Human Kinetics at the University of British Columbia, as well as a part-time instructor at Langara College for the Recreation Diploma program. Before teaching, she was a director of a municipal parks and recreation department. Her areas of interest are inclusion for disenfranchised groups in the field of sport and recreation, as well as organizational change.

Index

Hind, Margery, 143
histories. *See* case files; memories; oral
histories
H.L.W. and T.H.W., 206-7
homeless children, 245
Hoodless, Adelaide Hunter, 36
hopeless children. *See* marginalized
children
hospitals, 115-16
patient experiences, 148-49
See also Sainte-Justine Hospital
(Montreal)
human rights. *See* rights
Huntingdon (QC), 95, 109
Huston (TX)
juvenile delinquency, 76, 77-79, 87

ICSI. *See* reproductive technologies
ICWA. *See* Indian Child Welfare Act (1978,
US)
ILO. *See* International Labour
Organization
immigrant children
adolescents, 51; fear of, 59-60; Mexican
American, 73, 81, 82, 85, 86; suicide,
64
recreational activities: barriers to
participation, 223-24
immigrants, 216
with disabilities, 35, 40
Huston (TX), 76
See also immigrant children
In the Matter of Baby M, 204
in vitro fertilization. *See* reproductive
technologies
Indian Child Welfare Act (1978, US), 16,
22
Individuals with Disabilities Act (US), 169
industrial accidents, 237, 240-41
infant mortality, 138, 139-40, 213, 216-17
Ingram, Dorothea, 146-47
injuries
industrial accidents, 237, 240-41
institutional care, 48n52
abuse of children, 41
children with disabilities, 40-42, 49n85
See also hospitals; juvenile justice
systems
intelligence
racialization, 81-85, 161-65, 167, 170
testing: Texas juvenile justice system,
81-85
International Labour Organization (ILO),
231, 234-35, 239
intra-cytoplasmic sperm injection. *See*
reproductive technologies

IVF. *See* reproductive technologies

Jensen, Arthur, 167
Johnson, Lyndon, 164-65
Johnson, Walter, 82-83
Johnson v. Calvert, 204-5
Jones, Beverley, 97, 98, 99
Jordan's Principle, 38, 47n46
J.R. v. L.H., 206
juvenile delinquency, 52n1, 96
nighttime and, 99-101, 103, 105
shifts in portrayals of, 72-73
See also juvenile justice systems
juvenile justice systems, 159
black adolescents and, 51-52, 73-90
curfew laws, 104-8
Juvenile Delinquents Act (1908,
Canada), 52
Mexican American adolescents, 73, 81,
82, 85, 86
See also juvenile delinquency

Kelly, Peter, 22
Kelso, J.J., 97-103
Kerr, Walter Kingsolving, 73, 77, 84
K.G.T. v. P.D., 201-2
Kimelman, Edwin C., 22
Kimelman Inquiry. *See* Review Committee
on Indian and Métis Adoptions and
Placements
Knight, A.P., 144
Kramer vs. Kramer (film), 176, 178, 187

labour policies. *See* youth labour policies
labour relations
British Columbia, 231-32
See also youth labour policies
L'Arche homes, 40
Latimer, Tracy, 45
legal parenthood, 205-7, 211n39
leisure activities. *See* play; public recreational services; sports
lesbian mothers
child custody disputes between, 201-2
disputes with sperm donors, 197-201
Lewis, Oscar, 162-63
"The Little Brother" (short story), 136-37
local governments. *See* public recreational
services
The Lonely Ones (film), 87-89
lost children. *See* marginalized children
low-income children
adolescents, 51
education, 213; health education, 143-45
health issues, 143-45, 216-17; medical
care, 120-29, 132, 139, 142, 148-49, 213

Rebel without a Cause (film), 72
recreation centres, 219-20
recreational activities
working adolescents and, 236-37
See also play; public recreational services;
sports
reproductive technologies
disputes between sperm donors and
lesbian mothers, 197-201
legal regulation of parent-child relationships, 202-7
restaurant employment, 237
Review Committee on Indian and Métis
Adoptions and Placements, 22-23, 28
rights
children with disabilities, 37, 39, 165-66,
169-70
to desegregated education, 161-62, 165,
171, 174n52
juvenile justice systems, 1o4, 90, 95, 98,
107, 109
parental: biogenetic *vs.* social parents,
201-3; fathers, 194-96, 197, 199, 201;
legal parenthood, 205-7, 211n39;
mothers, 194-203; sperm donors,
198-201
United Nations Convention on the
Rights of the Child, 4, 39, 192, 234
Robillard, J.A., 106
Robitaille, Fernande, 130-32
RTs. *See* reproductive technologies
runaways, 60-61

Sainte-Anne-de-Bellevue (QC), 104-5
Sainte-Justine Hospital (Montreal),
120-22
educational services for patients, 118,
119, 122-26
parent visits, 131, 135n56
religious instruction for patients,
122-23, 125-26, 128-29
therapeutic services for patients, 118-19,
126-32
Sampson, Katelynn, 39
schools
children's health, 38, 119, 143-45
See also education
Scottsboro Boys, 161
Sheedy, Alexandra, 179-80, 189n14
Shelburne (ON), 106-7
Shriver, Eunice Kennedy, 165
"Sixties Scoop," 16, 23, 29, 29n3
Smith, George, 141
social classes. *See* low-income children;
middle-class values
Social Security Act (1935, US), 160-61

socio-economic conditions
children of divorced parents, 179,
181-83, 184-85, 188
See also low-income children; middle-
class values; poverty
sports
gendered participation, 218, 219, 221
international events, 219-20
state policies
children as "national assets," 54
citizen health, 138; fitness initiatives, 220
impact of American social policies on
children, 158-74
in loco parentis role, 101-2, 103
relations with Aboriginal peoples, 19
youth management, 54-55
See also Canada; United States: social
policies
sunset regulations. *See* curfew laws
surrogate parenthood. *See* reproductive
technologies

teenagers. *See* adolescence
Temporary Assistance for Needy Families,
169
Texas
juvenile justice system, 73-90
State Youth Development Council, 77,
79-86
Training School Code Commission, 76,
77
Youth Council, 77, 86-90
thalidomide, 37-38
This Child Is Rated X (TV documentary),
90
Thistledown Regional Centre (ON), 41
Thom, D.A., 58
Thomas, W.I., 61-62
Tierney, Jean, 146
Till, Emmett, 161
Tisdall, Frederick, 141
Toronto (ON)
adolescent suicide, 64-65
curfew laws, 104
emotionally disturbed children, 41
immigrant adolescents, 59
transnational adoption
of Aboriginal children, 18, 21-23, 30n19,
31n33
transracial adoption
of Aboriginal children, 13, 15-25, 26,
28-29, 42-43
of black children, 13, 15-18, 25-29
of Chinese children, 17
as instrument of colonization, 16, 17,
21; kidnap narrative, 20-21, 24, 25

Printed and bound in Canada by Friesens

Set in Stone by Artegraphica Design Co. Ltd.

Copy editor: Judy Phillips

Proofreader: Desne Ahlers

Indexer: Christine Jacobs